BYRON

The Erotic Liberal

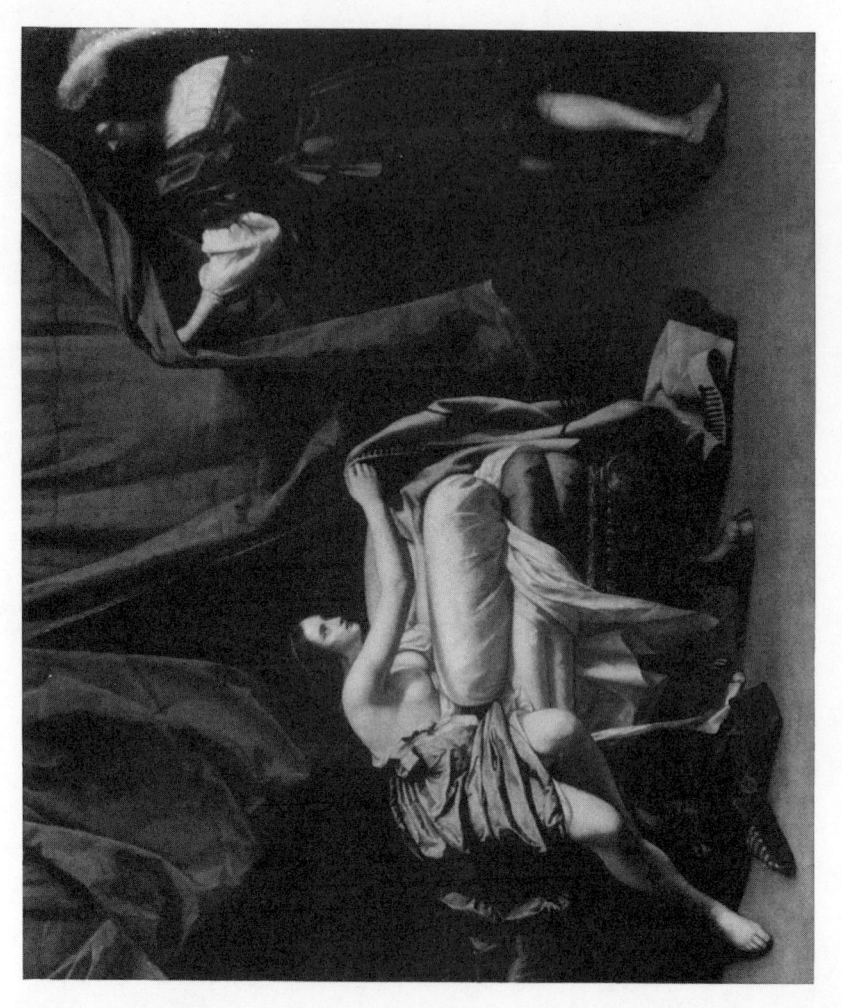

Orazio Gentileschi (1563–1647), *Joseph and Potiphar's Wife* (1630s). Paul Drey Gallery, New York.

BYRON

The Erotic Liberal

JONATHAN DAVID GROSS

ROWMAN & LITTLEFIELD PUBLISHERS, INC.
Lanham • Boulder • New York • Oxford

ROWMAN & LITTLEFIELD PUBLISHERS, INC.

Published in the United States of America
by Rowman & Littlefield Publishers, Inc.
4720 Boston Way, Lanham, Maryland 20706

12 Hid's Copse Road
Cumnor Hill, Oxford OX2 9JJ, England

Copyright © 2001 by Rowman & Littlefield Publishers, Inc.

All rights reserved. No part of this publication may be reproduced, stored in a retrieval system, or transmitted in any form or by any means, electronic, mechanical, photocopying, recording, or otherwise, without the prior permission of the publisher.

British Library Cataloguing in Publication Information Available

Library of Congress Cataloging-in-Publication Data
Gross, Jonathan David, 1962-
 Byron : the erotic liberal / Jonathan David Gross.
  p. cm.
 Includes bibliographical references and index.
 ISBN 0-7425-1161-8 (alk. paper) — ISBN 0-7425-1162-6 (pbk. : alk. paper)
  1. Byron, George Gordon Byron, Baron, 1788-1824—Political and social views. 2. Politics and literature—Great Britian—History—19th century. 3. Political poetry, English—History and criticism. 4. Sentimentalism in literature. 5. Liberalism in literature. 6. Emotions in literature. 7. Sex in literature. I. Title.

PR4392.P64 G76 2001
821'.7—dc21

00-046351

Printed in the United States of America

∞™ The paper used in this publication meets the minimum requirements of American National Standard for Information Sciences—Permanence of Paper for Printed Library Materials, ANSI/NISO Z39.48-1992.

For Jacqui and Shiri

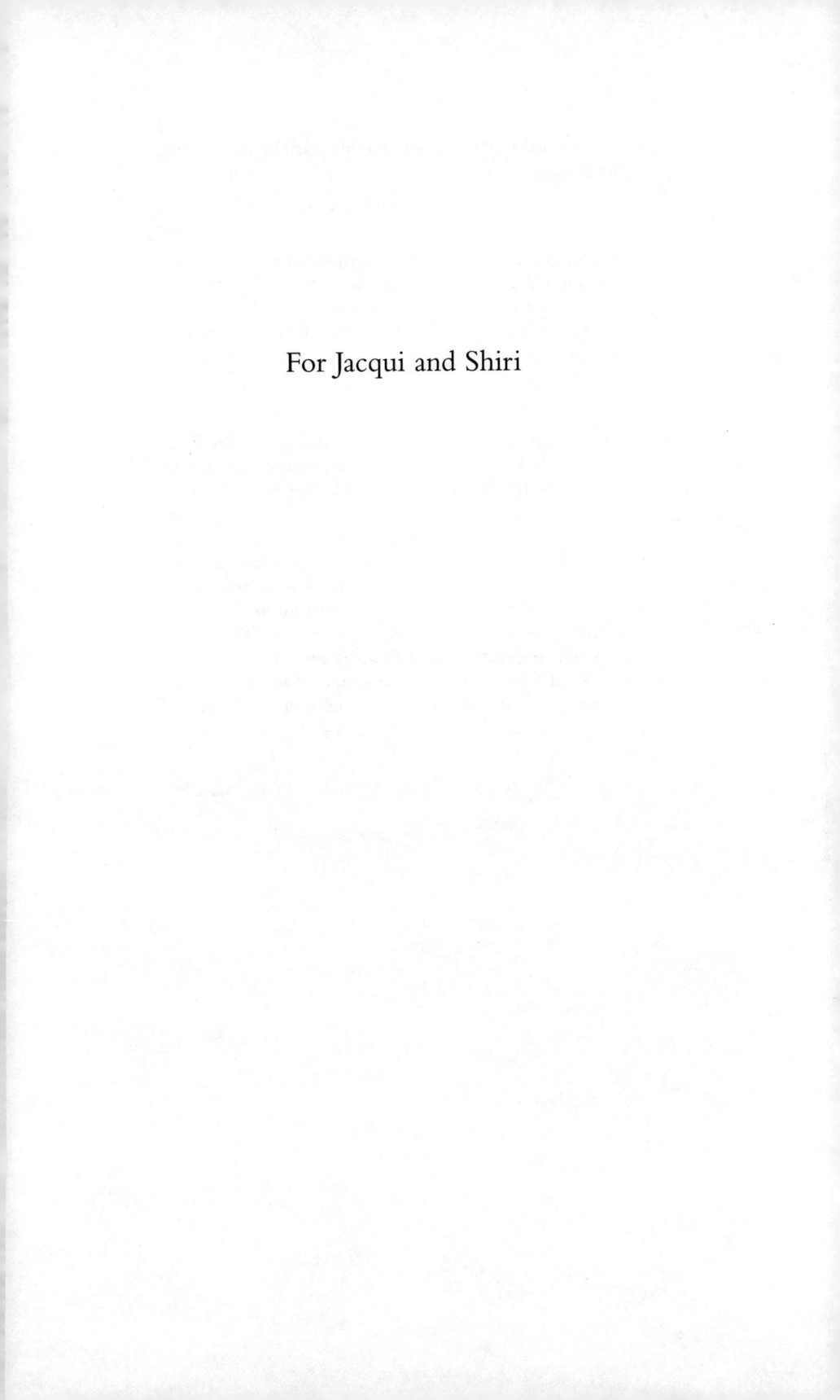

The degree and kind of a man's sexuality reach up into the ultimate pinnacle of his spirit.

Nietzsche, *Beyond Good and Evil*

He is, perhaps, more decidedly the creature of passion in its most intense and indomitable form, than any other living man;—and he certainly has it less under the governance of refined and enlightened intellect than any of the great poets of former times with whom, in other points, he may bear a comparison.

The Literary Gazette, February 1818

When a man is tired of what he is, by a natural perversity he sets up for what he is not. If he is a poet, he pretends to be a metaphysician: if he is a patrician in rank and feeling, he would fain be one of the people. His ruling motive is not the love of the people, but of distinction: not of truth, but of singularity. He patronizes men of letters out of vanity, and deserts them from caprice or from the advice of friends. He embarks in an obnoxious publication to provoke censure, and leaves it to shift for itself for fear of scandal. We do not like Sir Walter's gratuitous servility: we like Lord Byron's preposterous *liberalism* little better. He may affect the principles of equality, but he resumes the privilege of peerage, upon occasion. His Lordship has made great offers of service to the Greeks—money and horses. He is at present in Cephalonia, waiting the event!

William Hazlitt, *The Spirit of the Age*, April 1824

CONTENTS

Acknowledgments		ix
List of Abbreviations		xi
Introduction		1
1	Byron's Politics of Feeling	15
2	Byron's Politics of Sentimentalism	31
3	Byron and the Story of Joseph: "The Bride of Abydos," *Hebrew Melodies,* and *Don Juan*	55
4	Cosmopolitan Liberalism: *Childe Harold's Pilgrimage,* III, and *De l'Allemagne*	79
5	"Get[ting] into Lord's Ground": Byron's Aristocratic Liberalism in the Pope-Bowles Controversy and *Marino Faliero*	101
6	"One Half What I Should Say": Byron's Gay Narrator in *Don Juan*	129
7	Byron and *The Liberal:* Periodical and Political Posture	153
8	"Still let me love!": Byron in Greece	171
Afterword	Byron and the Liberal Imagination in America	189

Bibliography	*201*
Index	*221*
About the Author	*231*

ACKNOWLEDGMENTS

I would like to thank the University Research Council and College of Liberal Arts and Sciences at DePaul University for providing grant support for this project. Dean Michael Mezey and Helen Marlborough, chair of the Department of English, allowed me to complete this manuscript as a fellow in the DePaul Humanities Center, 1999–2000. My thanks to the director, Jackie Taylor, and her assistant, Anna Vaughn, for helping to make this year so productive; to fellows Eric Selinger, Dolores Wilber, and Maria Torres for their constructive comments; and to Shannon Siggeman for superb research assistance. For advice with specific chapters, I am grateful to Ted Anton, Jonathan Arac, Bernard Beatty, Jerome Christensen, Peter Cochran, Andrew Cooper, John Isbell, Helen Marlborough, Andrew Nicholson, Jacqui Russell, and Shailja Sharma. I really cannot adequately express my gratitude to John Clubbe, Peter Graham, Karl Kroeber, Malcolm Kelsall, James Soderholm, and Carl Woodring, who selflessly read the entire work at a late stage and provided important insights and suggestions. Any remaining errors are mine alone. Serena Leigh of Rowman & Littlefield provided very valuable editorial guidance, and Dorothy Bradley and Dave Compton helped turn my manuscript into a book.

I would also like to acknowledge Leonard Goldberg, Stephen Salkever, and Houston A. Baker, Jr. for their superb teaching at Haverford and Bryn Mawr colleges. They helped me think about Byron's poetry and politics in new ways. My greatest debts are to my wife, Jacqui Russell, whose love and support enabled me to finish this book, and to my father, Theodore L. Gross, whose erudition, scholarship, and liberalism have been an inspiration.

x   *Acknowledgments*

A briefer version of chapter 5 appeared as " 'One Half What I Should Say': Byron's Gay Narrator in *Don Juan,*" *European Romantic Review* 9 (Summer, 1998): 323–53; of chapter 7 as "Byron and The Liberal: Periodical as Political Posture," *Philological Quarterly* 72 (Fall 1993): 471–85. Chapter 3 is forthcoming as "Byron and the Story of Joseph" in *Byron: East and West* (Prague: Charles University Press, 1997). My thanks to the publishers of these journals and collections for permission to reprint earlier formulations of my argument. "Joseph and Potiphar's Wife," by Orazio Gentileschi, is reproduced on the cover jacket and in the book by permission of the Paul Drey Gallery, New York.

ABBREVIATIONS

BLJ   *Lord Byron's Letters and Journals.* Ed. Leslie A. Marchand. 12 vols. Cambridge: Harvard University Press, 1973–82.

CMP   *The Complete Miscellaneous Prose: Lord Byron.* Ed. Andrew Nicholson. Oxford: Oxford University Press, 1991.

CPW   *Lord Byron: The Complete Poetical Works.* Ed. Jerome McGann. 7 vols. Oxford: Clarendon Press, 1980–93.

DL   Laclos, Pierre Choderlos de. *Les Liaisons dangereuses.* Trans. Richard Aldington. New York: Signet, 1962.

DT   "Detached Thoughts." In *Lord Byron's Letters and Journals.* Ed. Leslie A. Marchand. 12 vols. Cambridge: Harvard University Press, 1973–82.

FL   First letter to John Murray, Esq., on Bowles, in *CMP,* 120–60.

Howe   *The Complete Works of William Hazlitt.* Ed. P. P. Howe. 20 vols. New York: AMS Press, 1967.

RR   Reiman, Donald, ed. *The Romantics Reviewed: Contemporary Reviews of British Romantic Writers.* 5 vols. New York: Garland Press, 1972.

SL   Second letter to John Murray, Esq., on Bowles, in *CMP,* 161–83.

SP   Shelley, Percy. *Shelley's Prose.* Ed. Fred Jones. 2 vols. Oxford: Clarendon Press, 1964.

INTRODUCTION

The sixteen-year-old Byron imagined himself as both an unfeeling libertine and a potential victim of Eros. Love was "a jargon of compliments, romance, and deceit; now for my part had I fifty mistresses, I should in the course of a fortnight, forget them all, and if by any chance I ever recollected one, should laugh at it as a dream, and bless my stars, for delivering me from the hands of the little mischievous Blind God" (*BLJ* October 24, 1804; 1:52).[1] Though he sometimes posed as an unfeeling libertine, Byron rarely escaped the "hands of the little mischievous Blind God." "I should like to know *who* has been carried off—except poor dear *me*," he wrote of Countess Guiccioli, fifteen years later. "I have been more ravished myself than any body since the Trojan war" (*BLJ* October 29, 1819; 6:237). Clearly *eros*, in tension with libertinism, shaped Byron's private and public life.

This study explores the relationship between Byron's erotic life and his political commitments. I argue that Byron used the Joseph story in "The Bride of Abydos," *Hebrew Melodies*, and *Don Juan* to resolve the tension between *eros* and libertinism in his own life. Throughout this volume, I offer close readings of "Lines to a Lady Weeping," *Childe Harold's Pilgrimage*, the Pope-Bowles controversy, *Marino Faliero*, and the periodical, *The Liberal*. My argument is that Byron resolved the tension between *eros* and libertinism, in part, by using his poetry to define a new political outlook—erotic liberalism—which he referred to in his letters as a "politics of feeling." Byron offered a unique literary contribution to liberalism in *Don Juan*, I suggest, by highlighting the double entendres of a "gay" narrator to parody social and sexual mores in Regency England. His contributions to *The Liberal* and his support for the Greek War of Independence represent one of the first articulations of liberal politics, a full eight years before the founding of the Liberal Party in 1832. Yet Byron's brand of liberalism was not popular during the Cold War in the United States. What does he have to teach Americans in the twenty-first century?

Malcolm Kelsall's *Byron's Politics* and Michael Foot's *The Politics of Paradise* offer divergent answers to the question of Byron's political legacy. Kelsall argues that Byron's life is of no political importance, while Foot sees him as a crucial champion of political liberty. This study offers yet another view by taking the question across the Atlantic. At a time when the personal has become increasingly political in the United States, what is the value of Byron's political example? I draw on Lady Melbourne's recently published responses to Byron's letters to answer this question, placing Byron's political perspective in the context of Madame de Staël's, and making use of feminism and gay studies to explain how Byron's sexuality shaped his political beliefs and literary style.

Though Byron ridiculed Plato as no more than a "go-between" in *Don Juan* (*CPW* 5:1:116),[2] Plato defines erotic love in ways central to my study. He uses the word *philia* to describe friendship and love of family; *eros* he most commonly reserves for "passionate love and desire, usually sexual, and the god who personified that state."[3] In the first speech of *Symposium*, Phaedrus calls Eros the oldest of the gods (178b); Agathon insists he is the youngest (195c); Diotima describes him as born of Poros and Penia, from resourcefulness and poverty (203c). Despite these divergent genealogies, all come to agree that Eros is a schemer after the good and the beautiful (203d). Perhaps the most striking image of all, however, is offered by Aristophanes. He explains that our ancestors were spherical balls consisting of two conjoined persons. Punished by the gods for their arrogance, they were split down the middle "like a flatfish"; man was separated from man, woman from woman, and man from woman (191e). Each of us searches for our lost half. *Eros* is the search for wholeness.

Sappho has a complementary view, equally relevant to Byron. For Sappho, *eros* is *glukipikron*, which can be translated as "sweetbitter." In fragment 31, Sappho explains the visceral emotions that attend the invasion of her body by *eros* as she watches a man talking to a woman she loves: "cold sweat holds me and shaking/grips me all, greener than grass/I am and dead—or almost/I seem to me."[4] *Eros* is a physical assault. In this poem and others by Archilochus and Anacreon, *eros* also denotes want, lack, desire for that which is missing—both the absent lover and the qualities he or she possesses. Surprised by *eros*, the lover strives to attain self-completion. "Reaching for an object that proves to be outside and beyond himself, the lover is provoked to notice that self and its limits," Anne Carson writes.[5] Byron's poetry exemplifies this theme, in short lyrics such as "The First Kiss of Love," which describes love as overpowering; in "There's Not a Joy the World Can Give," which represents love as sweetbitter (in that precise order). Even the cynical *Don Juan* begins with the famous phrase "I want a hero," which recalls Aristophanes' speech in *Symposium*. Byron strives to complete in fiction what he lacks in self.

Related to the erotic quest for self-completion is Plato's theory of knowledge as an act of mental recovery. "Studying exists because knowledge is leaving us," Diotima explains (208a). More fancifully, Diotima notes that some are pregnant in body, while others become pregnant in soul (209a): the first give birth to children, the second to wisdom. The latter sometimes plant ideas in students by teaching them (209c). Those who are in love with wisdom often find that lover and beloved exchange places so that the student comes to resemble his or her teacher in the search for knowledge, as in the case of Alcibiades, who falls in love with his teacher, Socrates (222b). Plato shows how *eros* and pedagogy are intimately related; both lead to a scale of love, from physical to ideal beauty. *Eros*, "which we first approached as the desire to possess sexually the body of another person," Alexander Nehamas argues, "turns out to be a desire for immortality, for wisdom, and for the contemplation of an object which is not in any way bodily or physical. Furthermore, only when a lover devotes himself to the pursuit of Beauty as a whole will it become possible for him to give birth not to images of virtue ... but to true virtue."[6] Byron's erotic relationships evince this desire for self-improvement. Lord Clare, John Edleston, Annabella Milbanke, Teresa Guiccioli, and Loukas Chalandritsanos challenged Byron to emulate qualities he longed to possess; all show the effect of *eros* on his life.

Byron's *eros* has little in common with libertinism. This is an important distinction. Where those driven by *eros* become dissatisfied with themselves and strive for self-improvement, libertines regard each new conquest as proof of their intellectual superiority. Erotic lovers are overwhelmed by passion, which they struggle in vain to control; libertines control others by controlling themselves. Plato explains how *eros* leads the lover from loving beautiful bodies to loving beautiful acts. The libertine's progress is toward hell and damnation. Prompted to serve the Greek cause by John Cam Hobhouse—and to "reform" himself in other ways by Annabella Milbanke and Teresa Guiccioli—Byron conformed to Plato's definition of *eros*, to an erotic ladder rather than a libertine descent.

The notion that Byron was not a libertine may need further elucidation and defense, which can be found in a historical understanding of the term. Libertinism flourished during two distinct periods. From the early Christian era to the seventeenth century, libertinism involved "a revolt against Christian asceticism, a rival conception of a Christian God."[7] The word was used as early as 1563 to criticize Anabaptists, Ranters, and Quakers, who were considered heretical for believing that sexual activity would bring them closer to God. The Blood Friends, a German sect, elevated sex into a sacrament, the sacrament of

Christerie. The *Homores Intelligentiae*, a Low Country sect of the early sixteenth century, called sex "the acclivity" (upward slope), which was a technical term of the mystical tradition meaning the ascent to God.[8] A second version of libertinism ran from 1700 to the French Revolution and involved a revolt against Christianity itself; "it had affinities with the systematic atheism of the Illumination. It was not a heresy, but an outright rejection of Christianity and Christian ethics." Baron d'Holbach, in *Système de la nature* (1770), derided religion and espoused an atheistic, deterministic Materialism; his circle included Helvetius, d'Alembert, Diderot, Buffon, and, for a while, Rousseau, as well as Garrick, Hume, Sterne, and Wilkes.[9] By 1812, the year Byron's *Childe Harold's Pilgrimage* appeared, libertinism was no longer influential: "in sooth he was a shameless wight," his narrator says of Harold and his "carnal companie"(*CPW* 2:1:14, 17). By the time Byron wrote *Childe Harold's Pilgrimage*, in other words, he could no longer endorse (without irony) the libertinism Laclos had condemned with the *ancien regime*. "That Nerciat, Sade, and others were still celebrating libertinism, ten or even twenty years after the appearance of *Les liaisons dangereuses* (1782) does not show the latter had no effect on society," Wayland Young explains; it did, "only not on those writers. Nobody was celebrating libertinism thirty years later."[10]

Born too late to be classified as a libertine, Byron did cultivate cosmopolitanism, a third concept which shaped Byron's political views. The word "cosmopolitan" is derived from the Greek (κόσμος, world, and πολιτης, citizen). Cosmopolitanism means "belong[ing] to all parts of the world, not restricted to any one country in its inhabitants." The word first appears as an English noun in 1645: "Every ground May be one's country—for by birth each man Is in this world a cosmopolitan," Howell wrote in his *Letters* (1645). By the mid-eighteenth century, Samuel Richardson, in *Sir Charles Grandison* (1751), dismissed cosmopolitanism and libertinism as practically synonymous: "wickedness and libertinism, called a knowledge of the world, a knowledge of human nature."[11] Here one might distinguish between cosmopolitanism defined as sexual licentiousness (perhaps gained from foreign travel) and cosmopolitanism as an emancipation from nationalism. Sixty years after Richardson's *Sir Charles Grandison*, Madame de Staël's *Corinne, or Italy*, and *De l'Allemagne* celebrated the virtues of this latter definition of cosmopolitanism, Byron's *Childe Harold's Pilgrimage* and *Don Juan* take a similar perspective that Byron first expressed to his mother in a letter of 1811: "I am so convinced of the advantages of looking at mankind instead of reading about them, and of the bitter effects of staying at home with all the narrow prejudices of an Islander, that I think there should be a law amongst us to set our young men abroad for a term among the few allies our wars have left us" (*BLJ* January 14, 1811; 2:34). Byron's cosmopolitanism is a type of internationalism. He cited Monbron's *Le Cosmopolite* in the epigraph to *Childe Harold's Pilgrimage*, alluded repeatedly to Goldsmith's *Citizen of the World* in his letters, and composed *Don Juan* and *The Liberal* in Italy, professing to gain a vantage point on England from the perspective of "the South."

How did Byron's *eros*, his rejection of libertinism, and his embrace of cosmopolitanism shape his liberal beliefs? All three words find resonance in a periodical Leigh Hunt edited from Pisa, Italy. Before discussing *The Liberal* (1822–23), however, I need to define the word "liberal" itself, explore Byron's usage, and explain why Byron's choice of this word as the title of a periodical is such a telling example of Byron's erotic liberalism.

The root of the word "liberal" is *liber*, which means free. The latin root describes someone who "acts according to his own will and pleasure, is his own master."[12] In the sixteenth century, for example, the English used "liberal" to describe men of leisure, "persons of superior social station," whose activities and education were "liberal." As a social term, its connotations could be positive or negative. "Liberal" could refer to a gentleman's generosity, but also to his licentiousness. Shakespeare captures both senses in *Much Ado about Nothing*, when he refers to "a liberal villaine" who "hath ... confest his vile encounters" (4:1:93).[13]

Increasingly, "liberals" who possessed personal wealth also displayed independent views. One of the first recorded uses of liberal, in 1375 to describe "Liberal arts" education, makes that connection explicit. "Liberal" meant "free in bestowing" as early as 1387; "made without stint" in 1433; "free from restraint," often in a bad sense, in the sixteenth and seventeenth centuries; "freely permitted, not interfered with" in 1530; "free from narrow prejudice" as early as 1781; and "free from bigotry" in 1823.[14] Not surprisingly, the Whigs associated their "independent" and "free" perspective in politics with the financial independence that made it possible.

Byron's life offers perhaps the most uniform and therefore helpful vista to explain how the adjective became a noun he used to describe his political perspective. Surprisingly, the word "liberal" appears in Byron's poetry only ten times,[15] but does so with a significant shift. Before 1818, Byron used the word as an adjective meaning "generous" in "Childish Recollections" (1806) ("Candid and liberal, with a heart of steel," *CPW* 1:ln.271), *Hints from Horace* (1811) ("Longman's liberal aid," *CPW* 1:ln.545), *Waltz: An Apostrophic Hymn* (1812) ("Liberal of feet," *CPW* 3:ln.114), and *Manfred* (1816) ("liberal air," *CPW* 4:1:2:50); after this date, he began to use the word to describe political generosity. In *Marino Faliero* (1821), Israel Bertuccio describes Faliero's "mind" as "liberal" (*CPW* 4:2.2.174) and Faliero's reluctant but nevertheless revolutionary decision to overthrow his aristocratic peers gives the word political resonance. In *The Age of Bronze* (1822), a poem Byron ultimately withdrew from

The Liberal, he reverted to the word's previous sense, as in "liberal thaw" (*CPW* 7:10:440). *Don Juan* was the first poem in which Byron began to depart from using "liberal" to mean tolerant ("This is a liberal age, and thoughts are free," *CPW* 5:4:7) or generous ("Thou, and the truly liberal Lafitte," *CPW* 5:12:6, and "liberal by nature" [*CPW* 5:15:52]) to using the word solely as a political label ("O'er congress, whether royalist or liberal" *CPW* 5:12:5).

Byron's prose illustrates a similar shift from the word's meaning as an adjective to the meaning it acquired as a noun. Before 1818, Byron used "liberal" to describe aristocratic comportment. In his suppressed preface to *Don Juan* (1818), however, he referred to the Spanish "Liberals," using the word as an English noun for the first time. He repeated the usage in a letter to Hobhouse, describing the Carbonari as "Liberals" (*BLJ* September 22, 1820; 7:235). By 1821, Byron was storing arms for this aristocratic group bent on driving the Austrians from Italy. He realized his extravagant claim, made in *Don Juan,* that he would war in "words" and "deeds" with "all who war/With Thought" (*CPW* 5:9:24), for he borrowed the title of *The Liberal* from a political movement in which he had become directly involved.

To trace Byron's forty seven uses of the word in his correspondence, in other words, is to chart his movement from an aristocratic to a revolutionary brand of liberalism. As a young boy, Byron defined liberalism as the conduct becoming a gentleman; as a man, he used the word to refer to his revolutionary activity with the Italian Carbonari (the "Liberals"). Byron united these two definitions, incompatible as they may seem, by adhering to the principles of Whiggery—resistance to royal power on the one hand, and to mob rule on the other. Byron defined a liberal gentleman as generous (in a Christian sense), aristocratic (because given to acts of *noblesse oblige*), cosmopolitan (because he had the finances to travel), literary (because educated in the liberal arts), and libertine (at least in a literary sense, because libertinism was sanctioned by literary precedent). With such a resilient definition, Byron was able to apply his term to changing historical events and to coin a political word that the Whigs themselves adopted when they regained office in 1832.

Having sketched provisional definitions of *eros,* libertinism, cosmopolitanism, and liberalism, I have still to explain the phrase "erotic liberal." Why yoke such seemingly disparate words together? One incident in Byron's life, the inspiration for this study, is emblematic. Byron's erotic attraction to Countess Teresa Guiccioli led him to support the cause of the Italian Carbonari (or "Liberals"), a group which her father and brother had joined. During (perhaps because of) his relationship with Teresa in 1821, Byron chose the title for *The Liberal* that same year and, through the naming of this ill-fated periodical, he introduced the word into the English vocabulary as a noun. Previously "liberal" had been used by Robert Southey and Lord Castlereagh as an abusive epithet, often in its Spanish or French forms, to characterize the government opposition. Now Byron's friendship with Teresa and her family, especially her brother and father, led him to sympathize with the Italians in their struggle to free themselves from Austrian rule and to use the English translation of an Italian political group (the Carbonari) to define an English political position. For Byron, *eros* and liberalism were mutually constitutive.

Erotic liberalism is a phrase that seeks to explain, by calling together, consistent themes and motives in Byron's verse.[16] I can perhaps best illustrate what I mean by erotic liberalism by offering a brief reading of "The Lament of Tasso" (1817), which Byron penned midway in his poetic career. Departing from the customary view of Tasso as mentally unstable, Byron portrays the author of *Jerusalem Liberated* as a victim of *eros* who fell in love with the wrong woman, the sister of the duke Alfonso II d'Este at Ferrara. Leonora's jealous brother shuts Tasso in prison, in part to separate the lovers. "That thou wert beautiful, and I not blind,/Hath been the sin which shuts me from mankind" (*CPW* 4:2:55–56), Tasso says in a dramatic monologue apparently addressed to the Princess. Tasso's love for Leonora intensifies precisely because he cannot possess her. "[N]o love-mate for a bard" (*CPW*, 4:5:123), she is "Worshipped at holy distance" (*CPW* 4:5:130). Paradoxically, this erotic relation to his love object releases him from his chains: "The very love which locked me to my chain/Hath lightened half its weight" (*CPW* 4:5:144–145), he observes, noting that it lends him "vigour to sustain,/And look to thee with undivided breast,/And foil the ingenuity of Pain" (*CPW* 4:5:146–148). Like Prometheus, Tasso is "lightened" by the burden of his chains, not weighed down by them. Cultivating a state of *eros*, Tasso finds that his pain is bittersweet.

Tasso's very susceptibility to beauty makes him an erotic liberal. That he has no particular political cause to espouse is precisely what he has in common with other Byronic heroes; his apolitical perspective, compassion, and sensitivity to beauty prove his moral integrity, his independent thought. "It is no marvel—from my very birth/My soul was drunk with love, which did pervade/ And mingle with whate'er I saw on earth" (*CPW* 4:6:149–151), he notes. His "whole heart exhaled into One Want" (*CPW* 4:6:168), until he meets his love object, who "annihilate[s]" the earth for him (*CPW* 4:6:173). Tasso's spirit is "proved" in the "tempering fire" of his love (*CPW* 4:8:204–205). If this "love" threatens his sanity, it is because he "feel[s]," not thinks, with his mind (*CPW* 4:8:189–190). Byron concludes by charting the "decay" of feeling itself, as if it were a separate faculty. "I once was quick in feeling—that is o'er;—/My scars are callous" (*CPW* 4:9:208–209). For adults, "feeling" can turn "callous" all too quickly.

Like Tasso, Byron remained faithful to *eros* by choosing to live his life in the role of a pursuer. The man who was the literary lion of England in 1812 and a fan carrier for Teresa Guiccioli in 1821 left Italy to participate in the Greek War of Independence; once in Greece, he fell in love with Loukas Chalandritsanos. In this sense, Byron differed from his own literary creation. Unlike the passive Don Juan of his epic poem, Byron expressed his liberalism by actively pursuing both erotic and political freedom.

Charismatic liberalism and physical beauty are closely intertwined and Byron had his share of both. Many politicians who pursue liberal politics—one thinks of Madame de Staël, Thomas Jefferson, John F. Kennedy, Martin Luther King, Jr., or even William Jefferson Clinton—have also had difficulty controlling the parameters of their erotic life, even as their magnetic personalities contributed to their political success. The charismatic Alcibiades of Plato's *Symposium* shows how this is quite natural. Properly channeled, "sexual desire [in politician, philosopher, or citizen] . . . leads not simply to gratification but to the good life."[17] Kennedy or Clinton's sexual "generosity," to borrow Henry Fielding's phrase, reflects the personal side of their public, political postures. Similarly, Byron's commitment to political liberty cannot be understood separately from his search for erotic freedom in his private life. What makes erotic liberals like Byron so compelling is their effort to connect their view of the political world with the liberty and freedom they long for privately. The erotic liberal is progressive because he or she is always in a position of pursuit, much like Byron's narrator in *Don Juan*. Such a person is grounded in reality, however, because he or she knows, as Byron knew, that the human form is made of "half dust, half deity" (*Manfred*; *CPW* 4:1:2:40). Byron's years of sexual and geographic exploration made him the great and sympathetic reader of human motives that he was. His aristocratic position merely gave him the opportunity to develop these traits of cosmopolitanism and understanding more fully than many of his contemporaries.

Distracted, perhaps, by Byron's flamboyant personality (his social class, his romantic affairs), fellow writers have not always taken Byron seriously as an intellectual or a liberal. "The moment he reflects, he is a child," Goethe observed. Emerson wrote that he "has manly superiority rather than intellectuality."[18] In fact, Byron's vast reading in Greek and Roman history, in the literature and history of Persia, Turkey, and Albania, in the Old and New Testaments challenges these assessments. His support for Catholic emancipation and for Italian, Spanish, and Greek independence movements provides crucial evidence for how one liberal responded to political events at the beginning of the nineteenth century. "Elite" and "liberal" have acquired almost exclusively pejorative connotations, and Byron was both. Yet Byron's aristocratic background shows the elitist inheritance of liberalism in its best light. What Byron offered the generation he inspired was an intellectually sophisticated response to world events that was uncompromising.

Byron's verse shows numerous examples of a broad-mindedness born of his vast reading, examples of his willingness to consider the wisdom and foolishness of Jewish, Islamic, and Christian perspectives. Much as literary theorists would like to view him as an orientalist, Byron was far more appreciative of Eastern culture than such a judgmental label would suggest. Byron did not colonize the East by writing about it, but complicated his own understanding of Christian forms of worship by visiting the countries he portrayed. Similarly, his marriage to Annabella Milbanke and his collaboration with Isaac Nathan on *Hebrew Melodies* were not simply moral and literary postures, but genuine efforts at self-reform and self-improvement. Byron was not consistently hostile to religion or religious people, and he was certainly not a closet anti-Semite, though poems like "The Age of Bronze" and a few stanzas from *Don Juan* criticizing the Rothschilds have led some to think so. Such a modern, suspicious reading, not historicized with the balance shown by Michael Scrivener,[19] fails to do justice to Byron's generous spirit in collaborating with Nathan at a time when Jews did not enjoy civil rights. Walter Scott and William Hazlitt began a tradition of faulting Byron for perversity and dishonesty in his politics. Such a view overlooks the consistency of Byron's liberal sympathies and the generosity of spirit that characterized many of his endeavors. To compare his politics to Madame de Staël's is to appreciate the extent to which Byron was a creature of his social class. Yet a close reading of "The Vision of Judgment" and his correspondence surrounding *The Liberal* shows that Byron tried to grow despite his class consciousness. Bertrand Russell viewed Byron's poetical ideas as a blueprint for fascism,[20] but Byron condemned tyranny in his own lifetime, whether incarnated by Lord Castlereagh, George III, or Napoleon Bonaparte. Throughout his life, Byron consistently favored liberal causes such as Catholic emancipation and Italian, Spanish, and Greek independence. "Judge me by my acts," he reputedly said, shortly before dying at Missolonghi.[21]

My study attempts to do just that. But even Byron knew that "acts" can be understood only by the words used to describe them. I discuss Byron's political speeches, correspondence, and poetry—his public and private conduct—in order to examine the full range of his political thought. I use the concept of erotic liberalism to illuminate Byron's unique political contribution, because such a concept draws on the reading—on Plato, Sappho, Montesquieu, Rousseau, Staël—that influenced Byron to behave the way that he did.

My first chapter examines Byron's parliamentary career, emphasizing the influence of Richard Sheridan and Beau Brummell. Struck by his failure as an orator in the House of Lords, Byron visited Leigh Hunt, editor of *The Examiner*, in the Surrey jail. As a poet who had become a political martyr for libeling the Prince Regent, Hunt taught Byron how to join the roles of poet and politician. By appending his name to "Lines to a Lady Weeping" in a new edition of "The Corsair" and by comparing himself to Napoleon, Byron fashioned an erotic liberalism which engaged in political critique by expressing personal feelings and desires.

I explore Byron's politics of feeling in my second chapter. Byron's antics at Newstead Abbey and his references to Laurence Sterne, the Medmenham monks, and Choderlos de Laclos show him emulating a version of eighteenth-century libertinism long after it was unfashionable, even politically dangerous, to do so. He continued this anachronistic libertinism in his letters, where he emulated Valmont's writing style and libertine strategies. I argue that Byron's references to Sterne and Laclos expose his sexual conservatism, which flourished, paradoxically, the same year he advocated liberal causes in the House of Lords.

In my third chapter, I note how Byron used the Joseph story to cure himself of mere libertinism. In writing "The Bride of Abydos" in November 1813, Byron drew on plot and imagery from Jami's "Yusef and Zuleika," a Persian poem based on the Koran version of the Joseph story; in *Hebrew Melodies* (1814), Byron explored biblical themes still further by collaborating with the Jewish composer, Isaac Nathan, on adaptations of Psalm 137; and in Canto 5 of *Don Juan*, begun on October 16, 1820, he used the Joseph story, in both its Jewish and Islamic forms, to challenge his Christian contemporaries' sexual mores while correcting his own libertine tendencies.

Byron's cosmopolitanism was an important aspect of his liberalism, the subject of my fourth chapter. This can best be understood by comparing Canto 3 of *Childe Harold's Pilgrimage* to Madame de Staël's *De l'Allemagne* in terms of the postures of cosmopolitanism, feeling, and self-mythology which they both employ. Joanne Wilkes examines how gender influenced their political brand of opposition and compares Canto 4 of *Childe Harold's Pilgrimage* with Staël's *Corinne*. My approach juxtaposes different works and discusses different themes. I argue that Staël's *De l'Allemagne* influenced the opening lines of "The Bride of Abydos" and helped shape Byron's cosmopolitanism in Canto 3 of *Childe Harold's Pilgrimage*. Suspicious of nationalism, especially in their own countries, Byron and Staël earned reputations for integrity which gave moral authority to the liberalism their work helped define.

Byron and Staël were both aristocratic liberals, and Byron's two letters on the Pope-Bowles controversy and his *Marino Faliero*, the subjects of my fifth chapter, show the peculiar paradox of Byron's position. Byron's defense of Pope reveals an aristocratic bias to his thought, his refusal to pander to the corrupted taste of the masses. A similar elitism is evident in Byron's *Marino Faliero*, which he refused to have judged by his contemporaries at Drury Lane. By using a neoclassical form to portray Faliero's "revolution," Byron subverted his play's ostensibly radical subject: the aborted effort of a Venetian doge to overthrow the Council of Ten. Faliero's numerous unrevolutionary and undemocratic remarks about his fellow conspirators also show the influence of Byron's social class.

My sixth chapter explores the implications of Byron's bisexuality, a more liberalizing influence on his politics. The poet's erotic life shaped *Don Juan*, for Byron created a narrator only marginally interested in the heterosexual plot he unfolds. The irony of *Don Juan* derives in large part from Byron's partial censoring of his narrator in a poem poised delicately between full disclosure and a more thoroughgoing and polite suppression of its homosexuality. Cecil Lang, Louis Crompton, and Jean Hagstrum[22] discuss Byron's homoeroticism in some detail. My chapter is the first to focus on how Byron's bisexuality influenced his use of what I call a "gay" narrator in *Don Juan*.

My seventh chapter focuses on Byron's joint editorship of *The Liberal*. I argue that Byron did not understand the meaning of the word he so famously selected as the title for this periodical. Though he fought with the Italian Carbonari (or "Liberals") for national sovereignty, he disapproved of English "liberals" like "Orator" Hunt, who advocated a form of social leveling. This chapter examines "The Vision of Judgment," first published in *The Liberal*, as a case study in Byron's liberalism. Byron's most anthologized satire exposes his liberalism by differentiating him from radicals and conservatives alike.

My eighth chapter, "'Still let me love!': Byron in Greece," draws on Stephen Minta's *On a Voiceless Shore* (1998) and Fred Rosen's *Bentham, Byron, and Greece* (1992) to contrast Byron's liberalism with Leicester Stanhope's utilitarianism during their involvement in the struggle for Greek independence.[23] Byron's distrust of systems in poetry and politics led him to sharp disagreements with the man he called the "topographical Colonel." I contrast Byron's ancient liberalism, as defined by William Hazlitt and Leo Strauss, with Stanhope's more modern variety, explicated by Benjamin Constant and Isaiah Berlin.[24] In love with Loukas Chalandritsanos, who inspired his military conduct in Greece, Byron contributes to contemporary understandings of political action (as Stephen Minta argues) by refusing to treat liberal politics as a purely ideological endeavor. In his poetry, as in his life, he cultivated an erotic liberalism.

My conclusion argues that American critics and politicians have not adequately recognized Byron's contribution to political liberalism. Lionel Trilling's *The Liberal Imagination* (1950) serves as a key text in explaining why a generation of American critics preferred Wordsworth's political quietism to Byron's more revolutionary commitments. I argue for Byron's political relevance during the Cold War, noting how Byron's *Don Juan* reveals the moral deficiencies of Henry Kissinger's congress diplomacy, which Kissinger (in *A World Restored* [1957], the published version of his Harvard doctoral dissertation) modeled on Byron's contemporary and nemesis, Lord Castlereagh.

NOTES

1. George Gordon, Lord Byron, *Lord Byron's Letters and Journals*, ed. Leslie A. Marchand, 12 vols. (Cambridge: Harvard University Press, 1973–82). All references are to this edition and include date, volume, and page number in the text.

2. Unless otherwise indicated, quotations from Byron's poetry are from *Lord Byron: The Complete Poetical Works*, ed. Jerome McGann, 6 vols. (Oxford: Clarendon Press, 1980–91). References in the text appear as *CPW* with volume, canto, and line number, except for references to *Hebrew Melodies,* which appear with volume and page number, and *Don Juan,* which list volume, canto, and stanza.

3. Plato, *Plato: The Symposium*, trans. and ed. Alexander Nehamas and Paul Woodruff (Indianapolis: Hackett Publishing Company, 1989), xiii.

4. Anne Carson, *Eros the Bittersweet: An Essay* (Princeton, N.J.: Princeton University Press, 1986), 32.

5. Carson, *Eros the Bittersweet*, 32.

6. Plato, *Symposium*, xxii.

7. Wayland Young, *Eros Denied: Sex in Western Society* (New York: Grove Press, 1964), 254.

8. Young, *Eros Denied*, 254.

9. Peter Wagner, *Eros Revived: Erotica of the Enlightenment in England and America* (London: Secker and Warburg, 1988), 213.

10. Young, *Eros Denied*, 274.

11. J. A. Simpson and E. S. C. Weiner, eds., *The Oxford English Dictionary*, 2d ed, vol. 3 (Oxford: Clarendon Press, 1989), 985.

12. Charlton Lewis and Charles Short, eds., *A Latin Dictionary* (Oxford: Clarendon Press, 1955), 1056.

13. Raymond Williams, *Keywords: A Vocabulary of Culture and Society* (New York: Oxford University Press, 1976), 180.

14. Simpson and Weiner, *The Oxford English Dictionary*, 10: 881–82.

15. Ione Dodson Young, *A Concordance to the Poetry of Byron*, 4 vols. (Austin: Best Printing Company, 1975), 2:825. Young's valuable concordance does not include Byron's prefaces, which would bring the number of uses of the word to fourteen.

16. For a suggestive study of Montesquieu's *Persian Letters,* from which my own book borrows its title, see Diana Schaub, *Erotic Liberalism* (Lanham, Md.: Rowman & Littlefield, 1995).

17. Plato, *Symposium*, xiii.

18. Matthew Arnold, quoting Goethe in his preface to his volume of selections, *Poetry of Byron* (1881), reprinted in *Essays in Criticism: Second Series* (1888); my source is *Byron: The Critical Heritage* (New York: Barnes & Noble, Inc., 1970), 452. For Emerson, see M. H. Abrams, et al., *The Norton Anthology of English Literature*, 6th ed., vol. 2 (New York: W. W. Norton & Company, 1993), 915.

19. Michael Scrivener, "'Zion Alone is Forbidden': Historicizing Antisemitism in Byron's *The Age of Bronze*," *Keats-Shelley Journal* 43 (1994): 94, 97.

20. Bertrand Russell, *A History of Western Philosophy* (New York: Touchstone, 1972), 747.

21. Harold Nicolson, *Byron: The Last Journey* (New York: Archon Books, 1969), 209.

22. Cecil Lang, "Narcissus Jilted: Byron, Don Juan, and the Biographical Imperative," in *Historical Studies and Literary Criticism*, ed. J. J. McGann (Madison: University of Wisconsin Press, 1985); Louis Crompton, *Byron and Greek Love: Homophobia in 19th-Century England* (Berkeley: University of California Press, 1985); Jean Hagstrum, "Byron's Songs of Innocence: The Songs to Thyrza," in *Eros and Vision: The Restoration to Romanticism* (Evanston, Ill.: Northwestern University Press, 1986), 177–192.

23. Stephen Minta, *On a Voiceless Shore: Byron in Greece* (New York: Holt Rinehart, 1997); Fred Rosen, *Byron, Bentham, and Greece* (Oxford: Oxford University Press, 1992).

24. William Hazlitt, "Advice to a Patriot," in *The Collected Works of William Hazlitt*, ed. A. R. Waller and Arnold Glover, 12 vols. (London: J. M. Dent & Co., 1902), 3:21; Leo Strauss, *Ancient and Modern Liberalism* (New York: Cornell University Press, 1968), 21; Benjamin Constant, "The Liberty of the Ancients Compared with That of the Moderns" (1819), in *Political Writings*, trans. and ed. Biancamaria Fontana (Cambridge: Cambridge University Press, 1988), 308–328; Isaiah Berlin, "Two Concepts of Liberty," in *Four Essays on Liberty* (New York: Oxford University Press, 1969), 118–172.

1

BYRON'S POLITICS OF FEELING

Four years after Byron died in Greece, Mary Shelley caricatured him as Lord Raymond in *The Last Man*. "'Verney,' said he, 'my first act when I become King of England, will be to unite with the Greeks, take Constantinople, and subdue all Asia. I intend to be a warrior, a conqueror; Napoleon's name shall vail to mine; and enthusiasts, instead of visiting his rocky grave, and exalting the merits of the fallen, shall adore my majesty, and magnify my illustrious achievements.'"[1] Mary Shelley understood that Lord Byron was not content with a parliamentary career. He saw himself as a man of action, signing his first order to his Suliote troops in Greece, "Generale Noel Byron."[2]

Mary Shelley and Lord Byron both supported Greek independence, but she nevertheless caricatured the egotism that motivated his political career. Recent critics present a similarly complex portrait of Byron's political motives. Michael Foot's *The Politics of Paradise* highlights Byron's political idealism, viewing him as an aristocratic rebel who championed the cause of the oppressed. Malcolm Kelsall's *Byron's Politics*, by contrast, debunks the legend of Byron's radicalism by demonstrating his debt to Whig principles. Byron's political speeches and diary of 1813 provide ample room for both interpretations.

Examining these documents, one realizes that Byron chose political models that proved to be more of an encumbrance than a help. He modeled his speeches on Richard Sheridan's, a fellow poet and playwright. Where Sheridan self-consciously separated the roles of writer and politician, Byron sought to combine them. His diary of 1813 shows that he visited Leigh Hunt in the Surrey jail in June of that year with the problem of his own political career firmly in mind. By February 1814, he elected to append his name to "Lines to a Lady

Weeping," reinventing himself as a political satirist. Departing from the epigrammatic wit which he had used in his maiden speech in 1812, Byron fashioned a new politics of feeling to reach a larger audience in 1814.

I

Byron began his political career as an eighteenth-century Whig. He made his first overtures to Lord Holland, nephew of Charles James Fox.[3] On February 27, 1812, he argued against making frame-breaking a capital offense; on April 21, 1812, he supported an extension of the franchise to Catholics; and on June 1, 1813, he presented Cartwright's petition for parliamentary reform. A decade later, Byron worried more about assessing his own eloquence[4] than ascertaining its effect. Seriousness of purpose did not characterize the gentleman orator of 1813. "I had been sent for in great haste to a Ball which I quitted I confess somewhat reluctantly to emancipate five Millions of people" (*DT* 9:28), he remembered, proudly displaying his jejune tone for posterity.

From 1812 to 1813, after all, Byron was a dandy.[5] The famous author of *Childe Harold's Pilgrimage* moved in circles with Scrope Davies and other dandies for whom the political was only one component of the social (*DT* 9:22). "I belonged to ... the Alfred, to the Cocoa tree—to Watier's ... to the Hampden political Club—and to the Italian Carbonari," Byron remembered, as if in order of importance (*DT* 9:23). Byron found himself accepted by the dandies at Watier's. "I had gamed—and drank—and taken my degrees in most dissipations—and having no pedantry and not being overbearing—we ran quietly together" (*DT* 9:22). The world of the dandy would not last forever, but the "tinge of Dandyism" Byron confessed to in his "minority" lasted long enough to set the tone for his political speeches.[6]

Beau Brummell exerted a formidable influence over English society. "In his own fashion, he ruled London," Connelly observes, "even after his quarrel with the Prince."[7] Though not an aristocrat, Brummell set the rules for London's most fashionable clubs. In 1799, he became a member of Brooks and shared power with an oligarchy of such "lady patronesses" as Lady Jersey, Lady Castlereagh, and Lady Willoughby d'Eresby. In conjunction with these women, Brummell managed to exclude three-quarters of the nobility from gatherings at Almack's. On one evening, Almack's closed its doors on the Duke of Wellington for appearing after the admission deadline of 11:00 P.M. Wednesday night balls at Almack's and Watier's soon became an aristocratic mating ground for those Brummell and others judged to have "ton."

Byron had little direct contact with Brummell, but he lived on Bennett Street, adjacent to St. James, and circulated in this world of high society, inheriting its prejudices and tone.[8] "I liked the dandies," he remembered, "we ran comfortably together." Both men were well-connected. Brummell numbered George Canning among his classmates at Eton and was bosom companion to the Prince Regent until their falling out.[9] Byron attended Harrow with Robert Peel and dined with Sheridan.[10] Like Brummell, Byron took great pride in his appearance, collected snuff boxes, and traveled in style. Both men were parvenus who used their impudence and wit, the one to establish a position in society, the other to convince himself that he belonged there.[11] In his Ravenna journal, written five years after his exile, Byron continued to see himself as a "dandy," now "broken" and in exile (like Brummell in Calais) from the fashionable world over which he had once reigned. "Brummell—at *Calais*—Scrope at Bruges—Buonaparte at St. Helena—you in—your new apartments—and I at Ravenna—only think so many great men!" Byron crowed in a letter to Hobhouse (*BLJ* March 3, 1820; 10:50). The comparison was apt. Both Byron and Brummell left England to escape creditors and scandals: Byron chose an ornate Napoleonic carriage which he had built especially for the occasion in 1816. Both Byron and Brummell tested the boundaries of social conventions without ever wishing to destroy them. Scorning the tastes of their countrymen, they never entirely escaped the influence of the culture they helped shape.[12]

Byron's speeches recall Brummell's witty repartee ("Who's your fat friend," Brummell once said to Lord Alvanley, who had appeared in a crowded room accompanied by the Prince Regent). Take, as an example, Byron's final peroration defending the Nottingham frame-breakers. Perhaps the most impressive of his rhetorical moments in the House of Lords, this speech succeeds stylistically even as it fails pragmatically. Byron sought to dissuade Tories from imposing the death penalty. Yet "nothing Byron said in the debate was going to affect the issue," Malcolm Kelsall observes. "The Whigs were in a minority. The death Bill had already passed in the Commons. Anyone looking at the benches of the Lords could count the heads, and would know that it would pass the Lords."[13] Far from ingratiating himself to his audience, Byron attacked them in a manner that recalls Brummell's scathing reference to the Prince Regent:

> But suppose it past, suppose one of these men, as I have seen them, meagre with famine sullen with despair, careless of a life,—which your Lordships are perhaps about to value at something less than the price of a stocking-frame,—suppose this man surrounded by those children for whom he is unable to procure bread at the hazard of his existence, about to be torn forever

from a family which he lately supported in peaceful industry, & which it is not his fault that he can no longer so support, suppose this man,—& there are ten thousand such from whom you may select your victims, dragged into court to be tried for this new offence by this new law, still there are two things wanting to convict & condemn him—& these are in my opinion, twelve butchers for a Jury, & a Jefferies for a Judge. (*CMP* 27)[14]

Like Beau Brummell, Byron insulted the very men he needed to persuade. In concluding his maiden speech, he referred to his colleagues as "careless" and implicitly compared their intolerance to that of Lord Jefferies, a "hanging judge" during the Glorious Revolution who brooked no political dissent (*CMP* 29, 289 n.6).

Like Burke, Byron memorized his speeches; like Sheridan, he delivered them theatrically. But Byron "altered the natural tone of his voice, which was sweet and round, into a formal drawl, and he prepared his features for a part," Robert Dallas remembered. "It was a youth declaiming a task," he noted.[15] No wonder Lord Holland found Byron's speech not "at all suited to our common notions of parliamentary eloquence."[16] Byron hoped to use his eloquence to cut a path to power in the House of Lords at a time when the sheer volume of legislation passing through both houses of Parliament made speech making less important, as Linda Colley points out.[17] Not particularly articulate themselves, Tory ministers dismissed Whig posturing.[18] In a comment he might have directed at Byron, Pitt regretted that Sheridan's speeches, Byron's great model, were not kept "to their proper stage."[19]

Sympathetic as he was to the plight of the weavers in his own district, Byron did not choose his own subject. John Cartwright urged Byron and Lord Holland to take up the cause of the Nottingham frame-breakers.[20] Holland was surveyor in this district and thus felt responsible for any legislation that might be passed against them. By contrast, when Byron returned from Athens in 1811, he seemed more concerned about his own fortune than his tenants'. Refusing to sell Newstead Abbey but unable to glean a profit from his disputed Rochdale coal mines, Byron doubled the rents of those living on his estate only several months before pleading the frame-breakers' cause.[21] In one breath he hoped to curb mob violence; in the other, he incited it. If his speech was not inflammatory enough, he published an "Ode to the Framers of the Frame Bill," which directed his readers' anger at the Tory legislators who "when asked for a remedy, sent down a rope."

The same preference for expressing generous principles rather than achieving practical results marks his defense of Catholic emancipation. Whigs shared Byron's support for extending the franchise to Catholics. In 1812, however, Byron's speech was politically inopportune. That April, Whigs still hoped to enter Perceval's administration. Even Charles James Fox had subordinated his support for Catholic emancipation to his desire to serve in the Talents ministry. Yet Byron showed no such pragmatism. A cynical critic might view Byron's speech as the work of a posturing demagogue. By referring to the Act of Union between Ireland and England as the union of the "shark with his prey," for example, he merely borrowed a trope from Sheridan's Begum speech ("it is the union of the vulture and its prey") at a time when it could achieve no practical result. Hobhouse noted that Byron's speech kept the House in a roar of laughter, but does not define its object. "Byron may have been wounded by it," Erdman notes. "He has made strangely few references to this speech, and when he says his parliamentary 'experiment' as far as it went . . . was not discouraging," he adds "particularly my first speech."[22]

Byron had good reason to be prouder of his first speech than his second. Where the frame-breaker's speech bore the stamp of Byron's charismatic liberalism, his Roman Catholic claims speech borrowed heavily from Sheridan. "Whenever any one proposes to you a specific plan of Reform [Sheridan] would say jokingly, always answer that you are for nothing short of Annual parliaments and Universal suffrage—there you are safe."[23] Fintan O'Toole views Sheridan's support for Catholic emancipation as his last will and testament,[24] but one of his first biographers, Thomas Moore, had his doubts. "He had often heard of people knocking out their brains against a wall," Sheridan reportedly said of the Whigs' defense of Catholic emancipation, "but never before knew of any one building a wall expressly for the purpose."[25]

Byron admired Sheridan's oratorical skills and found the former playwright's speech of August 13, 1807 particularly compelling. "The fact is, that the tyranny practised upon the Irish has been throughout unremitting," Sheridan began, before retailing an anecdote to call their distressed situation more vividly to mind.

> It was with respect to an Irish drummer, who was employed to inflict punishment upon a soldier. While he was flogging the soldier, the poor fellow, writhing with pain, intreated him to change his mode of lashing him. Sometimes he called to him to strike a little higher, and sometimes a little lower. The drummer endeavoured to accommodate him as far as it was in his power; but finding it to no purpose, at last cried out, "Upon my conscience, you are a discontented fellow, for whether I strike high or low, there is no such thing as pleasing you." This is precisely the case with respect to Ireland. Notwithstanding the infinite variety of oppression exercised against them, there are still a number of them who are so unreasonable as to be discontented. (*CMP* 304)

When Byron defended Catholic emancipation almost six years later in the upper house, he repeated, and only slightly recast, Sheridan's memorable anecdote.

> Those personages remind me of a story of a certain drummer, who being called upon in the course of duty to administer punishment to a friend tied to the halberts, he was requested to flog high, he did—to flog low, he did—to flog in the middle, he did—high, low, down the middle, and up again, but all in vain, the patient continued his complaints with the most provoking pertinacity, until the drummer, exhausted and angry, flung down his scourge, exclaiming, "the devil burn you, there's no pleasing you, flog where one will!" (*CMP* 39)

Sheridan focused attention on the oppressed, on the "poor" soldier, "writhing with pain." "There are still a number of them who are so unreasonable as to be discontented," he notes. Byron, by contrast, identified with the exasperated drummer who whips him. "[E]xhausted and angry," the drummer "flung down his scourge," "provok[ed]" by the "pertinacity" of his friend's "complaints": "the devil burn you, there's no pleasing you, flog where one will!" he says. Sheridan ridiculed the drummer; Byron mocked his "friend." As a dramatist conscious of his middle class origins, Sheridan expressed sympathy with victims more easily than Byron, who seemed as out of touch with suffering as Marino Faliero, Sardanapalus, or Sterne's Yorick (as I will argue in my next chapter).

Byron's third speech also suffered from Byron's effort to imitate Sheridan's theatrical style, a style more suited to the House of Commons than the House of Lords.[26] He intended to simply present Sir John Cartwright's petition for Reform, but Thomas Moore remembered how Byron

> continued to walk up and down . . . spouting forth for me, in a sort of mock-heroic voice, detached sentences of the speech he had just been delivering. "I told them," he said, "that it was a most flagrant violation of the Constitution—that, if such things were permitted, there was an end of English freedom, and that—" "But what was the dreadful grievance?" I asked, interrupting him in his eloquence.—"The grievance?" he repeated, pausing as if to consider—"Oh, *that* I forget." (*CMP* 311)

Andrew Nicholson justly observes that Byron's remark was "merely a display of bravado." The display is revealing, however, as are Byron's subsequent remarks about Cartwright and "the sort of reform for which he stood" (*BLJ* 6:165, 211–12; *BLJ* 8:240; *CMP* 311, 313). Remembering this last parliamentary speech in 1821, Byron recognized the futility of his actions. In his Ravenna journal, he displayed the pathos of supporting lost causes in Parliament; he used the journal form, in part, to gain recognition for his political efforts, long after the cause itself had failed.

At the time, Byron expressed considerable disappointment with his abbreviated political career,[27] and this judgment merits further scrutiny. "I have declined presenting the Debtor's Petition, being sick of parliamentary mummeries," he wrote in a diary entry of November 14, 1813.

I have spoken thrice; but I doubt my ever becoming an orator. My first was liked; the second and third—I don't know whether they succeeded or not. I have never yet set to it *con amore*. (3:206)

Byron's diary from November 14, 1813 to April 19, 1814 reveals why he doubted "ever becoming an orator."

II

Three conflicts recur. Byron fears that he cannot support political reform because of his social class, that he cannot be both a poet and a politician,[28] and that he has engaged in affairs too scandalous and public—with Lady Caroline Lamb in particular—to gain the respect of his colleagues in the House of Lords. As an aristocrat, Byron was reluctant to support the common people in Parliament. On February 25, 1812, for example, he "apologiz[ed]," however facetiously, for his frame-breakers' speech. "I am a little apprehensive that your Lordship will think me too lenient towards these men, & half a framebreaker myself" (*BLJ* 2:166), he wrote to Lord Holland. Visiting Leigh Hunt only intensified Byron's sense of impasse. How could an aristocrat support the causes Hunt defended without contradiction or impropriety?

Byron viewed libertinism as an equally formidable obstacle to political advancement. Here again, Leigh Hunt was an important foil. If Hunt was a political martyr, Byron disparaged himself as a libertine, pursuing affairs with his halfsister Augusta Leigh and other married women. "One must have some excuse to oneself for laziness, or inability, or both, and this is mine," he confessed to his diary several months after visiting Hunt. "'Company, villainous company, hath been the spoil of me;'—and then, I 'have drunk medicines,' not to make me love others, but certainly enough to hate myself" (*BLJ* November 14, 1813; 3:206).

Byron's diary shows that he felt poetry (especially satire) would compromise his political career. He renounced the poem that Richard Sheridan thought the most auspicious sign of his oratorical talent, "English Bards and Scotch Reviewers," to conciliate himself with the Whigs (*DT* 9:16). In the preface to "The Corsair," he even declared his intention to write no more. Politics and poetry were separate spheres, he reasoned, and acting was more manly than scribbling. Within a few months, however, Byron had reinvented himself as a political satirist, publishing "Lines to a Lady Weeping." In this poem, Byron criticized the Prince Regent for being a bad friend to the Whigs. He fashioned a new politics of feeling that emphasized passion rather than parliamentary procedure, genius rather than middle-class morality, and action rather than words.[29] Napoleon

Bonaparte's military success encouraged Byron politically by helping him overcome the binary oppositions of reformer/aristocrat, libertine/politician, words/actions. As Byron watched Napoleon's fortunes rise in late March 1814 (only to end in defeat that April at Waterloo), he identified closely with the French emperor: the world became his stage, poetry his political pursuit.

Byron first visited Leigh Hunt at the Surrey jail on May 19, 1813. To mark the occasion, Byron penned a facetious verse epistle to Thomas Moore, who had invited him:

> But now to my letter—to yours 'tis an answer—
> To-morrow be with me, as soon as you can, sir,
> All ready and dress'd for proceeding to spunge on
> (According to compact) the wit in the dungeon—
> Pray Phoebus at length our political malice
> May not get us lodgings within the same palace! (May 19, 1813; 3:49–50)

Byron could not resist ridiculing a man whose "wit" had landed him in a "dungeon," an irony he underscored yet again when John Cam Hobhouse was incarcerated at Newgate. In 1813, Byron still thought his "wit" would prove less self-destructive than theirs.

After beginning an extended affair with Augusta in the spring of 1813, however, Byron became "sunk" in his own estimation. No longer able to condescend to Hunt, Byron began to respect him. His diary entry of December 1, 1813 reflects this change. "Hunt is an extraordinary character, and not exactly of the present age. He reminds me more of the Pym and Hampden times—much talent, great independence of spirit, and an austere, yet not repulsive, aspect. If he goes on *qualis ab incepto,* I know few men who will deserve more praise or obtain it. I must go and see him again" (*BLJ* 3:228). Two paragraphs later, Byron contemplated his own political future:

> Baldwin is boring me to present their King's Bench petition. I presented Cartwright's last year; and Stanhope and I stood against the whole House, and mouthed it valiantly—and had some fun and a little abuse for our opposition. But "I am not i' th' vein" for this business. Now, had [Lady Oxford] been here, she would have made me do it. There is a woman, who, amid all her fascination, always urged a man to usefulness or glory. Had she remained, she had been my tutelar genius. (*BLJ* December 1, 1813; 3:229)

Without the erotic encouragement of Lady Oxford (their affair ended in late July, 1813), Byron had barely enough liberality to free a man from debtor's prison. Like Richard III, he is not "'i' th' vein' for this business."

But Byron had sounded the death knell for his political career too soon. On February 1, 1814, he published "Lines to a Lady Weeping" in the second issue of "The Corsair,"[30] appending his name to a work first published anonymously in *The Morning Chronicle* (March 7, 1812). Like Hunt's libeling of the Prince Regent, Byron's attack on England's ruler was *ad hominem*. The poem "fix[ed] his politics," according to Lord Holland,[31] and created a flurry of negative publicity. In 1812, one could still construe the Prince Regent's betrayal of his Whig friends as an act of loyalty to an ailing father. By 1814, however, any hope for George III's mental recovery was over, and Byron's attack on the Prince Regent's apostasy became notorious, in part, because Byron was so prophetic.[32]

He explained his eight-line poem in a manner that recalls Hunt's defense of his libel against the Prince Regent.[33] Both Byron and Hunt measured public figures by their private conduct. Hunt described the Prince Regent as a libertine "head over heels in debt," while Byron focused on the Prince Regent's relationship with his daughter: "It was asserted, in the beginning of the year 1812," he wrote in a letter to the *Courier* on February, 1814 (*BLJ* 4:41), "that the Prince discarded his friends and his opinions, and that on one occasion his daughter, whom he had educated in his former public principles and private friendships, finding it difficult at that early period of life when the heart is warm and the soul open, to revoke at once the best feelings of our nature, was so astonished at a convivial display of the new doctrines, that she shed tears" ("An answer to the *Courier*," *BLJ* February 1814?; 4:42). Byron contrasted "the new doctrines" with Princess Charlotte's candor; her soul was "too open" to conceal her astonishment at her father's behavior. The Prince, by contrast, abandoned his Whig friends with impunity. In the poem itself, Byron took the daughter's point of view:

> Weep, daughter of a royal line,
> A Sire's disgrace, a realm's decay;
> Ah, happy! if each tear of thine
> Could wash a father's fault away!
>
> Weep—for thy tears are Virtue's tears—
> Auspicious to these suffering isles;
> And be each drop in future years
> Repaid thee by thy people's smiles! (*CPW* 3:10)

Byron used possessives, five times in eight lines, to tie subjects to actions ("A sire's disgrace, a realm's decay;") as if insisting on the Prince Regent's moral responsibility ("father's fault"), which the "father" seemed determined to evade. Poor fathers make poor rulers, Byron suggested.

Byron forfeited a traditional political career when he acknowledged writing this poem.[34] With Napoleon's example before him, he defined politics as "a *feeling*," a natural extension of his personality. "Byron is concerned with specific abuses and particular tyrants and their sycophants," Karl Kroeber argues in *British Romantic Art*, "not abstractions such as political scientists devise. This specificity endeared him to many diverse kinds of patriots, who would not have found him so appealing had he not been so abusively *ad hominem* in his own voice."[35] In a letter to John Murray, Byron explained why he insisted on including his "weeping lines" over William Gifford's objection: "But—I cannot give up my weeping lines—and I do think them good & don't mind what 'it looks like.'—In politics he may be right too—but that with me is a feeling and I can't torify my nature" (*BLJ* January 22, 1814; 4:38). Byron combined his political and poetic pursuits by defining politics as a "feeling"; "simple concepts like liberty," to which Byron adhered, "are felt rather than defined," M. K. Joseph argues.[36] At least temporarily, Byron was now able to avoid political compromises. Poetry proved a more congenial method of self-expression for him than parliamentary "mummeries." "I have that within me that bounds against opposition," Byron informed Lady Melbourne. "I have quick feelings— & not very good nerves—but somehow they have more than once served me pretty well when I most wanted them—and may again—at any rate I shall try" (*BLJ* February 11, 1814; 4:53).

Yet feeling was a political strategy fraught with complications, Leigh Hunt argued. "This is one of the results of pushing our abstractions too far, and of that dangerous art which Mr. Wordsworth has claimed for his simpler pieces," Hunt wrote in his preface to *The Feast of the Poets*, "the giving importance to actions and situations by our feelings, instead of adapting our feelings to the importance they possess. The consequences of this, if carried into a system, would be, that we could make any thing or nothing important, just as diseased or healthy impulses told us;—a straw might awaken in us as many profound, but certainly not as useful reflections, as the fellow-creature that lay upon it."[37] Hunt thought that relying excessively on feelings would lead one from "thinking trifling things important, to thinking important things trifling" and end, as Wordsworth himself had ended, by becoming "government property," a stamp collector, insensitive to the plight of the poor.

Yet Byron's use of feelings as a guide to politics had more in common with Burke and Hunt than it did with Wordsworth. Like Burke's *Reflections on the Revolution in France*,[38] which used political feeling to secure sympathy for Marie Antoinette, Byron's letter to the *Courier* offered a glimpse of a private moment, a moment that Byron disingenuously claimed was not political at all: the prince's daughter's reaction to her father's abandonment of his friends. Byron privileged feelings, honor, and principle over narrow partisan concerns, knowing full well that one led inevitably to the other. "A child may lament a parent's error without disobedience—and the decay of a realm without rebellion," Byron wrote in his letter to *The Courier*. His "Answer to *The Courier*" (*BLJ* February 1814?; 4:42) explained the poem by drawing the distinction between public principles and private friendships sharply, but with a question mark rather than a line. The Prince's daughter found it difficult to revoke the "best feelings of our nature"; she was "astonished at a convivial display of the new doctrines"; she "shed tears" for which she was then criticized—"an unamiable weakness, and a formidable precedent for Heirs Apparent" (*BLJ* February 1814?; 4:43). Would the English not be better off if their political responses were as spontaneous as Princess Charlotte's? Byron seemed to ask. "An Heir Apparent may not be so justifiable in adopting and cherishing a friend's principles and promises for the purpose of denying them on his becoming Sovereign," he concluded. By the end of the paragraph, Byron's purely private observation became a forceful political critique.[39]

As a politician who was also a poet, Byron could maintain Whig positions without ingratiating himself to the Whigs, as he had with Lord Holland. He could be both libertine and liberal without contradiction or embarrassment. "'The lines to a Lady Weeping' must go with the Corsair," he wrote to his publisher. "I care nothing for consequences on this point—my politics are to me like a young mistress to an old man the worse they grow the fonder I become of them" (*BLJ* January 22, 1814; 4:37).[40] Politics became a form of transgression, perversity, and opposition, a "young mistress to an old man." Nor did he view poetry and politics as distinct spheres any longer, for he proudly sent a copy of "The Corsair" to Leigh Hunt, instructing Murray to include "the smaller poems" in it, that is, the poems that were explicitly political (*BLJ* February 10, 1814; 4:52).[41]

Byron's use of lyric poetry as a political weapon becomes clear through his response to the outcry "Lines to a Lady Weeping" produced. "As the wine is poured out, let it be drunk to the dregs," he wrote to Moore (*BLJ* February 10, 1814; 4:52); "as the wine is tapped it shall be drunk to the lees," he informed Lady Melbourne (*BLJ* February 11, 1814; 4:53). Both allusions, marked "unidentified" in Byron's letters, refer to Rabelais's "Prologue of the Author" in the *Third Book of Pantagruel*. "As much as you draw out at the tap, I will pour in at the bung ... if at times it seems to you to be emptied to the lees, still it will not be dry," Rabelais writes.[42] Like Byron, Rabelais instructed his audience to ignore *Pantagruel* if it displeased them. "If you do not like it, leave it alone," he wrote.[43] Byron offered similar advice to his Tory opponents and Whig friends. "'*Prosecute*,'" Byron wrote to Lady Melbourne, "Oh No—I am a great friend to the liberty of the press—even at the expence of myself" (*BLJ* March, 1814?; 4:75). Byron defended his poem by citing Rabelais, perhaps sensing that

Rabelais's multiple ironies and constantly shifting perspectives promoted diverse opinions and encouraged free expression, a fact not lost on Mikhail Bakhtin, who used Byron's commentary on Rabelais to criticize Stalinist Russia.[44]

Yet Byron feigned surprise that the newspapers took him seriously at all. "Did you ever know any thing like this?" he asked Lady Melbourne:

> at a time when peace & war—& Emperors & Napoleons—and the destinies of the things they have made of mankind are trembling in the balance—the Government Gazettes can devote half their attention & columns day after day to 8 lines written two years ago—& now republished only—(by an Individual) & suggest them for the consideration of Parliament probably about the same period with the treaty of Peace.—I really begin to think myself a most important personage. (*BLJ* February 11, 1814; 4:53)

Napoleon's return limned Byron's; the prospects for charismatic leadership seemed reborn.[45] When Napoleon lost all he had gained in a single battle at Waterloo, Byron identified with him still. "I want my books if you can find or cause them to be found for me," he informed his publisher, "if only to lend them to N[apoleo]n in the 'island of Elba' during his retirement" (*BLJ* April 9, 1814; 4:91). Napoleon became an alter ego. "I can't help suspecting that my little Pagod will play them some trick still," he wrote to Lady Melbourne. "If Wellington or one hero had beaten another—it would be nothing—but to be worried by brutes—& conquered by recruiting sergeants—why there is not a character amongst them" (*BLJ* April 8, 1814; 4:90).

Byron appealed to the press because he too was a "*character,*" one who attracted his own share of negative attention. "Oh—by the by, I had nearly forgot," he informed Thomas Moore nonchalantly,

> There is a long Poem, an "Anti-Byron," coming out, to prove that I have formed a conspiracy to overthrow, by rhyme, all religion and government, and have already made great progress. . . . I never felt myself important, till I saw and heard of my being such a little Voltaire as to induce such a production. Murray would not publish it, for which he was a fool, and so I told him; but some one else will, doubtless. (*BLJ* April 9, 1814; 4:93)

If Byron's amoral work inspired an "Anti-Byron," Napoleon's moral "revolution" produced an anti-Napoleon in the form of the Holy Alliance (*BLJ* January 12, 1814; 4:27). In a letter he wrote to his future wife, Byron greeted Napoleon's abdication by symbolically proffering his own. "I have brought my politics & paper to a close, and have only room to sign my abdication of both" (*BLJ* April 20, 1814; 4:102).

The dandies, Brummell, and Sheridan influenced Byron's parliamentary style, but Leigh Hunt altered Byron's political strategy. Visiting Leigh Hunt in jail forced Byron to realize that denouncing Lord Elgin in *Childe Harold's Pilgrimage* and pursuing his half-sister Augusta Leigh were not auspicious ways to launch a political career. Private conduct was beginning to matter. Napoleon's return during the hundred days renewed Byron's faith in the political process. He would not have to become a "bigot to virtue" like Hunt or a "poltroon" like Cicero (*BLJ* November 16, 1813; 3:207). He could follow the example of charismatic leaders like Napoleon instead. With Napoleon's fall, however, the balance of power in Europe and the class system it upheld appeared inexorable. Napoleon's "fall" disappointed Byron because tameness had triumphed over talent.

What Byron learned from Leigh Hunt, Rabelais, and Napoleon, however, was invaluable. The oppositions he had set up between poetry and politics, monarchies and republics, despots and heroes, suddenly dissolved. By writing squibs in *The Morning Chronicle*, Byron used his facility for poetic expression to advance the Whig cause. A reign of mediocrity had triumphed temporarily over talent, but Byron would not lose a second opportunity to combine poetry and politics. By the time a crack in the Holy Alliance appeared on October 1820 with the mutiny of King Ferdinand's army in Spain, Byron had already joined the Carbonari in August of that year.[46]

Leigh Hunt proved both catalyst and conscience to Byron: Hunt motivated Byron's return to the political arena in Greece, as surely as he altered Byron's self-conception in 1813, when Byron mistakenly believed his political career had ended in the House of Lords. Byron would have become a political poet without Leigh Hunt, but Hunt kept Byron on the liberal path and encouraged him to believe that poetry and politics were not distinct spheres. Byron's relationship with Hunt and its disintegration (which I explore in my seventh chapter), serve as an excellent yardstick to measure the progression of Byron's politics of feeling.

NOTES

1. Mary Shelley, *The Last Man*, ed. by Anne McWhir (Peterborough, Ontario: Broadview, 1996), 44–45.

2. Benita Eisler, *Byron: Child of Passion, Fool of Fame* (New York: Alfred A. Knopf, 1999), 740.

3. Eisler, *Byron*, 324.

4. George Gordon, Lord Byron, *Lord Byron's Letters and Journals*; 9:14; 16–17; 43.

5. See John Clubbe and Ernest Lovell's chapter on Byron in *English Romanticism: The Grounds of Belief* (De Kalb, Ill.: Northern Illinois University Press, 1983), 93–114; Ellen Moers, *The Dandy: Brummell to Beerbohm* (New York: Viking Press, 1960).

6. See J. B. Priestley, *The Prince of Pleasure and His Regency, 1811–20* (New York: Harper & Row Publishers, 1969), 145; Eisler, *Byron*, 326.

7. Willard Connelly, *The Reign of Beau Brummell* (New York: Greystone Press, 1940), ix.

8. I am indebted to Michael Rees, a long-standing member of the Byron Society, whose tour of "Byron's London" at the 18th International Byron Seminar (London, August 3, 1991) helped me to reconstruct the geography of Regency London.

9. Captain Jesse, *Beau Brummell* (London: Grolier Society, 1844), 140–150, 240. Contributors to Brummell's album included Byron, Sheridan, the Duchess of Devonshire, Lord Erskine, John Townshend, Charles James Fox, George Canning, and William Lamb.

10. Leslie Marchand, *Byron: A Portrait* (Chicago: University of Chicago Press, 1970), 24, 147.

11. Roger Sales, *English Literature in History: 1780–1830; Pastoral and Politics* (London: Hutchinson, 1983), 207.

12. Marchand, *Byron: A Portrait*, 322.

13. Malcolm Kelsall, *Byron's Politics* (Totowa, N.J.: Barnes and Noble, 1987), 45.

14. Andrew Nicholson, ed. *Lord Byron: The Complete Miscellaneous Prose* (Oxford: Clarendon Press, 1991). John Clubbe and Ernest Lovell have pointed to the use of parallelism and repetition that gives this speech its force. *English Romanticism*, 94. See also, Dora Neil Raymond, *The Political Career of Lord Byron* (New York: Henry Holt & Co., 1924), 41.

15. Eisler, *Byron*, 325.

16. David Erdman, "Lord Byron as Rinaldo," *Publications of the Modern Language Association* 57 (1942): 212.

17. Linda Colley, *Britons Forging the Nation*, 2d ed. (New Haven: Yale University Press, 1964), 32.

18. Kelsall, *Byron's Politics*, 50.

19. Michael T. H. Sadler, *The Political Career of Richard Brinsley Sheridan* (Oxford: B. H. Blackwell, 1912), 78.

20. Erdman, "Lord Byron as Rinaldo," 198; Raymond is misleading on this point, for she says simply that "Byron determined that he would speak on the occasion of the measure's second reading" *The Political Career of Lord Byron*, 39.

21. Erdman, "Lord Byron as Rinaldo," 199.

22. Erdman, "Lord Byron as Rinaldo," 197.

23. Linda Kelle, *Richard Brinsley Sheridan: A Life* (London: Pimlico, 1998), 96.

24. Fintan A. O'Toole, *A Traitor's Kiss: The Life of Richard Brinsley Sheridan* (New York: Farrar, Strauss, Giroux, 1997), 447.

25. Thomas Moore, *Life of Sheridan*, 2 vols., 1824 (New York: Redfield, 1853), 2:248–49. Malcolm Kelsall notes that Byron's Catholic Claims speech was highly literary, allusive, and patrician, adding that Byron bears responsibility for choosing such models as Sheridan (*Byron's Politics*, 36). In light of Kelsall's observation, Thomas Moore's comments concerning Sheridan's support for Catholic emancipation are revealing: "he was not altogether disposed to go those generous lengths in favor [of Catholic

emancipation] ... of which Mr. Fox and a few others of their less calculating friends were capable" (*Life of Sheridan*, 2:248–49).

26. Erdman, "Lord Byron as Rinaldo," 196.

27. Eisler, *Byron*, 328.

28. Jerome McGann also emphasizes the dilemma that confronted Byron as an unsatisfying choice between the careers of poet and politician and concludes that "he felt lost on both sides." *Don Juan in Context* (Chicago: University of Chicago Press, 1976), 22.

29. Elie Halevy, *The Growth of Philosophical Radicalism*, trans. A. D. Lindsay (London: Faber & Gwyer, 1928), 74. Byron's politics of "feeling," which I will treat in the next chapter, should be contrasted with the political approach of Bentham, who "mistrusted sensibility and opposed reason to sentiment: he had already so colored the philosophy of reform in England as to distinguish it for all time from the humanitarian philosophy which prevailed in the country of Rousseau, and even in that of Beccaria."

30. In contrast to Carl Woodring, Peter Manning and Frederick Beaty argue that Byron's poem was included in the first edition. By reconstructing Byron's correspondence with Murray, I tend to side with Woodring. If it is true that "the ten thousand copies sold on the day of publication represent several editions," however, as Manning asserts (203), then the debate itself does not seem particularly important. Carl Woodring, *Politics in English Romantic Poetry* (Cambridge: Harvard University Press, 1970), 168; Peter Manning, *Reading Romantics* (New York: Oxford University Press, 1990), 201, 203, 213; Frederick Beaty, *Byron the Satirist* (De Kalb: Northern Illinois University Press, 1985), 74.

31. Henry Richard Vassall, 3rd Lord Holland, *Further Memoirs of the Whig Party*, ed. Lord Stavordale (London: John Murray, 1905), 123. In *Reading Romantics*, Peter Manning argues that "Byron was not the man to be attached 'upon system' to any principle or party" (196). Yet previous critics have shown that Byron's politics were consistently Whig. E. D. H. Johnson, "Lord Byron in *Don Juan*: A Study in Digression" (Ph.D. diss., Yale University, 1939); Malcolm Kelsall, *Byron's Politics*; and J. Michael Robertson, "Aristocratic Individualism in Don Juan," *Studies in English Literature* 17 (autumn 1977): 639–55 and "The Byron of Don Juan as Whig Aristocrat," *Texas Studies in Language and Literature* 17 (winter 1976): 709–24.

32. John Murray, a Tory, was as critical of the Prince Regent as Byron. See his letter of August 1814 to Byron in Samuel Smiles, *A Publisher and His Friends: Memoir and Correspondence of the Late John Murray*, 2 vols. (London: John Murray, 1891), 1:232.

33. Leigh Hunt, *The Autobiography of Leigh Hunt with Reminiscences of Friends and Contemporaries*, 2 vols. (New York: Harper & Brothers, 1850), 1:320.

34. See Peter J. Manning, *Reading Romantics*, 216–37, for a keen reading of the contextual elements of "The Corsair." My argument develops Manning's point in another direction, for I note how Byron's decision to append his name to "Lines to a Lady Weeping" ended his political career in the House of Lords, but began his career as a political poet. Frederick Beaty finds Byron's other political squibs more "defamatory" than "Lines to a Lady Weeping" and would probably not agree with the idea that publishing the poem was a kind of political "forfeit." *Byron the Satirist*, 74.

35. Karl Kroeber, *British Romantic Art* (Berkeley: University of California Press, 1986), 217.

36. M. K. Joseph, *Byron the Poet* (London: Victor Gollancz, 1966), 326.

37. Leigh Hunt, *The Feast of the Poets, with Notes and Ocher Pieces of Verse* (London: James Cawthorn, 1814), 87.

38. See Edmund Burke, *Reflections on the Revolution in France and Thomas Paine, The Rights of Man* (New York: Doubleday, 1989), 89. "I thought ten thousand swords must have leaped from their scabbards to avenge even a look that threatened her with insult.— But the age of chivalry is gone.—That of sophisters, oeconomists, and calculators, has succeeded; and the glory of Europe is extinguished for ever."

39. Manning, *Reading Romantics*, 217.

40. Peter Manning notes that "The current standard editions of Byron disperse the poems that once appeared together, and so mask important elements of the impression the *Corsair* volume originally made" (*Reading Romantics*, 233). Even the new Oxford edition by Jerome McGann follows a chronological ordering, and places "To a Lady Weeping" in volume 1 and "The Corsair" in volume 3.

41. Byron would have only sent such a letter if the poems had been omitted in the first edition. For an opposing view, see Peter Manning, *Reading Romantics*, 216–37.

42. Leslie Marchand suggests that the quotation may be "adapted from *Macbeth*, Act II, scene 3, ll. 102–03" (4:52). The quotation appears in François Rabelais, *Gargantua & Pantagruel*, trans. J. M. Cohen (New York: Penguin, 1986), 286. Byron had read Rabelais by November 30, 1807, as Marchand notes. *Byron: A Biography*, 1:84–85.

43. Rabelais, *Gargantua & Pantagruel*, 286.

44. Mikhail Bakhtin, *Rabelais and His World*, trans. Helene Iswolsky (Bloomington: Indiana University Press, 1984), 3, 59–145. Richard M. Berrong, *Rabelais & Bakhtin: Popular Culture in Gargantua and Pantagruel* (Lincoln: University of Nebraska Press, 1986) offers a helpful counterargument.

45. Malcolm Kelsall notes how Byron's diary entries at this time resemble a Shakespearean soliloquy, while John Clubbe explores Byron's response to Edmund Kean in 1814. Kelsall, "Hamlet, Byron and 'an Age of Despair,'" in *Beyond the Suburbs of the Mind: Exploring English Romanticism*, ed. Michael Gassenmeier and Norman Platz (Essen, Germany: Verlag die Blaue Eule, 1987), 54. Clubbe, "Dramatic Hits: Napoleon and Shakespeare in Byron's 1813–1814 Journal," in *British Romantics as Readers: Intertextualities, Maps of Misreading, Reinterpretations, Festschrift for Horst Meller*, ed. by Michael Gassenmeier, Petre Bridzun, Jens Martin Gurr, and Frank Eric Pointner (Heidelberg: Universitätsverlag C. Winter, 1998), 271–94. My argument builds on Kelsall and Clubbe's insights, drawing the conclusion that Byron's political commitments were often more dramatic than genuine, though such a distinction can be hard to maintain with Byron.

46. Marchand, *Byron: A Portrait*, 330.

2

BYRON'S POLITICS OF SENTIMENTALISM

While critics have discussed Byron's politics in recent years, they have not always connected the politically liberal Byron of Mary Shelley's *The Last Man* with the more reactionary, libertine figure so evident in his correspondence. Michael Foot provides a very informative account of Byron's political writings, especially in relation to Hazlitt's, but does not treat Byron's sexual politics: "the story of his love affairs is not the subject of this book,"[1] he notes. So too, Malcolm Kelsall's *Byron's Politics* gives an excellent account of Byron's Whig inheritance, but remains focused on his public life. What such approaches overlook is the political significance of Byron's private conduct. At the very moment when Byron was beginning to speak out on liberal issues in the House of Lords, he began a series of notorious affairs with Lady Caroline Lamb, Lady Oxford, and Lady Frances Webster. While Byron exaggerated the extent to which libertinism impeded his political success in his diary entries, he correctly perceived the need to fashion himself differently from an eighteenth-century politician. The previous chapter argued that Byron modeled his political career on the conduct and example of the Dandies, Sheridan, Leigh Hunt, and Napoleon; equally revealing, however, are the poet's allusions to a series of epistolary novels in his correspondence with Annabella Milbanke, who taught him the danger of living up to his own illiberal self-fashionings.

Liberalism and libertinism are words with distinct pedigrees. When liberal gentlemen took their erotic privileges too far, however, their behavior could be characterized as licentious. "Liberty, though having an early general sense of freedom, had a strong sense from the fifteenth century of formal permission or privilege," Raymond Williams notes. "The other word for such a formal right was license, and the play of feeling, towards the sense of 'unrestrained,' can be clearly seen in the development, from the 16th century of licentious. Liberal . . . was close to licentious."[2]

In the late eighteenth century, before liberal became a noun with political connotations, the Whigs were notoriously licentious.[3] George III blamed his son's dissolute morals on the baneful influence of the Whig leaders in the House of Commons, Charles James Fox and Richard Sheridan. Nor were men the only libertines. Women felt free to pursue affairs with other men after they had produced a male heir for their husbands, as Lady Besford explained.[4] An easy marriage between libertine conduct and Whig politics existed at Devonshire House, Carlton House, and Melbourne House. Lady Melbourne (the model for Lady Besford) taught Byron how to conduct himself during their long talks at Whitehall, and it would not be too much to say that their extensive correspondence helped to shape his view of sexual politics. Byron remembered her as Lady Pinchbeck in *Don Juan*, a woman whose worldly experience made her more permissive of the transgressions of others than "prudes without a heart" (*CPW* 5:12:46). "Ladies in their youth a little gay,/Besides their knowledge of the world, and sense/Of the sad consequence of going astray,/Are wiser in their warning 'gainst the woe/Which the mere passionless can never know" (*CPW* 5:12:44), Byron's narrator observed. Coming of age in 1813 rather than, say, 1788, however, Byron did not mindlessly follow the libertine creed the sixty-two-year-old Lady Melbourne espoused in her correspondence with the young poet and at Whitehall; instead, he cautiously read the higher moral standards of a new age—the age of Leigh Hunt's *Examiner* and Byron's own "Lines to a Lady Weeping"—and conducted himself accordingly, eventually proposing to the formidably virtuous Annabella Milbanke.[5]

Byron's debt to the eighteenth century is clear. To begin with, he modeled his riotous behavior at Newstead Abbey on the Medmenham monks, or Hell-Fire Club, to which Sterne himself belonged from 1745 to 1768. In 1745, Sir Francis Dashwood led a society which adopted Rabelais's motto at the Abbey of Thelème—*Fay ce que tu voudras*, or do what you will. John Wilkes, Lord Sandwich, Paul Whitehead, George Selwyn, and several other members of this society, self-styled "The Monks of St. Francis," met at Dashwood's estate in West Wycombe on the site of the former Medmenham Abbey; their "activities comprised sexual orgies spiced with copious drinking and black magic."[6] Six decades later, in 1807, Byron invited John Cam Hobhouse, Scrope Davies, and a few close friends to Newstead Abbey to drink wine from skulls, the "riot most uncouth" Byron later depicted in *Childe Harold's Pilgrimage* (*CPW* 2:1:12). Leslie Marchand characterizes Byron's behavior at Newstead Abbey as mere "spirited horseplay."[7] What is interesting about Byron's conduct, however, is that he emulated the antics of Sir Francis Dashwood, John Wilkes, Charles Churchill, Laurence Sterne, and other eighteenth-century libertines at the precise moment when it had become an anachronism, even a political liability, to do so.

Tory leaders gained the patronage of George III, after all, because of their capacity to cultivate an image of self-restraint, sound judgment, and ordered lifestyles. William Pitt, Lord Castlereagh, Lord Sidmouth, and other Tory politicians were sexually conservative, seemingly uninterested in seducing women or keeping mistresses, as opposed to their more raucous Whig counterparts. The "angels all are Tories," Byron observed sarcastically in *The Vision of Judgment* (*CPW* 6:26:208), exaggerating what was already a confirmed impression. "Pitt was not only unmarried but was famously chaste and was said to have no interest in women," Fintan O'Toole observes; Sheridan referred to him, disparagingly, as "the virgin."[8] Sheridan's affair with Lady Bessborough, by contrast, almost ended his political career in the 1780s before resurfacing in embarrassing ways; Charles James Fox's "corruption" of the Prince Regent compromised the prince in the eyes of his fastidious father, George III, and helped to exclude Fox and the Prince Regent from office in the 1780s; while Lord Grey's affair with the duchess of Devonshire became notorious and inspired the Prince Regent's enduring dislike for him and reluctance to accept his administration after Perceval's assassination in 1812.

My argument is not that libertinism determines a liberal politics: there were probably as many conservative libertines as liberals—Sir Francis Dashwood and John Montagu, Earl of Sandwich, are good examples—and not all liberals or conservatives were *necessarily* libertine because of their political beliefs. My point is that the moral behavior expected of politicians changed at the beginning of the nineteenth century. Facts were often less important than perceptions. William Pitt, who died of gout at the age of forty-six, drank quite as avidly as Sheridan. Yet popular poems portrayed Pitt as the "Pilot who weathered the storm," while James Gillray ridiculed Sheridan as a drunken Irishman in "Uncorking Old Sherry." Though he was in the pay of the government,[9] Gillray, and cartoonists or journalists like him, contributed to the public's perhaps not unfounded perception of the Tories as more stable than their opponents.

Placed as he was at the end of the age of sensibility, Byron understood that political liberalism necessarily entailed a turning away from coarse libertinism to something more refined. Byron was an erotic liberal, after all, because he thought of politics as an expression of personal feelings and passions, and was loathe to conduct himself as Fox, Sheridan, or Wilkes had done, though he followed their political example in other ways. In order to formulate a political image palatable to his contemporaries, Byron emulated the conduct of male epistolary heroes, quoting Richardson, Rousseau, and Laclos frequently in his letters from 1812–14. Unfortunately, this decision was easier to make than to carry out.

Richardson's *Clarissa* (1748), Rousseau's *La nouvelle Héloïse* (1761), and Laclos's *Les liaisons dangereuses* (1782) approached, but did not quite attain, the erotic liberalism Byron espoused in his poetry.[10] The representation of a fully sexualized male who was not morally compromised was a long time in coming and this is perhaps Byron's contribution to the literature he absorbed. In most epistolary novels, women, not men, form the subject of moral investigation. Richardson's *Clarissa* focuses quite clearly on Clarissa's moral quandary. It shows how the moral compromises that church, state, and family demand of Clarissa portend her doom. In some respects, Richardson is not truly interested in Lovelace at all. Lovelace's outrageous conduct toward Clarissa is a product of social forces: he is an exemplary case, a social type. Rousseau's *Julie, ou La nouvelle Héloïse* similarly focuses on the moral situation of Julie, the titular heroine. Consistently read by Byron and Shelley as a celebration of romantic love, *Julie, ou La nouvelle Héloïse* also reflects Rousseau's interest in showing how erotic love outside the marriage bond must be sublimated in order to conform to the general will and lead to human happiness. St. Preux's erotic relationship to Julie, Byron and Shelley's great inspiration, merely serves as Rousseau's cautionary tale. Only Julie's marriage to Wolmar can provide a fitting counterpart to Rousseau's theory of the state as described in the *The Social Contract*.

In *Clarissa* and *La nouvelle Héloïse*, the more erotic a hero's orientation and sensibility the more morally suspect he appears. *Les liaisons dangereuses* is one of the first epistolary novels to take male eroticism seriously without condemning it out of hand. Yet, like *La nouvelle Héloïse*, it is also concerned with how dangerous the erotic relationship is to civil society, as Roger Shattuck has recently shown.[11] That Laclos's novel ends with Madame de Merteuil's political exile and Valmont's death by duel only underscores the danger their behavior represents. Laclos's playful allusion to the moral purpose of his novel in his brilliant editorial preface is not nearly as ironic as some critics have assumed. Published seven years before the fall of the Bastille, the novel reflects an aristocratic sense of license and complacency that the French Revolution did much to alter. Read allegorically, the most dangerous liaisons occur when the aristocracy begins to corrupt the chaster values of the middle class and the church, depicted in the characters of Danceny and Madame de Tourvel.

Though Byron liked to believe that *Les liaisons dangereuses* was the novel that most clearly represented his erotic outlook in 1813, his decision to marry Annabella Milbanke reflects his entrapment in the English system of morality outlined by Richardson's *Clarissa*. Byron despised Richardson's novel so much he could not complete it, but when it came time to marry, he informed Lady Melbourne that he still had enough Scotch and Norman prejudices to look upon Annabella's family and fortune very favorably. He accused Annabella of having been "Clarissa Harlowed" (*BLJ* September 5, 1813; 3:108) into an epistolary style and attitude that led to moral dishonesty. What he did not, perhaps, realize was the extent to which he had only barely escaped the same programmatic approach to morality himself by agreeing to marry her. In doing so, Byron wrote letters announcing his willingness to sacrifice his worldly pose, even his poetic persona, at the altar of his Englishness. Yet Byron knew that his persona, based as it was on novels set in Italy, could not survive on English soil alone. By using a French epistolary novel as the basis for his self-conception, Byron constructed a more cosmopolitan role for himself in English political life, as surely as he had once drawn on his extensive travels to compare the Luddites to Turkish workers abroad in his first parliamentary speech.

Lovelace is a villain in Richardson's *Clarissa*; St. Preux is a suffering and ineffectual character in Rousseau's *Julie, ou La nouvelle Héloïse;* only Laclos's libertine hero articulates a worldly philosophy that expresses Enlightenment ideals emancipated from religious scruples. Yet even Laclos's novel, *Les liaisons dangereuses*, condemns the libertine characters it so brilliantly delineates. Byron made his reputation by writing a poem, *Childe Harold's Pilgrimage*, that takes as its hero a man as satiated in worldly pleasure as Valmont himself. In his correspondence, as in his poetry, Byron tried to make something worthwhile out of the "very repulsive personage of Childe Harold" he had created. He did so by borrowing from aspects of all three epistolary novels outlined above, as well as from the gothic novel and from the historical example of Laurence Sterne. So appealing were his literary characters that Byron gave a dangerous cachet to the political views his heroes espoused. He established an erotic relationship with his (mostly female) readers that lured them into a brand of progressive politics that would find its ultimate expression in *The Liberal* and *Don Juan*.[12]

Though I underscore what Byron owed to his literary precursors, I also hope to show that Byron's method of "cross-writing" promised something new for English readers. Through fictional works set in foreign lands and sentiments placed in the mouths of foreign speakers, Byron showed his English readers how much more honest an erotic liberalism could be with respect to the passions than the type of life allowed for in England by restricting, confining, and hypocritical legislation pushed through Parliament by Castlereagh, Sidmouth, and Liverpool. Where English and French epistolary novels retreated in their final pages into a sentimental refusal of sexual passion, Byron insisted on *eros* as the very measure of political integrity. Politics was, above all, a feeling. When Byron tried to dissemble his feelings, as in his ill-fated marriage to Annabella Milbanke or his editorial pairing with Leigh Hunt on *The Liberal*, the result was predictably disastrous.

I

Byron's movement from an antiquated libertinism toward an erotic liberalism occurred in three distinct stages. The first is evident in his letters and journals for 1813, which reflect his sympathetic engagement with the erotic sentimentality of Sterne's Yorick; the second appears when he seems to embrace the calculated heartlessness of Laclos's Valmont; the third, when he follows Valmont's struggle (in the second half of Laclos's novel) to emancipate himself from the code of worldliness and feel the power of love he once ridiculed.

In 1813, the first stage I explore, Byron read his political inactivity in light of Laurence Sterne's *A Sentimental Journey*, condemning himself for not presenting William Baldwin's petition for prison reform before the House of Lords. In the same way that Byron was dishonest about his willingness to act (as opposed to speak) about the plight of the unfortunate, Yorick declares his intention to free a caged starling but soon lapses into selfish reflections on the dangers of his own impending confinement in the Bastille. "Baldwin is very importunate," Byron wrote in his diary entry,

> but, poor fellow, "I can't get out, I can't get out—said the starling." Ah, I am as bad as that dog Sterne, who preferred whining over "a dead ass to relieving a living mother"—villain—hypocrite—slave—sycophant! but *I* am no better. (*BLJ* December 1, 1813; 3:229)

In the same way that Byron felt unable to serve as an advocate for Baldwin's petition, Yorick could not free a caged starling. Byron mocked his inability to act decisively on another's behalf without lapsing into sentimental, and ineffectual, reflections. To be "as bad as that dog Sterne" is to embrace the politics of sentimentalism, to prefer "whining over 'a dead ass to relieving a living mother.'"[13] Byron was not a hypocrite. Rather, "what could be imputed to him," as Hazlitt observed, "was the voluntary prolongation or overcharging of a real sentiment."[14]

Byron compared himself to Sterne's Yorick because he was aware that he was using sentiment to mask *eros*. Byron's sexual feelings ("I cannot stimulate myself") swayed his political actions, and were just as transient as Yorick's.[15] He considered presenting Baldwin's petition, after all, not to relieve Baldwin's plight and that of other King's Bench prison inmates, but to win half a smile from Lady Oxford ("she would have *made* me do it," he confessed to his diary [*BLJ* December 1, 1813; 3:229]). After three adulterous affairs, however, Byron found his capacity for political sentiment as diminished as his sexual appetite. If Yorick feels too much for a mechanical bird, Byron no longer feels at all. Libertinism threatened Byron's liberality by encouraging him to substitute sexual for political "stimulat[ion]," vitiating both in the process. The theme was familiar for Byron, who wrote *Childe Harold's Pilgrimage*, in part, to show how "early perversion of mind and morals leads to satiety of past pleasures and disappointment in new ones" (Preface, *CPW* 2:6).

Like Sterne's Yorick, Byron saw a close relationship between erotic and political stimulation:

> 'Tis said—*Indifference* marks the present time,
> Then hear the reason—though 'tis told in rhyme—
> A King who *can't*—a Prince of Wales who *don't*—
> Patriots who *shan't*, and Ministers who *won't*—
> What matters who are *in* or *out* of place
> The *Mad*—the *Bad*—the *Useless*—or the *Base?*
> (*BLJ* September 21, 1813; 3:117)

The last line of Byron's poem recalls Lady Caroline Lamb's first impression of him as "Mad, bad, and dangerous to know." Yet Byron proved "useless" rather than "dangerous" to Lady Caroline Lamb. A mock Quixote tilting against windmills, he "disenchanted" Caroline (his Dulcinea) and used Lamb's own mother-in-law (Lady Melbourne) to do so. He was as politically useless to Baldwin as he was sexually "useless" to Caroline; he was "*Base*," not because of what he *tried* to do with her, but because of what he *would* not do: conduct their love affair according to a chivalric script.

Byron indicted himself by equating political and sexual uselessness—a theme he returned to in his suppressed dedication to *Don Juan*. Sexually he was out of place, an interloper in three marriages and a man whose object attachments were unstable ("I could love anything on earth that appeared to wish it," he wrote to Lady Melbourne, referring to Lady Caroline Lamb [*BLJ* November 26, 1812; 2:251]). Politically he felt equally displaced, for he was not a placeholder in a government run by Tories. Even his place as a writer of political squibs was suspect, for to write was to adopt the effeminate (in Byron's view) role of spectator. Unable to negotiate the shift from spectator to actor without Lady Oxford, Byron told his reasons in rhyme. He used "though" as the operative word in his poem, viewing writing as a moral capitulation. "No one should be a rhymer who could be any thing better" (*BLJ* November 23, 1813; 3:217), he declared.

Byron became convinced that libertinism had thwarted his political ambitions. He "could [not] be any thing better," he confessed. By 1813, however, Byron thought writing might liberate him from the political "*Indifference*" his libertine conduct had produced. In Sterne's novel, Yorick similarly "reason[ed]" that writing could "free" him from confinement in the Bastille: with "nine livres a day, and pen and ink and paper, and patience, albeit a man can't get out, he may do very well within." The caged starling, however, reminds Yorick that there is such a thing as real imprisonment and suffering. A mechanical bird that imitates a human pleading for liberty ("I can't get out"), the starling awakens Yorick's most tender sentiments. When he tries unsuccessfully to free the bird, however, Yorick confesses to finding a mechanical bird more moving than Bastille inmates. "I never had my affections more tenderly awakened," he observes, "or do I remember an incident in my life, where the dissipated spirits, to which my reason had been a bubble, were so suddenly called home."[16] Yorick is self-consciously ironic as he satirizes his inability to act. Sterne mocks him, even as both character and author tacitly endorse the aesthetic morality of the sentimentalist. By emphasizing that the bird is mechanical,[17] Sterne softens his satire's sting and absolves Yorick of moral responsibility for failing to free the starling.

By 1813, however, Sterne's sentimental posture toward mechanism was no longer available to Byron, who felt compelled, and yet unable, to protect human victims from industrialism's pernicious effects. On November 14, Byron wrote again to W. J. Baldwin to assure him that penal reform and the incarceration of debtors concerned him: "I have read your address—and I have read it with a hope almost for the sake of those to whom it is uttered—that their situation is less grievous than it would lead me to believe—not that I have any reason to doubt the statement—except the wish that in this—or in any other country—such oppression had never existed" (*BLJ* November 14, 1813; 3:165). He has no "reason to doubt" Baldwin's complaints, but prefers to do so, if only to maintain Yorick's pleasant sentimental posture. In place of advocating Baldwin's petition, Byron consoles himself with the "*wish* that such oppression had never existed" (my emphasis). Byron's tendency to view the plaintive cries of victims as bestial (uttered by birds and dead asses), however, betrays the condescension that his sentimental pose barely conceals. Both the cry and the failed response Sterne describes anticipate the age of "*Indifference*" Byron portrayed in his poem.

Both Yorick and Byron cultivate feminine feeling in order to heighten their political and moral sensitivity. Yet their feminine compassion renders them impotent to alter the circumstances they survey. "I am as weak as a woman," Yorick admits, "and I beg the world not to smile but to pity me."[18] Yorick's confession, of course, is not the whole truth. Both Yorick and Byron cultivate femininity to solidify class privilege,[19] distinguishing themselves from the bourgeoisie by refining their feelings. Byron found writing undignified precisely because it was effeminate. "I do think the preference of *writers* to *agents*—the mighty stir made about scribbling and scribes, by themselves and others—a sign of effeminacy, degeneracy, and weakness," he wrote in his journal. "Who would write, who had any thing better to do?" (*BLJ* November 24, 1813; 3:220). Yet Byron partook of the very degeneracy he criticized. Far from pursuing a life of political action, Byron chose to transform himself morally by reading new books. His turn from Sterne to Laclos is most evident in his letters to Lady Melbourne regarding his suspended engagement to Annabella Milbanke. As this literary genealogy might suggest, Byron's libertine correspondence deferred his political radicalism and encouraged him to embrace the social and class privileges he considered it his prerogative to enjoy. "Miss M[ilbanke] I admire because she is a clever woman, an amiable woman & of high blood, for I have still a few Norman & Scotch inherited prejudices on the last score, were I to marry," he wrote to Lady Melbourne. "As to *Love,* that is done in a week, (provided the Lady has a reasonable share)" (*BLJ* September 18, 1812; 2:199).

II

Yet marrying Annabella Milbanke proved more frustrating to Byron than he had anticipated. To begin with, she rejected his first marriage proposal. Secondly, Byron criticized Annabella for her choice of epistolary heroines. Having schooled himself in the sentimentalism of Laurence Sterne, Byron found Annabella's moral casuistry puzzling. He concluded that she had read too much Samuel Richardson, which left her "systematically Clarissa Harlowed into an awkward kind of correctness" (*BLJ* September 5, 1813; 3:108). R. F. Brissenden distinguishes Richardson from Sterne in ways that illuminate Byron's objection. "While Richardson clings desperately to his faith in man's ability to order and control life according to the conventional rules of prudent morality, to live, as Sir Charles Grandison does, strictly according to principle, Sterne begins by assuming, indeed insisting, that it is impossible ever fully to systematise life, or even completely to understand it."[20] Byron preferred Sterne to Richardson because he distrusted literary, moral, or political systems insufficiently alive to human complexity.[21] Alert to how he resembled Yorick's worst features (in his diary entry on Baldwin's petition, for example), Byron could not allow Annabella to emulate Clarissa Harlow with impunity.

In his letters to Lady Melbourne, Byron constructed two plots. According to the first, Annabella would enter "into some egregious blunder" because of her Clarissa-like systematizing; according to the second, she would realize her own wishes too completely. "She will find exactly what she wants," he explained, "& then discover that it is much more dignified than entertaining" (*BLJ* September 5, 1813; 3:108). But a third alternative existed. Byron could cast Annabella in the role of Madame de Tourvel; he could portray her as a paragon of virtue as well as the tragic victim of his epistolary designs. For two years, having seen Annabella less than a dozen times, Byron transformed her into a fictional character and altered his own moral character to conform to his epistolary portrait.

Published in 1782 and translated into English in 1784, Laclos's *Les liaisons dangereuses* circulated among members of Whig society: indeed, the Prince Regent[22] and Lady Caroline Lamb[23] both compared Byron to Laclos's hero. Byron alluded to the novel in his letters, quoting from it directly in his diary: "'one gets tired of every thing, my angel,' says Valmont" (*BLJ* November 24, 1813; 3:220).[24] For his correspondent, Byron chose a woman who seemed the very embodiment of Madame de Merteuil. During the separation proceedings between Annabella and Byron, for example, Annabella's mother wrote to her husband urging him to read the novel because "the Viscountess is exactly depicted in La Marquise."[25] Almost twenty years earlier (1793), Lady Holland also compared Lady Melbourne to Madame de Merteuil: "Our parties at Devonshire House were delightfully pleasant," she wrote. "Lady Melbourne is uncommonly sensible and amusing, though she often put me in mind of Madame de Merteuil in *Les liaisons dangereuses*."[26] Conscious of the vast differences between a French epistolary novel and the conduct of an English lord, I am not suggesting that Byron literally imitated Laclos's hero; I am more interested in what Byron's choice of models (and his ultimate repudiation of that choice) reveals about his politics.

III

Les liaisons dangereuses begins with a request. Madame de Merteuil asks Valmont, her former lover, to seduce Gercourt's bride, Cécile, in order to revenge herself on Gercourt for abandoning her. Valmont only assents when he has his own motive. Thwarted by Madame de Volanges in his plans to seduce Madame de Tourvel, Valmont resolves to strike at Madame de Volanges through "the object of her affection," Cécile. Valmont "obey[s]" Madame de Merteuil only when he can "use" her to achieve his own revenge.

The same struggle of wills marked Byron's relationship with Lady Melbourne: Byron used Lady Melbourne to extricate himself from his involvement with Lady Caroline Lamb and forward his proposal of marriage to her niece, Annabella Milbanke. Lady Melbourne, on the other hand, used Byron to end his affair with Lady Caroline Lamb and repair her son's marriage. "You will not regret to hear that I wish this [the affair with Caroline] to end," he wrote to Lady Melbourne. "It is not that I love another, but loving at all is quite out of my way; I am tired of being a fool" (*BLJ* September 10, 1812; 2:193). By taking Lady Melbourne as his confidante, Byron cast her in the role of Madame de Merteuil: "Write me a word and give me the cues for my part," Valmont implores Madame de Merteuil (*DL* 59:107).[27] "As I am one of the principal performers in this unfortunate drama, I should be glad to know what my part requires next?" Byron asked Lady Melbourne (*BLJ* August 12, 1812; 2:192). If Valmont flatters Madame de Merteuil ("You would make despotism attractive," he informs her [*DL* 4:13]), Byron exalted Lady Melbourne in similar terms. "So far from being ashamed of being governed like Lord Delawarr or any other Lord or master," he wrote, "I am always but too happy to find one to regulate or misregulate me, and I am as docile as a Dromedary and can bear almost as much" (*BLJ* September 13, 1812; 2:194).

In *Les liaisons dangereuses*, Madame de Merteuil both advises Cécile de Volanges and betrays her in a duplicitous correspondence with Valmont. "Is it not indeed amusing to console for and against, and to be the only agent of two directly opposite interests?" Merteuil asks (*DL* 63:112). Similarly, Lady Melbourne consoled her daughter-in-law in Ireland, but failed to inform her that Byron was now living with a new lover, Lady Oxford. "My dearest Aspasia," Lady Caroline Lamb wrote to Lady Oxford. "Byron is angry with me! Will you write to him, will you tell him I have not done one thing to displease him, and that I am miserable."[28] Such mistaken confidences recall Laclos distinctly and suggest other similarities. In *Les liaisons dangereuses*, Madame de Merteuil dictates a letter ending Valmont's affair with Madame de Tourvel, daring him to send it to prove his loyalty. I love another, Valmont writes at her urging, "It is not my fault" (*DL* 141:295). Similarly, Lady Oxford dictated Byron's letter to Lady Caroline Lamb. In *Glenarvon*, Lady Caroline Lamb represented Glenarvon's [Byron's] letter as "sealed and directed by Lady Mandeville [Lady Oxford]; but the hand that wrote it was Glenarvon's; and therefore it had its full effect."[29] I will return to this example of cross-writing; for now it is sufficient to note how Byron and Lady Caroline Lamb followed other ruses that recall *Les liaisons dangereuses*. "Would it not be amusing to steal a rival's letter or portrait," Valmont asks

(*DL* 40:79). Lady Caroline Lamb stole Byron's portrait from John Murray's, while Byron answered Lady Caroline Lamb's request for a lock of his hair with a lock of Lady Oxford's.

Though capable of such cruel comedy, Byron differed from Valmont in portraying himself as a gentleman. "She never did nor can describe a single reproach which must not fall with double justice and truth upon myself," he wrote of Lady Caroline Lamb. Byron's gentlemanly pose ("I have given you my word it shall be observed" [*BLJ* August 14, 1812; 2:189]) is far too English for the gallant Valmont, who could only write such a letter as a ruse. Valmont pretended that "the most adroit man can do no more than keep pace with the most sincere woman" (*DL* 25:50). Byron portrayed himself in similar terms. "Caroline is suspicious about our counter plots, and I am obliged to be as treacherous as Talleyrand, but remember that *treachery* is *truth* to you" (*BLJ* September 13, 1812; 2:196), he wrote. Byron absolves himself of responsibility by locating "treachery" elsewhere, with Lady Melbourne and a French diplomat. "Think me bad if you please," he writes, "but not meanly so." Valmont, by contrast, portrays himself as a sadist, determined to make Tourvel "expire in a slow agony" (*DL* 70:125).

As these passages from Laclos's novel suggest, Madame de Merteuil and Valmont turned chivalric conventions on their head. "Come, come as soon as you can and bring me a token of your triumph, like those gallant knights of old who used to lay at their ladies' feet the splendid fruits of their victory," Madame de Merteuil writes (*DL* 20:39). Byron was more facetious about Lady Oxford's charm. "Everything goes on 'sans peur & sans reproche' yet very unlike Bayard for all that," he confessed to Lady Melbourne (*BLJ* November 14, 1812; 2:246).

In *Les liaisons dangereuses*, Madame de Merteuil becomes jealous when Valmont falls in love with a woman she has not selected. "No matter how strong Madame de Tourvel's dominion over me," he writes, "I promise you that I shall never become so preoccupied with her that I do not have time to think about you a great deal" (*DL* 23:47). Byron patronized Lady Melbourne in similar terms. "Why are you silent?" he asked. "Do you doubt me in the 'bowers of Armida'?—I certainly am very much enchanted, but *your spells* will always retain their full force—try them" (*BLJ* October 30, 1812; 238).

Shortly after Lady Oxford departed for the continent, Byron began an incestuous liaison with Augusta Leigh and an adulterous one with James Wedderburn Webster's wife (*BLJ* September 28, 1813; 3:124). Of the latter affair, he boasted that his libertine method now had a moral purpose: he would seduce Webster's wife to expose his friend's vanity, and thus distract himself from pursuing a still more dangerous, because incestuous, affair with his half-sister. Accordingly, the sentimental but sly Danceny became his model. In *Les liaisons dan-*

gereuses, Danceny leaves his letters for Cécile in the strings of her harp. Similarly, Byron concealed his missives in a music book. "The most amusing part was the interchange of notes," he remembered,

> for we sat up all night scribbling to each other—& came down like Ghosts in the morning—I shall never forget the quiet manner in which she would pass her epistles in a music book—or any book—looking in [Webster]'s face with great tranquility the whole time—& taking mine in the same way (*BLJ* January 13, 1814; 4:29).

For Byron the "most amusing part" of seducing his friend's wife was writing about it. "I must tell you the place of declaration," he informed his sixty-two-year-old confidante,

> a billiard room!—I did not as C[aroline] says "kneel in the middle of the room" but like Corporal Trim to the Nun—"I made a speech"—which as you might not listen to it with the same patience—I shall not transcribe . . . I also observed that we went on with our game (of billiards) without *counting* the *hazards* (*BLJ* October 8, 1813; 3:134).

Byron embellished his letters with foolish *double entendres* ("*counting* the *hazards*"), which suggest that Byron's pleasure was as much textual as sexual. Despite the bravado of his letters, Byron forfeited his prey. "[W]as I wrong?" he asks. "I spared her.—There was something so very peculiar in her manner—a kind of mild decision—no scene—not even a struggle . . . & yet I know not whether I can regret it—she seems so very thankful for my forebearance" (*BLJ* October 17, 1813; 3:146). Byron's question ("Was I wrong?") is not tactical but moral, suggesting that he had refined his libertinism out of existence, in part, by writing about it.

Valmont defines pleasure as an endless anticipation of sexual satisfaction; after he conquers his victim, Tourvel will become only an "ordinary woman" to him. Byron, by contrast, felt that Webster would interest him more after he had successfully seduced her. "Do you remember what Rousseau says to somebody," he asked Lady Melbourne, quoting *La nouvelle Héloïse*. "'[I]f you would know that you are beloved—watch your lover as he leaves you—['] to me the most pleasing moments have generally been—when there is nothing more to be required . . . when you are secure of the past yet without regret or disappointment" (*BLJ* October 21, 1813; 3:151–2). Byron clearly replaced even the "reformed" Valmont (of the second half of Laclos's novel) with Rousseau as his model during his affair with Lady Frances Webster. In doing so, he adopted an increasingly sentimental posture which Lady Melbourne partially encouraged by rebuking him for his heartlessness.

IV

Byron's correspondence with Annabella Milbanke was marked by dramatic epistolary revisions that both resemble and differ from Valmont's. Valmont attempted to rewrite himself in order to seduce Madame de Tourvel. I say "attempted" because Valmont begins to use the idealistic language of Rousseau in place of his professed libertinism: he "feels" the rhetoric he uses.[30] Thus Valmont portrays himself as repentant in his letters to Tourvel and urges her not to confound "what I once was with what I now am" (*DL* 52:117). Like Valmont, Byron rewrites his past in an effort to obtain Annabella's hand in marriage and ends by having to live up to the self-portrait. He denies that he was ever a poet by vocation, declares that his imagination has led him astray, and subordinates himself completely to Annabella. "I am," he writes, "whatever you please to make me" (*BLJ* September 26, 1814; 4:184). Like Valmont, Byron will reform his conduct, "compress" his identity as he compressed his letters into envelopes (4:184), and become "good and true." He will renounce his poetic vocation, sell Newstead Abbey, that symbol of his wastrel youth, and arrange for the sale of his Rochdale estates in order to settle his debts. "Few prospective wives could hope to receive a more docile, frankly uxorious letter from a prospective husband," James Soderholm observes.[31]

The closer Byron came to marrying Annabella, however, the more he worried about the wisdom of sacrificing his literary voice on the altar of marriage. Byronic poetry, after all, will be impossible without Byronism. By marrying Annabella, he obliterates his own literary voice as surely as by selling Newstead Abbey he retails his own ancestry. Byron himself pointed to the self-effacement of Byronism that his marriage imposed. After he arrived at Annabella's house before the marriage and was surrounded by lawyers, he realized he had become the victim of his own epistolary imagination. Having created a persona in his letters to Annabella, he now had to live up to it. "The die is cast," he informed Lady Melbourne. "Neither party can recede—the lawyers are here—mine & all—& I presume the parchment once scribbled I shall become Lord Annabella" (*BLJ* November 4, 1814; 4:229).

Byron's fear of becoming "Lord Annabella" recalls his anxiety in 1813 about being Lord Byron.[32] On November 24 of that year, Byron alluded to Laclos's text, however inaccurately, to explain his growing disenchantment with effeminate authorship and his preference for a more manly life of action: "'One gets tired of everything my angel,' says Valmont." The true speaker of these words, however, is Madame de Merteuil.[33] Byron's effort to denounce the effeminate role of author is ironically subverted by his unwitting allusion to a woman's words to do so.

Byron's misquotation is an example of what I call cross-writing.[34] In the same way that Valmont uses Madame de Merteuil's words to end his affair with Tourvel, Byron used Lady Oxford's language to end his affair with Caroline. Both writers cross gender boundaries in order to abandon or seduce. Far from showing the fluidity of these boundaries, however, Laclos's novel and Byron's correspondence illustrate their rigidity, for while it is true that each writer can appropriate a feminine style, the decision to do so ends the relationship with a woman irrevocably.[35]

Providing a fuller context for Byron's quotation from Laclos may help reveal the perils and limits of cross-writing. After appropriating Madame de Merteuil's letter in order to end his affair with Tourvel, Valmont believes he can resume his own voice and seduce her once again. This soon proves impossible. Only Madame de Merteuil understands the devastating impact of the line that Valmont borrowed from her in his letter to Tourvel: "when a woman strikes at another woman's heart," Merteuil explains, "she rarely fails to find the sensitive place, and the wound is incurable" (*DL* 145:331). *Les liaisons dangereuses* would thus seem to both endorse and deny the possibilities of cross-writing. A man can borrow a woman's prose style (as Byron borrowed that of Lady Melbourne), but only a woman can strike "at another woman's heart" in this irreversible way. The natural counterpart to Merteuil's wounding of Tourvel (with a pen), of course, is Danceny's phallic wounding of Valmont (with a sword); the only person who can kill Valmont is another man, in this case a younger one. Despite Laclos's title, the fatal (as opposed to dangerous) liaisons in his novel occur within the sexes: Valmont and Madame de Tourvel die by daggers, whether sword or pen, guided by members of their own sex.

Perhaps Byron's most striking example of cross-writing occurred when he wrote to his fiancée from an inn. Byron had already delayed his arrival in Seaham, and his hasty departure from Annabella necessitated the production of several letters in a highly romantic style. Romance soon gave way to farce, however, as Byron found his friend, Francis Hodgson, engaged in the identical pursuit. "Opposite to me at this moment is a friend of mine," he wrote to Annabella:

> I believe—in the very act of writing to *his* spouse—elect—and complaining like me of his pen & paper to say nothing of absence & being obliged to scribble instead of speak . . . "My last will have made you anxious to hear again—and indeed I am so myself" this is a sentence which I have borrowed by permission from my neighbouring suitor's epistle to his Ladye—I think it does very well in a dearth of periods of mine own. (*BLJ* November 22, 1814; 4:233)

In the same way that he borrowed a page from Sterne's *A Sentimental Journey* to explain his political indifference, Byron borrows a sentence from his "neighbouring suitor" to reveal his romantic ennui. By taking his "words of love" from a friend who is also a minister, Byron turns romantic confession to quotation. It is almost as if Byron saw that his role as a romantic male was redundant, as outdated as Sterne's sentimentalism. In his marriage and his fiction, Byron parodied romance in order to create something new.

What Byron in fact created is a striking example of "male homosocial desire."[36] As he writes to Annabella, it is worth remembering, Byron's immediate audience is *another man*, Francis Hodgson. Byron is bound to Hodgson by a literary language that ostensibly worships women but actually depends upon their absence. To put this another way, what both the man of feeling and the libertine have in common is that they try to appropriate the feminine by construing it as part of their own personalities. Byron rejected the "puling" sonnets of Petrarch (*BLJ* December 17–18, 1813; 3:240), but his own letters to Annabella (with a reverend as muse and mentor) participate in this same tradition of courtly love.[37]

Annabella understood her irrelevance to this literary exchange between men when she commented on how she had been misrecognized by Byron and, I would argue, cast into the role of an English Tourvel. "Before you pass sentence on me finally, wait to see myself. Myself is by no means the grave, didactic, deplorable person that I have appeared to you . . . help me out of that atmosphere of sober sadness in which I was almost suffocated."[38] But Byron did not—could not—help Annabella out of the suffocating "atmosphere" he had himself helped to create. He could not "see" her because he had predicated their epistolary romance upon her absence. Only through such an absence could Byron make Annabella "everything that you and I wish."[39] By December 4, 1814, Annabella realized that her union with the author of their epistolary engagement was in serious jeopardy. "I begin to think that after the great cake is baked, and the epithalamium composed," she wrote, "the part of Spouse, like that of Hamlet, will be omitted 'by particular desire.'"[40]

Annabella's theatrical metaphor underscores Byron's distance from the role he projected in his letters. It also alludes, however subtly, to the "unmanliness" of Byron's behavior toward her both before and during their marriage—his difference from his gendered role. "Unmanly" is Judith Milbanke's suggestive word.[41] But his indecisiveness about the logistics of meeting Annabella in Seaham even earned him the rebuke of Lady Melbourne.[42] Byron would hear the complaint about effeminacy repeated later in his life. On this occasion, Byron's behavior seemed suspect because he appeared to view marriage not as a bond with a woman, but as a negotiation about his own prestige with other men; in a letter to Thomas Moore, for example, he commented on "the superlative felicity of these foxes, who have cut off their tails, and would persuade the rest to part with their brushes to keep them in countenance" (*BLJ* August 3, 1814; 4:151–52).[43] When he was rejected by Annabella as a suitor, Byron consoled himself by sharing his experiences with William Bankes, who had been similarly rejected (*BLJ* August 31, 1813; 3:103). Byron could not conceal the odd exhilaration he felt in reporting this to Annabella, even as he realized that it bordered on "impertinen[ce]" (*BLJ* February 19, 1814; 4:66). Annabella's rejection bound him closer to his friend, even as his engagement bound him closer to Hodgson.

Not only Byron's marriage, but also his adulterous affairs, amount to a "traffic in women" in order to enhance his prestige with other men. René Girard and Eve Sedgwick have helped modern readers understand "triangulation" and erotic love. In this instance, Byron conducted his affair with Frances Webster not out of a direct attraction to her so much as to teach "Bold" Webster, his own male friend, tact and humility (*BLJ* October 8, 1813; 3:135). Determined as he was to defeat his rivals and win Annabella's hand, Byron expressed little interest in seeing Annabella once they were engaged. "Never was a lover less in haste," his friend Hobhouse observed.[44] When Byron's marriage finally did take place, the tension between the claims of this homosocial world and the demands of matrimony (that is, the implicit rivalry between Hobhouse as best man and Annabella as wife) created a scene at once ludicrous and pathetic. "Byron was unwilling to leave my hand," Hobhouse records in his journal, "and I had hold of his out of the window as the carriage drove off."[45] Ethel Mayne observes that the young men, clinging to each other's hands, obscured the bride from view.[46]

Byron worried that marriage would curtail his contact with male literary and social society. In fact, his anxiety about becoming "Lord Annabella" was most acute as he continued his letter alongside Hodgson. "I have stolen another pen," he wrote, "but it is worse than the last—& am writing at an Inn—with noise 'around above and underneath' with the worst & most intractable of implements—ink like water—& sand like sawdust" (*BLJ* November 22, 1814; 4:233–34). No sooner does he "steal" what he once possessed (the pen or phallus as symbol of authorship), but he loses his potency in the act of writing and his ink turns to water. This conversion foreshadows Byron's authorial silence for the year of his marriage: "If rhymes be omens what a fate is ours," he wrote in a game of "bout-rimés" with his wife.[47] As Byron imagined and enacted it, to become Lord Annabella was to disengender oneself—to unwrite one's own sex—thus checking the sexual urge and the creative impulse that went along with it. At the same time, however, his marriage involved the engendering of a child. Unlike the "monstrous" progeny of his affair with Augusta ("it is *not* an *'Ape'* "[48] he felt compelled to tell Lady Melbourne [*BLJ* April 25, 1814; 4:104]), Byron's child with Annabella was "proof" that he had set himself straight, though his marriage, of course, only intensified his search for sexual self-discovery.

V

Having pointed to some of the similarities and differences between Byron's libertinism and Valmont's, I would like to conclude this chapter by assessing libertinism's political importance. Byron had barely achieved entry into aristocratic society at Holland House and Melbourne House when revolutions throughout Europe began threatening to take away aristocratic privilege.[49] In Laclos's novel, Byron found an ideal representation of the magnificent class prerogatives that had once existed in late-eighteenth-century England. Laclos's aristocrats were corrupt, but there was something appealing about their scandalous intrigues. They were liberally educated, after all, and their self-awareness redeemed their sins. The libertine did not fall prey to the senses. He or she controlled them and thus controlled others. The rhetorical control of Valmont and Merteuil—and the letters of Laclos's protagonists are highly rhetorical, masterful letters—is the counterpart to their sexual control of their victims and themselves. Their liberal education facilitates their libertinism.

In one sense, then, the literary tradition of libertinism coincided quite well with a liberal education. In a letter to Valmont, Madame de Merteuil tells him how she read the greatest philosophers and moralists in order to justify and facilitate her sexual conduct (*DL* 81:175–84). Madame de Tourvel's piety, on the other hand, is prompted at least in part by her limited reading: she never manages to finish Richardson's *Clarissa,* which would have helped her defend herself against Valmont. As a pious middle-class woman, Madame de Tourvel consults the bible and biblical commentaries (*DL* 107:250). By following the example of Laclos's well-read aristocrats, Byron behaved in a manner that resembled the conduct of the French upper classes before the Revolution.

As similar as the England Byron inhabited was to the social milieu of Valmont, the poet's emulation of Valmont's conduct was not so easily achieved. Brought up by a devout (though profligate) nurse, Byron inherited her Calvinist outlook as well as the Scottish prejudices of his mother. He felt deep remorse for his affair with Augusta, and though Lady Melbourne was his guide to conduct, his own moral sense was more highly developed, if not always realized. A second obstacle to Byron's libertinism was his definition of liberalism. To be a liberal in Byron's view was to embrace Christian morality. My equation of liberalism and Christianity might puzzle modern liberals who view separation of church and state as a basic tenet of that creed. Such a secular, modern view, however, overlooks the Christian roots of liberalism. For Byron, certainly, liberalism's religious origins were determinative: to be a gentleman in Byron's view was to be a Christian. When Byron could not support Baldwin's petition in the House of Lords, after all, he used religious language ("no more charity than a cruet of vinegar" [*BLJ* December 6, 1813; 3:233]) to describe the failure: a liberal political stance, for Byron, grew out of his sense of Christian duty.[50]

The more he followed the epistolary style of the unrepentant Valmont in the early pages of *Les liaisons dangereuses*, the more he began to write through that style and seek more enduring forms of commitment. Byron thought he could reform his character by renouncing authorship, yet his marriage proved to him the impossibility of living up to the epistolary portrait he had created for Annabella Milbanke in his letters. Byron's seduction of Annabella forced him to forfeit the epistolary style (and political attitudes) of the worldly Valmont, the very style that made such a seduction possible; he had to relinquish his Byronic persona and his career as a writer.

Byron struggled to combine an emerging form of liberalism—one associated with parliamentary reform, Catholic emancipation, and national sovereignty—with a sexual lifestyle commensurate with his sense of political morality.[51] Like Yorick and Valmont, he failed in his quest: neither sentimentalism, nor libertinism, nor Annabella's Christian morality proved sufficient to guide him. It would not be an exaggeration to suggest that Byron felt validated in his failure by the charismatic literary characters (Rochester, St. Preux, Valmont) who preceded him. *Their* moral quests, after all, were interesting precisely to the extent that they were unsuccessful. Yet Byron's effort to create a counterfeit self for Annabella did not end with his marriage. In some ways, his epistolary engagements, with their curious blend of libertinism and sentiment, served as provisional texts for the complex moral code evinced in such disparate works as *The Hebrew Melodies, Childe Harold* 3 and 4, and *Manfred*.

In his poetry as in his personal life, Byron did much to complicate his era's understanding of what liberalism, shorn of aristocratic wealth, might look like. He did this in part through a sophisticated engagement with Sterne, Richardson, Rousseau, Laclos, and what I would term the politics of sentimentalism in his letters and journals. Certainly, his marriage to the formidably virtuous Annabella Milbanke tested the sincerity of his desire for self-reform. But their separation was also a national test, one that led to one of those "periodical fits of morality" that the British public undergoes, as Macaulay put it,[52] when Byron left the country in disgrace in 1816. In his poetry, especially *Don Juan*,

Byron interpreted that scandal to his readers. He did so by usurping Annabella Milbanke's voice, but in the process he also learned to question his own libertine lifestyle through his narrator's commentary. The moral of his poem, we learn, is directed to those whose "headlong passions form their proper woes" (*CPW* 5:6:87).

Byron abandoned Valmont's libertine style in his letters between 1812 and 1815, though he never fully abandoned libertine affairs while in Italy. What his correspondence leading to his engagement taught him was to question his own libertine morality, and Byron's erotic liberalism existed, in the future, in dialectical relationship with the libertinism he struggled to overcome. One might argue that Byron's heroic sacrifices in Italy and Greece were made possible by such acts of self-overcoming. For Byron in 1813, libertinism had involved, among other things, a turning away from the sphere of public politics and a retreat into class privilege. His involvement in revolutionary movements in Italy and Greece, on the other hand, gave a new idealism to the liberal cause, the more so because Byron overcame his own well-publicized and guilty libertinism to embrace them.

NOTES

1. Michael Foot, *The Politics of Paradise* (New York: Harper & Row, 1988), 147.
2. Williams, *Keywords*, 149.
3. For Byron's distinction between license and liberty, see Lady Blessington, *Conversations with Lord Byron,* ed. Ernest Lovell, Jr. (Princeton: Princeton University Press, 1968), 174.
4. Duchess of Devonshire, *The Sylph,* 2 vols. (London: T. & W. Lowndes, 1779), 1:135–38.
5. For my discussion of Whig society, I am primarily indebted to Leslie Mitchell, *Holland House* (London: Duckworth, 1980) and *Lord Melbourne* (Oxford: Oxford University Press, 1997); Countess Mabell Airlie, *In Whig Society* (London: Hodder and Stoughton, 1921); and David Cecil, *The Young Melbourne* (New York: Bobbs-Merrill, 1954).
6. Charles Johnstone, *Chrysalis*, or the Adventures of a Guinea (London, 1760) describes Wilkes's induction; see also Daniel P. Mannix, *The Hell-Fire Club* (London: Four-Square, 1961), 152. Arthur M. Cash, *Laurence Sterne: The Later Years* (London: Methuen & Co. Ltd., 1986), 182 does not state that Sterne was a member, but cites Donald McCormick, *The Hell-Fire Club* (London: 1958) who lists Sterne's close friend John Hall-Stevenson as among one of the "probable" members. Sterne was also close friends with John Wilkes, who is listed as a member in Peter D. G. Thomas, *John Wilkes: A Friend to Liberty* (Oxford: Oxford University Press, 1992).

7. Leslie Marchand, *Byron: A Portrait* (Chicago: University of Chicago Press, 1970), 58.

8. O'Toole, *A Traitor's Kiss*, 208.

9. O'Toole, *A Traitor's Kiss*, 286.

10. Jean-Jacques Rousseau, *Julie ou la nouvelle Héloïse* (Paris: Garnier Freres, 1973); Samuel Richardson, *Clarissa: or the History of a Young Lady*, ed. Angus Ross, 1747–48 (New York: Penguin, 1985); Pierre Choderlos de Laclos, *Les liaisons dangereuses*, ed. with an introd. by Andrew Maurois, trans. Lowell Bair (New York: Bantam, 1962). Subsequent references are made to Bair's translation and include both letter and page number as parenthetical citations in the text.

11. Roger Shattuck, *Forbidden Knowledge* (New York: St. Martin's Press, 1996), 117.

12. See Andrew Elfenbein, *Byron and the Victorians* (Cambridge: Cambridge University Press, 1995), passim.

13. Marchand mentions the reference to Sterne's *A Sentimental Journey through France and Italy* (ed. Graham Petrie [New York: Penguin, 1967]), but Byron may also be quoting Horace Walpole, as Arthur Hill Cash (*Sterne's Comedy of Moral Sentiments: The Ethical Dimension of the Journey* [Pittsburgh: Duquesne University Press, 1966], 27) and Alan B. Howes, (Alan B. Howes, ed., *Sterne: The Critical Heritage* [London: Routledge & Kegan Paul, 1974], 305) suggest. If so, Walpole's quotation makes Byron's reference to Sterne even more suggestive, for Byron identified with Walpole's status as a nobleman, gentleman, and man of feeling. "It is the fashion to underrate Horace Walpole," Byron wrote in his preface to *Marino Faliero*, "firstly, because he was a nobleman, and secondly, because he was a gentleman" (*CPW* 4:305).

14. Quoted in *The Life and Letters of Anne Isabella Lady Noel Byron: From Unpublished Papers in the Possession of the Late Ralph, Earl of Lovelace* (New York: Charles Scribner's Sons, 1929), 116.

15. R. F. Brissenden provides an illuminating discussion of the relationship between erotic vivacity and moral sensitivity. *Virtue in Distress: Studies in the Novel of Sentiment from Richardson to Sade* (New York: Harper & Row Publishers, 1974), 87.

16. Sterne, *Sentimental Journey*, 95.

17. Sterne, *Sentimental Journey*, 95, 96. As Judith Frank has shown, Sterne's bird may be profitably compared to Jacques de Vaucanson's mechanical duck, which the French inventor (1709–82) had exhibited in Paris in 1753. Judith Frank, "'A Man Who Laughs Is Never Dangerous': Character and Class in Sterne's A Sentimental Journey," *ELH* 56 (spring 1989): 111. See also, Hugh Kenner, *The Counterfeiters: An Historical Comedy* (Baltimore: Johns Hopkins University Press, 1985), 29.

18. Brissenden, *Virtue in Distress*, 91; Sterne, *Sentimental Journey*, 95.

19. Anthony Vital, "Lord Byron's Embarrassment: Poesy and the Feminine," *Bulletin of Research in the Humanities* 86.3 (1983–85): 269–90. My argument strives to unite Vital's discussion of "the feminine" (276) with what he sees as Robertson's antithetical account of "aristocratic individualism."

20. Brissenden, *Virtue in Distress*, 122.

21. Marchand, *Byron: A Portrait*, 284.

22. Malcolm Elwin, *Lord Byron's Wife* (London: Macdonald, 1962), 147.

23. George Paston and Peter Quennell, *"To Lord Byron": Feminine Profiles, Based upon Unpublished Letters; 1807–1824* (New York: Charles Scribner's Sons, 1939), 63.

24. The copy of Byron's 1816 Sales Catalog at the Meyer Davis Collection at the University of Pennsylvania shows no record of Laclos's *Dangerous Liaisons*, nor does Nicholson's account of Byron's reading (*CMP* 279). That Byron could quote, however inaccurately, from a phrase that appears so late in Laclos's novel, is perhaps one indication that he read the entire work. Byron could not finish reading *Clarissa* (according to his diary of November 1813), preferred Fielding to Richardson (*Detached Thoughts*, diary of 1819), and rarely read French in the original. I have not been able to confirm the translation Byron read.

25. Ethel Mayne, *The Life and Letters of Anne Isabella Lady Noel Byron: From Unpublished Papers in the Possession of the Late Ralph, Earl of Lovelace* (New York: Charles Scribner's Sons, 1929), 209. Judith Milbanke's reference to the novel with its English title shows that the work had been translated. *The British Museum General Catalogue of Printed Books*, vol. 38 (London: Trustees of the British Museum, 1966) lists *Dangerous Connections* in a four-volume edition, published and translated as early as 1784.

26. Airlie, *In Whig Society*, 5.

27. I have taken all quotations from Pierre Choderlos de Laclos, *Les liaisons dangereuses*, trans. Lowell Bair (New York: Bantam, 1962), 81:151–160.

28. Paston and Quennell, *"To Lord Byron,"* 122.

29. Caroline Lamb, *Glenarvon*, a facsimile reproduction, with an introduction by James L. Ruff (New York: Scholars' Facsimiles & Reprints, 1972) 3:80. Byron ended his affair with Lady Caroline Lamb in a letter that recalls Valmont's. "Lady Caroline—our affections are not in our own power—mine are engaged. I love another" (*BLJ* November 1812?; 2:242).

30. For a reading of Valmont that stresses his entrapment in libertine values rather than his transformation, see Peter Brooks, *The Novel of Worldliness: Crebillon, Marivaux, Laclos, Stendhal* (Princeton: Princeton University Press, 1969), 206.

31. James Soderholm, *Fantasy, Forgery, and the Byron Legend* (Lexington: University Press of Kentucky, 1996), 84.

32. It also recalls his description of the marriage state in *Don Juan:* "that moral centaur, man and wife" (*CPW* 5:1264).

33. Marchand's edition of Byron's letters points out that Madame de Merteuil, not Valmont, quotes these lines in a letter to Valmont (*BLJ* November 24, 1813; 3:220n.1). A reader could be forgiven for attributing the remark to Valmont, however, since Valmont simply copies Merteuil's letter and sends it to Tourvel (*DL* 141:325).

34. In using this term, I have in mind Wolfson's suggestive reading of cross-dressing in *Don Juan*, in her article, "'Their She Condition': Cross-Dressing and the Politics of Gender in Don Juan," *ELH* 54 (fall 1987): 585–617.

35. Byron's letter made such an impact on Caroline that, in perhaps another example of cross-writing, she included it in her novel *Glenarvon*. Byron's method of ending their affair may well have prompted her to compare him to Valmont (Paston and Quennell, *To Lord Byron,* 63). For an illuminating discussion of *Glenarvon*, see Peter

Graham, *Don Juan and Regency England* (Charlottesville: University Press of Virginia, 1990), 89–124.

36. I borrow the term from Eve Sedgwick's *Between Men: English Literature and Male Homosocial Desire* (New York: Columbia University Press, 1985), 20, but also have in mind Louis Crompton's important study, *Byron and Greek Love: Homophobia in 19th-Century England* (Berkeley: University of California, 1985).

37. McGann sees in Byron's early poetry "a misogynist inversion of a central myth of the sentimentalist programme." I differ from McGann in viewing the "sentimentalist programme" itself, rather than just Byron's variety of it, as implicitly misogynist. As Terry Eagleton observes, "For the eighteenth-century woman, as indeed for women of any epoch, the pedestal is never very far from the pit." Jerome McGann, "'My Brain Is Feminine': Byron and the Poetry of Deception," in *Byron: Augustan and Romantic*, ed. Andrew Rutherford (New York: St. Martin's Press, 1990), 32; Terry Eagleton, *The Rape of Clarissa: Writing, Sexuality and Class Struggle in Samuel Richardson* (Minneapolis: University of Minnesota Press, 1982), 15.

38. Mayne, *Life and Letters*, 128–29.

39. Mayne, *Life and Letters*, 134.

40. Mayne, *Life and Letters*, 138.

41. Mayne, *Life and Letters*, 208.

42. See Lady Melbourne's previously unpublished letter of October 19, 1814, in Jonathan David Gross, ed., *Byron's "Corbeau Blanc": The Life and Letters of Lady Melbourne* (Houston: Rice University Press, 1997), 184–86.

43. In another letter, this time to Henry Fox, Byron used the same metaphor: "It is now six weeks and a day since I subsided into matrimony—since which period I have become duly domestic—and shall be happy to hear of the amputation of any further foxes—(particularly Hodgson's) tails in the same trap" (*BLJ* February 14, 1815; 4:271).

44. Mayne, *Life and Letters*, 154.

45. Mayne, *Life and Letters*, 158.

46. Mayne, *Life and Letters*, 158.

47. "[Bout-rimes from Seaham]," *CPW* 3:283:11. Byron, of course, wrote *Parisina* and *The Siege of Corinth,* and also published *Hebrew Melodies* during 1815, but even these works were derivative. *Parisina* and *The Siege of Corinth,* McGann argues, "developed out of an original MS. tale, begun in 1812 and continued in 1813 . . . possibly even before *Giaour*" (*CPW* 3:479–480). More importantly, Byron seemed to view his marriage as a partial renunciation of the persona of libertine author he had established in his early verse. "In course I mean to reform most thoroughly & become 'a good man and true,'" he wrote to Lady Melbourne upon informing her that he had been "accepted" by Annabella (*BLJ* September 18, 1814; 4:175).

48. "The mediaeval superstition [was] that the child of incest must be a kind of monster," Ethel Mayne notes in *Life and Letters,* 93; see also Phyllis Grosskurth, *Byron: The Flawed Angel* (New York: Houghton Mifflin, 1997), 192n.

49. Cecil, *The Young Lord Melbourne*, 18.

50. Foot, *Politics of Paradise*, 351.

51. For a provocative discussion of the relationship between political and sexual liberation in Byron, see Jerome Christensen's *Lord Byron's Strength: Romantic Writing and Commercial Society* (Baltimore: Johns Hopkins University Press, 1993), 55.

52. Thomas Macaulay, *Critical, Historical and Miscellaneous Essays by Lord Macaulay,* 6 vols. (New York: Sheldon and Company, 1860), 2:329.

3

BYRON AND THE STORY OF JOSEPH: "THE BRIDE OF ABYDOS," *HEBREW MELODIES*, AND *DON JUAN*

My account of Byron's developing liberalism has taken him to 1816. Before discussing this important date in Byron's political development, which I treat in my next chapter, I would like to provide an overview of Byron's erotic liberalism by tracing a theme he used with surprising consistency throughout his poetic career. Byron's eastern tales, *Hebrew Melodies*, and *Don Juan* show the poet making use of a cosmopolitan perspective gained from his travels of 1809–11. In these three works, he represented erotic passion to his English readers in new ways by adapting the Joseph story as told in Jami's "Yusef and Zuleika," the Koran, and Genesis for his own literary and political purposes. The Joseph story helped Byron consider the consequences of erotic passion, the ways in which *eros* can both compromise and enable generous actions.

Byron's "The Bride of Abydos" shares several striking similarities with Jami's "Yusef and Zuleika" and the Koran. In both poems, Zuleika takes the sexual initiative, offering her lover a rose to "calm" his cares. Her erotic attachment to a man whose white "capote" signals his legendary status improves her ethically as she strives to woo him with her generous gifts. For the next two years, Byron contemplated the meaning of the Joseph story as told in Genesis, which Fielding's *Joseph Andrews* and a recently published letter of Lady Melbourne's kept firmly in Byron's mind. That same year he developed his knowledge of Judaic themes by collaborating with Isaac Nathan on *Hebrew Melodies* before leaving England in 1816 to become, like Joseph, a stranger in a strange land. When Byron used the Joseph story as a leitmotif in *Don Juan* (1818), he recognized its personal application. Thematically, the story of Joseph helped Byron explain his hero's brushes with sexual temptation, and Juan's otherwise random transformation from an innocent Spanish roué into a diplomat for Catherine the Great. Like Juan, Joseph overcomes his struggles in a foreign land. Both young men escape near seduction by another man's wife to serve as a potentate's most trusted adviser. *The Literary Gazette* noted this allusion in canto 5, but failed to detect Byron's reliance upon Jami's poem and the Koran for such incidents as the purchasing of Juan at a slave market.[1] Recently, Byron scholars have benefited from the important work of Mohammed Sharafuddin, Anahid Melikian, and Naji B. Oueijan, who have helped explain Eastern allusions in Byron's poetry.[2] My chapter is the first to recover Jami as a source for "The Bride of Abydos" and canto 5 of *Don Juan*.

Byron's use of Jami's "Yusef and Zuleika" and the Koran in "The Bride of Abydos," *Hebrew Melodies*, and the canto 5 of *Don Juan* complicates his reader's response to the story of Joseph. Byron only partly fits Said's argument in *Orientalism* that English writers took a textual attitude toward the East.[3] Western sources, like Beckford's *Vathek*, influenced Byron's view of the East, but he was also familiar with Albanian and Turkish poetry and with these countries as well, having resided in them for months at a time (October–November 1809 and May–July 1810); in his extended grand tour, he even planned to visit Persia and India.[4] Byron represented these countries sympathetically, moreover, often exaggerating his admiration for Muslim Turkey in order to embarrass English Protestants. His pluralist account of the Joseph story resists the bourgeois assumptions of Western superiority evident in many of Robert Southey's verse tales, evident, for instance, in his first three footnotes to *Thalaba the Destroyer*. Where Samuel Johnson allowed his Tory values to suffuse *Rasselas,* Byron espoused a "realistic Orientalism."[5] He wrote "The Bride of Abydos," *Hebrew Melodies*, and canto 5 of *Don Juan* as a cultural comparativist, and his poetic fictions encourage attentive readers to question Western complacency as well as Eastern despotism. For this reason, Byron must have found the praise of *The Literary Gazette* disturbingly parochial.

> it is, perhaps, the greatest compliment we can pay Lord Byron, to affirm, that his talent has been omnipotent, to overcome the defects of his subject;—that the rays of his genius have been able to form a halo round the head of deformity, which he has so environed and emblazoned with the divinity of his muse, that, like the ugliness of an Eastern idol, we can gaze upon it with pleasure, on account of the costliness and magnificence of the shrine in which it is incased. (*RR* 523)

Unlike his reviewers, Byron did not assume that Western political and religious institutions were superior to their Eastern counterparts. He followed Montesquieu in viewing political structures as a response to the culture, climate, and national characteristics of the peoples and places that gave birth to them.[6]

I

JAMI'S "YUSEF AND ZULEIKA"

Critics assume that Byron wrote "The Bride of Abydos" to escape an incestuous liaison with his half-sister Augusta Leigh, and an equally intense relationship with Lady Frances Webster.[7] In the Oxford edition of the poem, for example, Jerome McGann states that Byron's "relations with Lady Frances entered *Bride* in the poem's specific allusion (insisted upon in the notes) to the story of Potiphar's wife, which in Turkish literature formed the story of the love of Zuleika and Mejnoun" (*CPW* 3:435). Yet Byron's letter of October 17, 1813 shows that he first compared Potiphar's wife to Lady Oxford, not Lady Frances Webster. Secondly, there is no "story of the love of Zuleika and Mejnoun" (*CPW* 3:435); Persian literature celebrates a romance between Yusef and Zuleika, and Laila and Majnoun.

"Zuleika," "the Persian poetical name for Potiphar's wife," was Byron's first title for "The Bride of Abydos," but he changed it before publication.[8] Byron borrowed the preliminary title (*BLJ* November 14, 1813; 3:205) from Persian poetry, possibly from Jami, or from D'Herbelot's entry in his *Bibliothèque Orientale*.[9] Byron's sales catalog (*CMP* 231–254) does not mention Jami's work, but Byron alludes to the Yusef and Zuleika story as "one of the finest poems in their language" in a footnote to "The Bride of Abydos" (*CPW* 3:440). Byron may have come across Jami in translations by Langles (1788), Samuel Rousseau (1801), or A. L. Chezy (1807), or during his two years in the East (1809–11), which took him through Turkey, Greece, and Albania. In his *Reading List* (1807), Byron notes, "Ferdausi, author of the Shah Nameh the Persian Iliad, Sadi, and Hafiz, the immortal Hafiz the oriental Anacreon, the last is reverenced beyond any Bard of ancient or modern times by the Persians, who resort to his tomb near Schiraz to celebrate his memory, a splendid copy of his works is chained to his Monument" (*CMP* 1–2).

Harold Wiener argues that Byron lifted these opinions from secondary sources rather than from perusing Persian manuscripts,[10] yet several translations of Jami, Hafiz, and Sadi were readily available by 1813, making such perusal unnecessary. Persian poetry, like travel literature, had become a "fad" when Byron wrote "The Bride of Abydos."[11] William Jones translated "An Ode of Jami, in the Persian Form and Measure" and "A Song, from Persia";[12] he also wrote a preface to his own translation of "Laila and Majnun" by Abdullah, surnamed Hatifi, nephew of Jami (or Nurudin).[13] *Asiatic Researches* (vols. 1–10) and *Journal of the Royal Asiatic Society* also provided a wealth of information on Eastern verse that was available to Byron. Volumes 3, 6, and 7 of *Asiatic Researches* contain articles bearing on Jami. In a letter to Charles Reviczky, Jones singled out Jami's poem for special praise, though he never published it. "One I like especially is Jami's poem called Yusef va Zulaikha. Each couplet of the poem, which has about 4,070 of them, has the pure brilliance of a little star. At Oxford we have six very beautiful copies of this work, one of which is accurately copied, with the vowels marked, and illustrated by Golius's notes. Another copy is in my possession, and I shall have it published if I can find the time."[14]

In "The Bride of Abydos," Selim and Zuleika are reading "Mejnoun's tale and Sadi's song," which indicates Byron's familiarity with the most popular of Persian stories, Sadi's *Leila and Majnoun*, published in French in 1807. Having lived in the East for over two years, Byron may well have borrowed the name Zuleika from a poem he had read, rather than solely from one of the works that appear in his sales catalog. Though Wiener notes that Byron did not read Persian, Byron certainly had access to English translations. "The works of the European[s], and some of the Asiatic[s], I have perused," Byron wrote, "either in the original, or Translations" (*CMP* 2).[15] In any case, too much in Byron's "The Bride of Abydos" resembles incidents in "Yusef and Zuleika" and the Koran to ignore the obvious similarities, which I summarize below.

Jami's "Yusef and Zuleika" differs from Genesis in several important respects. To begin with, Jami's poem—the fifth and most famous of his *Sab'a* ("Septet") or Haft Awrang ("Seven Thrones"), composed in the *hazaj* meter in 1483—follows the Joseph story as told in the 12th Sura of the Koran.[16] Punished by her Egyptian husband for seducing Yusef, Potiphar's wife defends herself in the Koran by citing Yusef's extraordinary beauty. She gains social acceptance for her actions by inviting the women of Memphis to a feast of oranges and other delicacies.[17] When they see him, they cut their hands with a knife, distracted by his beauty. They no longer condemn Zuleika, but desire Yusef themselves.

For Zuleika, loving Yusef is not sinful but redemptive, for her unrequited love leads her from pagan idolatry to monotheism. Yusef unwittingly saves Zuleika's soul by refusing her advances, a theme D'Herbelot, one of Byron's sources, underscores.[18] Even Jami improves morally, for he writes inspired poetry describing Zuleika's desire for Yusef, which Jami interprets as a form of divine communion. For Jami, E. G. Browne reminds the reader, "Love of the creature . . . [is] the bridge leading to love of the Creator,"[19] a theme George Sale underscores in a note to his translation of the Koran (194, note a). By relying on the Koran and Jami's poem, in other words, Byron humanized the contemptible pagan seductress who appears in the *Old Testament* and the *Agaddah*.[20] "I also wished to try my hand on a female character in Zuleika," he explained to the travel writer, Edward Clarke, "& have endeavored as far as ye. grossness of our masculine ideas will allow—to preserve her purity without impairing the ardour of her attachment" (*BLJ* December 15, 1813; 3:199). Jami's poem follows the Koran in portraying Joseph and Zuleika as passionate. Joseph would have slept with Zuleika had he not seen "the evident demonstration of his Lord,"[21] while Zuleika falls for Joseph because of his striking beauty. The women Zuleika invites to the feast at Memphis confirm her good taste.[22]

Byron must have found Jami's poem congenial, especially given his intention to portray his own Zuleika as morally pure (*BLJ* December 15, 1813; 3:199). Jami humanized Zuleika, in part, by telling his story from her vantage point, a strategy Byron only partly followed.[23] By relying on Jami's poem, however, Byron challenged Western readers to keep Genesis and the Koran in their minds at the same time. Byron's interest in narrative complexity had the perhaps inadvertent effect of leading him to espouse cultural pluralism. His interest in Jami's poem shows how seminal the story of Joseph was for him in composing "The Bride of Abydos," which corresponds with Jami's religious allegory in several striking respects.

In "Yusef and Zulaikha," Zuleika has three visions of a handsome young man who tells her that he is Egypt's Grand Vizir. She persuades her father to send a marriage embassy to the Vizir, who accepts the offer. When she arrives in Egypt, she peeps through the Vizir's tent and discovers, to her horror, that he is not the man in her prophetic dream. The Archangel Gabriel persuades her to marry him nevertheless, holding out the promise that she will eventually meet Yusef. She complies. Returning home with her new husband on the day of her marriage, she sees Yusef on the auction block, recently sold into slavery by his brothers. She persuades her husband to purchase him. They adopt him as a son, and Zuleika woos him as a lover.[24]

Like Jami's "Yusef and Zulaikha," "The Bride of Abydos" begins with an arranged marriage, Zuleika's betrothal to Osman, "kinsman of the Bey Oglou" (*CPW* 3:1:206). Giaffir announces his daughter's imminent marriage to a "nobleman" (*CPW* 3:437) as if setting a date for her execution, as Caroline Franklin argues.[25] At the same time, Giaffir harbors an erotic, perhaps incestuous, passion for her. She is "more . . . dear" to Giaffir than "her mother," and the sweetness of her lips are "cooled" just "in time to save" him from considering his sublimated passion for his daughter too intensely. "She is the offspring of my choice," he says. "Oh! more than even her mother dear,/With all to hope, and nought to fear,/My Peri! ever welcome here!/Sweet, as the desart-fountain's wave/To lips just cooled in time to save—"(*CPW* 3:1: 148–153).[26] Zuleika loves her cousin Selim, but Giaffir refuses to consent to their marriage because he considers his nephew too effeminate. "I would not have thee wed a boy," Giaffir says. "[H]is arm is little worth,/And scarcely in the chace could cope/With timid fawn or antelope" (*CPW* 3:1:135–137). Zuleika's father challenges his nephew's masculinity: "If thy beard had manlier length,/And if thy hand had skill and strength,/I'd joy to see thee break a lance,/Albeit against my own perchance" (*CPW* 3:1:122–125). Confronted by Zuleika's impending marriage, Selim prepares to take military action to prevent it.

Shortly after Giaffir's rebuke, Selim invites Zuleika to a grotto, where he appears before her dressed as a galiongée. "I said I was not what I seemed," he says, alluding to more than his outfit (CPW 3:2:151). He reveals that they are cousins. The two can wed, but not before Selim defeats Giaffir in battle. As Selim's ships are about to embark, however, Giaffir kills Selim with a single musket shot (*CPW* 3:2:570–580). When Zuleika dies of grief, a white rose blooms where she expired (*CPW* 3:2:715).

Robert Ogle has shown that Byron's poem is indebted to Ovid's *Heroides*, specifically to the story of Hero and Leander, but "The Bride of Abydos" also resembles Jami's "Yusef and Zuleika." Both Yusef and Selim are "beardless" men wooed by women of higher social station; both are offered "roses" by their loved ones which they reject. Jami compares Zuleika to a youth who wanders through a garden, "His heart marked like a tulip, for love of the rose,/First on its petals he looks with delight,/And then plucks the fair flower that has charmed his sight."[27] Jami's "Yusef and Zuleika" recounts their love in a manner that anticipates Zuleika's wooing of Selim in Byron's poem. Griffith's translation of the passage was illustrated by Thomas Stothard and set to music by Isaac Nathan:

> With winning art would Zulaikha woo;
> But Yusuf far from her gaze withdrew.
> Tears of hot blood would Zulaikha shed;
> But her tears were idle, for Yusuf fled.
> Zulaikha's soul with deep wounds was scarred:
> But the heart of Yusuf was cold and hard.
> Still on his cheek would Zulaikha gaze;
> But Yusuf never his eye would raise.
> For a glance from her darling Zulaikha burned;
> But Yusuf's look from her look was turned.
> His eye he kept lest his heart might err,
> And no fond glance would he bend on her.
> (Yohannan 167; Griffith 162)

Zulaikha woos Yusef in a manner that recalls Zuleika offering Selim a "rose to calm [her] brother's cares" (*CPW* 3:1:281–294). When Selim is unresponsive, she utters the phrase Thomas Stothard chose as the caption for his illustration of Byron's poem. "What—not receive my foolish flower?" she asks, "Nay then I am indeed unblest" (*CPW* 3:1:295–6). *La Belle Assemblée* professed to be shocked by Zuleika's expression of passion and commented on her want of "delicacy."[28] Perhaps anticipating reviewers' objections, Byron foregrounded Joseph's chastity, symbolized by his cloak, rather than Zuleika's seduction, as portrayed in the Koran and in Jami's poem. In perhaps his most important departure from his Eastern source, Byron made Selim rather than "Zuleika" the center of his poem's dramatic and erotic interest. By doing so, he restored the poem's Judeo-Christian context, making references to the Joseph story from Genesis.

Selim most resembles the *Old Testament* Joseph in the cloak he wears in the grotto scene:

> And from his belt a sabre swung,
> And from his shoulder loosely hung
> The cloak of white—the thin capote
> That decks the wandering Candiote
> (*CPW* 3:2:139–142)

While obviously different from Joseph's coat of many colors, Selim's "white" cloak recalls it symbolically. Both garments distinguish and (figuratively) destroy the possessor. By comparing Selim's "cloak of white" to the "thin capote/That decks the wandering Candiote" (*CPW* 3:2:141–142), Byron implicitly compares him to a nomad (*CPW* 3:2:387–490), like the wandering Jew, whose absence of a father is emblematic of the Jews' lack of a fatherland. Selim is the "nephew of a Cain" (*CPW* 3:2:204), whose utopia is not a Promised Land, but the "tent" and the ship. As a companionless Noah, Selim asks Zuleika to be the "dove" and rainbow to his ark. Through these references, Byron connects Selim to Cain, Noah, and Joseph, and, by implication, to the Old Testament.

Or the Koran. Tempting as it is to see Selim as a wandering Jew, Byron compares Selim's wandering with that of Arab nomads, preventing his reader from seeing the Joseph story through the lens of only one sacred text. "The wandering life of the Arabs, Tartars, and Turkomans, will be found well detailed in any book of Eastern travels," he writes in a footnote to this passage. In another note, he reminds readers that "every allusion to any thing or personage in the Old Testament, such as the Ark, or Cain, is equally the privilege of Mussulman and Jew: indeed the former profess to be much better acquainted with the lives, true and fabulous, of the patriarchs, than is warranted by our own

Sacred writ, and not content with Adam, they have a biography of Pre-Adamites.... Zuleika is the Persian name of Potiphar's wife, and her amour with Joseph constitutes one of the finest poems in their language. It is therefore no violation of costume to put the names of Cain, or Noah, into the mouth of a Moslem" (*CPW* 3:440; Byron's note to ln. 204 in canto 2).

These endnotes suggest that Byron saw the Joseph story as central to his design in "The Bride of Abydos"; he wished to stress both Jewish and Moslem versions, without relying exclusively on either. This tension between Jewish and Islamic representations of the Joseph story becomes clear in the poem itself, for Genesis and the Koran represent Joseph's coat in different ways. In Genesis, the cloak symbolizes Joseph's death at the hands of his brothers; he is thrown into a pit and reborn. In the Koran, however, Joseph's brothers pretend that a wolf devoured him and stained "his inner garment" (12:18) with blood.[29] Both deaths are figurative. Byron alters his sources by making Selim's death literal, linking the slain Yusef to his white capote.

> A broken torch—an oarless boat—
> And tangled on the weeds that heap
> The beach where shelving to the deep—
> There lies a white Capote!
> 'Tis rent in twain—one dark-red stain
> The wave yet ripples o'er in vain (*CPW* 3:2:592–597)

For Byron, the "white Capote" comes at the end of the tale to signal the death of the hero. Jami begins his poem with Yusef's torn garment to underscore a different theme: Zuleika's self-improvement.

> She clutches his skirt as he fled amain,
> and the coat from his shoulders was rent in twain
> Reft of his garment he slipp'd from her hand
> Like a bud from its sheath when the leaves expand.
> (Yohannan 185; Griffiths 212)

If Joseph escapes from Potiphar's wife in Genesis, Zuleika falls in love with, and ultimately worships, Yusef's beauty in Jami's poem. Departing from Genesis, Jami does not portray Zuleika as vile. Zuleika seduces Yusef, in part, to protect him, "like a bud from its sheath when the leaves expand." Acting as first lover and then surrogate mother to Yusef, Zuleika improves herself ethically, transforming *eros* into *philia*, by having her erotic advances thwarted. Most nineteenth-century translators omit Jami's fanciful tropes. Doing so can prevent Western readers from perceiving how Jami's "decorative" language underscores his heroine's psychological growth. Where Zuleika matures ethically by protecting Yusef like a "sheath," Byron's heroine remains psychologically stagnant, a frozen Niobe.

Both Jami and Byron depict the tearing of Yusef or Selim's cloak, but do so in different ways. In Byron's poem, the waves claim Selim's body, his white capote "rent" not from Zuleika's sexual desire, but from his failed conflict with her father, "the print of many a struggling hand" (*CPW* 3:2:590). His "broken torch" and "oarless boat" suggest his impotent struggle. Unlike Yusef, who escapes from Zuleika with his honor and integrity intact, Selim fails both to wed Zuleika and to overcome her father's superior force. If the poem allegorizes Whig failures, as Nigel Leask convincingly maintains,[30] then Selim's failure is as personal as it was political, as much a matter of failed masculinity as of failed political strategy.

Though Byron had represented feminine desire rather reticently in "The Bride of Abydos," the poem embarrassed him nevertheless. He disparaged his effort in a letter to Lord Holland. "The very *wild* stanzas are more like Southey or King David—'By the waters of Babylon' &c. than anything English, but that is thoroughly Eastern and partly from the Koran" (*BLJ* November 17, 1813; 3:168), he wrote. Perhaps Byron penned such letters to deny connections between Joseph's trials of temptation and Byron's own difficulties resisting his half-sister Augusta's charms. Byron could still distinguish his own personality from the "wildness" of the Old Testament and the "sullenness" of the Jews (*CMP* 67). Yet the grotto scene that opens canto 2, where Selim wears "from his shoulder" a "thin capote," also anticipates Thomas Phillips's portrait of Byron in Albanian dress, exhibited publically in 1814, three years after he returned from the East. In a letter to his mother, Byron first described the "very 'magnifique' Albanian dresses" he saw there. He included an anecdote about how he overcame his own fear of mortality during a dreadful storm aboard a Turkish ship of war: "I ... wrapped myself up in my Albanian capote (an immense cloak) & lay down to wait the worst, I have learnt to philosophize on my travels" (*BLJ* November 12, 1809; 1:229). Like Selim, Byron often imagined himself as a doomed hero, stoically facing his death.

Byron's poem reflects aspects of Jami's "Yusef and Zuleika" not found in Genesis. He had immersed himself so deeply in Eastern culture that his Eastern tales reflected complex attitudes toward passion and self-restraint. George Sale taught Byron that "poems," not "written laws," illuminate a culture's mores.[31] Like the followers of Mohammed, Byron communicates moral teachings even through such apparently sensational verse as "The Bride of Abydos." Judeo-Christian sources were not his sole guide. Reviewers who complained of Byron's arcane diction[32] failed to recognize that he attached as much importance to his Eastern costume as he did to his poem's themes. By using competing versions of the Joseph story, Byron indirectly endorsed cultural pluralism.

64   Chapter 3

II

Shortly after completing "The Bride of Abydos," Byron moved into the Albany; Lady Melbourne, who first lived in the elegant brick structure, reminded him of a painting of Joseph that had once hung on the walls (fig. 1).

> Opposite to the fire hung the view of Constantinople which you see here [Whitehall], & over the Chimney a painting of Joseph turning in disgust from Potiphar's Wife—Thus on one side you would have been delighted with the resemblance to *ce beau Ciel* you love so much, & on the other you would have seen a moral precept—of which I do not mean to say you stand in need—but there can be no disadvantage in having a good example always before your Eyes.[33]

Byron would link Constantinople with the slave market selling of Joseph in canto 5 of *Don Juan,* perhaps with this previously unpublished letter of Lady Melbourne's firmly in mind.

Though it had last graced Lady Melbourne's walls in 1792, Gentileschi's "Joseph and Potiphar's Wife" (if that is the painting to which Lady Melbourne refers) could still help Byron understand his erotic experience. Gentileschi emphasizes the Joseph story's didactic theme. Joseph's balladic posture suggests his moral superiority; just outside, a public world waits to judge the woman whose chamber he leaves. Potiphar's wife wears "a dark blue garment" and holds "Joseph's cloak of golden brown with its blue lining."[34] Though he does not quite turn "in disgust" from Potiphar's wife, as Lady Melbourne suggests, Gentileschi's Joseph does successfully resist her demands. Joseph's sanctimonious glance captures perfectly Byron's attitude toward Lady Frances Webster. The woman "once falling/Forever must fall," he wrote in a poem meant to describe her (*CPW* 3:320). Like Joseph, Byron resisted Lady Frances Webster's advances, though Byron differed from Joseph by precipitating the seduction. Other paintings show Joseph before or after the encounter with Potiphar's wife, and most of these were not in England in 1792, the year this painting hung in Melbourne House.[35]

If Lady Melbourne alluded to Orazio Gentileschi's version of the story of Joseph (as seems likely), then she proved herself a shrewd reader of *Childe Harold's Pilgrimage.* There, Byron had already implicitly compared himself (by comparing Harold) to the wandering Jew: "that settled, ceaseless gloom/The fabled Hebrew wanderer bore;/That will not look beyond the tomb,/But cannot hope for rest before" ("To Inez," *CPW* 2:1:853–856). Perhaps Lady Melbourne speculated that Byron would find further playful comparisons to the *Old Testament* congenial. But she did not want Byron to believe himself damned as

Calvinist or Jew. Instead, she sought to ease his transition into Regency society by schooling him in the moral hypocrisies of Charles I's court. At a time when Byron was pursuing Augusta Leigh and Lady Frances Webster, Lady Melbourne encouraged his erotic self-restraint by reminding him of Gentileschi's work. Both mother-figure and procurer, Lady Melbourne sensed Byron's wish to forsake the very libertine conduct with Lady Frances Webster he so humorously described in his letters. These letters continually allude to his need to reform and marry a woman who could improve him, such as Lady Melbourne's own niece, Annabella Milbanke.

Byron's *Hebrew Melodies* reveal his tendency to see his erotic encounters through the lens of religious scripture. Byron collaborated with the composer Isaac Nathan on *Hebrew Melodies*, in part, to please his prospective bride,[36] Annabella Milbanke, but the project also sharpened his identification with the Joseph story, which he had explored in "Bride of Abydos." "They will call me a *Jew* next," he wrote to Annabella (*BLJ* October 20, 1814; 4:220).[37] As this letter suggests, Byron initially found the Jews' exile as foreign as their moral self-righteousness, and cast their lamentations in the third person.

> Oh! weep for those that wept by Babel's stream,
> Whose shrines are desolate, whose land a dream;
> (*CPW* 3:292)

By the time he returned to Psalm 137, however, Byron had warmed to his subject. He was truly collaborating with Nathan in April 1814 rather than sending him poems he had previously written. In "By the Rivers of Babylon We Sat Down and Wept," he expressed his increasing identification with Jewish expatriation in the psalm of David by using the first person plural:

> We sate down and wept by the waters
> Of Babel, and thought of the day
> When our foe, in the hue of his slaughters,
> Made Salem's high places his prey
> (*CPW* 3:308)

During his honeymoon at Halnaby, when Annabella Milbanke copied out this poem, Byron felt increasingly drawn to the Jewish experience of exile. He came to see "the Hebraic strain, bound up with his Calvinistic fatalism."[38]

In both *Childe Harold's Pilgrimage* and *Hebrew Melodies*, exile was a convenient fiction. By April 1816, however, Byron left England's shores for good, separating from his wife whose "good example," like Joseph's, he found impossible to follow. Shortly before Byron departed, Isaac Nathan thanked his collaborator by giving him a gift of *matzos*.[39] Perhaps Nathan's gift reminded Byron that his own hasty departure from England was not unlike the Hebrews' flight from Egypt. In *Don Juan*, Byron compared Juan's exile to the Hebrews' precipitous departure:

> So Juan wept, as wept the captive Jews
> By Babel's waters, still remembering Sion
> (*CPW* 5:2:16)

Byron teased his readers with such comparisons only to undermine them. "I'd weep," Byron's narrator quickly adds, but "mine is not a weeping muse" (*CPW* 5:2:16). If Byron saw Hebrew poetry as sublime, he disassociated himself from Hebraic gloom in his mock-epic, hoping he would not become as "dumb and dreary as the Israelites" (*BLJ* 4:167).

III

"I want a hero: an uncommon want," Byron's narrator announces in *Don Juan*'s opening line. He runs through a Rabelaisian list of Christian surnames, but, dissatisfied with these, takes as his hero "Don Juan," a legendary figure whose name Byron encourages his reader to mispronounce: the Spanish "Juan" becomes the British "Jew-one." Byron forces readers to anglicize Juan's name,[40] which ironically renders him more Hebraic than before. This act of mispronunciation provides the first hint of Byron's religious allegory. By underscoring Jóse's ancient lineage, Byron's narrator leaves open the possibility that he is a *converso*. The impression gathers force when the narrator asserts the opposite. Jóse is "a true Hidalgo, free from every stain/Of Moor or Hebrew blood" (*CPW* 5:1:9), he assures the reader in the first of a series of ironic utterances. In fact, the Spanish inquisition made Spanish ancestry almost impossible to trace. One could never be certain that a true hidalgo was not a *converso*, or a Hebrew in disguise who had converted to Christianity under duress. Cervantes's *Don Quixote* reminds us of this persistent problem by calling attention to Sancho's insupportable distinctions between "old" and "new" Christians.

In *Don Juan*, Byron used the Joseph story as a leitmotif, a counter-myth to the story of the seducing Catholic libertine which Moyra Haslett traces in *Byron's Don Juan and the Don Juan Legend*.[41] In Byron's poem, Juan is a failed Joseph who succumbs to the temptation that Joseph resisted. Both Joseph and Juan are young, attractive men described as beardless (Genesis 41:14; *CPW* 5:14:66:525). One is seventeen (Genesis 37:2), the other sixteen (*CPW* 5:1:54) at the time their narratives begin. Joseph is "well-built and good looking" (Genesis 39:6)[42] and Juan's "beauteous" appearance (*CPW* 5:9:53) makes him "As fair a thing as e'er was form'd of clay" (*CPW* 5:2:110). Joseph curls his hair as a sign of his vanity (Midrash 807), while Haidée runs her hand through Juan's "locks so curly" (*CPW* 5:2:168); the narrator dismisses him as a "curly-headed, good-for-nothing" rascal (*CPW* 5:1:25). Both heroes are passive. Joseph falls prey to the machinations of others: his brothers, Potiphar's wife, and the Pharaoh (Genesis 41:14). Similarly, Juan is the dupe of numerous women—Julia, Haidée, Gulbeyaz, Catherine, and Lady Adeline Amundeville; his "mobility" (*CPW* 5:16:97) leads him from one misadventure to another. Where Joseph deflects the advances of Potiphar's wife (Genesis 39:8–9), Juan succumbs to Julia (*CPW* 5:1:117). Both men have garments torn in the process. After being sold into slavery, both men rise to high diplomatic office in a foreign land. Joseph serves the Pharaoh as a minister distributing grain in a time of famine (Genesis 41:56), while Juan becomes a foreign ambassador for Catherine's court (*CPW* 5:10:46). Where Joseph proves himself indispensable to Potiphar and the Pharaoh (Genesis 41:40), however, Juan is not indispensable to Catherine. In "four-and-twenty hours" Catherine finds "twice that number/Of candidates requesting to be placed" (*CPW* 5:10:48) in Juan's shoes.

Both characters are ethical models: Joseph for his self-restraint and Juan for his social tact. Juan's morality, in fact, transvalues moral codes. Byron's narrator encourages his readers to believe that Juan, though the unwitting cause of a divorce in Seville, is more virtuous than the Catholic family he has left behind; more knowledgeable and courageous than Pedrillo his tutor; more sympathetic to human life than his cannibalistic compatriots on the "Trinidada," the ship destroyed in a storm. Juan shares the dietary precautions of the Jews in refusing, at first, to eat either his spaniel's forepaw or his fellow passengers (*CPW* 5:2:78).[43] He also refuses to "dine with them on his pastor and his master" Pedrillo (*CPW* 5:2:78), an act of cannibalism which the narrator blasphemously compares to the sacrament of transubstantiation. Throughout the first two cantos, the narrator compares Juan to David, Noah, Daniel, Jacob, and Joseph,[44] whom he most resembles in his combination of diplomatic tact, personal charm, and sexual self-restraint (like Joseph Andrews, Juan is a failed Joseph).

For Byron, Joseph's rise to high diplomatic office recalls the careers of Robert Southey and William Wordsworth, who rose to government positions by buttering their bread on both sides. Southey became poet laureate and Wordsworth received the sinecure of distributor of stamps for Westmorland, which carried the salary of four hundred pounds a year. In his dedication to Don Juan (unpublished in Byron's lifetime), Byron lambasts both for changing their revolutionary politics along with their political appointments (*CPW* 5:6:44–46). Lord Castlereagh, another target in Byron's dedication, approximated the lakers' susceptibility to political expediency for he steeped his hands in "Erin's gore" ("Dedication," *CPW* 5:12:90) to advance to the position of foreign secretary he enjoyed when Byron wrote his dedication. Others have praised Castlereagh for minimizing bloodshed in Ireland during the Act of Union, but Byron was particularly bothered by the fact that Castlereagh could brutally suppress an Irish revolt, though he was himself half-Irish.[45]

Byron may have sensed the relevance of Joseph's story to such circumstances. Like the Marranos of Spain, to whom the narrator indirectly alludes (*CPW* 5:1:9), or the Jews in England during the Georgian period, Joseph seems all too willing to assimilate and "convert."[46] He forgets his father's house (41:51) and serves the Egyptians, turning his "very talent to a crime" (*CPW* 5:5:10) as Castlereagh abandoned the Irish and served the English. Joseph has better reasons for the betrayal than Castlereagh—as a slave, he has no choice—but both serve a foreign government. Joseph understands the mixed blessing of his earthly rewards. As if to call attention to his own apostasy, he names his first son Manasseh: "For God, said he, hath made me forget all my toil, and all my father's house" (Genesis 41:51). His second he names Ephraim: "For God hath caused me to be fruitful in the land of my affliction" (Genesis 41:52).

Juan is shipwrecked near Greece (*CPW* 5:2:105), sold into slavery in Constantinople (*CPW* 5:4:79), forced into the Russian army (*CPW* 5:7:62), and almost mugged in England (*CPW* 5:11:10). His suffering in a foreign land resembles Joseph's. Like Joseph, he is also fruitful: he sports a diamond ring from Catherine the Great (*CPW* 5:11:39) and inspires the love of Julia, Haidée, Gulbeyaz, Dudu, Catherine, Lady Adeline, and the Duchess Fitz-Fulke. To become fruitful in the land of one's affliction is to achieve what Byron and his hero achieve, an ambivalent inheritance.

IV

Byron compares Joseph and Juan explicitly. The first comparison occurs after Alfonso discovers Juan in bed with Julia.

> Juan contrived to give an awkward blow,
> And then his only garment quite gave way:
> He fled, like Joseph, leaving it; but there,
> I doubt, all likeness ends between the pair.
> (*CPW* 5:1:186)

Byron reduces the serious encounter between a young man and a (slightly) older woman to farce, as Alfonso, not Julia, holds the garment of the now naked

Juan. The narrator both alludes to Joseph and denies the allusion ("there,/I doubt, all likeness ends between the pair"), since "doubt" means both to believe and to question.

His second reference to the Joseph story occurs in canto 5. Having been sold on the human auction block in Turkey, Juan resists Gulbeyaz's command to lie with her. "Christian, canst thou love?" she asks Juan (*CPW* 5:5:116), whom she has purchased for this purpose. The narrator records Gulbeyaz's indignant reaction to Juan's answer, that "Love is for the free" (*CPW* 5:5:116):

> Suppose, but you already have supposed,
> The spouse of Potiphar, the Lady Booby,
> Phedra, and all which story has disclosed
> Of good examples; pity that so few by
> Poets and private tutors are exposed,
> But when you have supposed the few we know,
> You can't suppose Gulbeyaz' angry brow
> (*CPW* 5:5:131)

Byron both presents his Jewish source material and withdraws it, deflecting attention to Euripides, Henry Fielding, and Racine. As late as canto 7, however, Byron refers to Juan as "He with the beardless chin and garments torn?" (*CPW* 5:7:62), which alludes plainly to the biblical Joseph.

If readers of Byron's first two cantos have come to expect references to Western versions of the story of Joseph,—Fielding's *Joseph Andrews*, Racine's *Phaedra*—Byron surprises them by drawing on Jami's "Yusef and Zuleika" and the Koran in his fifth canto. Only the Islamic versions of the story of Joseph describe the purchasing of Joseph for Zuleika's erotic enjoyment, as Byron depicts it in canto 5. Where Byron attempted to take Zuleika's perspective in "The Bride of Abydos," he wrote *Don Juan* from his hero's vantage point. Perhaps Jami's idealized treatment of Zuleika no longer appealed to a poet intent on satirizing a wife from whom he had recently separated, or perhaps Byron's "misogynist" narrator in Don Juan is to blame, a hypothesis I explore in my sixth chapter. If Byron relied upon Genesis for his version of the Joseph story in cantos 1 and 2, however, he returned to Jami's "Yusef and Zuleika" to depict the Turkish harem sequence in canto 5. In the remainder of this chapter, I focus on how Byron's treatment of the story of Joseph shifts in canto 5 from allusions to the Old Testament and Western literature (Fielding, Racine), which critics have discussed, to borrowings from Jami, which complicate the satire of the Joseph story.

Perhaps Byron's most important reference to the story of Joseph occurs in canto 5 of *Don Juan*, where he interweaves narrative threads from Genesis, the Koran, and Jami's poem. Borrowing from Jami in canto 5, Byron portrays Juan being purchased at a slave market by a eunuch named Baba.[47] In Jami's poem, Zuleika purchases Yusef herself after returning with her new husband, the Grand Vizier of Egypt. She recognizes Yusef in the slave market as the man she dreamed would be her husband. She then explains her behavior to her nurse:

> At each word I say must my bosom ache.
> Thou sawest that youth in the midst of the press,
> While the people were praising his loveliness.
> It is he, my beloved, so long adored,
> My life and my treasure, my love and my lord,
> Whose face in my vision I saw when my soul,
> Lured by his splendour burst forth from control.
> (Rogers 96; Griffith 135)

One line later, Jami describes Joseph on the auction block, in a scene that recalls Byron's poem, though Jami romanticizes what Byron turns to farce.

> Blest is the time, of all hours most sweet,
> When two fond lovers, long parted, meet.
> When love's touch burns with a steady ray,
> And the pangs of longing have passed away.
> The beauty of Yusuf so charmed each eye
> That thousands of Memphis came round to buy.
> Each one his costliest treasure sold,
> And ran to the mart with the ready gold.
> (Rogers 97–98; Griffith 138)

Gulbeyaz, like Zuleika, saw Juan and admired him, ordering Baba to obtain the young man for her pleasure.

> Juan, the latest of her whims, had caught
> Her eye in passing on his way to sale;
> She order'd him directly to be bought,
> And Baba, who had ne'er been known to fail
> In any kind of mischief to be wrought,
> At all such auctions knew how to prevail:
> She had no prudence, but he had; and this
> Explains the garb which Juan took amiss
> (*CPW* 5:5:114)

The "pruden[t]" Baba sneaks Juan into the oriental palace disguised as a woman. All goes according to plan until Baba attempts to persuade Juan and his companion, Johnson, to submit to circumcision. Johnson feigns cooperation but Juan refuses to have anything to do with the ceremony. "Strike me dead," he says, "But they as soon shall circumcise my head!" (*CPW* 5:5:71).

Byron aligns Juan with the Jewish Joseph only to have his hero renounce the most sacred rite of the Jewish religion. Inured to the ritual significance of this ceremony, Juan hopes to protect his private parts from mutilation. Byron exploits this scene for all its comic potential, but also explores its serious ramifications.[48] For the Jews, circumcision was "an initiation into adult life, perhaps also a substitute for castration as practiced by some heathen religions in honor of their gods, and by some early Christians as exemplified by those 'who made themselves eunuchs for the kingdom of heaven'" (Matthew 19:12). The biblical justification for circumcision first occurs in Genesis (17:10–13), when God instructs Abraham that "You shall circumcise the flesh of your foreskin, and that shall be the sign of the covenant between Me and you. Throughout the generations, every male among you shall be circumcised at the age of eight days. Thus shall my covenant be marked in your flesh as an everlasting covenant" (Genesis 17:10–13). "The home-born slave and the one purchased from the outside" (Genesis 17:12)—Don Juan, in other words—should also undergo circumcision. Though Juan balks at the idea, circumcision "sanctif[ied] the human body and aid[ed] it in its fight against erotic indulgence, as exemplified by the cults of Astarte and Dionysus."[49] In having his hero reject this rite, Byron symbolically severs the ties to Joseph and Judaism he has already established. The frequent references to the Old Testament[50] that characterized cantos 1 and 2 begin to taper off. Even the narrator becomes disenchanted with the hero he has chosen.

One moral for Byron's poem is that people's "headlong passions form their proper woes" (*CPW* 5:6:87). Juan must learn this lesson, refusing to become the slave to any passion (including sexual passion) before he can truly liberate himself. This is what the story of Joseph teaches, but the lesson is not uniquely Jewish. In fact, Baba's proposed circumcision of Juan follows Muslim practice. In a note to "The Bride of Abydos," Byron reminded his readers that allusions to Adam, Noah, and even Joseph are "equally the privilege of Mussulman and Jew" (*CPW* 3:440). Byron shifts contexts to complicate the easy identification of Juan and Joseph that his first two cantos encouraged. English readers would be inclined to think of circumcision as Jewish, of the slave trade as taking place in Africa,[51] of libertinism as male, of sexual ravishment as the unfortunate lot of females. In Byron's poem, however, a Jew procures a Gentile (CPW 5:4:116); a black man purchases a white slave (*CPW* 5:5:26–27); a woman, Gulbeyaz, purchases a male concubine and makes advances on a man who (according to the legend, if not Byron's poem) is considered the most aggressive heterosexual in history, Don Juan. Or tries. Juan rejects Gulbeyaz's advances and delivers a short speech, telling her that "love is for the free" (*CPW* 5:5:127).

Byron sees slavery—whether sexual, political, or mental—as a condition shared by all.[52] Byron foregrounds Juan's "Jewishness" by comparing him to Joseph, using Juan's "chosen" status, as Fielding did, to expose Christian (though not just Christian) hypocrites. But he also portrays Juan rebelling against Jewish laws by refusing to undergo circumcision. He complicates the readers' identification of Juan and Joseph still further by reminding them that Muslims also practice circumcision.[53] He treats the Joseph story itself as similarly complex. Joseph is both hero and hypocrite, leader of the Jewish people, and apostate who served the Egyptian Pharaohs. If Byron's Juan is "a little superficial" (*CPW* 5:11:51:401) and grows "a little dissipated" (*CPW* 5:10:23) by the end of the poem, Joseph is not above humiliating his brothers after he gains a diplomatic post similar to Juan's. Joseph falsely accuses his brothers of stealing a silver drinking cup he planted in Benjamin's sack (Genesis 44:2–12), in much the way Potiphar's wife falsely accused Joseph.[54]

In "The Bride of Abydos," *Hebrew Melodies*, and the fifth canto of *Don Juan*, Byron shifts ethical and religious contexts to look through or beyond his culture's norms. Where Southey's *Letters from England* promised to present an outsider's view of England along the lines of Montesquieu's *Lettres persanes*,[55] these poems, especially *Don Juan*, came closer to achieving it, for Byron's self-exile in Italy ensured that his work would be more truly comparative than Southey's. In his unpublished dedication to *Don Juan*, Byron used his cosmopolitanism—a slur when leveled at Jews—to critique Wordsworth, Southey, and Coleridge's insularity. Then, too, his skepticism forced him to look beyond Christians, to Islamic and Jewish "others," in order to find alternative measures of moral valuation. Perhaps it is only by cultivating this cosmopolitan *eros*—a sense of bittersweet dissatisfaction with one's own culture—that a writer can create a code of conduct worth emulating.

NOTES

1. Donald Reiman, ed., *The Romantics Reviewed: Contemporary Reviews of British Romantic Writers*, 5 vols. (New York: Garland Press, 1972), 1428.
2. Mohammed Sharafuddin, *Islam and Romantic Orientalism: Literary Encounters with the Orient* (London: Tauris, 1994); Anahid Melikian, *Byron and the East* (Beirut: American University of Beirut, 1977); Naji B. Oueijan, *The Progress of an Image: The East in English Literature* (New York: Peter Lang, 1996).
3. *Orientalism* (New York: Pantheon, 1978).
4. William Borst, *Lord Byron's Pilgrimage* (New York: Archon Books, 1969; Re 1948), 125.

5. Mohammed Sharafuddin, *Islam and Romantic Orientalism: Literary encounters with the Orient* (London: New York: Tauris, 1994), ix.

6. See Part 3 of Baron de Montesquieu, *The Spirit of Laws*, trans. and ed. Anne M. Cohler, Basia Carolyn Miller, Harold Samuel Stone (New York: Cambridge University Press, 1989), 231–336.

7. *BLJ* November 4, 1813; 3:157, 205; Marchand, *Byron: A Biography*, 421.

8. Marchand, *Byron: A Biography*, 419.

9. William Jones, ed., *The Collected Works of Sir William Jones*, 13 vols. (New York: New York University Press, 1993), 3:315, 324, 369; 11:418. Barthelemy D'Herbelot, *Bibliothèque Orientale ou Dictionnaire Universel*, 4 vols. (Paris: J. Neaulme and N. van Daalen, 1777), 4:353.

10. Howard Wiener, "Byron and the East: Literary Sources of the 'Turkish Tales,'" in *Nineteenth-Century Studies*, ed. Herbert John Davis, William Clyde De Vane, and Robert Cecil Bald. 2d ed. (New York: Greenwood, 1968), 109.

11. John D. Yohannan, "The Persian Poetry Fad in England, 1770–1825," *Comparative Literature* (1952):137.

12. Jones, *Collected Works*, 2:501–02.

13. Garland Cannon, *The Life and Mind of Oriental Jones: Sir William Jones, the Father of Modern Linguistics* (Cambridge: Cambridge University Press, 1990), 46, 248, 291.

14. Jones, *Collected Works*, 13:389–397.

15. Though not mentioned in Byron's sales catalog, John Richardson's *Dictionary, Persian, Arabic, and English; to Which Is Prefixed, a Dissertation on the Languages, Literature and Manners of Eastern Nations*, 2 vols. (Oxford, 1777), as well as his *A Dissertation on the Languages, Literature, and Manners of Eastern Nations* [Richardson on Eastern Nations], 2 parts (Oxford: Clarendon Press, 1778) (published separately), also influenced Byron, as Howard Wiener points out in "Byron and the East," 96; see also *CMP* 241. In a more conservative estimate of the influence of Persian poetry on Byron, one should note that his sales catalog indicates that he owned William Beckford's *Vathek: The English Translation by Samuel Henley (1786)*, which mentions Jami (see the 1972 edition with an introd. by Robert J. Gemmett [New York: Scholars' Facsimiles & Reprints], 276). He also owned Barthelemy D'Herbelot's *Bibliothèque Orientale ou Dictionnaire Universel*, which was particularly noteworthy for its entries on Mejnoun (2:598), Leila (2:480), Giami (2:131), Esthekhar (1:660), Jousouf ben Jacob (2:332–334), and Zuleika (4:354); George Sale's preliminary essay to and translation of the Koran (1734); Jonathan Scott's introductory essay and edition of *The Arabian Nights: Tales, Anecdotes, and Letters*, 6 vols. (London: Cadell and Davies, 1800); William Jones's *Collected Works;* and various Turkish histories. Among the latter were Richard Knolles, *The Generall Historie of the Turkes* (1603) and its continuation by Sir Paul Rycaut, *The Historie of the Turkish Empire from 1623 to 1677* (1680); Demetrius Cantemir, *The History of the Growth and Decay of the Ottoman Empire* (1756); *Memoirs of the Baron de Tott, on the Turks and the Tartars*, translated from the French, 2 vols. (London, 1785); Lady Mary Wortley Montagu, *Works*, 5 vols. (1803); and Vincent Mignot, *The History of the Turkish, or Ottoman Empire*, trans. A. Hawkins, 4 vols. (London, 1787). (*CMP* 4).

16. E. G. Browne, *A Literary History of Persia*, 4 vols. (New York: Scribner, 1902), 3:516; Muhib Opeloye, "The Account of Joseph (Yusuf [A. S.]) in the Qur'an and the Bible," *Hamdard Islamicus* 18, no. 3: 85–96.

17. Koran, trans. N. J. Dawood (London: Penguin, 1956), 165–174; George Sale, *Preliminary Essay to the Koran*, 1763 (New York: Garland, 1984), 191; Jami, *Yusef and Zulaikha: A Poem*, trans. R. T. Griffith (London: Trubner & Co., Ludgate Hill, 1882), 168.

18. D'Herbelot, *Bibliothèque Orientale*, 333. "Les Musulmans ont este intruits de cette fable par un Chapitre de l'Alcoran qui ponte le nom de Joseph, et ils se servent souvent de leurs noms, et de leurs exemples pour élever le coeur des hommes a un amour plus excellent que celuy du vulgaire, prétendants que ces deux amants ne sont que la figure de l'âme fidèle qui s'éleve par amour jusques à Dieu, de même que les Livres sacrez employent les noms de l'époux and de l'épouse dans le Cantique des Cantiques." See also *CMP* 238, 231–254.

19. Browne, *A Literary History of Persia*, 3:531.

20. Cecil Roth, ed., *Encyclopedia Judaica* (Jerusalem: Keter Publishing House, 1971), 10:210–11.

21. Sale, *A Preliminary Essay to the Koran*, 190.

22. Sale, *A Preliminary Essay to the Koran*, 191; E. G. Browne, *Literary History of Persia*, 3:516.

23. See Jerome McGann, *Fiery Dust: Byron's Poetic Development* (Chicago: University of Chicago Press, 1968), 162. McGann correctly points out that each of the Eastern tales "centers around an exploration of the nature and consequences of a life that is Eros-directed," but "The Bride of Abydos" differs from "The Corsair," "Lara," and "Parisina" in portraying *eros* from the woman's vantage point.

24. I have consulted Griffith's translation, *Yusef and Zulaikha*, trans. R. T. Griffith; *The Book of Joseph and Zuleikha, Historical Romantic Persian Poem*, trans. Alexander Rogers (London: David Nutt, 1892); and *Analysis and Specimens of the Joseph and Zulaikha, A Historical-Romantic Poem, by the Persian Poet Jami*, trans. Samuel Robinson (London: Williams and Norgate, 1873), but relied chiefly on Griffith's, which is the most poetic and faithful of the three. Robinson's translation is based on the German translation of Franz Rosenzweig (*Joseph und Suleicha; historisch-romantisches gedicht aus dem Persischen des Abdurrahman Dschami* [Vienna: Anton Schmid, 1824]), to which Griffith (vii) and, to a lesser extent, Rogers (viii) also indicate their indebtedness. The most readily available text of the poem is contained in John D. Yohannan, ed., *Joseph and Potiphar's Wife in World Literature: An Anthology of the Story of The Chaste Youth and the Lustful Stepmother* ([New York: New Directions, 1968], 166–220), which makes use of the excellent translation of Griffith, supplemented by Rogers, who translates the very end of the poem differently from Griffith. Yohannan's translation, it should be noted, is an abridgement of Griffith's to one fourth its size.

25. Caroline Franklin, *Byron's Heroines* (Oxford: Clarendon Press, 1992), 41.

26. Byron's dash ("to save—") encourages a double reading. On the one hand, Zuleika is as sweet as a fountain's wave to a traveller whose lips are "just cool'd in time to save—": the traveller saves his life by procuring a drink at a propitious moment. On

the other hand, Giaffir's passion for his daughter is incestuous; he prefers Zuleika to his wife and his regard for her "Sweet[ness]" barely saves him from enacting his passion for his daughter sexually, as Manfred did so disastrously with Astarte; i.e., Giaffir is himself "just cool'd in time to save—[himself]" from acting on his passion for his daughter. I am indebted to Prof. Martin Prochazka for calling this second reading to my attention.

27. Yohannan, *Joseph and Potiphar's Wife*, 167; Griffith, *Yusef and Zulaikha*, 162.

28. Franklin, *Byron's Heroines*, 56; Reiman, *Romantics Reviewed*, 571.

29. Sale, *A Preliminary Essay to the Koran*, 189.

30. Nigel Leask, *Romantic Writers and the East* (Cambridge: Cambridge University Press, 1992).

31. Sale, *A Preliminary Essay to the Koran*, vi.

32. *The Monthly Museum; or, Dublin Literary Repertory of Arts, Sciences, Literature, and Miscellaneous Information*, I (February 1814), 287–290, 290; Reiman, *Romantics Reviewed*, 1718.

33. Gross, *Byron's "Corbeau Blanc,"* April 1, 1814; 170.

34. R. Ward Bissell, *Orazio Gentileschi and the Poetic Tradition in Caravaggesque Painting* (University Park: Penn State University Press, 1981), 191, fig. 1; see also Mieke Bal, *Reading "Rembrandt": Beyond the Word-Image Opposition* (Cambridge: Cambridge University Press, 1991), 105–08.

35. Clifton Harby notes fifteen paintings that allude to the story of Joseph. Of these, only five were painted before 1791, the year Lady Melbourne was living in Melbourne Hall, Piccadilly. Only one of these ("The Wife of Potiphar Beguiles Joseph," by Gerard de Jode, sixteenth century) alludes to Joseph and Potiphar's wife. Harby, ed., *The Bible in Art: Twenty Centuries of Famous Bible Paintings* (New York: Covics Friede, 1936), 39.

Evidence that Lady Melbourne had Gentileschi's conversation painting in mind is strong. Howard Usher notes that Lady Melbourne's family was connected to Orazio Gentileschi through John Coke's patronage of Matthew Lamb, Lady Melbourne's father-in-law. Coke negotiated with Gentileschi's son for the gift of his father's painting to the King of Spain. He may have received a second copy of "Joseph and Potiphar's Wife" as a gift which found its way to Melbourne House in Piccadilly, London; then to the Paul Drey gallery in New York in the late twentieth century; and later to a private owner in the United States. The other, larger, copy still resides at Hampton Court, England. *The Owners of Melbourne Hall* (Derby, England: J. H. Hall & Sons, 1993), 7. For a superb study of Orazio Gentileschi, see R. Ward Bissell's *Orazio Gentileschi and the Poetic Tradition in Caravaggesque Painting*, 191.

36. Marchand, *Byron: A Biography*, 488.

37. Thomas Ashton, *Byron's Hebrew Melodies* (Austin: University of Texas Press, 1972), 14.

38. Marchand, *Byron: A Biography*, 532.

39. Isaac Nathan, *Fugitive Pieces* (London: Whittaker, Treacher, and Co., 1829), 89.

40. Graham, *Don Juan and Regency England*, 13.

41. Moyra Haslett, *Byron's Don Juan and the Don Juan Legend* (New York: Clarendon Press, 1997).

76   Chapter 3

42. Midrash Rabbah sees Potiphar's wife's attempted seduction of Joseph as a test of his vanity. *Midrash Rabbah,* trans. H. Freedman (London: Soncino Press, 1939), 807. The medieval exegete Rashi draws a similar conclusion. *The Metsudah Chumash: A New Linear Translation,* trans. Avrohom Davis (Hoboken, N.J.: KTAV Publishing House, 1994), 441.

43. In *Lord Byron's Strength,* Jerome Christensen finds this reluctance inexplicable (250), but the allegory I am exploring does much (perhaps too much!) to explain it.

44. David (1:168:1344); Noah (2:8:62; 2:66:526; 2:95:757); Daniel (9:69:548); Jacob (7:52:415). For a fuller account of Byron's use of the Old Testament in *Don Juan* and elsewhere, see Travis Looper, *Byron and the Bible: A Compendium of Biblical Usage in the Poetry of Byron* (Metuchen: Scarecrow Press, 1978).

45. See Carl Woodring, *Politics in English Romantic Poetry,* 197. Wendy Hinde notes that "the fact that he was an Irishman made him a traitor as well as an oppressor" transforming his name into "one of the most hated in Irish history." Castlereagh (London: Collins, 1981), 57. For a more positive assessment of Castlereagh's career, see John Derry, *Castlereagh* (New York: St. Martin's Press, 1976), 45–99, and Henry Kissinger, *A World Restored: Metternich, Castlereagh and the Problems of Peace, 1812–1822* (Boston: Houghton Mifflin Company, 1957), 35, and *Diplomacy* (New York: Simon & Schuster, 1994), 88–90.

46. "Conversion" is a key word in Byron's dedication to *Don Juan* (*CPW* 5:6:43) and, I would argue, in understanding the poem as a whole. "Honest men from Iceland to Barbadoes," the narrator writes, "should not veer round with every breath, nor seize/To pain, the moment when you cease to please" (CPW 5:10:13). Todd Endelman discusses conversion as it relates to Byron's Jewish contemporaries in *Radical Assimilation in English Jewish History, 1656–1945* (Indianapolis: Indiana University Press, 1990).

47. Baba's name and race may have been suggested by Babalouk in Beckford's *Vathek* and by the entry under Baba in D'Herbelot's *Bibliothèque Orientale,* 77, 284. In his notes to Beckford's *Vathek,* Henley notes that black eunuchs were used to guard queens and princesses, quoting the *Arabian Nights* (4:189). William Beckford, *Vathek: The English Translation by Samuel Hemley (1786),* introd. by Robert J. Gemmett (New York: Scholar's Facsimiles & Reprints, 1972). D'Herbelot, *Bibliothèque Orientale,* 77, 284.

48. Roth, ed., *Encyclopedia Judaica,* 5:576.

49. Roth, ed., *Encyclopedia Judaica,* 5:576.

50. Looper, in *Byron and the Bible* (56–89), lists the following references to the Old Testament. I have compiled them in a way that reflects the frequency with which they occur in each canto: 1:28, 2:25, 3:11, 4:11, 5:14, 6:9, 7:14, 8:16, 9:22, 10:11, 11:13, 12:7, 13:14, 14:18, 15:8, 16:9. Byron's most frequent references to the Hebrew Bible are in cantos 1 and 2. During the course of the poem, he most often refers to Job, Daniel, David, Lot's Wife, Adam, Eve, Jacob, Babel, Semiramis, and Nebuchadnezzar.

51. Midrash Rabbah comments explicitly on the fact that an Ethiopian buys Joseph. It also notes the cunning of this Egyptian (803). The Egyptian assumes that because a black man is selling Joseph, that Joseph must be stolen. "Everywhere a white man sells an Ethiopian [black-skinned], while here an Ethiopian is selling a white man! He is no slave. 'Bring me a surety [that he is not stolen],' he demanded." R. Levi commented:

"A slave buys, the son of a bondmaid sells, and a freeborn son is slave to both." Levi's proverb is explained as follows: "Potiphar, Pharaoh's slave (servant), bought him, while an Ishmaelite descended from Ishmael the son of Hagar (the bondmaid), sold him."

52. Whereas Susan Wolfson reads canto 5 primarily as a meditation on the politics of gender, I would extend her remarks to include the importance of racial and religious cross-dressing as well. In canto 5:67, the clothes Baba buys are fit for a Mussulman, but also for a Christian. It is in this religious context that the theme of cross-dressing is introduced. The sexuality of the narrator, who seems to get much satisfaction out of seeing his hero dressed as a woman, also has more of a bearing on the narrator's treatment of Juan and gender than Wolfson allows. Susan Wolfson, "'Their She Condition': Cross-Dressing and the Politics of Gender in Don Juan," *ELH* 54 (fall 1987): 585.

53. Mircea Eliade, ed., *The Encyclopedia of Religion* (New York: Macmillan Publication Company, 1987), 3:512. "While circumcision is not discussed in the Qur'an, Muslims agree that it must occur before marriage and require it of male converts."

54. In Jami's poem, Yusef shows his own humanity by clutching Zuleika's garment in the same way she once clutched his. The couple is now married, but this passage shows that Yusef can be as susceptible to beauty as Zuleika (Rogers 209; Yohannan 220). This episode is not included in Griffith's translation.

55. Baron de Montesquieu, *Persian Letters,* trans. C. J. Betts (New York: Penguin, 1973); Robert Southey, *Letters from England: By Don Manuel Alvarez Espriella, Translated from the Spanish,* ed. Jack Simmons (London: Cresset Press, 1951). See Graham, *Don Juan and Regency England,* 34–60.

4

COSMOPOLITAN LIBERALISM: *CHILDE HAROLD'S PILGRIMAGE*, III, AND *DE L'ALLEMAGNE*

In the previous three chapters of this study, I explored Byron's liberalism as he defined it in his poetry and letters through his encounters with English, French, and Persian literature. Byron's career as a poet would not have been possible without the two years he spent in Albania, Turkey, and Greece. He deliberately cultivated a cosmopolitan outlook in order to begin his career as a politician. When that political career failed, Byron reaped the rewards of his travels by setting his Eastern tales in the countries he had visited. References to his own love affairs—to his possible involvement in the rescuing of a Muslim woman about to be drowned for adultery, for example, alluded to in "The Giaour"—lent authenticity to Byron's exploration of *eros* in Eastern cultures. Byron was the man. He had been there.

So convincing was Byron's immersion in the East, however, that suggesting that Byron exploited his adventures to advance a political agenda can seem rather cynical. Yet in England, cultivating cosmopolitanism, as Benjamin Disraeli pointed out fifty years after Byron's death, had a long liberal pedigree. In 1872, Disraeli accused Liberals of cosmopolitan interests and argued that Conservatives were the party of the nation. He identified cosmopolitanism with Continental ideas and nationalism with the British Empire. "Disraeli thus viewed liberalism and cosmopolitanism as constitutive of a European, not an English, national identity," Maura O'Connor argues.[1] It is ironic that Disraeli, whose *Vivian Grey* reflects Byron's influence, could so fully disown the liberal tradition Byron had come to represent. Yet the English premier was perhaps right in viewing Byron, certainly in the poet's work after 1816, as a European writer. Disraeli shrewdly perceived that liberalism has a foreign, Italian and Spanish, derivation. Yet he might have traced the cosmopolitan roots of liberalism back more than half a century, to two works published within a year of each other.

As the author of *Childe Harold's Pilgrimage,* Byron became famous one year before Madame de Staël, who visited England in 1813. They met each other at salons in England and discussed Napoleon, nationalism, and the possibility of maintaining a consistently liberal outlook. They also discussed the relative merits of their works. Byron read Staël's *De l'Allemagne* with approval and Staël advised Byron to continue his eastern tales. They met in 1812 and again in 1816. The third canto of *Childe Harold's Pilgrimage,* the subject of the present chapter, reflects the influence of Staël's *De l'Allemagne,* which Byron read attentively, not to say minutely. He included a reference to *De l'Allemagne* in a footnote to "The Bride of Abydos," and wrote a gracious account of her death in a footnote to the fourth canto of *Childe Harold's Pilgrimage.* Madelyn Gutwirth and Joanne Wilkes have considered the influence of Staël's gender on her political liberalism, and Byron's response to Staël's gender significantly colored his assessment of her importance as a writer. Through his numerous conversations with Madame de Staël and his close perusal of *De l'Allemagne,* however, Byron also came to understand the relationship between his antinationalism and his political liberalism. Enjoying but ultimately rejecting the outlook of Staël's *Corinne* as too sentimental, Byron found Staël's critique of Napoleon through her celebration of undiscovered German writers in *De l'Allemagne* far more interesting and congenial. In the third canto of *Childe Harold's Pilgrimage,* he profited from this lesson and learned how to use cosmopolitanism as a political weapon.

In the decade following his encounter with Madame de Staël, Byron rejected Napoleon as a political model, used his own cosmopolitanism to attack the lake poets, and cultivated a politics of feeling in his poetry. Staël advised Byron about how to comport himself at dinner, warned him about mistreating Lady Caroline Lamb, and attempted to reconcile him with his wife. Lady Melbourne and Madame de Staël are the most important older women who advised him during his residence in England and they form a striking contrast. Lady Melbourne never abandoned the values of the late eighteenth century that made her personality and spectacular success as a political hostess possible. Madame de Staël, by contrast, in *De l'Allemagne* defined romanticism, the literary movement that did more than any other event to make Enlightenment values obsolete. One woman acceded to society's strictures; the other flouted them. In long letters to Byron, Lady Melbourne inveighed against Madame de Staël's gift for *tracasseries.* Madame de Staël had braved "the opinion of the World" and thus violated Lady Melbourne's cardinal maxim: "sooner or later [Staël, like Caroline Lamb, would] feel the consequences of it" (*BLJ* April 13, 1810).[2]

Byron admired Lady Melbourne, but he attracted too many scandals to follow her advice. In truth, he had more in common with Madame de Staël. Her political courage earned Byron's grudging admiration and provided him, however indirectly, with a compelling blueprint for liberal principles during the age of Napoleon. By celebrating Germany in *De l'Allemagne*, Staël hoped to embarrass French chauvinists. By celebrating Italy in canto 4 of *Childe Harold's Pilgrimage*, the canto that most reflects Staël's influence, Byron cultivated a similar cosmopolitanism. Self-mythology, chivalry, and feeling are three themes or political postures that appear in *De l'Allemagne* and in canto 3 of *Childe Harold's Pilgrimage*. Byron and Staël employed similar strategies in combating a pernicious nationalism. By examining both works together, I hope to show not Staël's influence on Byron's subsequent political thought, but the surprising similarities they shared as fellow travelers, as shown in the contemporaneous works they composed before 1816.

A final word on nationalism before beginning my comparative study of Byron and Staël's liberalism. Byron and Staël understood the important role that authors play in creating a sense of national identity. Homer, Virgil, Petrarch, and Dante contributed to a sense of nation by writing in the vernacular of their countries. In *Childe Harold's Pilgrimage* and *De l'Allemagne*, Byron and Staël honored such contributions. If these works suggest that political liberalism is a by-product of nationalism, they also imply that it is a political creed most memorably articulated by men and women of letters. The disciplinary boundaries scholars impose on their study of the past obscure the intimate relationship between literature and politics that helped make liberalism palatable to a new generation of readers. Though most studies of liberalism fail to mention their contribution, Byron and Staël are perhaps the most important example of liberals who influenced their generation through the power of the written word.

I

"Stick to the East;—the oracle, Staël, told me it was the only poetical policy," Byron wrote to Thomas Moore on August 28, 1813. "The North, South, and West, have all been exhausted; but from the East, we have nothing but S★★'s [Southey's] unsaleables" (*BLJ* 3:101). Two months later, Byron "followed" Madame de Staël's advice by beginning "The Bride of Abydos" on November 1, 1813 as a sequel to the "The Giaour"; but he may have taken more from her than literary advice. Accused of plagiarizing the opening lines of "The Bride of Abydos" from Goethe's *Wilhelm Meister*, Byron confessed that Madame de Staël's *De l'Allemagne*, not Goethe's travel book, was the probable source. "Do you know de Staël's lines?" he reputedly asked Lady Blessington. "For if I am a thief, she must be the plundered, as I don't read German and do French: yet I could almost swear that I never saw her verses when I wrote mine."[3] I mention this incident not because the issue of plagiarism is important, but because it shows how much Madame de Staël's *De l'Allemagne* occupied Byron's thoughts during and after her visit to England, and how profoundly she shaped his early career as a political thinker.

Though reading *De l'Allemagne* prompted Byron to pronounce Staël "the first female writer of this, perhaps, of any age" in a footnote to "The Bride of Abydos" (*CPW* 3:436), Byron nevertheless ridiculed Staël for ingratiating herself with an English audience when she visited his country on June 20, 1813 (*BLJ* January 31, 1815; Lovelace 377; Gross 49).[4] "Yesterday I dined in company with Staël, the 'Epicene,' whose politics are sadly changed," Byron wrote after first meeting her.

> She is for the Lord of Israel, and the Lord of Liverpool—a vile antithesis of a Methodist and a Tory—talks of nothing but devotion and the ministry, and, I presume, expects that God and the government will help her to a pension. (*BLJ* June 22, 1813; 3:66)[5]

What Byron did not perhaps realize, or chose to overlook, was that Staël had consistently opposed Napoleon since 1801, when she could no longer influence his policies.[6] As a constitutional liberal, and erstwhile republican, whose support for political structures depended on the historical moment when they were proposed, Staël should have appealed to Byron, who wavered between supporting a republic and criticizing mob rule. Like Staël, who knew what it was to be both praised and excoriated in the press, Byron found that being of no party he "offend[ed] all parties" (*CPW* 5:9:26).

What the two writers ended up doing in 1813 was offending each other. Byron admired Staël intellectually but could not accept her expansive personality. "What the devil shall I say about 'De l'Allemagne?'" he confessed to his diary, after defending it at Holland House (*BLJ* November 17, 1813; 3:211). "I like it prodigiously; but unless I can twist my admiration into some fantastical expression, she won't believe me, and I know, by experience, I shall be overwhelmed with fine things about rhyme, etc. etc." (*BLJ* December 5, 1813; 3:231). Several awkward encounters followed which left Staël in "bad odour," to use Hobhouse's phrase,[7] though Byron retained his high opinion of her work. "I do not love Madame de Staël," Byron confessed to John Murray, "but depend upon it, she beats all your natives hollow as an authoress, in my opinion; and I would not say this if I could help it" (*BLJ* January 11, 1814; 4:25).

Byron did not record a meeting with Staël again until July 12, 1816[8] near Geneva, in circumstances far different from when he knew her during the

1813–14 season in London. The exact date when Madame de Staël met Lord Byron is of some interest as a key to understanding her influence over canto 3 of *Childe Harold's Pilgrimage*. Byron began canto 3 of *Childe Harold's Pilgrimage* on April 28 and completed it by June 8, 1816, a month before he saw Staël again in Switzerland, so direct personal influence on the poem is out of the question. Yet reading *De l'Allemagne* and reviews of her work in 1813, and conversing with the author intermittently from June 1813 to March 1814, must have had some influence on his poem, which he began on April 28, 1816, only twelve days after leaving England. From June 10 until November 1, he was staying in the Villa Diodati,[9] which was ten minutes from Shelley's residence at Montalegre by foot[10] and diagonally across the lake from Staël's at Coppet. "Since he boasted of his skill as a swimmer and sailor," Victor de Broglie remembered, "he incessantly crossed the lake in every direction and came to Coppet rather frequently"[11] after July 12.[12] This moment was a crucial one in Byron's personal and political history because that summer Madame de Staël attempted to reconcile Byron with Annabella Milbanke,[13] a debt Byron directly acknowledged in a note to stanza 54 of canto 4 by calling her "the patroness of all distress" (*CPW* 2:235–236). Though Byron's English contemporaries shunned him, Staël embraced him as a persecuted genius. "Byron, whom no one here receives except me, is nevertheless the man who occupies everyone most," Staël wrote to the Countess of Albany. When he first appeared at Coppet, for example, a female guest (Mrs. Hervey, a novelist) was carried out in a "dead faint." Entering, he "found the room full of strangers, who had come to stare at me as at some outlandish beast in a raree show."[14]

Though he disliked her when he first met her in England in 1813, Byron came to appreciate how much he shared with Madame de Staël both personally and politically in 1816. Exile had become an important metaphor for both of them; each writer resisted political tyranny, cultivated cosmopolitanism, criticized excessive nationalism, and linked the quality of a national literature to its political independence. Most of all, both writers prided themselves on "feeling" as they wrote, and doing so at a time when their closest contemporaries, such as Talleyrand and Constant, Annabella Milbanke and Lord Castlereagh, could exhibit a marked absence of feeling in their personal and public conduct.

II

Byron's *Childe Harold's Pilgrimage* (1812) and Madame de Staël's *De l'Allemagne* (1813) excoriated of unchecked nationalism. "The kind of unjust power to which both Staël and Byron were most unambiguously opposed was that exercised over states by foreign powers," Joanne Wilkes observes, "and the desire to combat such power motivates much of their writing."[15] Both authors question their fellow citizens' nationalism. The stanzas treating the battle of Talavera (*CPW* 2:1:40–42) "run directly counter to very many of our national passions, and most favoured propensities," *The Edinburgh Review* observed.[16] Napoleon's minister of police condemned Staël's work as "not French," exiling the author on twenty-four hour's notice and destroying what he believed to be the only remaining copies. Though such responses seem harsh, they were not unjustified. Byron celebrated every form of nationalism but his own in the first two cantos of *Childe Harold's Pilgrimage*, urging the Spanish, Portuguese, and Greeks to recover their dignity by fighting for national sovereignty. Though vocal about the need for European countries to throw off the Napoleonic yoke, Byron criticized England's efforts to assist Spanish nationalists in the Peninsular War, questioned Lord Elgin's right to ship Greek statuary to England (*CPW* 2:11–15),[17] and attacked Lord Wellesley at some length for his role in the Convention of Cintra, before removing four gratuitous stanzas in the poem's final draft (*CPW* 2:1:24).

Madame de Staël was equally critical of France, questioning its foreign policy and cultural contributions.[18] In *De l'Allemagne*, Staël equated French neoclassicism with French despotism and linked German romanticism with the potential for German liberalism. In defining a literary romanticism, Staël saw Germany, not France, as the country pregnant with futurity. Consistently, Staël idealized Germany[19] to criticize Napoleonic France, overlooking the liberal changes Napoleon brought to Germany.[20] "The good lady saw in our country only what she wanted to see," Heinrich Heine complained, "a misty land of spirits, where human beings without bodies, wholly virtuous, wander over snowy meadows and discourse on morals and metaphysics."[21] Byron might have agreed, but preferred Staël's "feeling" cosmopolitanism to cold pedantry. "She is sometimes right, and often wrong, about Italy and England," he wrote of *Corinne, or Italy*,[22] "but almost always true in delineating the heart, which is of but one nation, and of no country,—or, rather of all."[23]

Both Byron and Staël thought nationalism was not a fiction easily discarded.[24] They treated writers as the willing architects of national identity: important enough to be exiled, influential enough to alter public opinion. Byron describes Francesco Petrarch as one such figure, a man who "arose/To raise a language, and his land reclaim/From the dull yoke of her barbaric foes" (*CPW* 24:266–268), while Staël urged German writers such as Goethe, Lessing, and Klopstock to a similar enterprise. Though separated in age by more than two decades, they shaped their nation's response to world events without holding official government positions. Byron and Staël expressed their charismatic liberalism, then, not as an airless doctrine, but as an historicized polemic inspired, in part, by the vicissitudes of their emotional life and ever-shifting feelings. By remaining true to those feelings, both articulated a compelling version of liberalism that tempered their nationalistic impulses with an aristocratic cosmopolitanism.

Lord Byron and Madame de Staël troped cosmopolitanism as worldly and nationalism as parochial. Where Staël praised German romantic writers to embarrass French neoclassicists, Byron quoted Monbron's hero's cosmopolitan sentiments to embarrass English jingoists. Like *De l'Allemagne*,[25] which Staël based on five visits to Germany over a thirteen-year period (1789–1812),[26] *Childe Harold's Pilgrimage* was written "amidst the scenes [in 1809–11] which it attempts to describe" (*CPW* 2:3). Both writers used their cosmopolitan vantage points to interpret English and French nationalism. "J'haïssais ma patrie," Byron (or is it Harold?) announces in the epigraph from Monbron's *Le Cosmopolite*, but travel reconciles him to it, for "The universe is a kind of book of which one has read only the first page when one has seen only one's own country. I have leafed through a large enough number, which I have found equally bad" (*CPW* 2:3).

Staël could never say "J'haïssais ma patrie," for she had paid the bitter price of exile, which Byron had only imagined in his poem. Byron's "boat was always on the shore," as William Borst puts it,[27] but Staël became a reluctant cosmopolitan. Staël's Swiss Protestant[28] background complicated her identification with Catholic France, for she preferred the Parisian culture she criticized to the seclusion of Coppet, Switzerland. Banished by Napoleon for publishing *De l'Allemagne* in 1810, she found herself escorted by armed guards to the French border with less than ten days notice as she began her travels through war-torn Europe.[29] While Byron chose to leave his native country in 1809, departing for Spain and the East as part of an extended grand tour, Madame de Staël found herself *forced* by Napoleon to achieve the very cosmopolitan perspective she used to critique the French emperor. Byron's second exile was just as dramatic as Staël's, with Hobhouse and Thomas Moore disputing whether Byron left the country of his own volition.[30]

Victimized by Napoleon's censors (as Staël was), or muted by a Tory publisher (as Byron was), Byron and Staël valued free speech, while using exile to test its limits. To be sure, Byron relied upon aristocratic privilege to avoid prosecution, and Staël used her diplomatic immunity as the wife of the Swedish ambassador to escape becoming a political prisoner. Yet both writers believed that all citizens should enjoy free speech. Byron's harsh critique of England's foreign policy reached a moral crescendo in his preface to the fourth canto of *Childe Harold's Pilgrimage:* "What Italy has gained by the late transfer of nations, it were useless for Englishmen to enquire, till it becomes ascertained that England has acquired something more than a permanent army and a suspended Habeas

Corpus: it is enough for them to look at home. For what they have done abroad, and especially in the South, 'Verily they *will have* their reward,' and at no very distant period" (*CPW* 2:124). Writing from "abroad," Byron could criticize English foreign policy in Italy with new authority, even as Tories found his patriotism increasingly suspect.

Staël's preface was similarly polemical; she used inverted commas and page layout "to mark the passages which the censors of Paris . . . suppressed."[31] She wrote that "a sensible woman has said, that Paris is, of all the world, the place where men can most easily dispense with being happy." A footnote explains that "this line has been suppressed by the literary censorship; because there must be happiness in Paris, where the emperor lives."[32] Staël underscored Napoleon's excisions through a series of tendentious footnotes. She counteracts Napoleon's assault on her text, reducing his efforts at excision to marginalia.

Yet Byron and Staël's cosmopolitanism was also self-contradictory. *Childe Harold's Pilgrimage* supports Portuguese, Spanish, Italian, and Greek efforts to free themselves from their enslavers (Joseph II, Charles IV, Godoy, Ferdinand, Murat, Metternich, and Turkish sultans) while condemning English military aid to Spain. The poem is both nationalist, encouraging nations to return to their linguistic and literary origins, and cosmopolitan, broadcasting an Englishman's concern with the welfare of European literatures and the fate of foreign nations. Staël exhibited the same contradictory tendencies. Praised today for her "cultural liberalism,"[33] she paradoxically celebrated Goethe as a great *German* writer who showed his gift most clearly when he wrote as a cosmopolitan. He "pleases in the national songs of each nation; he becomes when he chooses it, a Greek, an Indian, or a Morlachian."[34] Thus Staël praised Goethe's cosmopolitanism, while urging Germans to reject French literary influence, a clear call to nationalism.

Neither writer could separate literary from military might. In order for Spaniards to develop their national literature, Byron argued, they must first defend their country's national honor. Yet in other passages the poet clearly deplored blood spilled in military campaigns. He invoked chivalry to fault Spanish cowardice in the maid of Saragossa passage, but dismissed it as a moral guide in his "Addition to the Preface." "The vows of chivalry were no better kept than any other vows whatsoever, and the songs of the Troubadours were not more decent."

III

"There [is] no country where Christians have been better knights, or knights better Christians, than in France"[35]

Staël, *De l'Allemagne*

Long before Byron accused Cervantes of "smil[ing] Spain's Chivalry away" (*CPW* 5:13:11), Byron wrote poems praising this medieval institution. At times, he mixed chivalry with libertinism. In "To Ianthe," for example, Byron opens *Childe Harold's Pilgrimage* by dedicating it to Lady Oxford's daughter in an erotic tone ("nor question why/To one so young my strain I would commend" [*CPW* 2:7: 35]), while two stanzas later he condemns Harold's morals, describing him as "a shameless wight,/Sore given to revel and ungodly glee" (*CPW* 2:1:2). The values of the poet and his poetic narrator collide.

Madame de Staël was guilty of a similar tension between her private and public conduct. Her notorious affairs with Louis Comte de Narbonne, Adolf Ludwig Count Ribbing, and Benjamin Constant must have made her defense of chivalry in *De l'Allemagne* appear rather ludicrous. Yet both Byron and Staël's genders affected their divergent attitudes toward libertinism. Byron quoted Valmont approvingly in his diary in 1813, the year Staël visited England. Staël cited the identical passage from Laclos's novel—"One grows tired of every thing, my angel"—to register the opposite response; the novel, she wrote in her chapter on "Chivalry," "makes one shudder at the refinements of immorality which it displays."[36]

Byron alluded facetiously to chivalric institutions; Madame de Staël devoted a whole chapter of *De l'Allemagne* to lamenting their decline. Byron mocked Burke's defense of Marie Antoinette in his "Addition to the Preface" to *Childe Harold's Pilgrimage* (cantos 1 and 2); Staël tried to rescue the French queen personally. Byron dismissed Bayard as "'sans peurs,' but not 'sans reproche'" (*CPW* 2:5); Staël observed that "the spirit of chivalry in France" was "extinct" since "she possessed no longer a Godefroi, a Saint Louis, or a Bayard, to protect weakness."[37] Consistently, Staël used the fiction of German chivalry to expose Napoleon's decidedly unchivalrous conduct. "The spirit of chivalry still reigns among the Germans," she wrote to draw the contrast sharply. "They are incapable of deceit, and their integrity discovers itself in all the intimate relations of life."[38]

Both Byron and Madame de Staël praised chivalric institutions for providing aristocratic men with a sense of social purpose and decorum. Byron's first name for Harold was Childe Burun, which shows, in part, that Byron identified with, and valued, his aristocratic knight's romantic quest. "Harold's degeneracy and departure suggest that since its development into a modern nation-state Britain offers no satisfactory public role for the young aristocrat," Franklin writes. "The object of the pilgrimage is to recover such a role in Europe if not for Harold then for his poet."[39] Byron criticized those who failed to fulfill such a lofty goal. He related Portugal's fall to the failure of Portuguese noblemen. "Here all were noble, save Nobility;/None hugg'd a Conqueror's chain, save fallen Chivalry!" (*CPW* 2:1:85). Chivalry is "fallen" as surely as the aristocratic warrior falls to his knees to hug, not a woman, but the knees of the man who has conquered him. Like Portuguese peasants, Spain's "vassals combat when their chieftains flee" (*CPW* 2:1:86). Byron spoke "in a very slight and sarcastic manner of wars, and victories, and military heroes in general,"[40] *The Edinburgh Review* charged. The review perhaps overlooked the fact that Byron invoked chivalry, even if only as a fallen standard. Staël concurred with such idealism, calling chivalry "the military religion of Europe,"[41] though Byron and Staël thought liberalism would historically supplant it.

For all their praise of chivalry, Byron and Staël knew such aristocratic values were becoming obsolete. Byron nevertheless believed men should defend their country's honor,[42] and Madame de Staël criticized Germans for accepting foreign rule too easily. "Individuals ought to submit to destiny, but nations never," she wrote. "The submission of one people to another is contrary to nature. Who would now believe in the possibility of subduing Spain, Russia, England, or France? Why should it not be the same with Germany?"[43] Staël praised German chivalry and tried to cultivate German nationalism.[44] She argued for educational reforms that would encourage such sentiments, as if to imply that Prussian and Austrian defeats were caused by poor *esprit de corps*.

Yet both writers tempered their militarism. Though they used the standard of chivalry to criticize national leaders, they did not urge their own countrymen to pursue military glory. Staël showed her cosmopolitanism by praising other countries at the expense of her own. England "has been seen like a knight armed for the defence of social order," Staël wrote in *De l'Allemagne*, "preserving Europe during ten years of anarchy, and ten years more of despotism."[45]

IV

Both Madame de Staël and Lord Byron mythologized themselves, in part, to make their political views more palatable. Madame de Staël "linked her fame to Napoleon: like Byron, she thus create[d] her own myth, both in her life and in her books," John Isbell argues. "*De l'Allemagne's* great impact upon the nineteenth century cannot be interpreted without taking that myth into account."[46] Where Staël published *Corinne* and became known by that name and several others (Phèdre, Sappho), Byron referred to himself as "the grand Napoleon of the realms of Rhyme" (*CPW* 5:11:56).[47] Byron swam from Sestos to Abydos in imitation of Leander, commissioned busts by foreign nationals like Thorwaldsen, and explained the significance of exotic locations[48] in *Childe Harold's Pilgrimage* in such a way as to celebrate his personal accomplishments on foreign shores. Jerome McGann argues that "a literary 'cult of personality' had begun to flourish in the eighteenth century" in the work of Young, Burns, Chatterton and Cowper.[49] Thus, Byron posed as an English lord in *Childe Harold's Pilgrimage*, but also as a private person whose feelings and personal character are important.[50]

One can easily forget that Byron was not a significant personality when he wrote cantos 1 and 2. Despite the minor scandal produced by Henry Brougham's scathing review of *Hours of Idleness* and Byron's response in *English Bards and Scotch Reviewers*, Byron awoke to find himself famous *after* he published *Childe Harold*, not before. For this reason, one notes with surprise how often Harold responds personally to political events, or comments on the Convention of Cintra, the fallen state of Greece, and Lord Elgin's marbles. Why did Byron assume his readers would care about Harold's opinions, especially when he insists that Harold is only a poetical Zeluco, a borrowed type, a Gothic villain?

In part, Byron, and to a lesser extent Harold and his narrator, derive their moral authority from exotic travel. The preface to canto 1 insists upon this, noting that the poem "was begun in Albania; and the parts relative to Spain and Portugal were composed from the author's observations in those countries" (*CPW* 2:3). As Byron moved from topography to biography, however, the poem gained new moral authority. This shift is evident even in the poem's dedication. Byron dedicated canto 1 to Ianthe, the child of his mistress, Lady Oxford, and canto 3 to his own daughter, Ada. The first dedication compromised Byron's ability to criticize Harold's libertinism; the second showed Byron renewing his (and Harold's) political idealism. Byron replaced Harold's political *ennui* and disgust in canto 1 with expressions of filial love in canto 3.

Byron planted the seeds for this shift in sensibility as early as canto 1 with the libertine Harold's idealistic wish that Greece "might still be free." If the narrator exposes Harold's passive cynicism in cantos 1 and 2, in canto 3 he praises men like Rousseau, Napoleon, and Voltaire, men who altered their nation's destiny despite personal limitations. Agency enters the poem. Byron's narrator begins to use events in his own life in canto 3 to explain how governments and nations might comport themselves in adverse times. Byron articulated Harold's moral vision, what I am calling his erotic liberalism, most fully in canto 3, as he moved from using Harold as a moral commentator to speaking in his own voice to praise those who actively shaped the world around them.

Madame de Staël had less trouble imagining herself as a world historical individual. While Byron was almost without social connections before he became a peer, Staël was famous from birth as the daughter of M. Necker, Louis XVI's finance minister. Staël's father helped precipitate the fall of the Bastille by absenting himself from his government post. "C'est M. Necker qui a fait le Révolution," Napoleon informed Madame de Staël's son. "Vous ne l'avez pas vue, et moi j'y étais." Napoleon's chief of police recognized Staël's importance by blaming her for Napoleon's fall: "Elle a été la chaînon de l'entrevue d'Åbo. . . . Voilà comment Madame Staël a servi la restauration."[51] If Necker helped to bring down the Bastille, Staël mobilized public opinion against Napoleon by portraying herself as a victim in *De l'Allemagne* and underscoring the parts of her book which Napoleon excised.[52] In *De l'Allemagne*, Staël used Napoleon's persecution of her ("such a weak . . . being as myself")[53] as a synecdoche for his persecution of liberal intellectuals everywhere. Through this synecdoche, Staël hoped to encourage Germans to resist Napoleon's forces and assert their incipient nationhood.

The Corsican Napoleon's minister of police, Savery, censored *De l'Allemagne* as "not French," troping Madame de Staël as a foreigner, yet Staël used such persecution to gain renewed prestige for her political opinions.[54] She contrasts Germany's recognition of her literary importance with Napoleon's unchivalrous exile. If Germany is a faithful lover, Napoleon is a boor too crude to value her opinions. In one particularly notorious exchange, Napoleon interrupted Staël by examining her décolletage and asking if she breast-fed her children. In retaliation for such sexist remarks and for her exile, Staël used synecdoche in *De l'Allemagne,* using the national shortcomings of France to illustrate the personal failings of Napoleon.

During Staël's brief visit to England in 1813, Byron was an amused, if slightly coldhearted, witness to her talent for self-display. "Corinne [Madame de Staël] is doubtless very much affected," Byron wrote to Lady Melbourne when Staël's son Albert died in a duel. "Yet methinks—I should conjecture—she will want some spectators to testify how graceful her grief will be—& to relate what fine things she can say on a subject where commonplace mourners would be silent.—Do I err in my judgment of the woman think you?" (*BLJ* August 8, 1813; 3:87). By comparing Staël to her heroine Corinne, Byron mocks her, portraying her as a woman who behaves like an exaggerated character in one of her own novels.

Yet Byron commemorated the death of his cousin Frederick Howard (1785–1815) at Waterloo in similarly histrionic terms. He compared his cousin's death to a "broken mirror" which captures both the fragility of human life and the poet's capacity to immortalize human suffering.

> Even as a broken mirror, which the glass
> In every fragment multiplies; and makes
> A thousand images of one that was,

> The same, and still the more, the more it breaks;
> And thus the heart will do which not forsakes,
> Living in shattered guise, and still, and cold,
> And bloodless, with its sleepless sorrow aches,
> Yet withers on till all without is old,
> Showing no visible sign, for such things are untold
> (*CPW* 2:3:33)

Byron makes his cousin's death emblematic of the pain of others, indeed the pain of Europe as a whole. Byron's heart, which is "broken" by this death, attracts more attention than a whole heart, because as a poet he can multiply its fragments into "a thousand images of one that was." His heart's brokenness (his grief over his cousin's death) is a "shatter'd guise" for authorial vanity that reflects pain outward like "a broken mirror."

So intense was their desire for self-mythology that both Byron and Staël became distrustful of the other's claim on immortality. During their turbulent encounters at London social gatherings in 1813 and 1814, Staël welcomed Byron as a member of the aristocracy of letters. Yet on one occasion, she criticized his treatment of Caroline Lamb, claiming that he knew nothing of "la belle passion"(*BLJ* July 13, 1813; 3:76). Byron's response to Staël was equally ambivalent. Though he praised her in a footnote to "The Bride of Abydos" as "the most eminent woman writer of this or indeed of any century," he referred to her as the "Epicene" in his correspondence, remembering her "with her pen behind her ears and her mouth full of *ink*" (*BLJ* January 8, 1814; 4:19). In fact, Byron never truly accepted Staël as an author. After Staël's death, he rewrote her myth, remembering her in a note to canto 4 of *Childe Harold's Pilgrimage* as a gracious hostess, a "patroness of ... distress." He remembered how she consoled him in Switzerland shortly after his separation from Annabella. One would never know that she was also an author.

Both Byron and Staël mythologized themselves as outsiders, exiles, and lonely individualists persecuted for their liberal beliefs. They used fictional characters such as Harold and Corinne to make their political views more palatable. Byron's *Childe Harold's Pilgrimage* and Staël's *De l'Allemagne* exploded distinctions between author and character. Byron expressed his misanthropy through Harold and Madame de Staël displayed her dejected feelings in *Corinne*. Yet *De l'Allemagne* resembles *Childe Harold's Pilgrimage* even more than Staël's novel about Italy. In the same way that Byron dropped the literary persona of Harold in canto 3, Staël abandoned the mask of Delphine and Corinne in *De l'Allemagne* to speak in her own voice. Both authors became the literary personae they wrote about. They used this strategy of self-mythology to make their criticisms of Napoleon and George III compelling. Never have two writers come to such sweeping conclusions based on such personal perspectives. Never has "feeling" struggled to assume such cosmopolitan prestige.

V

"She thinks like a man, but . . . alas! she feels like a woman"[55]
Byron of Madame de Staël

Byron shared the trait for which he criticized Staël: "feel[ing] like a woman." "I cannot separate my ideas from my feelings," Madame de Staël confessed in her conclusion to *Literature Considered in its Relation to Social Institutions*,[56] and Byron complained to John Murray that politics "with me is a *feeling* . . . I can't *torify* my nature" (*BLJ* January 22, 1814; 4:38). Sainte Beuve characterized Staël as the "Empress of Mind" and Napoleon as the "Emperor of Matter," but such a portrait (of Staël at least) is incomplete.[57] Staël parodied Talleyrand's opportunistic rationalism in *Delphine*, embraced feeling as a guide to moral action in *Corinne*, and endorsed romanticism as a worthy successor to the Enlightenment in *De l'Allemagne*.[58] "The first requisite in writing is a strong and lively feeling," Staël reminded her readers of *De l'Allemagne*, a work that did more than any other to define romanticism as a literary movement.

Both writers traveled, and their visits to foreign countries stimulated the political feelings they expressed in their work. Staël developed a sense of historical imagination and memory, in part, to improve her understanding of the art of foreign countries and the feelings that art inspired.[59] "We can give life to objects of art only by an intimate acquaintance with the country and with the epoch in which they existed,"[60] she observed. Similarly, Byron wrote sections of the third canto of *Childe Harold* at Lake Leman in order to achieve an "intimate acquaintance" with the places Rousseau lived and felt (*CPW* 2:3:312).

Byron first uses the word "feeling" in *Childe Harold's Pilgrimage* in the sixth stanza of canto 3. The word helps him define his reason for writing at all:

> 'Tis to create, and in creating live
> A being more intense, that we endow
> With form our fancy, gaining as we give
> The life we image, even as I do now.
> What am I? Nothing: but not so art thou,
> Soul of my thought! with whom I traverse earth,
> Invisible but gazing, as I glow
> Mix'd with thy spirit, blended with thy birth,
> And feeling still with thee in my crush'd feelings' dearth.
> (*CPW* 2:3:46–54)

Jerome McGann treats this passage as a meditation on the act of writing.[61] Yet the poet also refers to "creating" his daughter,[62] a reference Byron underscores by alluding to Ada directly in the first stanza.[63] Through Ada (and even, perhaps, Medora), he "lives a being more intense"—he endows her form with his fancy; her eyes "gaze" at him as he "glows" with literary fame. "[G]aze" suggests a child innocently watching her father, much as Byron's readers became spellbound by his physical and literary presence.[64]

By the end of canto 3, the poet must confess that this effort to embrace feeling only makes him more aware of his moral shortcomings. His daughter gives shape to his moral imagination and reminds him of another daughter he has neglected:[65]

> to feel
> We are not what we have been, and to deem
> We are not what we should be,—and to steel
> The heart against itself; and to conceal,
> With a proud caution, love, or hate, or aught,—
> Passion or feeling, purpose, grief or zeal,—
> (*CPW* 2:3:1032–38)

Byron personifies Italy and Greece, countries that "feel" they are not what they have been nor should be. But he also refers to his relationship with his wife, and possibly even Augusta, noting his own failure to reform his libertinism and become a liberal gentleman. This latter theme is everywhere evident in Byron's correspondence before, during, and after his marriage to Annabella Milbanke. His feeling for his daughter(s) leads Byron to mix moral declamation with self-critique.

In the canto's final stanza, Byron returns to the idea of his daughter living through him, making the creation of his poem possible. She is an invisible presence who allows him to live "A being more intense" (*CPW* 2:3:47).

> I see thee not,—I hear thee not,—but none
> Can be so wrapt up in thee; thou art the friend
> To whom the shadows of far years extend:
> Albeit my brow thou never should'st behold,
> My voice shall with thy future visions blend,
> And reach into thy heart,—when mine is cold,—
> (*CPW* 2:3:1069–74)

Harold's *eros* ("none/Can be so wrapt up in thee") promises to cure his grief. Whatever his *other* problems, the narrator's heart is not "cold." He still has enough feeling to continue writing.

If Wordsworth finds himself revitalized by his sister's presence in "Tintern Abbey," Byron must live with the painful consequences of his daughter's absence.[66]

He almost forgets that he is writing about his *daughter* (she was barely three months old when he saw her last) and uses her as a literary prop. Converting *philia* into *eros*, Byron stresses that absence is a condition of literary composition, the writer creating fanciful forms to fit his imagination. Byron's *eros* is all the more tragic because he senses that he will never see the real beings of his flesh and blood again.

Byron used the word "feeling" on sixteen occasions in the third and fourth cantos of *Childe Harold's Pilgrimage*, and not at all in the first two.[67] Perhaps politics *became* a "feeling" for the poet (*BLJ* January 22, 1814; 4:38), developing in response to his separation and self-imposed exile. Byron altered his stagily sentimental poem into one that expressed his politics of feeling. In canto 3 of *Childe Harold's Pilgrimage,* Byron most often employed the word "feeling" to connect Harold's personal unhappiness with the scenes of political nostalgia and *eros* that the fallen states of Spain, Italy, and Greece evoke.

VI

Byron's third canto lends itself to more cynical interpretations. In 1816, Byron knew that dedicating canto 3 to his daughter Ada was one way of criticizing Annabella and her lawyers for separating them forever. Byron used his daughter as a pawn, even as a stand-in for Augusta Leigh, to turn what Annabella called "the Tide of public opinion" in his favor.[68]

One could go further with this approach and question the sincerity of Byron and Staël's cosmopolitanism. Byron's much vaunted "hatred" for his country, for example, barely conceals his jingoism. At times Byron resembles Southey in assuming that his own moral character is sounder than that of the Portuguese, Italians, or Greeks he describes. "To talk, as the Greeks themselves do, of their rising again to their pristine superiority, would be ridiculous," he writes in the notes to cantos 1 and 2, "as the rest of the world must resume its barbarism, after re-asserting the sovereignty of Greece; but there seems to be no very great obstacle, except in the apathy of the Franks, to their becoming an useful dependency" (*CPW* 2:202). Byron barters for Greece's fate with France ("useful dependency") in the tone of a dissenting Protestant, uttering his opinions in a cosmopolitan but patronizing tone (*CPW* 2:201).[69] He moves beyond his country, but never beyond his culture.

Madame de Staël praised England's political institutions, one reason her manuscript could not be published in France until three years after she wrote it. Yet one can hardly read a page of *De l'Allemagne* without noting how French chauvinism shines through her coy praise of Germany. Like Byron, who describes Greeks as heterodox, Staël depicts German citizens as "noble savages."[70]

The French have the best conversation, the most advanced European civilization. Unfortunately, their very achievements spring from defects such as overrefinement. The French apply neoclassical standards too minutely. The Germans, by contrast, tolerate melodrama too readily; they are too sincere.[71] Staël encourages Germany to pursue its own cultural destiny. Perhaps she can do so because she is convinced that no country can threaten French cultural supremacy.

Neither Byron nor Staël enjoyed hearing a foreign writer practice this complacent brand of cosmopolitanism. "She interrupted Whitbread; she declaimed to Lord L.; she misunderstood Sheridan's jokes for assent," Byron remembered of Staël's visit to England in 1813. "[S]he harangued, she lectured, she preached English politics to the first of our English Whig politicians, the day after her arrival in England; and (if I am not much misinformed) preached politics no less to our Tory politicians the day after. The Sovereign himself, if I am not in error, was not exempt from this flow of eloquence."[72] Staël felt her national pride equally injured when Byron described *Delphine* and *Corinne* as "very dangerous productions to be put into the hands of young women." According to Byron, "all the moral world thought, that her representing all the virtuous characters in 'Corinne' as being dull, commonplace, and tedious, was a most insidious blow aimed at virtue, and calculated to throw it into the shade. She was so excited and impatient to attempt a refutation, that it was only by my volubility I could keep her silent."[73] Given Byron and Staël's discomfort with visitors making sweeping generalizations about foreign countries and their literary works, why should their own arguments about nationalism be heeded?

Posing the same question, Staël's biographer, J. C. Herold, finds *De l'Allemagne* "replete with ulterior motives, scarcely concealed propaganda, and willful blindness." He finds this work of stunning erudition "an apostasy from the liberal, rationalist position" of Staël's *On Literature Considered in its Relationship to Social Institutions* and *Considerations on the Principal Events of the French Revolution*.[74] "The theme of *De l'Allemagne* is essentially polemical and for the day," he concludes.[75] Yet these weaknesses are also strengths. Byron's *Childe Harold's Pilgrimage* (canto 3) and Staël's *De l'Allemagne* show liberalism functioning as both personal polemic and political philosophy. Perhaps liberalism is at its most effective when doing both at the same time.

Homi Bhabha,[76] Ernest Gellner,[77] and Benedict Anderson do not consider Lord Byron and Madame de Staël's theories of nationalism in constructing their own. Yet Byron and Staël understood that nations, though imagined communities, are not imaginary. Nations are, and will continue to be, entities for which human beings give their lives and which they surrender at their peril. Lord Byron and Madame de Staël used their cosmopolitan liberalism to critique nationalism. If they betrayed their own crass opinions, cultural biases, and downright ignorance (on rare occasions) in order to do so, their experiment was worthwhile. They knew that language, race, and cultural identity provide the impetus for literary production. Literary works do not merely reflect national values, as Madame de Staël knew, but create them. Finally, writers, not anthropologists, imagine a community. Madame de Staël's sociological approach to literature in *De l'Allemagne* is as strikingly complex as Byron's literary approach to politics in *Childe Harold's Pilgrimage*. Focusing on Indonesian culture to explain nationalism in Europe, Benedict Anderson's *Imagined Communities* does not do full justice to European writers' contributions to the formation of national identities. Certainly any theory of nationalism that omits discussing literary culture will be incomplete. And it is perhaps to Nancy Rosenblum's treatment of literary culture—to writers themselves—that one might more profitably turn to define the relationship between nationalism and liberalism.[78] Lord Byron and Madame de Staël showed how writers can offer a nuanced (because cosmopolitan) approach to nationalism while remaining quintessentially liberal in their political outlook.[79] Byron's cosmopolitan liberalism (like Staël's), shorn of abstract theory and inspired by political passions and feelings, makes his brand of political liberalism particularly compelling at the beginning of the twenty-first century.

NOTES

1. Maura O'Connor, *The Romance of Italy and the English Political Imagination* (New York: St. Martin's Press, 1998), 45.
2. Gross, ed., *Byron's "Corbeau Blanc,"* 104.
3. Roberta Forsberg, *Madame de Staël and the English* (New York: Astra Books, 1967), 49.
4. John Isbell (*The Birth of European Romanticism* [Cambridge: Cambridge University Press, 1994], 2) notes that the book was published in June, 1813 and sold 2,250 copies. Gretchen Rous Besser (*Germaine de Staël Revisited* [New York: Twayne Publishers, 1994], 93) states that *De l'Allemagne* came out in June 1813, but that the first edition, which came out in October 1813, sold out in three days (107). Isbell mentions that the book was published in 1813 but does not specify the month. Staël's preface reads "1st October, 1813" in the edition I am using: *Germany*, ed. by O. W. Wight, 2 vols. (New York: Derby and Jackson, 1859). Wight's edition is based on John Murray's of 1813, with slight alterations. My assumption is that Byron read the work in an English translation, as his quotation from "Bride of Abydos" would suggest.
5. Forsberg, *Madame de Staël*, 47. In referring to her as "the Epicene," Byron endorsed a satire of Staël entitled "The New Morality," which appeared in *The Anti-Jacobin Review* and was possibly penned by George Canning:

> And Ah, what verse can grace thy stately mien,
> Guide of the world, preferment's golden queen,
> Necker's fair daughter, Staël the Epicene!
> Bright o'er whose flaming cheek and purple nose
> The bloom of young desire unceasing glows!
> Fain would the Muse—but ah! she dares no more,
> A mournful voice from lone Guyana's shore,
> Sad Quatremer, the bold presumption checks,
> Forbid the question thy ambiguous sex!

Canning refers to Antoine Quatremer's censure of Staël's conduct in the Council of the Five Hundred under the Government of the Directory (1795–99).

6. Marchand accuses Staël of being inconsistent politically. "He did not fail to observe that this heroine of the persecutions of Napoleon, this liberal expounder of the new German sensibility and 'Romanticism,' had quite changed her face politically when she reached English shores" (Marchand, *Byron: A Biography*, 393). Staël maintained a consistent opposition to Napoleon for ten years. It was, in fact, Byron who changed his mind about the French emperor, as his "Ode to Napoleon Bonaparte" shows. Ultimately, Byron came to agree with Staël about Napoleon's limitations.

7. Forsberg, *Madame de Staël*, 54.

8. Forsberg (*Madame de Staël*, 55) gives a date of July 29 and Joanne Wilkes (*Lord Byron and Madame de Staël: Born for Opposition* [London: Ashgate, 1999], 6) cites Byron's letter of July 29, 1816 (5:86), though Marchand states that Madame de Staël "returned to her chateau at Coppet across the lake, and from the *second week* in July Byron was a frequent visitor there. He enjoyed the society of the Shelleys, but now would gladly have dispensed with their company for the sake of getting Claire out of the way" (italics mine; Marchand, *Byron: A Biography*, 634). Later, he adds that "Byron was nevertheless pleased with the society at Coppet, and found Mme de Staël more agreeable at home than she had been in London. . . . The chatelaine was cordial and invited him oftener than he cared to go, but he did frequently cross the water to her hospitable chateau in July and August, and more frequently yet after Hobhouse's arrival. It was a much more congenial atmosphere than he had found in the drawing rooms of Geneva, which were filled with English people" (635).

9. Marchand, *Byron: A Biography*, 625.

10. The Shelleys were at Chamonix from July 21 to July 27. According to Marchand's edition of Byron's letters and journals, Byron visited Staël as early as July 12 (3:338–9), for he wrote to Murray that he had been at Coppet "ten days ago" (Marchand 634).

11. J. C. Herold, *Madame de Staël: Mistress to an Age* (New York: Harmony Books, 1958).

12. Marchand, *Byron: A Biography*, 635.

13. Staël made the mistake of choosing Byron's most implacable enemy, Henry Brougham, to do so. Brougham's double-dealing, evident in his letters to Annabella in the Lovelace Collection, illustrates the hypocrisy Byron noted in him. Marchand blames Staël for choosing Brougham as an intermediary, but Brougham's unpublished letter of August 23, 1816 in the Lovelace collection shows him to be all too willing to deceive Staël and pose as Byron's friend.

14. Herold, *Madame de Staël*, 465; Marchand, *Byron: A Biography*, 635. At Coppet, Byron may have met his old nemesis Brougham, who added to a negative review of *Hours of Idleness* the dubious distinction of interfering in the poet's effort to reconcile with his wife, though Byron did not know of any of this at the time.

15. Wilkes, *Lord Byron and Madame de Staël*, 180.

16. Reiman, *Romantics Reviewed*, 482.

17. Lord Elgin's activities have been recently defended by critics as diverse as William Borst *(Lord Byron's Pilgrimage)*, Maura O'Connor *(The Romance of Italy)*, William St. Clair *(That Greece Might Still Be Free: The Philhellenes in the War of Independence* [New York: Oxford University Press, 1972]), and Benita Eisler *(Byron)*.

18. Isbell, *Birth of European Romanticism*, 2.

19. John Isbell notes that Germany was an invented term, since no German nation existed in 1810; "in 1916, they called her *la prussolatre*" (6).

20. Isbell, *Birth of European Romanticism*, 55–107.

21. Quoted in Emma Gertrude Jaeck, *Madame de Staël and the Spread of German Literature* (New York, 1915), 64, and in Morroe Berger, ed., *Madame de Staël: On Politics, Literature, and National Character* (New York: Doubleday, 1964), 84.

22. Byron read the novel in 1819, two years after Staël's death. He was inspired to read the work because Teresa Guiccioli looked upon it as one of her favorites. See Marchand, *Byron: A Portrait*, 311, and Wilkes, *Lord Byron and Madame de Staël*, chapter 3.

23. Thomas Moore, *The Life of Lord Byron* (London, 1854), 407 n.1, quoted in Berger, *Madame de Staël*, 51.

24. For a different view, see Benedict Anderson, *Imagined Communities* (New York: Verso, 1983), 5–6. Timothy Brennan offers, I think, a more nuanced interpretation of cosmopolitanism. Brennan, *At Home in the World: Cosmopolitanism Now* (Cambridge: Harvard University Press, 1997).

25. The work was composed in 1810 and published in October 1813 in England and May 1814 in France. Besser, *Germaine de Staël Revisited*, 106.

26. Isbell, *Birth of European Romanticism*, 10.

27. Borst, *Lord Byron's Pilgrimage*, 154.

28. Besser, *Germaine de Staël Revisited*, 93. Wilkes(*Lord Byron and Madame de Staël*, 3) mentions her Swiss-German parentage.

29. Isbell, *Birth of European Romanticism*, 3.

30. "Some Observations Upon An Article in *Blackwood's Edinburgh Magazine* (1820)," *Complete Miscellaneous Prose*, 95.

31. Wight, ed., *Germany*, 1:24.

32. Wight, ed., *Germany*, 1:23.

33. Besser, *Germaine de Staël Revisited*, 95.

34. Wight, ed., *Germany*, 1:228.

35. Wight, ed, *Germany*, 1:47.

36. Wight, ed., *Germany*, 1:50.

37. Wight, ed., *Germany*, 1:49.

38. Wight, ed., *Germany*, 1:51.

39. Caroline Franklin, "Cosmopolitan Masculinity and the British Female Reader of Childe Harold's Pilgrimage," in *Byron, the European: Essays from the International Byron Society*, ed. Richard A. Cardwell (Lewiston, N.Y.: Edwin Mellen Press, 1997), 112.

40. Review of *Childe Harold's Pilgrimage*, *Edinburgh Review*, Reiman, *Romantics Reviewed*, 467.

41. Wight, ed., *Germany*, 1:48.

42. Benjamin Constant, "The Spirit of Conquest and Usurpation and their Relation to European Civilization," in *The Political Writings*, trans. and ed. Biancamaria Fontana (Cambridge: Cambridge University Press, 1988), 51–80.

43. Wight, ed., *Germany*, 1:19.

44. Wight, ed., *Germany*, 1:118.

45. Wight, ed., *Germany*, 1:17.

46. Isbell, *Birth of European Romanticism*, 106.

47. See John Clubbe, "Dramatic Hits: Napoleon and Shakespeare in Byron's 1813–1814 Journal," in *British Romantics as Readers: Intertextualities, Maps of Misreading, Reinterpretations, Festschrift for Horst Meller*, ed. Michael Gassenmeier, Petre Bridzun, Jens Martin Gurr, and Frank Eric Pointner (Heidelberg: Universitätsverlag C. Winter, 1998), 271–94, and chapter 1 of the present study, which discusses Byron's turn away from Leigh Hunt in order to identify himself with the heroic individualism of Napoleon Bonaparte.

48. See Byron's note to line 674 in canto 4, where he recalls that his years at Harrow were "the happiest of my life; and my preceptor (the Rev. Dr. Joseph Drury), was the best and worthiest friend I ever possessed" (*CPW* 2:249).

49. McGann, *Fiery Dust*, 7.

50. Christensen, *Lord Byron's Strength*.

51. Isbell, *Birth of European Romanticism*, 101.

52. Isbell, *Birth of European Romanticism*, passim.

53. Wight, ed., *Germany*, 1:16.

54. Isbell, *Birth of European Romanticism*, 14–20.

55. Marchand, *Byron: A Biography*, 1:393.

56. Morroe Berger, ed., *Madame de Staël: On Politics, Literature, and National Character*, 87.

57. Herold, *Madame de Staël*, 192.

58. Herold, *Madame de Staël*, 193.

59. Wight, ed., *Germany*, 1:147.

60. Wight, ed., *Germany*, 1:172. For a discussion of cosmopolitanism in *De l'Allemagne*, see Kirsten Daly, "'Worlds Beyond England': Don Juan and the Legacy of Enlightenment Cosmopolitanism,'" *Romanticism* 4, no. 2 (1998): 189–202.

61. McGann, *Fiery Dust*, 114.

62. Richard Sha, *The Verbal and Visual Sketch in Romanticism* (Philadelphia: University of Pennsylvania Press, 1998), 192.

63. McGann, *Fiery Dust*, 114, 118.

64. "The act of conjuring up the face of his absent daughter becomes an example and image of poetic inspiration," as Caroline Franklin notes. Franklin, "Cosmopolitan Masculinity," 121.

65. At least some biographers concur that Medora was Byron's child. Marchand (*Byron: A Portrait*, 166n) leaves the matter open, while Phyllis Grosskurth (*Byron*, 475) and Benita Eisler (*Byron*, 423) assume Byron was the father. Byron's letter to Lady Melbourne, in which he says that the child is not "an Ape," as well as numerous other guilt-ridden letters and hints seem inexplicable otherwise.

66. McGann, *Fiery Dust*, 117.

67. Byron used the word "feel" six times in cantos 1 and 2, and fourteen times in cantos 3 and 4. The increased usage of this word would seem to indicate its importance when Byron elected to continue writing the poem in 1816.

68. Grosskurth, *Byron*, 131.

69. O'Connor, *The Romance of Italy*, 112.

70. Herold, *Madame de Staël*, 390.

71. Wight, ed., *Germany*, 1:28.

72. Marchand, *Byron: A Biography*, 393; *CMP* 193.

73. Marchand, *Byron: A Biography*, 394; *CMP* 194.

74. Herold, *Madame de Staël*, 390, 389; Madame de Staël, *On Literature Considered in its Relationship to Social Institutions*, 2 vols. (London, 1793) and *Considerations on the Principal Events of the French Revolution*, 3 vols. (London: Baldwin, Cradock, and Joy, 1818).

75. Herold, *Madame de Staël*, 390.

76. Homi K. Bhabha, "DissemiNation: time, narrative, and the margins of the modern nation," in *Nations and Narration*, ed. Homi K. Bhabha (New York: Routledge, 1990), 291–322.

77. Ernest Gellner, ed., *Nationalism* (New York: New York University Press, 1997).

78. Nancy Rosenblum, *Another Liberalism: Romanticism and the Reconstruction of Liberal Thought* (Cambridge: Harvard University Press, 1987), 187.

79. My argument challenges (or perhaps supports) Linda Colley's *Britons* which argues that Britons forged a nation by imagining themselves in relationship to an Other. Always idiosyncratic, Byron incorporated the "Other" into his poetry precisely to challenge the jingoism of his English contemporaries.

5

"GET[TING] INTO LORD'S GROUND": BYRON'S ARISTOCRATIC LIBERALISM IN THE POPE-BOWLES CONTROVERSY AND *MARINO FALIERO*

In the years that followed Madame de Staël's death in 1818, Byron became involved in aesthetic controversies in which he struggled, like Staël, to unite classical and romantic taste. If Staël defined romanticism in *De l'Allemagne*, Byron challenged her definition in his letters on the Pope-Bowles controversy and the neoclassical form of *Marino Faliero*.

Despite their differences, however, Staël and Byron shared an aristocratic suspicion of romanticism as a dangerously unbridled literary style. Staël attacked German melodrama and Byron criticized the Cockney school of Hunt and Keats.[1] What needs to be emphasized is that Byron's liberalism was never really democratic. Following the lead of Samuel Chew, historical critics from the 1920s and, especially, the 1940s perpetuated a myth of Byron as an aristocratic rebel who left behind the assumptions of his social class and championed great democratic movements.[2] Yet Byron's role in the Pope-Bowles controversy reveals an elitist, aristocratic side to his thought. In two letters he wrote to his publisher, John Murray, Byron defended Alexander Pope by attacking William Bowles and the Cockney poets for their social class (*CMP* 88–119).[3] Byron's elitism is also evident in *Marino Faliero*, which, in both its aesthetic theory and in the personal and political circumstances it dramatizes, demonstrates the difficulties Byron faced supporting democracy from his class position as an aristocratic rebel. Byron wrote a defense of Pope as early as March 15, 1820 in an unpublished letter to *Blackwood's Edinburgh Magazine*[4] and began *Marino Faliero* the next month, on April 4 (*CPW* 4:522), though he meditated on it as early as February 25, 1817 (*BLJ* 5:174). Juxtaposing Byron's prose and poetry in 1820, I hope to consider how Byron's conservative aesthetics and aristocratic birth inflect his political liberalism.

THE POPE-BOWLES CONTROVERSY

William Bowles was a vicar of Bremhill whose *Sonnets* (1789) exerted an important influence on Southey, Lamb, Wordsworth, and Coleridge. Bowles's introduction to Pope's *Collected Works* (1806), which censured Pope's moral (i:xv–cxxxi) and poetical character (10:363–80), sparked a debate that lasted well into the next decade. A writer from Blackwood's *Edinburgh Review* (11:22) was the first to attack Bowles's new edition of Pope in 1808. Next, Lord Byron mocked the edition in *English Bards and Scotch Reviewers* in 1809. The most serious attack, however, came from Thomas Campbell, in *Specimens of the British Poets*, in 1819. To answer Campbell, Bowles wrote an open letter which he published as a pamphlet entitled "Invariable Principles of Poetry" in that same year.[5] What did Bowles say that caused so much controversy?

Both in his original introduction to Pope's works and in his subsequent letter to Campbell, Bowles discussed Pope's limitations as a man and as a poet. As a man, Pope was vain and licentious, Bowles argued: Pope had compromised his moral character in his "libertine" love for Martha Blount and in his relentless pursuit of Lady Wortley Montagu. As a poet, Pope occupied a secondary rank. The reasons Bowles gave for this assessment became known as his "Invariable Principles of Poetry." Though Pope wrote excellent didactic verse, Bowles argued, he did not treat subjects suited to higher orders of poetry, as Shakespeare and Milton did. According to Bowles, Shakespeare and Milton's works were "higher," not only because of their genre but because of their subject matter. Unlike Shakespeare or Milton, Pope was concerned with art more often than with nature and, in Bowles's view, sublime objects taken from art were less poetical than sublime objects taken from nature.

In two letters he wrote to Bowles in 1821, Byron took issue with Bowles's invariable principles of poetry. He argued that the poet's powers of execution, not his subject matter, formed the ultimate test of a poet's merit, and he denied that nature formed a more suitable subject for poetry than art. In both points, Byron misunderstood Bowles's position. Bowles had never denied that the poet's powers of execution determined his or her merits: in fact he had written, "Be the subject what it may, the poet's merit must depend on the execution." Byron was equally misguided in his second line of attack. Tirelessly enumerating examples of poetic objects in nature, Byron never challenged Bowles's invariable principle, that *sublime* objects taken from nature are more poetic than those taken from art (*CMP* 400). Byron may have deliberately misunderstood his opponent. Bowles's preference for the "open, enjambed couplet," as William Keach has shown, "exacerbat[ed] Byron's antipathy to Bowles as it did his antipathy to Keats."[6]

But the arguments of Bowles and Byron were almost beside the point, for "the form and content of a novel or poem became political declarations," as Leslie Mitchell has observed in *Holland House*. To the Whigs, the poetry of Pope was as sacrosanct as the work of Tasso, Ariosto, and Dryden. These were the authors admired by Charles James Fox and his nephew, Lord Holland. To a large extent, Byron, though a reluctant pioneer of the new style of poetry, was an eighteenth-century Whig where literary matters were concerned and shared Holland's classical tastes,[7] as Byron's unpublished "Observations Upon An Article In *Blackwood's Edinburgh Magazine*" (1820) reveals (*CMP* 88–119). E. D. H. Johnson has shown that "the poet's much-maligned defence of the neo-classic as opposed to the romantic movement in literature was in full accord with the prevailing critical sentiment,"[8] yet Andrew Nicholson argues that Byron's "manifesto aimed directly at the poetical (and political) taste and tenets of the day" (*CMP* 408). Perhaps the best way to reconcile these points of view is to suggest that different social classes held different aesthetic principles dear at different times between 1790 and 1818. As Nicholson points out, the controversy "documents a long-held and firm belief in the sovereignty of the classical tradition of literature" (*CMP* 408). But the "belief" was held by the Whig aristocrats and the upper classes, rather than the middle class or Cockney school of Hunt and Keats, and this belief changed over two decades, as the political principles of the French Revolution made themselves felt in English verse, as William Hazlitt argued had happened with Wordsworth's poetry.

My concern, however, is not with Whig tastes in literature—or even with Pope as a symbol of English nationalism,[9] the subject of an illuminating article by James Chandler—but with Byron's class consciousness as betrayed in a literary quarrel. In discussing matters of taste, Byron informed his publisher, Bowles had entered onto "Lord's ground" and Byron intended to show his opponent how such matters should be discussed: "Bowles must be *bowled* down—'tis a sad match at Cricket—if that fellow can get any Notches at Pope's expence.—If he once gets into 'Lord's Ground' (to continue the pun because it is foolish) I think I could beat him in one Innings" (*BLJ* September 18, 1820; 7:229). Through his use of puns based on the game of cricket, Byron reveals his class consciousness, referring both to his own social status as a Lord and to a cricket field called "Lord's Ground." Socially, Byron will protect his higher social "ground," and as a cricket player he will not allow Bowles to "get into 'Lord's ground'" (or score runs at the expense of Pope). As if to signal his seamless passage from "metaphorical" to "literal" meaning, Byron continues his postscript by adding that he was "once—(not *metaphorically* but really) a good Cricketeer—particularly in *batting*—and I played in the Harrow match against the Etonians in 1805, gaining more notches (as one of our chosen Eleven) than any except Ld. Ipswich and Brookman on our side" (September 9, 1820; 7:225).

The same rules that applied in cricket, in other words, could be applied to the social world. "The games which public schoolmen took up or invented, the rules which they laid down for them, the clothes which they wore, the settings and equipment which they devised, the language which they used and the seriousness with which they took the whole business gradually spread down the social scale," Mark Girouard argues. By applying the analogy of cricket to literary criticism, Byron implicitly excluded Bowles from the game ("not *metaphorically* but really"), anticipating a usage that would become popular at the end of the nineteenth century. "It became commonplace, in an everyday rather than a sporting contest," Mark Girouard points out, "to condemn an action as 'not cricket' or to commend someone for being a sportsman or for playing the game."[10]

Like Lord Holland, Byron rejected the democratical proscriptions of these new poetasters and used their shabby origins, not to mention their democratical subjects, to drive them from Lord's ground. According to the Whigs, poetry and politics were only possible with "the leisure and education that came with property holding."[11] To accept views on matters of taste from a vicar at Bremhill, however logical, involved an inversion of the social hierarchy, the same hierarchy that made such pleasant diversions as the enjoyment of poetry possible.[12]

In his essay on the Pope-Bowles controversy, Hazlitt noted the aristocratic tone of Byron's debate with Bowles, the "cavalier assumptions of patrician manners" that Byron assumed; he described Byron as "throwing out a number of pert, smart, flashy things, with the air of a man who sees company in matters of taste" (Howe 19:63).[13] By foregrounding manners, Byron served as Bowles's judge and jury. He commented on Bowles's "good humour," his "gentlemanly manners and agreeable conversation" (*FL* 121), only so he could reprove his poor manners elsewhere. In his second letter, he then upbraided Bowles for attacking his opponent's profession and attempted to instruct Bowles on the literary manners appropriate to Christian reviewers. "Mr. G's Station . . . which might conduct him to the highest civic honours—and to boundless wealth—has nothing to require apology,—but even if it had—such a reproach was not very gracious on the part of a clergyman—nor graceful on that of a gentleman" (*SL* 165). The key phrase in this sentence, of course, is "even if it had." By introducing his criticism of Bowles with this phrase, Byron does not fault Bowles's class snobbery, only his manner of expressing it.

Byron's private letter to Murray of February 1, 1821, which was unavailable to Hazlitt, exposes the hypocrisy of Byron's democratic advice to Bowles. "You are an excellent fellow—mio Caro Moray," he wrote on that occasion, "but there is still a little leaven of Fleet-street about you now and then—a crumb of the old loaf" (*BLJ* February 1, 1821; 8:72). Byron refered to his publisher as a "tradesman" who does not "understand civility" in one breath—a tradesman "with a little leaven of Fleet-street about you now and then"—and criticized Bowles for that same class snobbery in another.[14] Byron exercised his lordly prerogative when he criticized "tradesmen," but Bowles was ungracious and unchristian when he did the same.

By referring to Bowles's manner of conducting his argument with Gilchrist, Byron maintained his posture as an indifferent judge, commenting on the manners of both participants. "[I]t is to be regretted that he has lost his temper—," Byron wrote of Bowles. "Whatever the language of his antagonist may have been—I fear that his replies have afforded more pleasure to them than to the Public" (*SL* 161). As a judge, Byron weighed the relative merits of both Bowles's and Gilchrist's position, though he clearly preferred Gilchrist's honest indignation to Bowles's indignant honesty. "Mr. B . . . charges Mr. Gilchrist with 'slang' and 'slander'—besides a small subsidiary indictment of 'Abuse, Ignorance, Malice'—and so forth.—Mr. Gilchrist has indeed shown some anger—but it is an honest indignation—which rises up in defence of the illustrious dead" (*SL* 162). Byron even corrected Bowles for his failure to put Gilchrist's name before his own. "Courtesy requires, in speaking of others and ourselves, that we should place the name of the former first—and not 'Ego et Rex meus.' Mr. B should have written 'Mr. Gilchrist's name and *his*'" (*SL* 163).

Perhaps Byron's most significant arguments challenged Bowles's statement that Pope was licentious. He attributed Bowles's attack on Pope's moral character to the "cant" of nineteenth-century Englishmen.

> The truth is, that in these days the grand "primum mobile" of England is *Cant*—Cant political—Cant poetical—Cant religious—Cant moral—but always Cant—multiplied through all the varieties of life—It is the fashion—& while it lasts—will be too powerful for those who can only exist by taking the tone of the times—I say *Cant* because it is a thing of words—without the smallest influence upon human actions—the English being no wiser—no better—and much poorer—and more divided amongst themselves—as well as far less moral—than they were before the prevalence of this verbal decorum. (*FL* 128)

Byron's aristocratic birth and classical education enabled him to resist "the tone of the times" and to offer a more forgiving, liberal assessment of licentiousness.

For the diatribe against cant quoted above, Byron won high marks from William Hazlitt (Howe 19:65, 70) and Matthew Arnold.[15]

Less honorable, perhaps, was Byron's tendency to dismiss Bowles's arguments as parochial. To rebut Bowles's view that the sea is a more poetical object than a ship, for example, Byron emphasized his own cosmopolitanism: "I look upon myself as entitled to talk of naval matters," he wrote, "at least to poets—with the exception of Walter Scott—Moore—and Southey—perhaps—who have been voyagers I have *swum* more miles—than all the rest of them together now living ever *sailed*—and have lived for months and months on Shipboard;—and during the whole period of my life abroad—have scarcely ever passed a month out of sight of the Ocean.—Besides being brought up from two years till ten on the brink of it" (*FL* 131). In his letter to Bowles, he described scenes in Attica, Pentelicus, and Anclesmus which he had seen personally, as if travelling broadly made his argument about the value of Pope's poetry any more compelling.

Byron's cosmopolitanism was also his excuse for judging the manners of others. "In these things (in private life at least)—I pretend to some small experience—because in the course of my youth—I have seen a little of all sorts of Society—from the Christian—Prince—and the Mussulman Sultan and Pacha—& the higher ranks of their countries,—down to the London boxer, 'the *Flash and the Swell*'—the Spanish Muleteer—the wandering Turkish Dervise—the Scotch Highlander—and the Albanian robber;—to say nothing of the curious varieties of Italian social life" (*FL* 159). Great poets were those who knew life, Byron informed Bowles, not those who lied to hide their ignorance. But since a knowledge of life depended on a knowledge of all classes of life, Byron was particularly well suited to the task of critic. By seeing all aspects of culture, he positioned himself beyond culture, travelling both horizontally and vertically, accreting experiences in order to establish himself as a cosmopolite. He was at the same time English and not-English, Italian and not-Italian, romantic and not-romantic, as his letters to his mother boasting of his cosmopolitanism and his allusions to Turkey in his "Framebreakers" speech suggested (*CMP* 26).

In his first letter to Bowles, Byron argued that Bowles was too parochial to judge Pope's conduct. "[A]ll men of the world who know what life is—or at least what is [*sic*] was to them in their youth—must laugh at such a ludicrous foundation of the charge of 'a libertine sort of love'" *(FL* 128). Now he added an additional argument: an unnatural adherence to moral purity could do more damage than the licentiousness with which Bowles charged Pope. Byron noted how Madame Cottins's virtue caused two suicides. "Virtuous she was, and the consequences of this inveterate Virtue—were that two different admirers (one an elderly Gentleman) killed themselves in despair" (*FL* 167). Morality was not a system of rules to be determined by ministers, but a state of responsiveness that depended as much upon an individual's experiences in the world as it did upon his or her knowledge of moral precepts. In fact, moral precepts such as his wife Annabella Milbanke possessed were not in themselves a guarantee of living a moral life. In his satire of Madame Cottins, Byron showed how moral innocence, or a too close regard for one's own virtue, could be a form of selfishness. In the Pope-Bowles controversy, then, Byron not only exposed his class consciousness, but enunciated his erotic liberalism, his sense that sexual generosity was more "moral" than a selfish regard for one's own virtue.

Defending Alexander Pope provided Byron with the opportunity to defend his own licentiousness in *Don Juan* and in his private life by declaring that he adhered to an aristocratic and cosmopolitan standard of virtue that was less parochial than Wordsworth's and Hunt's. Pope even shared with Byron an innate physical deformity that Byron believed strengthened the libido: the lame animal covers best, Byron reminded his readers (*SL* 170). He then went on to defend Pope's licentious language by noting that it was a form of sociability in the eighteenth century. "[F]or seventeen years the prime Minister of the country—was [licentious] at his own table," Byron wrote. As his excuse, he said "that everybody understood *that*—but few could talk rationally upon less common topics" (*SL* 171). Byron found the refinement of his own day more contemptible than the bawdiness of the past, for it shows "the consequence of vice, which wishes to mask and soften itself, as much as of virtuous civilization" (*FL* 170). In his second letter to Bowles, he alluded ironically to "this immaculate period [in Regency England], this Moral Millennium of expurgated editions in books, manners—and royal trials of divorce" *(FL* 170). The "*Delicacy* of the day" was "not a whit more moral—than, & not half so honourable—*as*—the coarser candour of our less polished ancestors" (*FL* 170), an argument Byron resorted to frequently in his letters in order to defend the licentious language of *Don Juan*.

Human beings are fallen. Pope knew this, yet Madame de Staël and Jean-Jacques Rousseau—and now Bowles—acted as if it were not so.[16] Surveying the contributions of classicism and romanticism, two schools of poetry which Madame de Staël had defined in *De l'Allemagne*, Byron criticized Rousseau and Staël for their pretensions to "Optimism": "The Sentimental Anatomy—of Rousseau and Made. de Staël—are far more formidable than any quantity of verse.—They are so—because they sap the principles—by *reasoning* upon the *passions*—whereas poetry is in itself passion—and does not systematize—It assails—but does not argue; it may be wrong, but it does not assume pretensions to Optimism" (*FL* 178).

In criticizing Pope for a libertine sort of love, Byron argued, Bowles did not expose Pope's licentiousness but his own moral fanaticism and hypocrisy. Critics like William Bowles attacked Pope's licentiousness because they were overly optimistic about man's moral possibilities; classicists were more honest about human frailty and human passion. Though he did not use the word romanticism, Byron found the "Sentimental Anatomy" of popular writers morally parochial; he preferred classicists because they had read more and, Byron implied, lived more.

To a certain extent, Byron's aesthetic critique of Pope's detractors had become indistinguishable from his political critique. By exaggerating the importance of imagination, Pope's detractors had become too populist. "It is the fashion of the day to lay great stress upon what they call 'Imagination' and 'Invention' the two commonest of qualities," he wrote in his first letter to Bowles. "[A]n Irish peasant with a little whiskey in his head will imagine and invent more than would furnish forth a modern poem" (FL, 143). Byron mocked those who would endorse imagination, the "commonest of all qualities," as an aesthetic standard, in part, because all social classes, even the "Irish peasant," had access to it.

Classicists, by contrast, did not stress the imagination's importance. By imitating the ancients, classicists implicitly engaged in a form of literary practice restricted to "the man of education the gentleman and the Scholar sporting with his subject,—it's Master—not it's Slave" (FL 160). Mere passion and invention, the virtues of the "Irish peasant," would not permit one to enter the hushed sanctuary of classicist poets. Education and refinement were necessary for that.

There was thus a political dimension to Byron's critique of Pope's critics as well as an aesthetic one. "Byron's idea that imagination is not the source of poetry but merely one of the tools at an author's disposal is plainly conservative, not to say reactionary," McGann argues.[17] To understand the reasons for Byron's conservative reaction, it is necessary to reconstruct the historical events to which it was a response. In England, the agitation for parliamentary reform had reached a violent pinnacle in 1820 and Byron, alarmed by his friend Hobhouse's involvement in the reformers' cause, wrote him letters criticizing him for the "low" company he was keeping. "Byron persisted in believing, in spite of all Hobhouse had told him, that the Whigs were still the liberal party in England, whereas they had sided with the Tories whenever it was necessary to beat the Westminster Reformers," Marchand explains. Byron dismissed Henry Hunt as a "rabble-rouser" and became increasingly hostile to the efforts of the lower middle class to obtain greater representation in parliament.[18]

Both the political and poetic reformers were "blackguards" in Byron's view. A democracy, Byron had written in his diary, was "an aristocracy of blackguards." Equally "blackguard" was a poetic movement that denied Pope his proper station in the poetic hierarchy. "I have at last lost all patience with the atrocious cant and nonsense about Pope with which our present blackguards are overflowing," he wrote to John Murray, "and am determined to make such head against it, as an Individual can by prose or verse—and I will at least do it with good will—There is no bearing it any longer, and if it goes on, it will destroy what little good writing or taste remains amongst us" (*BLJ* March 20, 1820; 7:61). Yet Byron had never meant to include Revd. Bowles in his attack on these levelers. "What I say of the *democracy* of poetry cannot apply to Mr. Bowles," he wrote to Murray, "but to the Cockney and Water washing-tub Schools" (*BLJ* May 10, 1821; 8:111). For his attack on the democracy of poets, Byron shifted his focus from William Bowles to John Keats and Leigh Hunt.

It is true that Byron himself had written poetry in a style that debased the public taste. He distinguished between himself, a repentant author who still admired Pope, however, from blackguards like Leigh Hunt and John Keats, who deliberately defied Pope's poetic example. "Of the praises of that little dirty blackguard KEATES in the Edinburgh—I shall observe as Johnson did when Sheridan the actor got a *pension*. 'What has *he* got a pension? Then it is time that I should give up *mine*.'—Nobody could be prouder of the praises of the Edinburgh than I was—or more alive to their censure—as I showed in English Bards and Scotch Reviewers—at present *all the men* they have ever praised are degraded by that insane article" (*BLJ* September 18, 1820; 7:229). Byron's threat to abandon the *Edinburgh* for the *Quarterly*, a Whig for a Tory magazine, illustrates the political subtext behind his attack on poetic blackguards.

The political subtext to Byron's two letters to Bowles is most apparent in an addendum to his letter (*BLJ* March 12, 1821), which he later (*BLJ* March 13, 1821; 8:93) asked Murray to remove. In the second letter, Byron objected to the social class of Pope's detractors and to the movement they had helped to found. By asking Murray to remove this addendum to his second letter, Byron both said and unsaid the elitism that had been the subtext to his two letters to Bowles.

> Far be it from me to presume that there ever was or can be such a thing as an *Aristocracy* of *Poets* ... but there *is* a Nobility of thought and of Style—open to all Stations—and derived partly from talent—& partly from education,—which is to be found in Shakespeare—and Pope—and Burns—no less than in Dante and Alfieri—but which is no-where to be perceived in the Mockbirds & bards of Mr. Hunt['s] little chorus.—If I were asked to define what this Gentlemanliness is—I should say that it is only to be defined by *examples*,—of those who have it,—& those who have it not.—In *Life*,—I should say that most *military* men have it,—& few *Naval*;—that several men of rank have

> it—and few lawyers—that it is more frequent among authors than divines . . . and that . . . it is far more generally diffused among women than among men. . . . Your vulgar Writer is always most vulgar—the higher his subject. . . . (*FL* 160)

The phrase, "*Aristocracy of Poets*" shows how Byron used the connotations of one word to define another. He expunged, or attempted to expunge, the language of its social connotations: his aristocracy was open to all stations; his nobility was not of rank but of "thought and of Style"; the quality of gentlemanliness was more prevalent among women than men. Though he seemed to be purifying language of its class and gender bias, however, Byron actually reinscribed bias by choosing words with distinct social connotations such as "vulgar," "noble," "gentleman," and "aristocracy." His use of social terms to conduct an aesthetic argument was his method of dismissing Pope's opponents on the basis of their social class.

Arguing from a weak theoretical position, Byron attempted to overawe Bowles with examples proving the existence of an aristocracy of poets. Yet Byron admitted that "Gentlemanliness," the very term that gained one entry into this aristocracy, was undefinable. "If I were asked to define what this Gentlemanliness is," he wrote, "I should say that it is only to be defined by *examples,*—of those who have it, and those who have it not." Byron's definition of gentlemanliness, in other words, is indistinguishable from his definition of the aristocracy itself: "several men of rank have it, and few lawyers." Using social distinctions to justify his aesthetic categories, reinforcing one hierarchy with another, Byron showed how gentlemanliness in poetry was most often found among gentlemen in real life. Though he would never "presume to assert" that there is an aristocracy of poets—"Far be it from me," he says—he uses phrases like "a Nobility of thought and of style" that amount to the same thing.

The same effort to use social class as a means of determining aesthetic worth is apparent at the close of Byron's second letter to Bowles. Here the language of social class was most pronounced. At first Byron distinguished between the words "coarse" and "vulgar." He soon found he could not maintain this distinction without using other labels such as "shabby-genteel" to support it.[19] "The grand distinction of the Under forms of the New School of poets is their *Vulgarity,*" he wrote. "By this I do not mean that they are *Coarse*—but 'shabby-genteel'—as it is termed.—A man may be *coarse* & yet not *vulgar*—and the reverse.—Burns is often coarse—but never *vulgar.*—Chatterton is never vulgar;—nor Wordsworth—nor the higher of the Lake school, though they treat of low life in all it's branches" (*FL* 159). Coarse poets, content with their own social station, do not threaten the status of the aristocrat. Only the social climbers, the "Shabby-genteel" poets, can do that.

Byron thus made the social pretension of the "Under forms of the New School of poets" (*CMP* 159) the consummate expression of their "vulgarity." The more the "shabby-genteel" (*CMP* 159) poets tried to rise in social class, the more vulgar they proved themselves to be. The lower middle class, of course, became most tellingly vulgar when they threatened the status of aristocrats by wearing finery that obscured their social station. "It is in their *finery* that the New-under School—are most vulgar," Byron instructed the reader, "and they may be known by this at once—as what we called at Harrow 'a Sunday Blood' might be easily distinguished from a Gentleman—although his cloathes might be the better-cut—and his boots the best-blackened of the two—probably because he made the one—or cleaned the other with his own hands" (*FL* 159). The labor the lower-middle-class man expended in mimicking the gentleman disqualified him for the title he struggled to achieve. Yet appearances were deceptive. The clothes of a "Sunday Blood" were better cut than those of the gentleman. Throughout his debate with Bowles, Byron decoded such appearances. He had to expose the poetic imposters who mocked Pope as surely as he explained the vulgarity of the Sunday Blood's clothing.

Byron repeatedly cast his aesthetic distinctions in the language of social class. He expended so much energy comparing Hunt and Keats to "shabby-genteel" members of society that he no longer seemed to be discussing poetry at all. "[I]t is a thing to be felt—more than explained," Byron wrote:

> let any man take up a volume of Mr. Hunt's subordinate writers—read (if possible) a couple of pages & pronounce for himself if they contain not the kind of writing—which may be likened to "shabby-genteel" in actual life.— When he has done this let him take up Pope—and when he has laid him down—take up the Cockneys again;—if he can—. (*FL* 160)

What Byron never makes clear is how writing may be termed "shabby-genteel." And here Byron's argument is at its weakest. For most of the writers he describes as shabby-genteel (Burns is an exception) are middle class, too anxious to dress up their language in "finery." Byron's argument is hopelessly circular.

But there was another reason Byron's argument was ineffective. Repeatedly, he encouraged his readers to subject authors to the same class considerations they used to judge each other socially. He alluded to an ideal of gentility which the Cockney poets had violated. But with the rise of a wealthy manufacturing class, these considerations were becoming less important. Even from Italy, Byron could perceive the change in social structure that was occurring in England. Perhaps sensing the weakness of his position, Byron wrote to his publisher carefully specifying that Murray remove the class-conscious addendum to his second letter to Bowles. By reading the omitted sections of his attack on Bowles, we can see how Byron's defense of Pope was, at least in part, an attempt to bolster social distinctions that were in the process of dissolving.

By March 1820, Byron's neoclassical dramatic principles conflicted with his own poetic practice. On the one hand, he had defended Pope's poetry against William Bowles. On the other hand, he was writing *Don Juan*, a poem that was innovative aesthetically, if not politically. By searching for a form for his fictions, Byron sought, analogously, a form for his political ideas. The question of political form is central to his thoughts at the time of his writing *Don Juan* and *Marino Faliero*. In a diary entry, for example, he wondered which form of government was the worst and concluded that it was impossible to say, "all are so bad.—As for democracy it is the worst of the whole—for *what is (in fact)* democracy? an Aristocracy of Blackguards" (*BLJ* May 1, 1821; 8:107). Byron's search for an aesthetic form in his debate with Bowles reveals the complexity of his politics, for Byron, despite his battles for liberty, was not consistently democratic any more than he was consistently romantic. Perhaps it is not unfair to say that Byron's attempt to defend an aristocracy of poets in his debate with Bowles was his oblique way of making public his distaste for an aristocracy of blackguards. Not even a poetic aristocracy such as Byron had described, however, could prevent William Bowles and a new generation of poets like Keats and Hunt from "get[ting] into Lord's Ground."

MARINO FALIERO

There is an obvious similarity between Byron's championing of Pope in his poetry and his defense of the unities in the introduction to *Marino Faliero*. In both cases, he showed a preference for the work of an eighteenth-century writer like Pope over the romantic license exhibited by his own generation. Not surprisingly, he matched his aesthetic preferences for neoclassical poetry and drama with nostalgia for the political systems of that time. Writing to Hobhouse and Murray, Byron remembered with fondness the power of the Whigs in eighteenth-century England to lead and shape social change. Both the aesthetic preference for Augustan dramas and the political views which that preference implies will form the subject for the second half of this chapter. Richard Lansdowne has shown how Byron championed neoclassicism and rejected Shakespeare's example, but nevertheless alluded frequently to *Julius Caesar* in *Marino Faliero*.[20] Byron's involvement in the Pope-Bowles controversy and the Italian struggle for independence provide further examples of the tension between his theory and practice. Byron's aesthetic and political views cannot be separated, for Byron chose to obey the unities at the precise moment when he was becoming involved in the cause of Italian liberty.

When Byron began *Marino Faliero* in 1820, he modeled his play after classical principles and intended it as closet drama, "for the reader, not for the stage."[21] In drama as in poetry, Byron wished to change the taste of his day. Having read a number of plays as a member of the subcommittee of the Drury Lane Board of Managers in 1815, Byron had seen the danger of romantic license when applied to the theatre. *Marino Faliero* was immune from these faults. "There are neither rings, nor mistakes, nor starts, nor outrageous ranting villains, nor melodrama in it," he wrote to John Murray. "All this will prevent its popularity, but does not persuade me that it is *therefore* faulty. Whatever faults it has will arise from deficiency in the conduct, rather than in the conception, which is simple and severe" (*BLJ* February 16, 1821; 8:78). The unified, coherent form of classical drama appealed strongly to Byron. "If you want to have a notion of what I am trying to do, take up a translation of any of the Greek tragedians," he wrote in an earlier letter (*BLJ* January 4, 1821; 8:57).[22]

Byron's ambivalent attitude toward his own audience was readily apparent in his decision to write closet drama, as David Erdman observes.[23] In the introduction to *Marino Faliero*, Byron explained why his play would not be performed: "the trampling of an intelligent or of an ignorant audience on a production which, be it good or bad, has been a mental labour to the writer, is a palpable and immediate grievance, heightened by a man's doubt of their competency to judge, and his certainty of his own imprudence in electing them his judges" (*CPW* 4:305).[24] Byron wrote closet drama for the elite in taste and judgment. Though he wished to reform drama he did not want to subject himself to an audience's direct rebuke.

By writing what he called "mental theatre," in other words, Byron resisted the democratic implications of having his play performed (*BLJ* August 23, 1821; 8:187). Byron doubted the competency of his audience to judge him as surely as he doubted their capacity to lead their own revolution. The writer who elected an audience to be his judge was in the same position as a patrician who divested himself of political power and granted that power to others through political reform. Such a man—whether his name was Marino Faliero or Lord Byron—submitted himself to his inferiors and became aware of "his own imprudence in electing them his judges."

The phrase "electing them his judges" deserves consideration, since it betrays Byron's class consciousness, as does his use of the word "swine" to describe them. "You see what it is to throw pearls to swine," he informed Shelley. "As long as I write the exaggerated nonsense which has corrupted the public taste, they applauded to the very echo, and, now that I have really composed, within these three or four years, some things which [they] should 'not willingly let die,' the whole herd snort and grumble" (*BLJ* September 19, 1818; 6:67). Byron justified his snobbery toward his audience by arguing that this attitude was reciprocal. According to Byron, the public preferred work by men of low birth such as Hunt and Keats to that of aristocrats like Horace Walpole and himself. "It is the fashion to underrate Horace Walpole; firstly, because he was a nobleman, and secondly, because he was a gentleman" (*CPW* 4:305), he wrote in the introduction to *Marino Faliero*. Concerned that he would receive similar treatment, Byron inveighed against this egalitarian strain in romanticism which had corrupted the taste of readers. "Shakespeare and Otway had a million of advantages over me," Byron told John Murray, "besides the incalculable one of having been *dead* from one to two Centuries—and having been both born blackguards (which *are* such attractions to the Gentle living reader)" (*BLJ* August 8, 1820; 7:194). By adhering to the unities in *Marino Faliero* and arguing for dramatic reform, Byron registered his disapproval of a certain leveling strain of romanticism.

Byron's decision to obey the unities also influenced his play's political content. Observing the unities led him "to represent the conspiracy as already formed, and the Doge [as merely] acceding to it," he wrote in his introduction, "whereas in fact it was of his own preparation and that of Israel Bertuccio" (*CPW* 4:306). The difference between acceding to a rebellion, however, and actually forming one is crucial, since it influences the audience's view of whether the doge was actively or only passively involved in the conspiracy. The conservative aesthetic form Byron chose for his play, in other words, coopted and contained its disruptive political content, turning his hero from a man who starts a rebellion into one who resists the collective action of the citizens to which he has only "acceded."[25]

Certainly, a revolutionary play written in a neoclassical form would seem to be pointing in two different directions at the same time. Aesthetically, the poet respects and reveres tradition; politically, Byron wrote a play that was so revolutionary it could not be performed in London without an "uproar."[26] In order to explain Byron's ambivalent attitude toward tradition, I will turn now from the aesthetic theories that inform the play to the play itself.

Marino Faliero concerns the failed attempt of a fourteenth-century Venetian doge to overthrow the state of which he was reigning chief. Faliero assumes his revolutionary role because of an insult he receives at the hands of Michel Steno. As doge, Faliero cannot revenge himself on Steno, but must wait for the Council of Forty to pronounce judgment upon him. When Steno is sentenced to a month "in close arrest," Faliero is unsatisfied. He resolves to avenge his honor against Steno's insult and the lenient punishment imposed by the Council of Forty, his aristocratic peers. At the same time, he expresses his desire to liberate Venice from the tyrannical rule of a corrupt aristocracy.[27] Faliero will both avenge his wrongs and free Venice—the relative importance of each objective for Faliero is not clear.

Samuel Chew and G. Wilson Knight stress Byron's political idealism in *Marino Faliero*. For Samuel Chew, Faliero is a revolutionary hero and Byron is "here, as always,... the poet of revolution"; Knight calls the play Byron's "greatest political work," because of the democratic values it expresses.[28] Far from asserting the value of liberty, however, *Marino Faliero* actually charts the hero's progressive disenchantment with the democratic cause. "Despite his statements of sympathy," Peter Manning observes, "Byron provides little evidence in *Marino Faliero* from which it can be decided whether the revolution Faliero embarks upon is justified."[29] Motivated by aristocratic pride, Faliero seeks to overthrow the Council of Forty when he discovers that they will not avenge his honor against the ribaldry of Michel Steno. In a letter to his publisher, John Murray, Byron specified Faliero's motives as "a private grievance against one of the Patricians" (*BLJ* February 25, 1817; 5:174). Faliero's contempt for law, his respect for social hierarchy and for the natural hierarchy that reaffirms it, reveal a hero more concerned with his own honor than with the cause of the people he pretends to defend. Nowhere in *Marino Faliero* does the hero commit himself to rash equality.[30] Rather, he leads a revolutionary movement but soon becomes as alienated by democrats as he was by aristocrats.

What first attracted Byron to the story of *Marino Faliero* was not the struggle for liberty as such, but the aristocrat's role in a rebellion. "I mean to write a tragedy upon the subject, which appears to me very dramatic," Byron wrote to John Murray as early as February 25, 1817. "An old man, jealous, and conspiring against the state of which he was actually reigning chief. The last circumstance makes it the most remarkable and only fact of the kind in all the history of all nations" (*BLJ* February 25, 1817; 5:174). By focusing on the aristocratic rebel's perspective, Byron undermined the democratic assumptions that the play would seem to affirm, showing his readers the danger of violating social hierarchies.

Throughout the play, Faliero feels superior not only to other aristocrats but to the citizens whose cause he actually joins.[31] When Israel Bertuccio seeks Faliero's active participation in the revolutionary plot, the doge shows how reluctant he is to act collectively. "We!—We!" he says facetiously, "no matter— you have earn'd the right,/To talk of *us*" (*CPW* 4:3.1.65–66). But this right is never quite earned. The doge's ambivalent attitude toward the conspirators can be seen by his inability to gracefully decline their offer to elect him as their leader. "I cannot stoop—that is, I am not fit/To lead a band of—patriots" (*CPW* 4:3.2.220–21). He corrects himself, substituting the word "fit" for "stoop," but the implication is obvious: Faliero still retains enough class pride to condescend to his compatriots. As he is tried for his crimes, Faliero refers to Bertuccio and Calendaro by the aristocratic names they have adopted. Yet the doge's act of renaming only underscores the differences between them, since he calls them "the plebeian Brutus . . . And the quick Cassius of the arsenal" (*CPW* 4:5.1.177–8).

As he meets with the revolutionaries for the first time, Faliero underscores the self-destructive aspect of his liberalism. Fittingly, he delivers his speech dedicating himself to the radical cause in a graveyard, beneath a statue of his dead ancestors. "The interview before the embodiment of his patrimony brings out the doge's ambivalence toward the rebellion," Manning notes in *Lord Byron and His Fictions*, "and to highlight it Byron happily departed from the historical accuracy and the unities he touted; he told Murray that 'all that is said of his *Ancestral Doges*, as buried at St. John's and Paul's, is altered from the fact, *they being in St. Mark's*'" (*BLJ* October 12, 1820; 7:201).[32]

The doge feels watched by his dead relatives as he plots to overthrow the Forty, an oligarchy which his family has served and been part of for so long. "Think you that he looks down on us, or no?" he asks Israel. When Bertuccio replies that "there are/No eyes in marble," the doge is still unconvinced.

> Deem'st thou the souls of such a race as mine
> Can rest, when he, their last descendant chief,
> Stands plotting on the brink of their pure graves
> With stung plebeians?
> (CPW 4:3.1.99–102)

he asks Israel. By the end of his speech, Faliero has answered his own question: "Each stab to them will seem my suicide" (*CPW* 4:3.2.472), he says.

Alienated from his own class deliberately, Faliero is no less estranged from the common people whose cause he has championed. When Faliero is executed after the plot has failed, two citizens strain to hear the hero's last words:

> 'Twas but a murmur—Curse upon the distance!
> His words are inarticulate, but the voice
> Swells up like mutter'd thunder; would we could
> But gather a sole sentence!
> (*CPW* 4:5.4.11–14)

That the citizens cannot hear the words of their great champion, the doge,— that their experience of his execution is both temporally and spatially different from that of the patricians—underscores the "distance" between aristocrats and plebeians that Byron's play was pointing to all along.[33]

In 1820, it seemed to Byron, a "radical" could not express his political views without sacrificing himself to the mob. When Hobhouse was imprisoned for publishing an attack on Lord Erskine that was deemed a breach of privilege,[34] Byron found confirmation for his fears of self-sacrifice and lampooned his friend for his expedient method of getting elected to parliament.[35]

> Would you go to the House by the true gate—
>   Much faster than ever Whig Charley went
> Let the Parliament send you to Newgate,
>   And Newgate will send you to Parliament.
> (*BLJ* April 18, 1820; 7:78)

By relying on the radicals to get elected, Byron argued, Hobhouse curtailed his capacity for effective leadership once he had arrived. "You see the blackguards have brought in Hobhouse for Westminster," he wrote to Richard Hoppner on April 18, 1820, "[but] it will eventually be a millstone round his neck, for what can he do? he can't take place? he can't take power in any case—if he succeeds in reforming—he will be stoned for his pains—and if he fails—there he is stationary as Lecturer for Westminster" (*BLJ* 7:78).[36]

In *Marino Faliero*, Byron dramatized the degrading effects of political office. Faliero returns from the battlefield to find that he has been named Duke of Venice by his peers. Far from greeting this as a promotion, however, Faliero recognizes that a position in government is a "flattering fetter." Like Hobhouse, Faliero is interested in establishing a direct connection with the people. Unlike Hobhouse, however, Faliero knows enough not to seek such enslavement in the senate. "I sought it not," he informs Israel, "the flattering fetters met me/Returning from my Roman embassy,/And never having hitherto refused/Toil, charge, or duty for the state, I did not,/At these late years, decline what was the highest/Of all in seeming, but of all most base/In what we have to do and to endure" (*CPW* 4:1.2.445–451). Faliero finds the pageant of power he has been granted as a politician an insult to the dignity he has earned as a soldier. Repeatedly, Faliero distinguishes between the two roles. "I have lived and toiled a soldier and a servant/Of Venice and her peoples, not the senate," he says. At another point, he contrasts his valor in battle with the cowardly patricians who have given him a title but no power. "From my equality with you in birth,/And my superiority in action,/You drew me from my honorable toils/In distant lands . . . to/Stand crown'd, but bound and helpless, at the altar" (*CPW* 4:5.1.202–7), he tells them. As doge, Faliero is both "crowned" and "bound" by his civic responsibilities. Faliero's search for power has ended with a form of enslavement, precisely the fate Byron predicted for Hobhouse.

Though doge, Faliero prides himself on his military background rather than on his political office. Angiolina flatters Faliero's self-conception at his trial. While Faliero was protecting the commonwealth of Venice and fighting for its glory, she argues, the men who sat in judgment upon him were seeking their own political advancement. Without Faliero, she insists, there would be no commonwealth of Venice and no legal system to condemn him. For Angiolina, the conqueror is more important for a republic than the politician, the man of action superior to the man of words.

Despite Angiolina's defense, Byron and Faliero's militarist brand of liberalism is problematic. In "Ode to Napoleon Bonaparte" and in his correspondence, Byron chastised Napoleon for allowing the quest for military glory to divert him from the more important task of liberating the people from tyrannical rule.

> But thou forsooth must be a king,
> And don the purple vest,—
> As if that foolish robe could wring
> Remembrance from thy breast.
> Where is that faded garment? where
> The gewgaws thou wert fond to wear,
> The star—the string—the crest?
> Vain froward child of empire! say,
> Are all thy playthings snatch'd away?
> (*CPW* 3:18)

Like Napoleon, Faliero finds himself fascinated with the "gewgaws" of power; he longs to exchange his ducal bonnet for a crown. "I pray you to resume what you have spurn'd," Bertuccio says of the ducal bonnet, "Till you can change it haply for a crown" (*CPW* 4:1.2.253–54). After Bertuccio departs, the doge addresses his ducal cap. "Beset with all the thorns that line a crown," he says, "Without investing the insulted brow/With the all-swaying majesty of kings;/Thou idle, gilded, and degraded toy" (*CPW* 4:1.2.260–63). Even Israel describes the doge as one "Who would become a throne, or overthrow one" (*CPW* 4:2.2.163). When he is asked by Israel and others his motives for joining a plebeian rebellion, the doge replies that he wishes to be sovereign of the people but only if the people are happy. He believes in "equal rights," he says on another occasion, but "not rash equality" (*CPW* 4:3.2.170). No democrat, Faliero fights to become king of Venice, to punish his peers for their lax sentence on Steno, and to elevate himself above the other nobles.

Like Faliero, Byron sought a political career not only to achieve liberal social policies but to prove himself the first of men. Though he was concerned with the plight of the Nottinghamshire weavers, he was, arguably, more concerned with the credit he would win by the speech he delivered on their behalf. Byron noted the reactions assiduously in his diary and letters. Sir Francis Burdett told him it was "the best speech by a *Lord* since the 'Lord knows when,'" while Lord Grenville informed him that the "constructions of some of [his] periods are very like Burke's!!" (*BLJ* March 5, 1812, 2:167). Eight years later, Byron distinguished his political views from those of Hobhouse by participating in a revolutionary rather than a parliamentary struggle. English radicals adopted dubious causes, Byron argued, such as defending Queen Caroline against the charge of infidelity, while Italian liberty was a cause worthy of a man of action.[37]

The schism in Byron's politics—between his attitude toward events in England and Italy—is never more apparent than when he discusses the intended audience for his play. *Marino Faliero* was not meant for England, he tells Murray, but was "purely Venetian." Despite this disclaimer, Byron knew that English and Venetian politics were not so easily separated. Thomas Otway's *Venice Preserved*, a model for Byron's play, drew parallels between the system of government shared by the two countries. Even William Hazlitt found Venice an important model for English political institutions and dedicated over fourteen hundred pages to the subject in *The Venetian Republic: Its Rise, Its Growth, and Its Fall*. Historically, the English Whigs looked to the Venetian oligarchy of the Renaissance as a precedent for their own oligarchical rule in England. Like the Venetian nobility, English noblemen protected their political rights from royal encroachments in 1688 and, less successfully, in 1820. In situating his play in Venice, in other words, Byron invited comparisons between the Venetian revolution of 1455 and the English revolution that seemed imminent. So volatile were political events in England, in fact, that a vague reference to virtue in Byron's play caused a furor when it was performed in London because it was interpreted as a defence of the Queen in the scandal created by the divorce proceedings.[38] The *Morning Chronicle* (April 26) declared that "the times . . . prepare the minds of men for the bold and daring sentiments with which it abounds," while the *European Magazine and London Review* (79 [January–June, 1821], 453) observed that "the anti-patriotic sentiments scattered throughout the play seemed to constitute its strongest, and almost only, hold upon public opinion."[39]

Yet Byron saw his support for the Italian revolution as an extension of his Whig principles. In his letter to the Neapolitan insurgents, for example, Byron made this connection explicit. "As a member of the English House of Peers," he wrote, "he would be a traitor to the principles which placed the reigning family of England, if he were not grateful for the noble lesson so lately given both to people and to kings" (*BLJ* October ? 1820; 7:187–88). Byron portrayed himself as a "friend to liberty" who was merely exhibiting "the enthusiasm natural to a cultivated man" in assisting the Neapolitans in their "determination ... to assert their well-won independence." Far from being suicidal, Byron's revolutionary activity in Italy actually perpetuated the political principles of the Whigs: he would have been a traitor to "the principles which placed the reigning family of England" if he had acted otherwise.

The more Byron struggled to represent his politics in Italy as an extension of the political principles of England, the less continuous they seemed. What was "natural" about Byron's enthusiasm for the Italian cause? What stake did an Englishman have in Italian independence? Why should an English peer be "enthusiastic" about a revolution? Why should "both people and kings" be grateful for the lesson of liberty? How could he support Italian independence with this brand of inclusive rhetoric but not English political reform? Byron's statement of support, in other words, was marked by distinctions which were only partially resolved: member/traitor, well-won/assert. By casting his declaration to the insurgents in the third person, moreover, Byron distanced himself from their cause in the very act of supporting it.

To examine Byron's play from a purely political point of view, however, obscures the personal context in which he composed it. Byron bragged to his publisher that he could not copy out a scene of the play without Teresa Guiccioli interrupting his labors to request an assignation in the house of her husband (*BLJ* October 8, 1820; 9:24). Byron even joined the Carbonari, in part, because Teresa's father and brother were members, and the dramatic personae of the play reflect Byron's personal history. Like Teresa Guiccioli, Angiolina married a man three times her age; like Steno, Byron was a "rank, rash patrician" of sorts who came between the elderly man and his bride; and like the doge, the count reacted with a certain degree of antagonism toward Lord Byron. A minor character in the drama, moreover, bears the same name as Teresa's brother, Pietro. Teresa's father, Count Ruggero Gamba Ghiselli, and Pietro "were among the staunchest supporters of libertarian principles in Ravenna, and soon became leaders of the revolutionary society of the Carbonari," Marchand explains.[40] Though Byron lived the life of a domesticated libertine in Venice during his affair with Teresa, he wrote a play that would seem to condemn youthful libertinism outright. It is almost as if Byron took revenge on his own sexual passion by denying it to his hero. No Byronic hero, Faliero is the diametrical opposite of the libertine Childe Harold and, to a lesser extent, of Don Juan,[41] whom Byron was creating at the same time. In *Marino Faliero*, controlling one's sexual passion is a symptom of self-control.

BYRON'S PURITANICAL DOGE

Marino Faliero is indeed quite puritanical in its defense of the doge and Angiolina's sexless marriage. Though Faliero has many passions, sexual passion never predominates. "For in my fieriest youth," the doge tells Angiolina in Act 2, "I sway'd such passions; nor was this my age/Infected with that leprosy of lust/ Which taints the hoariest years of vicious men" (*CPW* 4:2.1.313–316).[42] Even Faliero's curse on Venice is puritanical, connecting Venice's political corruption with its sexual sins. He warns of a time when Venice will be left to the bastard offspring of the adulteress and the libertine. "The few who still retain a wreck/Of their great fathers' heritage shall fawn," and others "Proud of some name they have disgraced, or sprung/From an adulteress boastful of her guilt/With some large gondolier or foreign soldier,/Shall bear about their bastardy in triumph/To the third spurious generation" (*CPW* 4:5.3.64–65, 69–72).

I have said that Byron took revenge on his own libertine conduct by denying it to the hero of his play. As a puritanical figure, the doge repeatedly decries female inconstancy. "Vice cannot fix, and virtue cannot change," he tells Angiolina. "The once fall'n woman must for ever fall;/For vice must have variety, while virtue/Stands like the sun, and all which rolls around/Drinks life, and light, and glory from her aspect" (*CPW* 4:2:1.394–398). The personal significance of Faliero's speech for Byron becomes readily apparent when we read Byron's letters. Specifically, the speech recalls a poem Byron wrote to Lady Melbourne describing his affair with Caroline Lamb.

> The first step of error none e'er could recall
> And the woman once fallen forever must fall,
> Pursue to the last the career she begun,
> And be false unto many, as faithless to one
> (*BLJ* September 18, 1812; 2:200)

In both his play and in the poem that predates it, Byron emphasizes the woman's fallenness: "The woman once fallen forever must fall." Yet it was not only women who fell. As both writer and libertine, Byron repeated his sin, "fall[ing] forever" and forever writing ("recall[ing]") that fall. His next affair, for example, was with Lady Frances Webster, who received the following words of advice, words Byron might have more aptly penned to himself.

> Then fare thee well, Fanny,
> Now doubly undone,
> To prove false unto many
> As faithless to one.
> Thou art past all recalling,

> Even would I recall,
> For the woman once falling
> Forever must fall.⁴³
> (CPW 3:320–24)

In this unpublished stanza from "When We Two Parted" (1814), Byron transfers the Calvinist conceit of irredeemable sin to Lady Caroline Lamb and then Lady Frances Webster as if to escape the moral consequences of his own involvement in these affairs.⁴⁴

Byron's prose, poetry, and drama show him fascinated by the relationship between libertine conduct and moral turpitude. In *Marino Faliero*, Byron pits libertines against liberals, contrasting Steno and Bertram with Faliero.⁴⁵ Steno is a man who does not know how "to demean himself in ducal chambers," Faliero tells Angiolina (*CPW* 4:2.1.425), while Bertram is suspected of lurking "in narrow places," with "Disbanded soldiers, discontented ruffians/And desperate libertines who brawl in taverns" (*CPW* 4:4.1.225–28). He is "a patrician,/Young, galliard, gay, and haughty," his nephew observes (*CPW* 4:1:2:21). As such, Steno is not unlike the Byron of 1812 (whose squibs in the *Morning Chronicle* were an attack on royal prerogatives) or the Byron of 1820 (who was playing a libertine and disruptive role in Teresa and especially Alessandro's life by breaking the very convention of *cavalier servente* to which he pretended to adhere). The play is a hymn to inconstancy and all that it inherits. For libertinism is not only a sexual but a political sin: it is the betrayal of the patriarchy.

The other villain of Byron's play, Bertram, is an orphan who has no sense of patriarchy, no father to give him a sense of civic responsibility.⁴⁶ He betrays the conspirators and is, as Faliero asserts, a double villain, unfaithful to the conspirators and the aristocracy alike. Though he did not repeat Bertram's apostasy, Byron used his fatherless upbringing to excuse his libertine affairs in 1812. "What better can be expected of me?" he asked Augusta. In the fourth act, Lioni suspects that Bertram's libertine lifestyle has somehow led him to revolutionary actions:⁴⁷

> I know that there are angry spirits
> And turbulent mutterers of stifled treason
> Who lurk in narrow palaces, and walk out
> Muffled to whisper curses to the night;
> Disbanded soldiers, discontented ruffians,
> And desperate libertines who brawl in taverns;
> *Thou* herdest not with such: 'tis true, of late
> I have lost sight of thee, but thou were wont
> To lead a temperate life, and break thy bread
> With honest mates, and bear a cheerful aspect.
> What hath come to thee? in thy hollow eye

And hueless cheek, and thine unquiet motions,
Sorrow and shame and conscience seem at war
To waste thee?
(*CPW* 4:4.1.223–33)

Byron faults Hobhouse for the same libertine associations. "Why write it?" Byron asked Hobhouse, concerning the letter to Lord Erskine, "why lend yourself to Hunt and Cobbett—and the bones of Tom Paine? . . . You used to be thought a prudent man . . . but methinks you are waxed somewhat rash at least in politics" (*BLJ* March 3, 1820; 7:50). In the early 1820s, not only Hobhouse, imprisoned in Newgate, but the Spenceans and Cato Street conspirators showed Byron how licentious conduct could lead to revolutionary actions.

In contrast to these libertine men is Marino Faliero, the liberal of Byron's play. "[H]is mind is liberal," Israel Bertuccio says of him in act 2, scene 2. "He sees and feels the people are oppress'd,/And shares their sufferings" (*CPW* 4: 2.2.175). Byron is careful to use the word "liberal" to describe Faliero, distinguishing him from the radical and libertine conspirators whose cause he joins. As a liberal Whig, in other words, Faliero leads the revolution with discretion: he is a gentleman bred to the business. If he sympathizes with the oppressed, he also sympathizes with the members of his own social class. As a liberal, he "feels" the crime he commits; he has only contempt for the conspirators who, like butchers, would murder the aristocrats without compunction. Unlike Bertram, Faliero can overcome his liberal sympathies to perform revolutionary actions for the good of the state.

In *Marino Faliero*, Byron was able to separate liberals and libertines quite tidily. Faliero's only liberal failing is his inability to forgive Steno. Angiolina goes the furthest toward explaining the reason for this failure by distinguishing between Steno and Faliero, the libertine and the liberal. "The vile are only vain," Angiolina notes, "the great are proud" (*CPW* 4:2.1.210). In his own life, however, Byron was both libertine and liberal. One example of Byron's tendency to achieve a moral purity in his play which he could not achieve in his own life concerns the dichotomy he draws between words and actions. Certainly, soldiers fare much better than writers in this play. Byron associated Steno, whose only action appears to be linguistic, with all that's base in Venice. Faliero has led a life of virtue; he has "swept kings from their thrones," only to have these actions blasted away by "A miscreant's angry breath" (*CPW* 4:2.1.421).

Yet the doge believes that "true *words* are *things*" (*CPW* 4:5.1.288). If he did not, he would not bother to curse Venice or to add that "walls have ears—nay, more, they have tongues" (*CPW* 4:5.1.279). For Faliero as for Byron, true words have lasting, even prophetic value. Byron seems to recuperate his poetic vocation in Faliero's assertion that "[T]rue *words* are *things,*/And dying men's are things which long outlive,/And oftentimes avenge them" (*CPW* 4: 5.1.288–290). Throughout his poetic career, Byron used the phrase, "words are things," and did so with an increasing respect for the poet's vocation. In an 1813 diary entry, Byron preferred Anthony the conqueror to Cicero the politician (*BLJ* November 16, 1813; 3:207) and he later repeated this preference, facetiously, by noting that words were not "things" to Sheridan as they had been for the Comte de Mirabeau (*BLJ* February 27, 1814; 4:74); in canto 3 of *Don Juan* (1820), however, he marveled at the effect which one drop of ink could have on men's minds (*CPW* 5:3:88); in *Marino Faliero*, completed later that same year, he was most optimistic of all, identifying with Faliero's assertion that words can outlive even the actions of the dying man who utters them (5.1.289). His four uses of the phrase "words are things," then, illustrated the development of his liberal imagination (a development that mirrored that of Mirabeau): he moved from a stance of hostility toward the writer to one of admiration.

Byron's decisions to fight for a liberal cause, to continue his liberal style of poetry, and to write for a periodical he named *The Liberal* all occurred within two years. Clearly, Byron was adapting to the times. In his debate with Bowles, as in *Marino Faliero*, Byron was deeply distrustful of the new relationship to words that poets were forging. He worried that the poetic systems of Hunt and Keats would degrade and thereby enslave a generation of writers. Similarly, he was skeptical of the new political vocabulary emerging in England and attacked his friend Hobhouse for associating with the radicals. He worried that libertinism led inevitably to radicalism. Only when he found his own cause to champion (liberty in Italy) and a word to describe it (liberal), did he abandon the reactionary rhetoric that marked his letters to Hobhouse. Only when he felt more confident about the new poetic style of *Don Juan* did he become less concerned with attacking the works of his contemporaries. Now he could assume a more liberal posture. In drama, his aesthetic theories and his regard for Pope gave way to a romantic poem written in a new style, for *Don Juan* was not simply another *Dunciad*.[48] In politics, his preference for Whig leadership gave way to the belief that the people could lead themselves. Though the Whig ideal of an aristocratic ruler had died, as surely as the Neapolitan revolution would fail, Byron was still guided by that ideal, even as he knew that the noble energy of the Italians would ultimately make them capable of governing themselves. "And yet there are materials in this people," he wrote of the Italians during their revolution, "and a noble energy, if well directed. But who is to direct them? No matter. Out of such times heroes spring. Difficulties are the hot-beds of high spirits, and Freedom the mother of the few virtues incident to human nature" (*BLJ* January 9, 1821; 8:19).

NOTES

1. For a groundbreaking discussion of Keats and social class, see Marjorie Levinson, *Keats's Life of Allegory: The Origins of a Style* (Oxford and Cambridge, Mass.: Blackwell, 1990), 4 and passim, and "A Question of Taste: Keats and Byron," in *Rereading Byron: Essays Selected from the Hofstra University's Byron Bicentennial Conference*, ed. by Alice Levine and Robert N. Keane (New York: Garland, 1993), 187–204.

2. Bertrand Russell, *A History of Western Philosophy* (New York: Touchstone, 1972), 747. Wilfred S. Dowden states that "Byron's love of freedom would not let him stand idly by while there was fighting for the oppressed to be done." E. D. H. Johnson, by contrast, sees Byron as a true descendant of the eighteenth century, and not the "unreal hero" of the romantic revolt. Malcolm Kelsall states that "the life of Byron is of no political significance." Kelsall's book has influenced the present study considerably and is an important corrective to previously overblown accounts that portray Byron as a democratic liberal. Dowden, "Byron and the Austrian Censorship," *Keats-Shelley Journal* 4 (winter 1955): 67; Johnson, "Lord Byron in Don Juan: A Study in Digression" (Ph.D. diss., Yale University, 1939); Kelsall, *Byron's Politics*, 2.

3. For the slipperiness of "class" as a category, see Jeffrey N. Cox, *Poetry and Politics in the Cockney School* (Cambridge: Cambridge University Press, 1998), 48. Cox cites Raymond Williams, Asa Briggs, and Harold Perkin to show that society's divisions into "wage laborers, capitalists, and landlords was being historically enacted" during this time period.

4. For a history of the conflict, see J. Van Rennes, *Bowles, Byron and the Pope-Controversy* (Amsterdam: H. J. Paris, 1927), which contains excerpts from Bowles's letters, Byron's two letters in response, and Hazlitt's essay ridiculing the participants. Andrew Nicholson provides a more recent bibliography of the conflict (*CMP* 408–09), though he omits James Chandler's article in his discussion of critical literature on the topic (408). I have taken my references to Bowles's letters and Byron's response from Nicholson's edition, marking Byron's first letter *(FL)* and his second *(SL)* parenthetically in the text.

5. J. J. Rennes, *Bowles, Byron and the Pope-Controversy* (Amsterdam: H. J. Paris, 1927), 522–36; Nicholson, *CMP* 401.

6. William Keach, "Cockney Couplets: Keats and the Politics of Style," *Studies in Romanticism* 25 (summer 1986): 187. For an excellent discussion of Byron's personal motives in entering the Pope-Bowles controversy, see Frederick W. Shilstone, *Byron and the Myth of Tradition* (Lincoln: University of Nebraska Press, 1988), 234–42.

7. Leslie Mitchell, *Holland House* (London: Duckworth, 1980), 186; Jeffrey N. Cox, *Poetry and Politics in the Cockney School: Keats, Shelley, Hunt and their Circle* (Cambridge: Cambridge University Press, 1998), 55.

8. E. D. H. Johnson, "Lord Byron in 'Don Juan': A Study in Digression," 300.

9. James Chandler, "The Pope Controversy: Romantic Poetics and the English Canon," in *Canons*, ed. Robert von Hallberg (Chicago: University of Chicago Press, 1984), 43.

10. Mark Girouard, *The Return to Camelot: Chivalry and the English Gentleman* (New Haven: Yale University Press, 1981), 233. For a more elaborate argument concerning the

relationship between games and social codes in England, see Maurice Samuel, *The Gentleman and the Jew* (New York: Alfred A. Knopf, 1952), 1–50.

11. Mitchell, *Holland House*, 192.

12. For a similar line of attack, see John Wilson Croker's review of Keats, analyzed by William Keach in *Studies in Romanticism* 25 (summer 1986): 182–94. "In accusing Keats of playing at *bouts rimes*," Keach argues, "Croker insinuates that this low-born London 'neophyte' of Leigh Hunt is abusing Pope by taking seriously a parlor game with which his aristocratic betters merely while away their time on weekends" (184).

13. *The Complete Works of William Hazlitt*, ed. P. P. Howe, 20 vols. (New York: AMS Press, 1967), hereafter referred to as "Howe" with volume and page number.

14. In a letter to Kinnaird, Byron asserts that "a man's trade always brings out his worst qualities" (March 9, 1821; 8:91). He then refers to Murray, facetiously, as a gentleman: "There is one thing I wish to state to Mr. Murray—it was understood and exprest? (by his particular wish) that the *Copyright* of *Beppo* was to cancel all bills of his *up* to 1818 the date of that publication.—Now your House *date his bill* from March *1816*—If this is not a mistake—all I can say is it *ought* to *be one.*–but I have little more to say of that Gentleman" (*BLJ* March 13, 1821; 8:93).

15. Matthew Arnold, "Byron," in *Essays in Criticism: Second Series*. Reprinted in *Matthew Arnold: Selected Prose*, ed. J. Keating (New York: Penguin Books, 1970), 400.

16. For a discussion of how Rousseau's idealistic view of human nature led him to transform the Roman conception of virtue, see Carol Blum, *Rousseau and the Republic of Virtue: The Language of Politics in the French Revolution* (Ithaca, N.Y.: Cornell University Press, 1986), 27–35.

17. McGann, *Don Juan in Context*, 160.

18. Marchand, *Byron: A Biography*, 846. Marchand argues that Byron had an "18th century conception of liberalism as a revolt against tyranny which might go even so far as republicanism, but which always envisioned an aristocratic or gentlemanly leadership. This concept involved trust of the mob and lack of sympathy for democratic or proletarian, or even middle-class, control or participation in government" (*Byron: A Biography*, 841).

19. For a discussion of class conflict in this aesthetic debate, see David Erdman, "Byron and 'The New Force of the People,'" *Keats-Shelley Journal* 11 (1962): 54 and George Cheatham, "Byron's Dislike of Keats' Poetry," *Keats-Shelley Journal* 32 (1983): 20–25.

20. Richard Lansdowne, *Byron's Historical Dramas* (Oxford: Oxford University Press, 1992), 118–133.

21. Paul Trueblood, *Lord Byron* (Boston: Twayne Series, 1968), 108; Richard Lansdowne (*Byron's Historical Dramas* [Oxford: Oxford University Press, 1992], 118–133) focuses on Byron's use of Shakespeare's *Julius Caesar* as a model for *Marino Faliero*, whereas I focus on how Byron's decision to choose a neoclassical form for the play reflected Byron's aristocratic liberalism.

22. For a helpful discussion of Byron's use of the unities, see Samuel Chew's "Byron and the Dramatic Unities," an appendix to his *The Dramas of Lord Byron: A Critical Study* (New York: Russell & Russell, 1964), 165–73.

23. David Erdman, "Byron's Stage Fright: The History of His Ambition and Fear of Writing for the Stage," *ELH* 6 (1939): 219–45.

24. All quotations are taken from Jerome McGann's edition.

25. Other critics have commented on how the conservative aesthetic theory of Byron's play conflicts with its revolutionary practice, but they have not shown how that theory led Byron to alter the content of his play. For an interesting discussion of how form affects content in another work by Byron, see Susan Wolfson, "Couplets, Self, and 'The Corsair,'" *Studies in Romanticism* 27 (winter 1988): 491–515.

26. Erdman, "Byron's Stage Fright," 230.

27. McGann, *Fiery Dust*, 208, 212.

28. Samuel C. Chew, in *The Dramas of Lord Byron*, was reacting against a Victorian tradition which had seen Byron as consonant with "dandyism, Wertherism, scandal, pose" (164) and may have emphasized the idealism of the play in reaction to this kind of criticism. G. Wilson Knight lavishes praise on the play not for its intrinsic merits, but for the revolutionary idealism it espouses. Knight, *Lord Byron: Christian Virtues* (Oxford: Oxford University Press, 1953), 147–48.

29. Peter J. Manning, *Byron and his Fictions* (Detroit: Wayne State University Press, 1978), 110.

30. E. D. H. Johnson, "A Political Interpretation of Byron's 'Marino Faliero,'" *Modern Language Quarterly* 31 (1942): 420; Carl Woodring, *Politics in English Romantic Poetry*, 181–86.

31. Chew, in *The Dramas of Lord Byron*, adopts a different perspective than the one I outline above. He admits that Faliero has a feeling of "caste" about him, but ultimately dismisses the argument that he is as motivated by class consciousness and personal ambition as he is by a love of democracy and the common people (160).

32. Manning, *Byron and His Fictions*, 112.

33. For a discussion of Delacroix's representation of *Marino Faliero* and his use of the politics of space, see Martin Meisel, "Pictorial Engagements: Byron, Delacroix, Ford Madox Brown," *Studies in Romanticism* 27 (winter 1988): 551–62.

34. Hobhouse's "A Trifling Mistake in Lord Erskine's Recent Preface" was a response to Erskine's *A Preface to the Defences of the Whigs*. Robert Zegger has shown that Hobhouse was as distrustful of mob rule as Byron, though he does not draw the comparison. Hobhouse "reminded Erskine that the Radical proposals of 1819 hardly differed from those he and Grey had favored in 1793. . . . On nomination day of the 1819 election he claimed that the Radicals 'never were for annual parliaments and universal suffrage in the pure, bigotted, exclusive sense of the phrase.'" Zegger, *John Cam Hobhouse: A Political Life, 1819–1852* (Columbia: University of Missouri Press, 1973), 75.

35. In his letters to Hobhouse, Byron repeatedly separated the cause of reform from radicals like Hunt, whom he called "scoundrels," "ruffians," "blackguards," "unredeemed dirt," "miscreants," "dinnered blackguards," and "felons." Like Faliero, Byron saw movements as inseparable from the people who led them. For this reason, he distinguished Mirabeau and La Fayette from Robespierre and Marat; Tyler and Cade from Walworth and Iden, as Carl Woodring explains in *Politics in English Romantic Poetry*, 152.

36. And previously, on February 21, 1820. "By the king's death, Mr Hobhouse I hear will stand for Westminster," he informed Murray. "I shall be glad to hear of his standing any where except in the pillory—from which the company he must have lately kept (I always except Burdett—and Douglas K. and the genteel part of the reformers) was perhaps to be apprehended" (*BLJ* February 21, 1820; 7:44).

37. Woodring, *Politics in English Romantic Poetry*, 184–85.

38. David Erdman, "Byron and Revolt in England," *Science & Society* 11 (1947): 234–48.

39. Manning, *Byron and his Fictions*, 121.

40. Marchand, *Byron: A Portrait*, 299.

41. M. K. Joseph in *Byron the Poet* (London: Victor Gollancz, 1966), points out that Byron does not "write in the orthodox tradition of a Don Juan whose naturalism is the source of his wickedness.... He has, in a sense, 'de-Byronised' the Don himself" (307). I would extend Joseph's argument about the character of Don Juan, for I find Faliero equally "de-Byronised," or puritanical.

42. Peter Manning, in *Byron and His Fictions*, notes the "sexual defensiveness" (111) of Faliero, which he compares to Othello. "Unlike Othello, Faliero knows that his wife is chaste, and so his subsequent tirade on the horrors of infidelity is off the mark." Manning argues that "Faliero has retreated into the role of father to protect himself from sexual desires unacceptable to him" (112). My reading of the play is less Freudian and more autobiographical: Faliero's troubled attitude toward sexuality echoes Byron's own, especially his letters admonishing Teresa for submitting to her husband's "dotardly caresses."

43. Marchand, *Byron: A Biography*, 581.

44. *CWP* 3:479n.279. Byronic heroes escape moral judgment by concentrating on the woman's fall. Conrad is pursued by Gulnare, whose faithlessness to Seyd is a kind of "fall." The Giaour, though he initiates an affair with Leila, sees her brutally killed for her infidelity to Hassan. Manfred regrets having wrecked the woman he loves, but feels worse for the problems she faces in her moral existence (the fact that she must "forever fall") than for his own (which he can heroically confront). In each case, the loss of a woman signals the moment of moral epiphany for Byron's heroes, who thereby learn the moral consequences of their actions.

45. Peter Manning, in *Byron and His Fictions*, also observes that "Bertram is the symmetrical opposite of Faliero" (116).

46. Peter Manning, in *Byron and His Fictions*, notes the importance of an absent father on Byron's work (13). Though he does not read *Marino Faliero* autobiographically, he does point out the role of fathers and "patrimony" in bringing out the doge's ambivalence toward the rebellion (112).

47. For an insightful discussion of the relationship between Lioni and Bertram, see D. M. De Silva, "Byron's Politics and the History Plays," in *Byron: Poetry and Politics: Seventh International Byron Symposium, 1980,* ed. Erwin A. Sturzl and James Hogg (Austria: University of Salzburg, 1981), 118–25.

48. For an explanation of some of the differences between Pope's satire and Byron's, see Christensen, *Lord Byron's Strength*, 258–75.

6

"ONE HALF WHAT I SHOULD SAY": BYRON'S GAY NARRATOR IN *DON JUAN*

Byron began *Don Juan* in 1818, two years before he became involved in the Pope-Bowles controversy and penned *Marino Faliero*. A year after completing his neoclassical drama, Byron identified himself as a political liberal and collaborated with Leigh Hunt on *The Liberal*, making common cause with the very man he had attacked in his letters on Alexander Pope and William Bowles. Byron's shifting opinion of Hunt can be explained most effectively by considering the political and social nuances in his poetry of 1818–21. My argument in this chapter is that the style of Byron's *Don Juan*, his most personal and perhaps most successful work of art, yields important insights into Byron's vexed endorsement of political liberalism.

"Man is least himself when he talks in his own person," Oscar Wilde has written. "Give him a mask and he will tell you the truth." Wilde's insight illuminates not only Byron's narrative strategy in *Don Juan*, but the personal and political crises that made that style necessary. The narrator's closeted sexuality can help explain his digressive style, one of the poem's most debated features, and provides insight into his double entendres and puns. Byron's use of coded language in *Don Juan* focuses new light on what makes the poem so humorous, as well as what it owes to oral traditions. In the past, editors of the Oxford and Norton anthologies—constrained, in part, by page limits—have retained the heterosexual plot of *Don Juan* but omitted its homoerotic digressions. In the same way that "learned men" expurgate the young Juan's classical texts (*CPW* 5:1:44–45), editors bowdlerize *Don Juan* (especially cantos 1 and 2), excising the very stanzas that call attention to the theme of censorship (*CPW* 5:1: 44–45).[1] Byron's use of irony in *Don Juan* has received more critical attention than almost any other topic. Yet few monographs consider the narrator's ironic relationship to the very legend of Don Juan that he both narrates and subverts.

Byron's use of a gay narrator in *Don Juan* illuminates his aristocratic liberalism, but the poem's politics change. The repressed narrator who consistently exposes his aristocratic liberalism in cantos 1–5 becomes indistinguishable from Byron himself, and poses as a democrat in cantos 6–17. I say poses, because Byron only muted his narrator's aristocratic sensibility; it never disappears. Leigh Hunt, Walter Scott, Percy Shelley, and William Hazlitt all questioned the sincerity of Byron's liberal convictions, and Andrew Rutherford, Malcolm Kelsall, and Leslie Marchand have more recently portrayed him as ambivalently disposed toward revolutionary and democratic ideas,[2] an argument I make in the previous chapter. Byron's aristocratic form of sexual practice consistently inflected the poet's peculiar brand of liberal belief. "The noblest kind of Love is Love Platonical," the narrator announces, "To end or to begin with" (*CPW* 5:9:76). Byron means something more than idealized love in such passages.[3] When placed in the context of his love for Loukas Chalandritsanos, for example, Byron's support for Greek independence appears less democratic, more personal and aristocratic.

Though Byron's narrator is clearly bisexual—having had affairs with women in the past—I use the term "gay"[4] to foreground his homoeroticism, which precipitates some of the poem's most subversive moments. By referring to Byron's narrator as "gay," I do not mean to imply that his sexual character is fixed. Byron's narrator changes his tone and style throughout the poem's seventeen cantos, for Byron's friends urged him to abandon the narrator's lascivious asides and autobiographical references that characterized the first two cantos. The term "gay" explains the narrator's erotic presence in the poem, however, and has several advantages over "homosexual": it is not an etymological hybrid; it has not been used by doctors to describe a pathology; and it is used most often by homosexuals to define themselves. The word has obvious advantages over "sodomite," "third sex," or other abusive epithets popular in early-nineteenth-century English society. Though sometimes scorned as a neologism, as John Boswell observes, the word "gay" more accurately connotes a way of life than does "homosexual," which refers solely to a form of sexual practice.[5]

Byron's narrator has freed himself from heterosexual constraints: from the constraints of fatherhood, as well as from the strained seriousness of such patriarchal figures as Lambro and Lord Henry. Whereas a restrained and prudent Byron limited himself to ogling beautiful women in his poetry, Byron's gay narrator surveys both sexes with an eroticized eye. Juan and Haidée (*CPW* 5:2:105–20), Gulbeyaz and the Sultan (*CPW* 5:5:97), and Baba and

Catherine (*CPW* 5:9:53–66) intrigue him equally, though he gravitates more toward men than women, as details in his description of each gender show (*CPW* 5:2:105–20). The narrator once loved, and perhaps even respected, women, but now makes remarks that betray his casual and almost mechanical misogyny. Throughout *Don Juan,* the narrator suggests more than he reveals about his sexuality, and the narrator's pointed allusions may well explain the angry responses the poem elicited in reviews. *Bon-Ton* magazine, for example, referred to the "vulgar jargon" of *Don Juan,* its tendency to make "vice familiar with the public mind."[6] By employing this "jargon," the narrator assumes a mysterious sexual identity connected with such "vice," as Jerome Christensen and Andrew Elfenbein show.[7] The narrator's role in the poem deserves careful scrutiny, for once decoded his jargon deconstructs the very Don Juan legend he appears to expound.

I

On the eve of his departure for the Morea in 1809, Byron wrote a letter to Charles Skinner Matthews. He described his flirtatious attention to a young man from Falmouth, adopting the coded language that would later characterize his narrator's digressions in *Don Juan.* In this letter of June 22, Byron alluded to Petronius's *Satyricon* and declared his intention to pursue "Plen. and optabil. Coit.," or full intercourse to one's heart's content (*BLJ* 1:207). Matthews congratulated Byron on the "splendid success of his first efforts in *the mysterious,* that style in which more is meant than meets the Eye." In the same letter, Matthews used the word "method" to pun on homoerotic practice and the religious enthusiasm he connected with Methodism. "I positively decree that every one who professes *ma methode* do spell the term wch designates his calling with an e at the end of it—*methodiste,* not method*ist,* and pronounce the word in the French fashion."[8] Matthews underscores words to exploit the distinction between conversation and writing, a distinction Byron's narrator in *Don Juan* maintained as well. Louis Crompton believes "this letter unequivocally reveals the homosexual bond in the Cambridge circle."[9]

Yet Byron's sexuality formed a ripe area for investigation long before Crompton's important study appeared. In 1951, Doris Langley Moore suggested that the poet had homosexual experiences at Harrow;[10] in 1973, a popular undergraduate textbook edited by Harold Bloom and Lionel Trilling introduced him as "fundamentally homosexual";[11] and in 1985, Cecil Lang speculated that his homoerotic experience in Albania provided an important clue to explicating the ninth (and for him, central) canto of *Don Juan.* Cecil Lang's essay, published in the same year as *Byron and Greek Love,* was one of the first to show how Byron's homoeroticism manifested itself in his poetry.[12] Jerome McGann, Andrew Rutherford, and Robert Gleckner were more decorous.[13] Even recently, few readers of Byron have followed Crompton's lead. Susan Wolfson concentrates primarily on *Don Juan*'s heterosexual politics, for example, relegating Byron's homoeroticism to the status of a "more privately coded issue."[14] Yet Judith Butler's *Gender Trouble* and *Bodies That Matter* argue that treating homoeroticism as "private" perpetuates the notion that only heterosexuality is culturally intelligible.[15]

Byron's silence regarding his own homosocial desire became a theme during the poet's lifetime. In the December 6, 1814 edition of the *Morning Chronicle,* for example, "Ruhtra" accused Byron of subduing his "tuneful tongue" by not publicly lamenting the death of his friend, Charles Skinner Matthews, who drowned in the Cam River in 1811. Ruhtra attributes Byron's silence to his sincere grief, but also to his social snobbery: Byron is unwilling to remember someone beneath his social station.

In fact, Byron exhibited feelings for male friends reluctantly, as his retitling of numerous elegies suggests. Ruhtra's poem, which appears reprinted here for the first time, shows how a contemporary of Byron's viewed his relationships with other men:

To the Memory of
CHARLES SKINNER MATTHEWS, Esq.
SOMETIME FELLOW OF DOWNING COLLEGE, CAMBRIDGE,
DROWNED IN THE CAM, AUGUST, 1811

Why all our praises to the *titled* crew?
MATTHEWS, who never cringed, I sing to you!
Why all our art the *living* must engross?
Matthews, there are those who yet do weep thy loss,—
There are who loath the lies by flatt'ry bred,
But pay their willing homage to the dead!
To him, alas! our sighs who may not hear
Nor heed the load of anguish that we bear,
To him—whom numerous Byron hath not sung—
For grief sincere subdued his tuneful tongue!
Yet we who loved not less, will strive in song,
Not him to honour—but our tears prolong.
Who loved him living will lament him dead,
And heep unheeded praises on his head!
His was the soul erect—the manly mind—
With learning's lore,—and wit—and taste refin'd;
And fair sincerity's ennobling charm.

> A head so cool, and yet a heart so warm!
>   Cambridge, farewell! my sorrow has not pow'rs
> To tell thee, Granta, why I hate thy tow'rs!
> And thee, ungrateful Cam! whose waters flow
> Accursed ay—sad source of all my woe!
> Damn'd be thy sedgy current, and thy stream
> Of grief and hate the everlasting theme!
>   In vain do suns and waning moons decline—
> Untired my tears—unceasing sorrow mine.
> With him I saw my dearest joys depart—
> A frightful chasm still left within my heart;
> In vain the hours and days each other urge,
> For each revolving year I'll chant his dirge;
> His virtue and our grief will still rehearse,
> And pour the poor vain tribute of a verse!
> Ah! who shall speak the hopes for ever gone—
> The parent's heavy heart, and friends undone?
> For thee the choaking sob, the big tears roll,
> Side–piercing grief,—and pangs that reach the soul!
> But hold,—no more!—let sorrow be but sad—
> We must not think on't so—'twill make us mad.
> Yet there is comfort—we shall meet again—
> Byron!—there *is* a heav'n!—Amen, Amen!

4 Dec. 1814   RUHTRA

The phrase "numerous Byron" tropes the poet as the author of a large number of literary works. Yet the phrase also implicitly alludes to the consequences of Byron's libertine practice, as if he has so many lovers that he cannot spare the time to lament those who have died. The speaker's italics ("*titled* crew") imply that Byron refrained from singing Matthews's death because of his low birth (Byron's poems to Lord Clare and Lord Delawarr provide instructive contrasts). Ruhtra does not feel as hampered by social distinctions as Byron. In lamenting Matthews's unsung death, Ruhtra points to a larger theme: that something unintelligible, "untitled" or unentitled, prevents one man from singing his love for another.[16]

Ruhtra describes Matthews as one "who never cringed" in the face of social titles to expose Byron as one who had. Yet Ruhtra is only slightly more comfortable displaying his feelings for another male in verse. Conforming "cring[ingly]" to the *Morning Chronicle*'s conventions, he rearranges the letters of his own name before appending it to his poem. Arthur (or "Ruhtra") enters the literary marketplace backward, so to speak, adopting a literary mask that must be "read through" (or even read backward) to be understood. Where Byron silences his "tuneful" voice because of grief, Ruhtra renames himself. No one "heed[s] the load of anguish that we bear," Ruhtra complains; no one will "heep unheeded praises on [Matthews's] head." He uses the first person plural to underscore the fact that Matthews's mourners form a community. Even if they did not know Matthews well, they have lost other men they loved. English society renders such loss unintelligible by enforcing sexual hegemony.

As the poet begins his lament to Matthews, he insists that Cambridge, no less than the *Morning Chronicle,* frustrates the expression of homosocial desire. The poet connects the river that drowned his friend with an institution that supported loving relationships between men, "drown[ing]" such sentiments in a muddy bog of compulsory heterosexuality[17] when they grew up. He tropes his song as only slightly more nurturing than the Cam River, implicitly comparing the two by noting that stifling weeds replace the "choaking sob[s]" of Matthews's mourners. The poet alternates between images of restriction and flow ("choaking sob" and "big tears roll") to reflect his own difficulty speaking out, first signaled by signing his name as an anagram.[18] The speaker imagines a better place ("there *is* a heav'n") where all three men might meet unrestricted in their expressions of mutual regard, unhampered by social constraints.

Like the Byron depicted in Ruhtra's poem, the bachelor narrator of *Don Juan* has a similar difficulty speaking out. Despite the fact that he was living in Venice, a city attractive to English tourists for its relaxed laws governing sodomy,[19] Byron transferred some of his own English inhibitions to his Spanish-born narrator. A "moderate Presbyterian" misogynist, the narrator remains silent about his education, his own love affairs, and his particular interest in Don Juan's beauty (*CPW* 5:15:91). He is an avid reader of English preachers who rightly wonders how his English compatriots (he lived in England once) will receive his "moral" tale. From the very outset of the poem, then, he struggles to validate his own sexual preference and his effeminate protagonist. His wry perspective on matrimony leads him to mock an institution in which "*Wedlock* and a *Padlock*" mean the same (*CPW* 5:5:158), one that makes a "moral centaur" of a man and a woman. Byron's narrator nevertheless mutes his more heterodox opinions in the poem's early cantos, sensing his English audience's heterosexual bias clearly enough to narrate his story cautiously. John Murray obeyed the same impulse, removing the derogatory stanza about marriage quoted above (*CPW* 5:5:158) from the poem's first edition.[20]

Andrew Elfenbein argues that "the most challenging figure to analyze . . . in Byron's work is the narrator" and concludes that the narrator is "Byron himself." Like Elfenbein, who considers "Byron himself" to be more than a biographical person, I distinguish Byron's gay narrator, with his preoccupations about truth, constancy, and sexual education, from Byron, who advertises his heterosexuality through a deliberate and unconvincing bravado.[21] By distinguishing himself from his narrator, Byron displaces his gay identity onto another. The dialectic that occurs in this poem between Byron's homo- and heterosexual selves may help explain the relationship between two aspects of the poem that have puzzled critics for some time: the theme of metaphysical doubt and the poem's digressive method.[22]

II

I am not the first to discuss Byron's narrator in *Don Juan*. William Marshall found a "myriad of speakers" in the poem, while George Ridenour saw Byron's narrator as "self-consistent."[23] Nancy Benson has described the tension between Byron and his narrator in terms of Piaget's epistemological schema.[24] Less theoretical was David Parker's account of the narrator's "oblique style," which he connected with "rogue literature."[25] Following Paul de Man, Kim Michasiw saw Byron's narrator as aesthetically inconsistent and "effaced." I would agree that "his presence thins until it vanishes," and that the poem cannot "be read properly without breaking the code" of the narrator's silence. Where Michasiw viewed the narrator as a "sculpt[ed] . . . voice"[26] performed by some rhetorical sleight-of-hand, however, I argue (with Ridenour) that he is a fully fledged persona whose use of double entendre clearly differentiates him from Byron.

What *do* we know about the narrator? In the preface to his poem, Byron asks his readers to imagine his narrator "a Spanish gentleman in a village in the Sierra Morena on the road between Monasterio and Seville." He parodies Wordsworth's preface to "The Thorn," as well as Cervantes's chapter "Adventure in the Sierra Morena" in *Don Quixote*. Byron invokes the theme of indeterminate authorship by referring to these works, identifying himself as the narrator of his poem only to frustrate such identifications. Where Wordsworth uses the persona of a garrulous narrator and Cervantes alludes to an Arab historian, Cide Hamete Benengeli,[27] as the true authors of "The Thorn" and *Don Quixote* respectively, Byron suggests that a surrogate "Byron" composed *Don Juan*. His autobiographical references begin in the preface, where he describes two men who resemble Byron and Hobhouse touring Portugal, Spain, Italy, and the Morea. At this point, however, Byron deliberately distinguishes himself from "the storyteller."[28] "Byron," whose flirtations with Spanish women during his grand tour became legendary, watches the movements of a "tall peasant girl, whose whole soul is in her eyes and her heart in the dance." The narrator, on the other hand, recalls the story of Don Juan to a group of like-minded gentlemen, "without being much moved by the musical hilarity at the other end of the village green" (39). He sits *"at some distance"* (italics mine) with a small elderly audience, narrating his tale. Like Socrates, who banishes flute girls in Plato's *Symposium*, Byron's gay narrator avoids female companionship and "musical hilarity," preferring male company.

Byron continues to refer to the peculiar interests of his narrator in canto 1. The narrator imagines a heterosexual script, complete with a "*mistress* in some soft abode," and then deliberately departs from it.

> Most epic poets plunge in "medias res,"
> (Horace makes this the heroic turnpike road)
> And then your hero tells, whene'er you please,
> *What went before*—by way of episode,
> While seated after dinner at his ease,
> *Beside his mistress* in some soft abode,
> Palace, or garden, paradise, or cavern,
> Which serves the happy couple for a tavern.
>
> *That is the usual method, but not mine*—
> My way is to begin with the beginning;
> The *regularity of my design*
> Forbids all *wandering as the worst of sinning*,
> And therefore I shall open with a line
> (Although it cost me half an hour in spinning)
> Narrating somewhat of Don Juan's father,
> And also of his mother, if you'd rather.
> (*CPW* 5:1:6–7; italics mine)

In his letter to Lord Byron in 1809, quoted earlier, Charles Skinner Matthews referred to homosexuality as the "method"; he spelled it with an extra "e" and pronounced it with a French accent. In these stanzas, Byron's narrator uses double entendres to construct a similar code *("usual method, but not mine," "regularity of my design," "wandering as the worst of sinning")* that differs from more conventional, heterosexual narratives.

The speaker narrates of "Don Juan's father,/And also of his mother, if *you'd* rather" (italics mine) to emphasize that the audience's preferences are not his own. Byron stresses the heterosexual bias of his audience ("if *you'd* rather") by using enjambment and a caesura. He then makes several pointed remarks about Jóse. The narrator knew him "well," "very well": "a better cavalier ne'er mounted horse,/Or, being mounted, e'er got down again" (*CPW* 5:1:9). The narrator's gratuitous references to this relationship ("well," "very well"), as well as his play on "mounted" and "being mounted," invite supplemental readings that the narrator never fully clarifies. For some reason, Jóse's history costs the narrator "half an hour in spinning." Byron uses a stammering syntax to indicate the narrator's increasing discomfort. Jóse "who/Begot—but that's to come—

Well, to renew" (*CPW* 5:1:9). The narrator's elliptical style is obviously comic, but the stammering remains unexplained, inviting the reader to speculate about its cause. Readers who take the narrator's innuendos ("well," "very well") risk mistaking licentious language for licentious deeds. Those who overlook them, however, miss "half" of the meaning of the poem.

Regardless of how one interprets the narrator's remarks concerning Jóse—a difficult task without more explicit evidence—Byron's narrator calls attention to his own difficulty "beginning" his poem. "My way is to begin with the beginning," he writes, but soon finds this easier said than done.[29] "Nothing so difficult as a beginning" (*CPW* 5:4:1), he adds in canto 4. The narrator chooses canto 12 to return to this topos, at the very moment when Virgil's and Milton's epics end, and Homer's *Iliad* and *Odyssey* are half over. "Now I will begin my poem," the narrator states, in deliberate deadpan.

>   'Tis
> Perhaps a little strange, if not quite new,
> That from the first of Cantos up to this
> I've not begun what we have to go through.
> (*CPW* 5:12:54)

For *Don Juan*'s narrator, beginnings are always sexually charged, whether they involve poems, love affairs, or complex references to the poet's personal history. In this stanza, Byron appears *in propria persona* to recount his friendship with Lady Melbourne, disguised here as Lady Pinchbeck, in order to offer his readers a second, perhaps more definitively autobiographical, beginning to his poem. Discretion and decorousness, however, mandate that Byron's narrator can never quite "begin" his poem any more than he can "end" it. The narrator speaks in perpetuity, and the poem remains incomplete as long as the author who created him survives. Perhaps the narrator's difficulty "beginning" underscores his non-procreative form of sexual practice. If so, then his choice of the heterosexual Don Juan as his subject continually stymies his struggle "from the first of Cantos up to this" to "go through" the details of his own more complex sexual history. To compensate for his choice of legends, the narrator makes Don Juan the subject of his erotic gaze and transforms him and the Don Juan legend in the process.

Byron's closest confidante during his years of fame in England was Lady Melbourne. To her he recounted his affairs with married women and even with Augusta Leigh, yet he never confessed his homoeroticism to his sixty-two-year-old confidante.[30] Byron could only present an unacknowledged side of himself through a mask. In a letter to Murray, Byron repeatedly referred to *Don Juan's* secret moral which canting reviewers had missed. The narrator's suggestive asides regarding his close friendship with Don Juan and his father certainly support Byron's claim. His narrator imagines a *hypocrite lecteur* who understands double entendres, but feigns ignorance. To communicate with his "atrocious" (*CPW* 5:14:97) reader, the narrator constructs a guide that devolves into a series of sexual innuendos. "Firstly, begin with the beginning," the narrator announces,

> (though
> That clause is hard); and secondly, proceed;
> Thirdly, commence not with the end—or, sinning
> In this sort, end at least with the beginning.
> (*CPW* 5:13:73)[31]

At first glance, these lines function as a series of textual instructions, as in *Ars Poetica:* "the middle" should not be "discordant with the beginning, nor the end with the middle," Horace states.[32] Upon closer inspection, however, the narrator seems to be using words as metonymies ("beginning," "proceed," "commence," "end," "sinning/In this sort") to connect ways of reading with sexual acts. Like Rabelais, in his prefaces to *Gargantua* and *Pantagruel*, Byron's narrator views writing as an eminently physical act. He compares his epic poem to a human body that can be seduced or "read" from the front or back. As in other sections of the poem, the narrator undermines his ostensibly heterosexual plot[33] by suggesting that his anatomical book is male—its "front" is hard, and entry at its "end" is prohibited. "[C]ommence not with the end—or, sinning/In this sort, end at least with the beginning" (*CPW* 5:13:73). Such references can apply to women as well as men (as details of Byron's sexual history with Annabella Milbanke suggest), but homoeroticism is the narrator's dominant motif. Like Diotima, he ranks love in a *scala d'amore* that reinforces the homoerotic lessons of Plato's *Symposium*, which shares with *Don Juan* the presumption of a predominantly male audience (preface 39). In *Don Juan,* Byron satirized the moral hypocrisy of an English public school education that taught the Greek language by exposing impressionable boys to Greek sexual practice and then punished them with the pillory for practicing such behavior. Unlike Ruhtra, who commemorated the death of Matthews in a moving elegy, Byron converted such sentiments to farce, as one would expect in a mock epic rather than a lyric poem. His verbose and bawdy narrator delights in exposing social hypocrisies through double and triple rhymes ("Platonical"/"canonical;" "thing in hand"/ "Christian land"):

> The noblest kind of Love is Love Platonical,
> To end or to begin with; the next grand

> Is that which may be christened Love Canonical,
> Because the clergy take the thing in hand;
> The third sort to be noted in our Chronicle
> As flourishing in every Christian land,
> Is, when chaste Matrons to their other ties
> Add what may be call'd *marriage in disguise*.
> (*CPW* 5:9:76)

If "Platonic love" means friendship to the "common" reader (remembering the epigraph from Horace), "Love Platonical" suggests something closer to Pausanias's praise of male-male love in Plato's *Symposium* (181C). The narrator's inversion of word order to force a rhyme also inverts the reader's sense of what these words can mean, liberating them from conventional heterosexual connotations. The narrator inverts other words ("Love Canonical") to exploit the difference between "common" conceptions of the clergy as sanctifying marriage, and his own lewd suggestion, in the manner of Boccaccio's *Decameron,* that the clergy "take the thing in hand." The passage ends by implying that marriage "*disguise[s]*" the partners' proclivities, even as *cavalier serventissmo* disguises a woman's true affections. Clearly, the narrator's use of such phrases as "sinning/In this sort," "To end or to begin with," "take the thing in hand," and "*Marriage in Disguise*" invite such supplemental readings, as does a phrase like "That clause is hard."

Other readings of these phrases are certainly possible and can support the sexual innuendoes I have outlined. Byron's phrase, "That clause is hard," for example, also recalls Dante's reaction to the "hard" truth inscribed on the gates of Hell: "Dinanzi a me non fuor cose create/Se non etterne, e io etterna duro./Lasciate orgni speranza, voi ch'intrate" [Before me nothing but eternal things/ Were made, and I endure eternally./Abandon every hope, who enter here].[34] Dante turns to his guide, Virgil, and states, "Maestro, il senso lor m'e duro" [its meaning is hard to understand/accept], which plays off the other cognate of the word "duro," "io etterna duro" [eternal I endure]. Byron must have had such scenes in mind while composing *Don Juan,* for he saw a copy of Dante's *Inferno* on Teresa Guiccioli's desk in 1819, read the episode of Paolo and Francesca with her, and hoped to publish his translated excerpt from Dante's fifth canto alongside *The Prophecy of Dante*.[35] Far from disproving *Don Juan*'s homoerotic subtext, however, the narrator's allusion to Dante in canto 10 of Byron's poem only reinforces it. He implies that "Love Platonical" will be subject to eternal damnation in an inferno not unlike Dante's. Byron translated Dante's Paolo and Francesca passage into English; Byron's "narrator" uses Dante's poem for more subversive ends.

Byron's allusions to a homoerotic subtext to his poem are all the more remarkable because same-sex love was a capital offense in Regency England, punishable by public hanging or the pillory.[36] Introducing canto 6, he referred to Lord Castlereagh's suicide, which occurred, according to rumors, in part from Castlereagh's fear of being exposed as a sodomite. Hobhouse warned Byron against alluding directly to Castlereagh's motives in killing himself, for fear, perhaps, that journalists might expose salacious anecdotes about Byron's own conduct in Greece and Albania during his minority.[37]

Byron recognized that in order to speak of "common things in the *proper way*," as his epigraph from Horace commands, the narrator of his poem must rely upon dramatic conventions. "We have all seen him in the pantomime," the narrator says of Don Juan, "Sent to the devil, somewhat ere his time." Invoking the pantomime conventions of "Principal Boys" and "Breeches Parts," the narrator both pleases his audience's "common" tastes for cross-dressing males and satisfies his own more polymorphously perverse predilections.

In the eighteenth century, as Peter Graham has shown, pantomimes were not dumb shows, but a concatenation of ballet, dancing, and burlesque. They appealed to a broad audience, in part, by playing havoc with gender roles. Byron's invocation of pantomime traditions makes his narrator's effeminacy self-explanatory.[38] Byron's narrator fosters interest in Juan's cross-dressing by performing the function of a *corago*, or stage manager, who both encourages and conceals his spectators' view of his titillating hero, making this "beauteous boy" visible. In nineteenth-century theater and popular entertainments, a principal boy's costume speaks for itself. In Byron's poem, a gay narrator calls attention to his travestied hero. Byron absolves himself of responsibility for his corago's prurience by constructing a narrator more transgressive than himself.[39]

At the end of canto 2, the narrator describes a masquerade that resembles the pantomime. Both events underscore his view of gender as "inconstan[t]" and unstable.

> I hate inconstancy—I loathe, detest,
> Abhor, condemn, abjure the mortal made
> Of such quicksilver clay that in his breast
> No permanent foundations can be laid;
> Love, constant love, has been my constant guest,
> And yet last night, being at a masquerade,
> I saw the prettiest creature, fresh from Milan,
> Which gave me some sensations like a villain.
>
> But soon Philosophy came to my aid,
> And whisper'd "think of every sacred tie!"
> "I will, my dear Philosophy!" I said,
> "But then her teeth, and then, Oh heaven! her eye!

> I'll just inquire if she be wife or maid,
> Or neither—out of curiosity."
> "Stop!" cried Philosophy, with air so Grecian,
> (Though she was masqued then as a fair Venetian.)
> (*CPW* 5:2:209–10)

The narrator conceals his "creature['s]" gender, even as he calls attention to it: "I'll just inquire if she be wife or maid,/Or neither." He refers to Boethius's *Consolations of Philosophy* to exploit the ambiguity. Is it Philosophy masked as a "Venetian" or is it the "creature, fresh from Milan"? Is the Grecian character a woman, or a man? If Boethius's Philosophy is a man "masqued then as a fair Venetian," he implicitly warns the narrator against pursuing women; his air is "Grecian" and he says "Stop!" in part, because classical tradition teaches the inferiority of heterosexuality.[40]

While theatrical pantomime says nothing but shows everything, poetic pantomime says everything but shows nothing. The verbose narrator criticizes Juan's education, but remains silent about his own. His double negatives ("nothing—nothing . . . No—No . . . no matter *what*—/I never married") continually fall short of self-disclosure.

> For my part I say nothing—nothing—but
> *This* I will say—my reasons are my own—
> That if I had an only son to put
> To school (as God be praised that I have none)
> 'Tis not with Donna Inez I would shut
> Him up to learn his catechism alone,
> No—No—I'd send him out betimes to college,
> For there it was I pick'd up my own knowledge.
>
> For there one learns—'tis not for me to boast,
> Though I acquired—but I pass over *that,*
> As well as all the Greek I since have lost:
> I say that there's the place—but *"Verbum sat,"*
> I think I pick'd up too, as well as most,
> Knowledge of matters—but no matter *what*—
> I never married—but, I think, I know
> That sons should not be educated so.
> (*CPW* 5:1:52–53)

Most critics overlook the repeated innuendoes of this passage and the hyphens that call attention to the narrator's stammering style. Yet the narrator uses conversational ticks to both reveal and conceal crucial knowledge about himself. He passes over "all the Greek I since have lost," and tells the reader *"Verbum sat,"* or "a word to the wise is sufficient."

What might these stanzas mean? Who is the "wise" audience to which the narrator refers? What, exactly, is the narrator "pass[ing] over"? Lady Byron complained to Harriet Beecher Stowe that "there was everything in the classical course of the schools to develop an unhealthy growth of passion, and no moral influence of any kind to restrain it."[41] Parodying Lady Byron's editorial impulses, Byron portrays Donna Inez overseeing the censoring of Juan's Greek and Roman schoolbooks, for she "dreaded the mythology" (*CPW* 5:1:41). Though less judgmental about homoeroticism than his wife, Byron nevertheless maintained a judicious silence about the subject. Winckelmann confessed that he too would have "been able to say more [in his preface to *History*] if I had written for the Greeks, and not in a modern tongue, which imposes on me certain restrictions."[42] Byron's narrator feels a similar "restriction," using precisely this word to account for his chaste muse (*CPW* 5:11:88, 5:14:13).

Byron often uses "Greek" as a metonymy for "Greek love." His narrator states that he has picked up "Knowledge of matters—but no matter *what*—/I never married" (*CPW* 5:1:53). In a literal sense, then, the narrator remains silent about his own sexual history because English is not his native tongue: "Much English I cannot pretend to speak," he says (*CPW* 5:2:165), even though (perhaps because) he has learned the language from its "preachers" ("Barrow, South, Tillotson") and studies them "every week." Byron uses the English language as a metaphor for sexual repression. Following Montesquieu and Staël, he views the "nations of the moral North" as a group. For Byron, language becomes a metonymy for sexual performance. The narrator prefers the "strange tongue" of Greek to "English," as he confesses when narrating the Haidée episode.

> 'Tis pleasing to be school'd in a strange tongue
> By female lips and eyes—that is, I mean
> (*CPW* 5:2:164)

The enjambment of "By female lips and eyes" clarifies the sexual object choice too late, as do the stumbling qualifications, "that is, I mean." Though ironic in suggesting that he knows little of heterosexuality ("learned the little that I know by this"), the narrator's interest in women is chaste, in part, because it has "pass'd away." "As for the ladies," the narrator continues,

> I have nought to say,
> A wanderer from the British world of fashion,
> Where I, like other "dogs, have had my day,"
> Like other men too, may have had my passion—
> But that, like other things, has pass'd away,
> And all her fools whom I *could* lay the lash on:
> Foes, friends, men, women, now are nought to me

But dreams of what has been, no more to be.
(*CPW* 5:2:166)

A phrase in the fourth line of this stanza ("may have had my passion") suggests that the narrator's heterosexuality is as illusive as a romance, "*dreams* of what has been, no more to be" (italics mine). The narrator's sexual experience with women has not ended. Rather, his sexuality, like his selfhood, is unstable. The narrator must plead guilty to the charge Byron leveled against Robert Southey, of "struggling convulsively to deceive others without the power of lying to himself" (preface 40).

Byron's poem reaches a licentious peak in the first two cantos. After writing 180 octaves of *Don Juan*, however, Byron began to wonder whether "the poem was not—at least as far as it has yet gone—too free for these 'very modest days'" (*BLJ* September 19, 1818; 6:69–70). When his friends and publisher indicated that it would be "*impossible to publish this*" kind of verse in England, Byron lost his nerve and produced the more tepid third and fourth cantos.[43] Critics who discuss Byron's narrative strategy sometimes ignore the poem's serialized form. Yet the author responded directly to press reviews and the narrator distinguishes between the first two cantos and those that follow:

> Here I might enter on a chaste description.
> Having withstood temptation in my youth,
> But hear that several people take exception
> At the first two books having too much truth;
> Therefore I'll make Don Juan leave the ship soon,
> Because the publisher declares, in sooth,
> Through needles' eyes it easier for the camel is
> To pass, than those two cantos into families
> (*CPW* 5:4:97)

The poem cannot "pass" into families because John Cam Hobhouse, Scrope Davies, and others detect its secret code. Having read Byron's letters from Greece as a youth, Hobhouse and Davies were alert to the poet's double entendres; they objected to these as strenuously as to the stanzas about Lady Byron. In another sense, the poem cannot reproduce itself into cantos 3 and 4 ("families" of cantos) without being significantly altered: the poem is not "reproductive" because the narrator's perspective is discernibly homoerotic.

Shelley noted a similar change in the poem. Disapproving of Byron's cynicism in the first two cantos,[44] he found cantos 3, 4, and 5 "pregnant with immortality."[45] Pregnancy is an apt metaphor, for it corresponds with Byron's efforts to set himself straight in Venice. Where he once visited men who lacked the "gait and physiognomy" of man, as Shelley observed, Byron later "got rid of all those melancholy and degrading habits which he indulged at Venice"[46] and lived as an "altered man" as cavalier servente to "one woman," Teresa Guiccioli, whom he had met in April 1819 (December 18, 1818; SP 2:58).[47] He composed cantos 3, 4, and 5 to conform to English notions of propriety (BLJ February 7, 1820; 7:35, 82; CPW 5:694).[48] As early as October 26, 1819, he recognized that the narrator's allusive style—what Byron called "*that there* sort of writing" (BLJ 6:232)—accorded poorly with "family values." In subsequent cantos, Byron deliberately muted his outrageous narrator by assuming his identity. Yet a careful reader can still discern that the whole poem is written against "straight" life: against stifling marriages like Julia's (CPW 5:1:99); polygamous ones like Gulbeyaz's (CPW 5:6:24–25); and sexless, and more importantly soulless, ones like Adeline's (CPW 5:14:69).

When Teresa Guiccioli prevented Byron from continuing *Don Juan* on July 6, 1821 (8:147), she did so, Byron wrote, because the poem "strips off the tinsel of *Sentiment*."[49] In the absence of Teresa's direct testimony, one can only speculate that Teresa disapproved of the poem because it took Byron out of the closet. Teresa's "straight" lover assumed the persona of a narrator commenting cynically upon heterosexuality. By banning the poem, she shamed the "outed" Byron into silence, punishing him for his audacious wit and exposing his animus against women. Byron blamed women for censoring his muse. "I have been their martyr," he wrote to his publisher. "My whole life has been sacrificed *to* them & *by* them" (BLJ October 10, 1819; 6:257). The word "sacrifice" falls rather heavily, as does "martyr." Perhaps Byron blamed women (and English law) for his need to travel abroad for two years to pursue young boys in Greece and Albania; to feign love for Caroline Lamb, after their initial attraction subsided, to please her mother (BLJ November 4, 1812; 2:239); to propose marriage to Annabella in order to reform his character (BLJ September 20, 1814; 4:178); and to remain in Italy as a fan carrier for Teresa Guiccioli, even after he had set his sights on a political adventure in Greece (BLJ August 23, 1819; 6:214). Byron may well have created a career out of a myth, as Jerome Christensen argues,[50] but he also became a martyr to perhaps the greatest myth of all: his uncomplicated heterosexuality. Byron could find only limited satisfaction writing in the style and mores of a society that was too repressive to be vital, a place Byron referred to as the "tight little island" (BLJ November 27, 1816; 5:136).[51]

In Greece, by contrast, he pursued young men with impunity. One might even say that Byron died less for nationalism than for the idea of same-sex love. Because *Don Juan* only hinted at his frustrations, the poem (after canto 5) became less satisfying to Byron, who preferred shocking his audience to delighting them.

In *Don Juan*, the narrator conceals his sexual orientation. One sign of this is his heterosexual bravado. "I love the sex," a typical passage begins,

> and sometimes would reverse
> The tyrant's wish, "that mankind only had
> One neck, which he with one fell stroke might pierce:"
> My wish is quite as wide, but not so bad,
> And much more tender on the whole than fierce;
> It being (not *now*, but only while a lad)
> That Womankind had but one rosy mouth,
> To kiss them all at once from North to South.
> (*CPW* 5:6:27)

The narrator distinguishes between his heterosexual past and homoerotic present. He wished to kiss the "rosy mouth" of "Womankind" "not *now*, but only while a lad." Written after Teresa banned Byron from continuing the poem, this stanza shows the narrator masquerading as a heterosexual. He desired so many different women, he claims, that he hoped ("while a lad") to distill his passion into one kiss. One can read these overdetermined assertions in just the opposite way, however. The narrator wishes all womankind "had but one rosy mouth" so he could avoid kissing them individually. Byron exposes his anxiety about compulsory heterosexuality through a narrator who yokes violence and tenderness, one who implicitly compares kissing a woman to cutting off their necks.

Contrast this with Byron's letter. "It is true from early habit, one must make love mechanically as one swims," Byron informed Lady Melbourne on September 10, 1812. "I was once very fond of both, but now as I never swim unless I tumble into the water, I don't make love till almost obliged" (*BLJ* 2:193).[52] Unlike the "oblig[ing]" Byron, the gay narrator of *Don Juan* has refused women on more than one occasion, and will not "make love [as] mechanically as [he] swims." The narrator describes Gulbeyaz's reaction when Juan informs her "love is for the free":

> A tigress robb'd of young, a lioness,
> Or any interesting beast of prey,
> Are similes at hand for the distress
> Of ladies who cannot have their own way;
> But though my turn will not be served with less,
> These don't express one half what I should say:
> For what is stealing young ones, few or many,
> To cutting short their hopes of having any?
> (*CPW* 5:5:132)

Juan cuts short Gulbeyaz's hopes of having children by not lying with her. He charms the narrator, who has presumably been in a similar situation himself. Pederasty ("stealing young ones, few or many"), the narrator reasons, is not nearly so bad as "cutting short [a woman's] hopes of having any" by refusing to perform. The narrator indirectly validates a "purposeless" sexuality, while reinforcing his praise of other nonteleological activities such as the "great *end* of travel—which is driving" (*CPW* 5:10:72). But not Byron. His only purpose was "to giggle and make giggle" (*BLJ* August 12, 1819; 6:208), he informed Thomas Moore.

The narrator establishes his gay identity by comparing himself to other figures involved in homoerotic relationships and whose sexuality is ambiguous: Socrates' erotic friendship with Alcibiades; Tiresias's bisexual experience; and the narrator's own friendship with a monk who has gone to seed (*CPW* 5:14:81). He tells us that "Some truths are better kept behind a screen,/Especially when they would look like lies;/I therefore deal in generalities" (*CPW* 5:14:80). Byron made *Don Juan* a riddle of futurity, "happily" hiding what it pretends to reveal. In pointed digressions, Byron's narrator compares the poem to

> hieroglyphics on Egyptian stones,
> The pleasant riddles of Futurity—
> Guessing at what shall happily be hid,
> As the real purpose of a Pyramid.
> (*CPW* 5:8:137)

Leslie Marchand has noted that "the poem is . . . one in which the author 'speaks out' in his own person on whatever most concerns him at the moment,"[53] but Byron also silences his narrator's speech. Even behind his adopted mask, the poet remains reluctant to "*speak out*" (*CPW* 5:11:88). Instead, he uses his narrator to build a pyramid of a poem that hides homoerotic messages in "riddles of Futurity."

The narrator keeps up his screen, but only by avoiding the "finest ferocious Caravaggio style" of satire Byron employed in "The Vision of Judgment" (*BLJ* October 12, 1821; 8:240).[54] If the narrator has spoken of Juan as a "beauteous Boy" (*CPW* 5:9:53) and "paint[ed]" his beauty with more care than his portraits of Donna Julia, Haidée, Gulbeyaz, or Catherine, he has his reasons. His topic requires "the due restriction" of "proper courtesy" (*CPW* 5:11:88): "Ne'er doubt/ *This*—when I speak, I *don't hint* but *speak out*" (*CPW* 5:11:88). Clearly the statement is ironic, as the italicized words and pun on "doubt" suggest.

Contrast Byron's caution in the latter cantos of *Don Juan* with his poem addressed to his Greek servant, Loukas Chalandritsanos. Byron wrote "Love and Death" a year after he had substantially completed *Don Juan*. "Love and Death" recasts themes in "On This Day I Complete My Thirty-Sixth Year"—specifically, Byron's fear of no longer being loved: "Tread those reviving passions down,/Unworthy manhood!" Byron wrote on his birthday. Yet "Love and Death" goes further than "On this Day" to articulate what Byron's gay, but closeted, narrator could not say:

yet thou lov'st me not,
And never wilt—Love dwells not in our will.
Nor can I blame thee—though it be my lot
To strongly—wrongly—vainly—love thee still.
(*CPW* 5:7:82)

At the end of his life, Byron finally answered the anonymous critic of the *Morning Chronicle,* Ruhtra, who both rebuked and forgave him for "cring[ing]" and not singing of Charles Skinner Matthews's death. "To me he was much," Byron said of Matthews, "to Hobhouse every thing . . . /I did not love so much as I honoured him" (*BLJ* September 7, 1811; 2:93). In 1824, Byron wrote a poem that was unabashedly homoerotic—perhaps because he was now truly in love— and sang of his unrequited love without fear of "*speak[ing] out.*" To do so, Byron overcame the aristocratic scruples of one who could only express his love for a member of his social class.

In *Don Juan,* Byron both conformed to society's demand for heterosexual masquerade and alluded to a more dangerous and subversive self behind this heterosexual persona. When Horace Walpole complained to Horace Mann that "balls and masquerades supply the place of politics," he anticipated the great theme of Byron's poem: masquerade is inseparable from political life in Turkey, Russia, and England.[55] In a masquerade, according to Terry Castle, "the true self remained elusive and inaccessible—illegible—within its fantastical encasements. . . . [O]ne was obliged to impersonate a being opposite, in some essential feature, to oneself."[56] Set in the eighteenth century, Byron's poem continued this tradition; it achieved the same illegibility. By impersonating a being "opposite, in some essential feature," from himself as conventionally understood, Byron exploded the Don Juan legend he helped create. By doing so, he remained true not to the lyric voice of his poem to Loukas Chalandritsanos, but to the theatrical metaphor with which *Don Juan* began: "We all have seen him in the pantomime/Sent to the devil, somewhat ere his time" (*CPW* 5:1:1).

I have read *Don Juan* with an eye on his narrator and would like to conclude by noting several instances in which the poet's bisexuality informs his political and social views.[57] Clearly, Teresa Guiccioli's love was not enough for Byron even after she separated from her husband. In a letter to Hobhouse, Byron expressed his dissatisfaction with Italian efforts to domesticate the libido through conventions such as *cavalier serventissmo.* "But I feel & I feel it bitterly— that a man should not consume his life at the side and on the bosom—of a woman—and a stranger—that even the recompense and it is much—is not enough—and that this Cicisbean existence is to be condemned" (*BLJ* August 23, 1819; 6:214). Byron's dashes crescendo ("the bosom—of a woman—and a stranger"), just as the first dash calls attention to the problematic nature of Byron's gender choice ("bosom—of a woman"). That Byron ended his life trying to substitute Loukas's bosom for Teresa's gives this passage resonance. Such letters suggest that it may not have been libertinism, but rather compulsory forms of sexuality that troubled him. While motives are always obscure, Byron may have participated in the Greek struggle for independence as much to recover buried sexual impulses as to free Greece from Turkey. According to this reading, his presence in Greece was as personal as it was political, as aristocratic (a defense of his intellectual traditions at Harrow) as nationalistic. In the same way that Byron fought to free himself from Caroline Lamb,[58] he fought for his own sexual freedom in Italy, where he lived a "Cicisbean existence." "Byron felt life was slipping past him"[59] and hence sought a military adventure by way of compensation, as William St. Clair shows, but there were also more specific, erotic, motives for his Greek adventure.

Byron's sexual dissatisfaction prompted his first pilgrimage and extended residence in Greece. Benita Eisler traces the genesis of *Childe Harold's Pilgrimage* to Albania and his homosexual experiences there. This biography lends support to the thesis that Childe Harold's numerous ejaculations of political protest in cantos 1 and 2 also signal Byron's dissatisfaction with his country's restricted view of human sexuality, most clearly alluded to in the passage on William Beckford's exile (*CPW* 2:1:22).[60] Childe Harold's frustration, which he shares with the heroes of Byron's Eastern tales,[61] is not only social, then, as Daniel Watkins has ably argued, but erotic.[62] The Byronic hero's moody, almost chronic dissatisfaction appears as a rough draft for *Don Juan*'s more subversive, gay, narrator. Reading Byron's political disgust as an expression of displaced erotic frustration helps connect Byron's politics with Byronic gloom. Peter Thorslev views the Byronic hero as a concatenation of previous literary types and formulas, such as the Child of Nature, the Gothic Villain, the Hero of Sensibility, or the Noble Outlaw,[63] yet he also reflects Byron's frustrated sexuality.

Byron used a gay narrator in *Don Juan* to subvert increasingly restrictive modes of speech in England while outwardly conforming to heterosexual conventions. The true burlesque of *Don Juan* redounds upon the myth of *Don Juan* itself—not simply because Juan is more "pursued than pursuing" (as many have rightly argued)—but because the narrator's erotic relationship to his male hero differs radically from any treatment of the Don Juan legend that preceded it.[64]

NOTES

1. *Romantic Poetry and Prose* (Harold Bloom and Lionel Trilling, eds. [Oxford: Oxford University Press, 1973], 320–54), omits stanzas 2–4, 8–9, 11–12, 20–53, 67–68,

86–89, and 95–100, while *The Norton Anthology of English Literature*, 6th ed. (M. H. Abrams et al., eds [New York: W. W. Norton & Company, 1993] 2:566–628), omits stanzas 2–4, 14–21, 30–31, 34–36, 45–51, 66–68, 73–74, 80–85, 87–89, 95–102, and 108–112. Both the Oxford (stanzas 69–85) and Norton anthologies (stanzas 103–107 and 113–117) retain aspects of the heterosexual plot. *British Literature: 1780–1830* (Richard E. Matlak and Anne K. Mellor, eds. [New York: Harcourt Brace College Publishers, 1996], 954–96) and *Romanticism: An Anthology*, 2d ed. (Duncan Wu, ed. [London: Basil Blackwell, 1998], 752–812), do not contain such cuts and reflect, I think, the influence of gay studies and the renewed respect for Byron as a master of digression and tonal complexity.

2. Leigh Hunt, *Lord Byron and Some of His Contemporaries* (London: Henry Colburn, 1828), 35; Walter Scott quoted in Rowland E. Prothero, ed. *The Works of Lord Byron* (New York: Octagon Books, Inc., 1966), 3:412; Percy Shelley quoted in *Shelley's Prose*, ed. Fred Jones (Oxford: Clarendon Press, 1964), 2:345; William Hazlitt quoted in Andrew Rutherford, *Byron: The Critical Heritage* (New York: Barnes & Noble, 1970), 131. Three critics with divergent approaches, Andrew Rutherford, Malcolm Kelsall, and Leslie Marchand, all express their reservations about Byron's radicalism. Rutherford, *Byron: A Critical Study* (Stanford University Press, 1961), 182–97; Kelsall, *Byron's Politics*, 2; Marchand, *Byron: A Portrait*, 321.

3. See John Boswell, *Christianity, Social Tolerance, and Homosexuality* (Chicago: University of Chicago Press, 1980), 48.

4. On the distinction between gay and homosexual, see Jeffrey Weeks, *Sex, Politics, and Society: The Regulation of Sexuality since 1800* (London: Longman, 1981), 108–17, and John Boswell, *Christianity*, 44.

5. Boswell, *Christianity*, 195; Eve Kosofsky Sedgwick, *Between Men: English Literature and Male Homosocial Desire* (New York: Columbia University Press, 1985), 158.

6. August 1819; Reiman, *Romantics Reviewed*, 1843.

7. Christensen, *Lord Byron's Strength*, 376; Andrew Elfenbein, *Byron and the Victorians* (Cambridge: Cambridge University Press, 1995), 206.

8. Crompton, *Byron and Greek Love*, 129.

9. Crompton, *Byron and Greek Love*, 129.

10. Doris Langley Moore, *The Late Lord Byron* (Philadelphia: Lippincott's, 1957), 243.

11. Bloom and Trilling, *Romantic Poetry and Prose*, 243.

12. Cecil Lang, "Narcissus Jilted: Byron, Don Juan, and the Biographical Imperative," in *Historical Studies and Literary Criticism*, ed. J. J. McGann (Madison: University of Wisconsin Press, 1985), 166.

13. McGann, *Don Juan in Context*; Rutherford, *Byron: A Critical Study;* and Robert Gleckner, *Byron and the Ruins of Paradise* (Baltimore: Johns Hopkins Press, 1967). Peter Manning's Freudian study, *Byron and His Fictions*, comes closest to unmasking Byron's sexual imagination, but does not find his homoeroticism as compelling or important as I do. Even critics who have focused specifically on Byron's narrator have avoided coming to terms with his sexuality. See David Parker, "The Narrator of Don Juan," Ariel 5:1 (1974): 49–58; Leslie Marchand, "Narrator and Narration in *Don Juan*," Keats-Shelley Journal 25 (1976): 26–42; Kim Michasiw, "The Social Other: Don Juan and the Genesis

150   Chapter 6

of the Self," *Mosaic* 22 (spring 1989): 29–48; and Nancy Benson, "Hero and Narrator in Byron's *Don Juan:* A Piagetian Approach," *Centennial Review* 28–29 (1984–85): 48–57.

14. Wolfson, "'Their She Condition,'" 585–87.

15. Judith Butler, *Gender Trouble: Feminism and the Subversion of Identity* (New York: Routledge, 1990), 148; Judith Butler, *Bodies that Matter: On the Discursive Limits of Sex* (New York: Routledge, 1993).

16. Eve Sedgwick traces the roots of this unintelligiblity in *Billy Budd* and *Dorian Gray,* noting its origin in "St. Paul's . . . denomination of sodomy as the crime whose name is not to be uttered" and Lord Alfred Douglas's "epochal public utterance, in 1894, 'I *am* the Love that dare not speak its name.'" Segwick, *Epistemology of the Closet* (Los Angeles: University of California Press, 1990), 74.

17. I borrow this phrase from Adrienne Rich's essay "Compulsory Heterosexuality and Lesbian Existence," *Signs* (1980): 631–60.

18. On the use of cryptograms in *Don Juan,* see Cecil Lang, "Narcissus Jilted," 165.

19. David Greenberg, *The Construction of Homosexuality* (Chicago: University of Chicago Press, 1988), 310.

20. Marchand, *Byron: A Portrait,* 335.

21. Elfenbein, *Byron and the Victorians,* 44. In *Don Juan in Context,* McGann also equates Byron with the narrator (66). A biographical reading of the narrator is tempting, especially when we consider that Lady Blessington found Byron's "voice and accent . . . somewhat effeminate. . . . [H]e is too gay, too flippant for a poet," she observed (Ernest Lovell, *His Very Self and Voice: Collected Conversations of Lord Byron* [New York: Macmillan, 1954], 350). Blessington anticipates the constellation of characteristics now associated with the word "gay." The *Oxford English Dictionary* records 1935 as the first year in which the word "gay" was used to describe a "homosexual," quoting from N. Ersine's *Underworld & Prison Slang.* Simpson and Weiner, eds. *The Oxford English Dictionary,* 6:409.

22. Marchand, *Byron's Poetry: A Critical Introduction* (Boston: Houghton Mifflin, 1965), 159, by contrast, argues that "the new poem appealed to him as a medium for telling the truth in poetry in a more transparent way than he had ever attempted before." The "dialectic" I speak of here adds another dimension to the argument set forth in Terence Hoagwood, *Byron's Dialectic: Skepticism and the Critique of Culture* (Lewisburg: Bucknell University Press, 1983), 15, 152. Hoagwood's study illuminates the importance of Byron's skepticism.

23. William Marshall, *The Structure of Byron's Major Poems* (Philadelphia: University of Pennsylvania Press, 1962), 176; George Ridenour, "The Mode of Byron's Don Juan," *PMLA* 79 (September 1964): 443.

24. Nancy Benson, "Hero and Narrator in Byron's *Don Juan,*" 48–57. See note 12 of this chapter.

25. David Parker, "The Narrator of Don Juan," 49. See note 12 of this chapter.

26. Kim Michasiw, "The Social Other," 7. See note 12 of this chapter.

27. Miguel de Cervantes Saavedra, *Don Quixote,* trans. J. Cohen (New York: Penguin, 1950), 77. Byron, George Gordon, *Lord Byron: Don Juan,* ed T. G. Steffan, E. Steffan, and W. W. Pratt (London: Penguin, 1957), 38. I have used Steffan's edition for citations from

the preface because it is one of the few to include the preface as part of the poem. All page numbers for the preface refer to this edition. I follow Peter Graham (*Don Juan and Regency England*, 11–35) in making use of this preface to the poem in my analysis. The preface was not published with the poem, but it is clearly indispensable in explaining the narrator's persona that finally emerged.

28. Michasiw does not distinguish between the storyteller and the Byron figure.

29. Edward Said notes that "literature is full of the lore of beginnings despite the tyranny of starting a work in *medias res*, a convention that burdens the beginning with the pretence that it is not one." Said, *Beginnings: Intention and Method* (New York: Columbia University Press, 1985), 43.

30. Gross, *Byron's "Corbeau Blanc,"* 50.

31. Anne Barton argues that Byron is "insisting" in this stanza "that *Don Juan* needs to be experienced as an evolving whole." She does not highlight Byron's double-entendres, which show that Byron views reading itself as a sexual act. Barton, *Don Juan* (Cambridge: Cambridge University Press, 1992), 79–80.

32. Horace, *Horace: Satires, Epistles, and Ars Poetica*, ed. H. Rushton Fairclough (Cambridge: Harvard University Press, 1978), 463.

33. He also subverts the "beginning" of the poem, by referring to beginnings as late as canto 13.

34. Dante Alighieri, *Inferno*, trans. Allen Mandelbaum (Berkeley: University of California Press, 1980), 3:7–9.

35. Marchand, *Byron: A Portrait*, 305.

36. Crompton, *Byron and Greek Love*, 14.

37. Graham, *Don Juan and Regency England*, 76–80; Wolfson, "'Their She Condition,'" 585–617.

38. In "Don Juan's Earliest Scrape," which appeared as act 2 of *One Fatal Swoon*, at London's Jermyn Street Theater on December 4, 1995, adaptor Carole Bremson and director Mary Elliott Nelson depicted the narrator as erotically attracted to Don Juan, a performance that did much to confirm my own reading of the poem. Nelson's lecture after this performance clarified a number of directorial decisions that informed this wonderful production.

39. Boswell, *Christianity*, 48.

40. Plato, *Symposium*, 181b–d;191e–92.

41. Harriet Beecher Stowe, *Lady Byron Vindicated* (New York: Haskell House Publishers, 1970), 164.

42. Crompton, *Byron and Greek Love*, 87.

43. Marchand, *Byron: A Portrait*, 292.

44. Shelley, *Shelley's Prose*, 2:42; Rutherford, *Byron: The Critical Heritage*, 160.

45. Shelley, *Shelley's Prose*, 2:330.

46. Shelley, *Shelley's Prose*, 2:330.

47. Marchand, *Byron: A Portrait*, 298.

48. Cantos 1 and 2 were written between July 3 and September 6, 1818, while cantos 3, 4, and 5 were written between September 17, 1819 and December 26, 1820. My

152   Chapter 6

argument is that having met Teresa Guiccioli in April 1819, Byron responded to her influence, as well as to the suggestions of his friends, when he composed cantos 3–17.

49. Leslie Marchand notes that Teresa Guiccioli read the first two stanzas in a French translation and excerpts in the Milan *Gazzetta* (July 5–6, 1821). Marchand, *Byron: A Portrait*, 344.

50. Christensen, *Lord Byron's Strength*, xxiv.

51. Leslie Marchand points out that the phrase comes from a song by Charles Dibdin, "The Snug Little Island," in a musical play of 1797 called *The British Raft* (November 27, 1816; 5:136n.3).

52. In *Lord Byron's Strength*, Jerome Christensen has shown how two other letters connect swimming and homoeroticism in less "mechanical" ways (64–65). Byron's letter to Hobhouse describes Signore Nicolo as a "bad ... hand in the water" (*BLJ* August 23, 1810; 2:14); his second, to John Murray, recounts Shelley's refusal to allow Byron to "save him" from drowning during a storm (*BLJ* May 15, 1819; 6:126).

53. Leslie Marchand, "Review of Byron and Greek Love," *Keats-Shelley Journal* 45 (1986): 190–93.

54. My gratitude to Prof. Peter Graham and Prof. Carl Woodring, who helped me locate this source.

55. Horace Walpole, *The Yale Edition of Horace Walpole's Correspondence*, ed. W. S. Lewis (New Haven: Yale University Press, 1937), 1:343, letter of February 25, 1742.

56. Terry Castle, *Masquerade and Civilization: The Carnivalesque in Eighteenth-Century English Culture and Fiction* (Stanford: Stanford University Press, 1986), 4–5.

57. See Phyllis Grosskurth's treatment of this subject in her biography, *Byron* (223). During his honeymoon, Byron repeatedly alluded to the importance of John Edleston in his life, though he represented Edleston to his wife as a woman who had died. See also James Soderholm's discussion of the erotic confusion created by Byron's retitling of his poems in "Annabella Milbanke's 'Thyrza to Lord Byron'" (*The Byron Journal* 21 [1993]: 32).

58. Gross, *Byron's "Corbeau Blanc,"* 115–18.

59. William St. Clair, *That Greece Might Still Be Free*, 151.

60. Christensen, *Lord Byron's Strength*, 66.

61. "The Bride of Abydos," *CPW* 2:20:387–450; "The Corsair," *CPW* 3:19:567–97.

62. Watkins, in *Sexual Powers*, questions whether romanticism's "masculine identity" "appropriates and subordinates femininity" (xii). His concern with violence and sexual power, as well as his focus on Wordsworth, Coleridge, and Keats, differs from my own.

63. Peter Thorslev, *The Byronic Hero: Types and Prototypes* (Minneapolis: University of Minnesota Press, 1962), 27–83.

64. An earlier version of this chapter was presented in Chicago in 1995 at a special session of the Modern Language Association titled "Byron and His Narrators." My thanks to Prof. Andrew Elfenbein, Prof. John Clubbe, and Prof. Stuart Sperry for their insights and suggestions.

7

BYRON AND *THE LIBERAL*: PERIODICAL AND POLITICAL POSTURE

In *Don Juan*, Byron expressed his political views indirectly, through a Wildean "mask." On October 15, 1822, however, he contributed to a political journal that avoided the circumlocutions of fiction and narrative digression. *The Liberal* represents one of the first uses of the word as an English noun. "The title of *Liberal* was given it by Lord Byron," Leigh Hunt observed.[1] Byron's choice represents the apotheosis of a lifelong engagement with English and European political issues which began in Parliament, continued with *Childe Harold's Pilgrimage*, and flourished during his contact with Holland House. Having left England in 1816, however, Byron did not know what "liberal" meant in his own country when he chose the title for this ill-fated journal. As a member of the Italian Carbonari in 1821 (or "Liberals" as they called themselves), Byron thought liberals advocated national sovereignty, not social reform. Holland House inevitably influenced Byron's definition, for *El Espagñol*, financed by Lord Holland, brought the word "liberales" into the English vocabulary. Rather than assume the existence of a "post-Waterloo liberalism,"[2] I trace the shifting significance of the word "liberal" in Byron's poetry and prose before he contributed to this periodical. My purpose is to explain how *The Liberal* united, however temporarily, the diverse political views of the writers who published under its masthead: Lord Byron, Percy Shelley, Leigh Hunt, Mary Shelley, Charles Armitage Brown, Thomas Jefferson Hogg, and William Hazlitt.[3] Byron's *The Vision of Judgment*, a satire on radicalism, illustrates Byron's distance from his collaborators. Yet *The Liberal* transformed Byron's very definition of the word, pointing him in the direction of Greece, where he completed that redefinition.

I

Though he chose the word as the title for a periodical in 1822, Byron did not introduce the word "liberal" into the English political vocabulary singlehandedly. Long before Byron's journal appeared, Lord Holland had already educated a small coterie of English politicians about Spanish liberalism during the Peninsular War. Lord Holland inherited the responsibility of Whig leadership from his uncle, Charles James Fox, and became interested in Spanish politics through two celebrated journeys he made to that country. He took his wife during his first voyage (1802–05) and brought the future founder of the modern Liberal Party, Lord John Russell, along as well during the second (1808–09). Holland wrote a biography of Lope de Vega that mixed Spanish literature and politics. He also published his correspondence with Jovellanos and Infantado in a periodical that was "widely assumed to be a new avenue by which Holland House hoped to conduct a foreign policy independent of that preferred by the English government."[4]

Edited by Joseph Blanco White, *El Espagñol* appeared in eight issues (April 1810–June 1814). "The aim of this new venture was avowedly didactic," Leslie Mitchell argues. "It aimed both to influence English opinion in favour of the Spanish liberals and to offer advice and encouragement to the Spanish themselves. One of its principal customers was the British government, which was anxious to keep Holland House foreign policy under surveillance."[5] At a time when an overweening executive branch threatened to compromise his political influence, Holland viewed his correspondents as Spanish Whigs. Their fight against the abuse of power by Charles IV, Maria Luisa, and Ferdinand VII mirrored his own political battles in England.[6]

Byron's close association with Holland House affected his politics, poetry, and social connections. Though it would be impossible to measure Henry Holland's influence on Byron's attitude toward the Spanish *liberales*, Byron could not help becoming aware of their cause. When Byron resided in England (1811–16), the Holland House circle and members of Parliament watched the shifting fortunes of the Spanish *liberales*. In December 1814, Lord Castlereagh attacked "the Liberales" as "a perfectly Jacobinical party, in point of principle." They "had declared that they would not admit Ferdinand's right to the throne, unless he put his seal to the principles which they laid down, and among the rest to that of the sovereignty being in the people."[7]

Castlereagh's speech marks one of the first recorded uses of "liberal" in a political sense, a full two years before Robert Southey's entry, which is cited in the *Oxford English Dictionary*.[8] The Liberal Party would not emerge in England until Lord John Russell's administration in 1832. Yet Tory critics used the term "liberal," first in its Spanish and then in its English form, to describe the more radical members of the Whig opposition. In August 1819, for example, the *Courier* conflated "radical" with "liberal," using the latter term in its English form to designate an English political party for perhaps the first time: "The *liberals* of course attribute this peaceable and orderly conduct to the lamblike and gentle dispositions of the Reformers themselves." By September 28, 1821, the liberals in England had gained enough power to win the trust of their Spanish counterparts. "The Cortes . . . think the Liberal party is so strong amongst us that the Ministry, however they may love despotism and legitimacy, cannot act against them," E. Ward informed Lord Castlereagh.[9] As the party in power, the Tories foresaw how the Spanish "liberales" could galvanize English "liberals" at a time when the postwar depression exacerbated political unrest.

II

Byron's exile began in 1816, just when Tories began using "liberal" and "radical" synonymously. In a letter to Hobhouse, Byron criticized reformers like Orator Hunt, but felt compelled to confess his ignorance of new political terms. "Upon reform you have long known my opinion," he wrote to his friend Hobhouse, "but radical is a new word since my time—it was not in the political vocabulary in 1816—when I left England—and I don't know what it means—is it uprooting?" (*BLJ* April 22, 1820; 7:81). Had he known, however, he probably would not have referred to himself as a "radical," "reformer," or "liberal" for that matter. "I esteem and admire Burdett as you [Hobhouse] know—but with these and half a dozen more exceptions—I protest, not against *reform*—but my most thorough contempt and abhorrence—of all that I have seen, heard, or heard of the persons calling themselves *reformers, radicals,* and such other names,—I should look upon being free with such men, as much the same as being in bonds with felons" (*BLJ* April 22, 1820; 7:81). Like other Whigs—Henry Holland, Henry Brougham, and Samuel Romilly, for example—Byron envisioned political change coming from the top down. Henry Hunt ignored such protocol; he was perhaps too eager to lead.

Despite Byron's reservations, John Murray forced him into the company of radicals (the "blackguards" of Byron's letters). From 1818 until 1821, Murray would not publish *Werner, The Vision of Judgment,* and *Heaven and Earth,* and withdrew his name from the first two cantos of *Don Juan,* fearing prosecution by the Constitutional Association.[10] Byron ridiculed him as a coward, but Murray's fears were well grounded. In July 1819, the government arrested "several 'malicious, seditious, evil-minded persons,' including the editors of the *Black*

Dwarf and the Manchester *Observer*, as well as Major Cartwright, whose Radical Hampden Club Byron had joined in 1813."[11] By October 1819, the government won a further victory by convicting Carlisle for selling the "Theological Works of Thomas Paine." Given this political climate and the hostility of the government, John Murray would not risk prosecution by publishing further cantos of *Don Juan*. Murray's delays prompted Byron to make three proposals for a journal that would perform this function.

Byron first proposed that his friend edit a newspaper that would satirize radicals who supported Queen Caroline. He predicted that it would prove more popular than the Tory *Courier*, edited by Thomas George Street. "You should set up a radical Newspaper and call it 'the Bergami,'" he wrote to Douglas Kinnaird, alluding to the queen's alleged lover and "courier." "It would beat Mr. Street's nowadays" (*BLJ* October 26, 1820; 7:214). Naming this mock publication after a presumed adulterer, Byron clearly viewed radicalism itself as a subject of mirth. His journalistic project became a personal crusade. Criticized by the Tory *Courier* for publishing "Lines to a Lady Weeping" with "The Corsair," Byron facetiously aligned himself with the opposite camp to satirize radicals.

Two months later, Byron changed his stripes and proposed editing a Whig journal that would attack reformers. "They have no merit but practice and impudence," he wrote (this time to Thomas Moore), "both of which we may acquire, and, as for talent and culture, the devil's in't if such proofs as we have given of both can't furnish out something better than the 'funeral baked meats' which have coldly set forth the breakfast table of all Great Britain for so many years" (*BLJ* December 25, 1820; 7:254). Here again, Byron distinguishes himself and his friend from the radicals, hoping to correct the abuses of "common-place blackguards who have so long disgraced common sense and the common reader" (7:254).

Byron thought his more serious proposal to Thomas Moore could aid Moore financially, restore Pope's reputation, and exact political revenge. "Tenda Rossa," Byron's second title, for example, clearly recalls Alessandro Tassoni's mock-heroic poem *La Secchia Rapita* (the ravished pail), a precursor of Pope's *Rape of the Lock*. "Gli" or "I Carbonari," his other suggestions, are more political than Popean and anticipate *The Liberal*, his final choice (7:255).[12]

Byron was intent on returning poetry to its classical roots. "The journal will be as literary and classical a concern as you please," he wrote to Moore. He saw his involvement as an extension of his role in the Pope-Bowles controversy, to "give the age some new lights upon policy, poesy, biography, criticism, morality, theology, and all other *ism, ality,* and *ology* whatsoever" (7:254). The journal would enable the two poets to show their "independence" from the "present scoundrels, who degrade that department" (7:254). Moore declined the invitation, however, and Byron resolved not to return to England.

The plan that won the day, ironically, included Leigh Hunt, the very poet Byron had denounced as a Cockney a year before and visited in prison eight years earlier. Critics have remained as confused as Byron's own editor about the poet's commitment to *The Liberal*. After noting Byron's increasing distance from his "reforming acquaintances," for example, Hunt confessed his surprise when he received a letter from Shelley "which contained a proposal from my former acquaintance [Byron], inviting me to go over, and set up a work with him."[13] Shelley's letter to Hunt, communicating Byron's proposal, illustrates Byron's indecision. "Leigh Hunt was Shelley's fault entirely," Harold Nicolson writes. "Shelley was like that; he let one in for things."[14] More recently, Benita Eisler states that Shelley was the "project's prime mover,"[15] but Byron's three previous proposals demonstrate that he had some such journalistic enterprise in mind long before Shelley hatched his plan. Nevertheless, Byron certainly did not know that Shelley had proposed editing a journal with Hunt, nor was he aware of the extent of Hunt's indebtedness. According to Edward Trelawny, Byron only joined the project because he believed that Hunt could pay his own bills by editing *The Examiner*.[16] Barnette Miller goes further in stressing Byron's indifference; he argues that Shelley deceived Hunt about Byron's enthusiasm, misleading Byron by concealing Hunt's insolvency.[17]

The truth is that Byron remained undecided. At times, he portrayed himself as skeptical about collaborating with Hunt in order to avoid offending Moore: "Be assured that there is no such coalition as you apprehend" (*BLJ* February 19, 1822; 9:110), he wrote. Despite this disclaimer, Byron contributed £250 to assist Hunt's passage to Italy (*BLJ* February 23, 1822; 9:113). When Hunt arrived, "bilious and unwell," Byron finally admitted his plans to Moore, but continued to portray himself as ambivalent about their project. "Can you give us any thing?" he asked. "He [Hunt] seems sanguine about the matter, but (entre nous) I am not. I do not, however, like to put him out of spirits by saying so" (*BLJ* July 12, 1822; 9:183). A month and a half after writing this letter, Byron avoided identifying himself directly with Hunt's project. "Leigh Hunt is sweating articles for his new Journal," he wrote to Moore, "both he and I think it somewhat shabby in *you* not to contribute" (*BLJ* August 27, 1822; 9:197). On the one hand, he referred to the journal as "his" (Hunt's); on the other, he assured Moore of his involvement ("both he and I") and criticized his friend for not contributing.

Yet Shelley's endorsement of the project influenced Byron, who respected Shelley's views more than Moore's or Hunt's. Byron viewed Shelley's radicalism as the prerogative of the gentry; landholders like Sir Francis Burdett could speak out freely while publishers and writers feared prosecution.[18] Half-heartedly following Shelley's example, Byron faulted Moore for his conventionality. "The truth is, my dear Moore, you live near the *stove* of society, where you are unavoidably influenced by its heat and its vapours.... If you speak your *own* opinions [concerning Shelley], they ever had, and will have, the greatest weight with *me*. But if you merely *echo* the 'monde,' (and it is difficult not to do so, being in its favour and its ferment,) I can only regret that you should ever repeat any thing to which I cannot pay attention" (*BLJ* March 4, 1822; 9:119). Byron's use of the word "ferment" is striking. He connects the foaming that occurs during the manufacture of wine and beer with the political ferment in England that causes Moore to be uncharitable toward Shelley. In his earlier letter to Moore, for example, Byron referred to the "funeral baked meats" of "impuden[t]" English journalists. Comparing Moore's social views to "goods" baked in the oven of English political society, Byron declares his emancipation from that stove. Like Bacchus (Liber), who freed the cities of Boetia from slavery, Byron liberates *himself* from English cant. He accomplishes this self-liberation, interestingly enough, through geographic displacement. He views the South as the imaginative terrain of the second generation of romantics, as surely as he associates the moral North (or lake district) with the first generation.

Byron's letter to Moore defines liberalism as a function of place and position. The *location* of this periodical, stressed in its very subtitle *(Verse and Prose from the South)* is the site of revolutionary activity in Italy—and, through metonymy, Spain and Greece. Freed from the "stove" of society, Byron can edit *The Liberal* in an appropriate, perhaps the only appropriate, place.

III

Fred Rosen argues that *The Liberal*'s politics do not reflect Byron's. "Byron's involvement with Leigh Hunt in the publication of *The Liberal* in 1822–23 might also appear to fix Byron as a liberal," Rosen states, "except that Leigh Hunt's preface ... does not clearly state the review was meant to form the vanguard of a liberal doctrine. Instead Leigh Hunt uses the word in the older sense and advocates a literary journal."[19] In fact, Hunt states that "we go the full length in matters of opinion with large bodies of men who are called LIBERALS."[20] With Byron's blessing, Hunt attacked Lord Castlereagh, the Duke of Wellington, the Prince Regent, and George III directly, while disingenuously insisting on the journal's purely literary focus. "We wish to do our work quietly, if people will let us,—to contribute our liberalities in the shape of Poetry, Essays, Tales, Translations, and other amenities, of which kings themselves may read and profit, if they are not afraid of seeing their own faces in every species of inkstand."[21] The qualifications are important, because they are deliberately tendentious: "*if* people will let us"; "*if* they are not afraid . . ." (italics mine).

Percy Shelley had already died on July 8, 1822 before the first issue of *The Liberal* found its way into print the following October 15. Hunt defended his deceased friend's atheist and radical views in ways that helped establish the journal's "liberal doctrine."[22]

> Have the consequences of Lord CASTLEREAGH's actions died with him? are the Six Acts dead? Are thousands of the Irish *living*? We will give a specimen of the liberality of these new demanders of liberality. The other day, when one of the noblest of human beings, Percy Shelley, who had more religion in his very differences with religion, than thousands of your church-and-state men, was lost on the coast of Italy, the *Courier* said, that "Mr. Percy Shelley, *a writer of infidel poetry*, was drowned." Where was the liberality of this canting insinuation? Where was the decency, or as it turned out, the common sense of it? Mr. SHELLEY's death by the waves was followed by LORD CASTLEREAGH'S by his own hand; and the cry is for liberal constructions. How could we not turn such a death against the enemies of Mr. Shelley, if we could condescend to affect a moment's agreement with their hypocrisy?[23]

Hunt ridiculed those who would extol Lord Castlereagh's private virtues and omit discussing his public policies. Hunt's preface thus used literature as a stalking horse for liberal politics.

Despite Hunt's profession of political uniformity in the preface to *The Liberal*, English expatriates contributed more radical works than their counterparts who still resided in England. Mary Shelley's "Madame d'Houtetot" and "A Tale of the Passions," Percy Shelley's translations from Goethe, and Byron's own translation from Luigi Pulci's *Il Morgante Maggiore* reveal the journal's continental cast. Charles Armitage Brown's "Les Charmettes and Rousseau," by contrast, was only nominally about Rousseau's six years at "Les Charmettes," the home of Mme. de Warens, while Brown's "Shakespear's Fools" focused on English, as opposed to Continental themes.[24] William Hazlitt's "On the Spirit of Monarchy," "On Arguing in a Circle," "On Pulpit Oratory," "On the Scotch Character," and "My First Acquaintance with Poets" also reflect a Londoner's perspective.

Though torn between its continental and English contributors, "The Liberal" achieved a modicum of political coherence by attacking Lord Castlereagh and Lord Wellington in a number of works, including the preface, Byron's "Epigrams on Lord Castlereagh," and Leigh Hunt's "The Dogs." "Never was a greater outcry raised among the hypocrites of all classes, than against this publication," Hunt wrote in his "Advertisement to the second volume."[25] From a purely literary standpoint, what Phyllis Grosskurth characterizes as a mere "miscellany of disconnected writings"[26] included three of romanticism's most anthologized works: "The Vision of Judgment," "On the Spirit of Monarchy," and "My First Acquaintance with Poets"; Mary Shelley had even slated her husband's "Defence of Poetry" for the second issue, though for some reason it failed to appear. In truth, the journal's reputation suffered most from Leigh Hunt's *Lord Byron and Some of His Contemporaries*, which portrayed Byron as a hypocrite, one who had "become not very fond of his reforming acquaintances" since he left England.[27] Lampooned by Charles Dickens in *Bleak House* as a sponger (Harold Skimpole) who turned on his benefactors, Leigh Hunt earned Dickens's caricature by remembering Byron's generosity through the lens of his own literary jealousy. In a bitter biographical reminiscence, Hunt denies that Byron was a liberal.[28] I have chosen to focus on events leading to Byron's involvement with the journal in order to question Leigh Hunt's largely unchallenged account of Byron's commitment to *The Liberal*. In a book-length study devoted to the journal, William Marshall treats *The Liberal* as a literary rather than a political accomplishment; I stress how one grows out of the other.

IV

"The Vision of Judgment" was Byron's most distinguished contribution to *The Liberal*. In this poem, which appeared in the journal's first issue, Byron satirized Robert Southey's "A Vision of Judgement" and portrayed George III as the enemy of liberty movements in America and France. Murray's decision to omit Byron's preface in the proofs he forwarded to John Hunt left the poem open to misinterpretation, however, as a libel of George III rather than as a satire of Southey's poem. When read with its preface, "The Vision of Judgment" clearly satirizes radicalism rather than endorsing it.

Byron's treatment of John Wilkes and Junius,[29] the two witnesses Satan calls forward to denounce George III, underscores his satiric intent. A great champion of liberty, Wilkes was also a notorious opportunist. Elected Lord Mayor of London, he "ended as a prop of the establishment" and repeatedly called his supporters "Middlesex fools . . . the greatest scoundrels upon earth."[30] Byron presents Wilkes in precisely this light. When Satan calls Wilkes to testify against George III, Wilkes seeks to use the opportunity to garner votes for yet another parliamentary election. "If those are freeholders I see in shrouds," he says, "And 'tis for an election that they bawl,/Behold a candidate with Unturn'd coat!/Saint Peter, may I count upon your vote?" (*CPW* 6:67:535–36). But Wilkes's coat is far from "unturned," as the poem goes on to show.

Equally suspect in Byron's poem is Junius, Satan's next witness. An anonymous libeller of King George III, Junius attacked the king for his mother's relations with Lord Bute[31] and then hypocritically accused the king of "personal resentment" against him. Despite Junius's radical rhetoric, his ultimate aims were not the removal of the king and impeachment of the aristocracy, but dissolution of Parliament, triennial elections, an extension of county membership, and the return of the Whig administration.[32] Though he agreed with moderate Whig positions, Byron disagreed with the libels he uses to achieve his ends in "The Vision of Judgment." By attacking the king personally, Junius crosses the boundaries of Whig propriety, condemning himself to political oblivion. Byron exploits Junius's anonymity, his practice of not signing his name to his letters (common enough at the time), to expose Junius's place in the political wilderness and underscore the danger of abandoning one's party. Interpreting Junius's anonymity literally, Byron concludes that Junius[33] is *"really, truly,* nobody at all" (*CPW* 80:640).

> I don't see wherefore letters should not be
> Written without hands, since we daily view
> Them written without heads; and books we see,
> Are fill'd as well without the latter too:
> And really till we fix on somebody
> For certain sure to claim them as his due,
> Their author, like the Niger's mouth, will bother
> The world to say if *there* be mouth or author.
> (*CPW* 6:80:660–62)

As if to complete Byron's critique, Michael accuses Junius of "Exaggeration . . . Thou wast/Too bitter—is it not so?" The most Byron can say in Junius's favor is that he "loved [his] country, and hated [George III]."[34]

Far more gentlemanly than Junius or Wilkes are Michael and Satan. If Satan is an eighteenth-century Whig, Michael is a Tory, or "new man." "A familiarity between [these aristocratic leaders of different parties] . . . unites them as members of the same class, and separates them from the lower orders."[35] Byron emphasizes their similarities:

> He [Michael]
> turned as to an equal, not too low,
> But kindly; Sathan met his ancient friend
> With more hauteur, as might an old Castilian
> Poor noble meet a mushroom rich civilian.
> (*CPW* 6:36:288)

Michael is a gentleman, but he has come to his wealth and social position more recently than Satan, who Byron compares to a "Poor noble." Theologically,

Satan recalls Genesis and the Hebrew Bible, while Michael is a more novel religious figure who suggests the values of the New Testament in which he appears. Like early-nineteenth-century Tories, Michael is *nouveau riche* in more than one sense.

Whigs and Tories have become familiar adversaries. "[B]etween his Darkness and his Brightness," Byron notes, "There passed a mutual glance of great politeness" (*CPW* 6:35:280). By 1821, in fact, Whigs and Tories were almost parodies of one another,[36] distinguished more by opposing radicalism than by offering different legislative programs. Michael, after all, "ne'er mistake[s Satan] for a *personal* foe;/Our difference is *political*," he says, "and I/Trust that, whatever may occur below,/You know my great respect for you; and this/Makes me regret whate'er you do amiss" (*CPW* 62:492–496). Michael's dismissive phrase, "whatever may occur below," underscores the Tory and Whig hostility to reform, a hostility based on their "height" (Satan's height, of course, is borrowed: he is a guest in Heaven for the trial of King George III). Like the Whigs, Satan observes the "point of form" of parliamentary procedure that keeps him out of power, but closer to it than the radicals. He indicts George III, but does so in a perfunctory manner, criticizing him for warring with "freedom and the free" and for opposing "Catholic participation." "To me the matter is/Indifferent, in a personal point of view," Satan says of George's trial. "I can have fifty better souls than this/With far less trouble than we have gone through/Already; and I merely argued his/Late Majesty of Britain's case with you/Upon a point of form: you may dispose/Of him; I've kings enough below, God knows!" (*CPW* 6:64:505–511). Byron was similarly "[i]ndifferent" to George III's fate; he directed his poem primarily against radical apostates like Southey and Wilkes.

Byron's hostility toward radicalism is perhaps most evident in his decision to concentrate on issues and personages (Wilkes, Junius) who made their reputation before what Byron describes as "the Gallic era 'eighty-eight'" (*CPW* 6:1:5). By doing so, he ignores the political issues that undid the Whigs (parliamentary reform, the French Revolution, and collaboration with Napoleon). In the same way that he always thought of the Whigs as the party of Fox and Sheridan, Byron returned his poem to a time when these politicians were in their prime, fighting royal power, championing the cause of the common people, and doing both without jeopardizing their own political livelihood.[37] Since 1789, the Whigs' fall from power had seemed irrevocable: the Tories were always in power and the Whigs always out of it. In his preface to "A Vision of Judgement," Southey accused Byron and Shelley of belonging to the "Satanic school of poetry." Byron implicitly mocked this idea by identifying his Whig politics with Satan's. Wilkes and Southey's radicalism was far more dangerous than Satan's good-natured opposition, he suggests. Both were turncoats, after all.

Satan, at least, was consistent. Called as a witness, Wilkes refuses to indict George III. Instead, he votes his habeas corpus into heaven:

> "Wilkes," said the Devil, "I understand all this;
> You turn'd to half a courtier ere you died,
> And seem to think it would not be amiss
> To grow a whole one on the other side
> (*CPW* 6:72:569–72)

As a Whig, Satan reproves the radical Wilkes for his waywardness. The third radical in Byron's poem is Southey, another apostate:

> He had written praises of a regicide;
> He had written praises of all kings whatever;
> He had written for republics far and wide,
> And then against them bitterer than ever;
> For pantisocracy he once had cried
> Aloud, a scheme less moral than 'twas clever;
> Then grew a hearty antijacobin—
> Had turn'd his coat—and would have turn'd his skin.
> (*CPW* 6:97:769–76)

Wilkes and Southey's radicalism is a sham: the one alters his creed by firing on a London crowd while the other moves from "praises of a regicide" to "praises of all kings whatever." Byron's poem helps define the "integrity of the middle ground."[38]

Fittingly, Byron metes the worst punishment out to Robert Southey.

> Saint Peter, who has hitherto been known
> For an impetuous saint, upraised his keys,
> And at the fifth line knock'd the Poet down;
> Who fell like Phaeton, but more at ease,
> Into his lake, for there he did not drown,
> A different web being by the Destinies
> Woven for the Laureate's final wreath, whene'er
> Reform shall happen either here or there.
> (*CPW* 6:104:825–32)

Byron presents reform ironically, as a "web" or trap that will expose Southey as a hypocrite who lacks substantial political convictions: he supported "reform" as a youth, but as poet laureate he will be embarassed by such developments.[39] He diminishes Southey by portraying him as a perpetual youth whose *hubris* is as absurd as Phaeton's. Both Southey and Phaeton must realize that the reins of government, like the reins of Apollo's chariot, are best left in the hands of more experienced drivers.

Byron's radicals are disruptive. No sooner does Satan call them to bear witness against George III than he regrets his actions. Byron portrays them as "locusts" and "wild geese," as "Bitter as clubs in cards are against spades" (*CPW* 6:60:460, 462, 488). Their "bitter[ness]" is futile, Byron suggests, since all cards are in the same deck. Byron emphasizes the insolence of their "swearing" style, which undermines the effectiveness of their testimony. Satan, however, transforms the crowd's geese-like squabbling into an eloquent attack on George III. He does so by employing a typically Whig strategy: portraying the king as an enemy of liberty.

Byron found his companions on *The Liberal* no less vexing than the radicals he satirized in his poem. He contributed to *The Liberal* alongside William Hazlitt but attacked Hazlitt in his *Ravenna Journal* (January 28, 1821) as a man who "*talks pimples*—a red and white corruption rising up (in little imitation of mountains upon maps), but containing nothing, and discharging nothing except their own humours."[40] Byron admired Shelley the gentleman but distrusted Shelley the atheist. Rescuing his illegitimate daughter from the hands of his fellow editor on *The Liberal*, Byron placed Allegra in a convent, where she received a traditional Catholic education until her untimely death.[41]

V

When Shelley died on July 8, 1822, Byron could not maintain his posture of liberality toward Hunt, for his class consciousness and preference for classical literature inevitably reasserted themselves. The same year he sought to reach a broader audience as editor of *The Liberal*, Byron had narrowed the audience for his poetic work by completing the last of his classical dramas. *Marino Faliero* (1821), *The Two Foscari* (1821), and finally, *Sardanapalus* (1821) show the distance Byron meant to put between his classical Whig tastes in literature and the cloying style of Hunt's "The Story of Rimini" or Keats's "Eve of St. Agnes," both of which he criticized in his letters on the Pope-Bowles controversy.

Byron's break with Hunt shows how Shelley's death altered Byron's behavior. In a letter to Murray, Byron explained how distasteful he found his older definition of liberality. "I am afraid the Journal is a bad business," Byron wrote:

> and won't do—but in it I am sacrificing myself for others—I can have no advantage in it—I believe the *brothers* Hunt to be honest men—I am sure that they are poor ones.—They have not a rap—they pressed me to engage in this work—and in an evil hour I consented—still I shall not repent if I can do them the least service.—I have done all I can for Leigh Hunt—since he came here—but it is almost useless—his wife is ill—his six children not very tractable and in the affairs of this world he himself is a child—The death of

Shelley left them totally aground—and I could not see them in such a state without using the common feelings of humanity—& what means were in my power to set them afloat again. (*BLJ* October 9, 1822; 10:13)

Byron's metaphors betray him. He views the journal commercially, as "a bad business," and finds noblesse oblige antiquated. "I am sacrificing myself for others—I can have no advantage in it," he concludes, repudiating the aristocratic ethos he once used to define liberality.

Byron's close friendship with Shelley was the only political passion that kept *The Liberal* afloat. When Shelley died, Hunt was left "totally aground," and felt he had no choice but to appeal for Byron's financial help directly. Where he had once used Shelley as an intermediary with Hunt, Byron hoped to "set [Hunt's family] afloat again"—not for the purpose of welcoming the Hunt family's bark into his aristocratic harbor, but to dispatch Hunt and his family to some safe location. Ultimately, Byron, not Hunt, was the first to depart, but Byron could never escape viewing his role with Hunt as that of a lifeguard assigned the unenviable task of rescuing a man intent on drowning. "It is like pulling a man out of a river who directly throws himself in again," he wrote to Thomas Moore. "For the last three or four years, Shelley assisted, and had once actually extricated him. I have since his demise—and even before,—done what I could" (*BLJ* April 2, 1823; 10:138).

Byron's nautical metaphors betray his belief that liberality can be a thankless moral posture. Byron was not yet willing to act on this insight, but when he did he dissolved *The Liberal* as decisively as he altered his use of the word. Having moved from England to Italy, Byron had come to define liberality differently. In 1818, he still subscribed to the view that a gentleman should not receive payment for his literary work. By January 19, 1819, however, this was no longer the case: "Whatever Brain-money—you get on my account from Murray—pray remit me," he wrote to Kinnaird with a bawdiness that showed how Italian customs influenced his English manners. "I will never consent to pay away what I *earn*—that is *mine*—and what I get by my brains—I will spend on my b——ks—as long as I have a tester or a testicle remaining" (*BLJ* 6:92).

In 1818, Byron still felt uncomfortable about seeking payment for his literary works. To conceal his embarrassment, he exaggerated his greed in letters to Douglas Kinnaird, lacing his requests for money with quotations from *The Merchant of Venice*. As he wrote *Don Juan*, Byron continued to justify his avarice. "So for a good old gentlemanly vice," he wrote, "I think I must take up with avarice" (*CPW* 5:1:216). According to Hunt, Byron confessed his avarice to "secure the public against a suspicion of it."[42] Perhaps, but Byron's perspective had also altered by November 28, 1822. "You will smile at all this tirade upon business," he wrote to Douglas Kinnaird, "but it is time to mind it—at least for me to mind it—for without some method in it where or what is independence? the power of doing good to others or yourself" (*BLJ* November 28, 1822; 10:43). Byron's letters to Kinnaird became longer, filled with plans about how to invest his money. "I cast up my household accounts—and settle them daily myself— and you cannot imagine the difference" (*BLJ* October 19, 1822; 10:61). He informed Kinnaird of how earnest he was in his "frugalities." "I am selling two more horses—and dismissing two superfluous servants—My horses now amount to *four* instead of *nine*—and I have arranged my establishment on the same footing" (*BLJ* October 9, 1822; 10:51). "Send me a good Cocker," he wrote, "or the best Simplifier of arithmetic" (*BLJ* October 19, 1822; 10:61).

Ironically, Byron's involvement in *The Liberal* occurred when he was becoming more self-protective. Where Shelley had delighted in mixing up his financial affairs with Hunt's, Byron compelled Hunt to receive weekly payments from Byron's servant, Lega Zambelli. Hunt found this arrangement humiliating and had difficulty striking the right tone for his requests. "I must trouble you for another 'cool hundred' of your crowns," runs one such letter, "and shall speedily, I fear, come upon you for one more."[43] Where he had once given loans freely to Augusta, refused payment from Murray for his manuscripts, married Annabella without investigating her finances, and separated from her by offering a generous annuity, he was now more suspicious of his close friends' pecuniary motives. He feared acting generously and of not being repaid in kind. Murray's offer for the *Don Juan* cantos was too low; Annabella's family had not sent him money when Lady Noel died; Lord Lushington attempted to cheat him of a trifling amount; Hobhouse upbraided him for granting Thomas Moore free copyrights of his memoirs (*BLJ* July 6–September 26, 1822; 9:180–219, passim; October 4–9, 1822; 10:1–51, passim). He noted the lack of reciprocity among the "canaille" English when he attempted to recover money that his friend James Wedderburn Webster owed him. "I have never pressed Webster—but to say truth—he has behaved shabbily about it—and had the impudence to ask me the other day—whether 'my heirs' could act upon it.... I am sure that all my Creditors have been a good deal less patient" (*BLJ* October 10, 1822; 10:49).

Byron's attention to fiscal details weakened his sense of obligation toward Hunt. If Shelley's generous feelings for Hunt helped launch *The Liberal*, Byron's indifference spelled its demise. "I will do my duty by my intimates, upon the principle of doing as you would be done by," he informed Mary Shelley. "But as for friends and friendship, I have (as I already said) named the only remaining male [Lord Clare] for whom I feel any thing of the kind, excepting, perhaps, Thomas Moore" (*BLJ* November 16, 1822, 10:34).

As a young man, Byron did not pursue liberty in the political sphere alone. Like his Whig predecessors (Charles James Fox, Charles Grey, and Sir Francis Burdett), he conducted libertine affairs while committing himself to liberal causes. As his sexual passions waned, however, so too did his extravagant gifts. Robert Rushton, Augusta Leigh, and Nicolo Giraud[44] saw their fortunes decline with Byron's waning erotic attachment. "I always looked to about thirty as the barrier of any real or fierce delight in the passions," he wrote to Douglas Kinnaird, "and determined to work them out in the younger ore and better veins of the Mine—and I flatter myself (perhaps) that I have pretty well done so—and now the *dross* is coming—and I loves lucre—for one must love something" (*BLJ* January 18, 1823; 10:87–88).

Working on *The Liberal* altered Byron's very definition of the word. By the time he published the fourth issue with Leigh Hunt on July 30, 1823, the appeal of rescuing Leigh Hunt financially paled in comparison with devoting himself to the cause of Greek independence. "If my health gets better and there is a war," he wrote to Douglas Kinnaird, "it is not off the cards that I may go to Spain—in which case I must make all 'Sinews of War' (monies that is to say) go as far as they can—for if I *do* go—it will be to do what I can in the good cause" (*BLJ* March 1, 1823; 10:114).

As the periodical press noted, Byron's position was precisely the reverse of what it had been. Where he had borrowed money from Jews as a college spendthrift, he now served as Leigh Hunt's moneylender and compared himself to the Merchant of Venice; if he had joined *The Liberal* out of a sense of noblesse oblige, he now recognized that such an ethos was morally bankrupt. These reversals of fortune provide insight into how Byron defined the word "liberal" in a new way. He did so by committing himself to Greek independence, although his new self-conception ended with an unwitting self-immolation when he died of a fever at Missolonghi. Byron aided the Greeks by subordinating his personality to a larger cause. He believed in the Greeks, and perhaps the Jews, more than he believed in Leigh Hunt (*BLJ* June 1, 1818; 6:47–48),[45] and assumed a bewildering number of "liberal" postures before arriving at the "true one." Yet Byron's act of self-overcoming in Greece enabled him to convert his avarice to philanthropy, his noblesse oblige to noble action, and his failed journal into a triumph that forever altered how both Byron and *The Liberal* were seen.

NOTES

1. Hunt, *Lord Byron and Some of His Contemporaries*, 80; William Marshall "The Catalogue for the Sale of Byron's Books," 25. Perhaps distrusting Leigh Hunt as a source,

168 Chapter 7

Leslie Marchand, in his revised edition of his three-volume biography (*Byron: A Portrait*, 385) states that no documentary evidence exists for claiming that Byron chose the title, *The Liberal*; Grosskurth and Eisler provide no further information. Yet Byron's role in choosing the title (his first was "Hesperides") is documented by Anne Blainey (*Immortal Boy: A Portrait of Leigh Hunt* [Philadelphia: University of Pennsylvania Press, 1968], 134), William Marshall (*Byron, Shelley, Hunt, and the Liberal* [Philadelphia: University of Pennsylvania Press], 71), Elie Halevy (*A History of the English People: The Liberal Awakening (1815–1830)*, trans. E. I. Watkin [New York: Peter Smith, 1949], 81), and Raymond Williams (*Keywords*, 180), who stresses the importance of this event.

2. Peter Thorslev, "Post-Waterloo Liberalism," *Studies in Romanticism* 28 (fall, 1989): 437–41.

3. I stress differences among contributors. For an excellent discussion of what this group had in common, see Jeffrey N. Cox, *Poetry and Politics in the Cockney School*, 50.

4. Mitchell, *Holland House*, 232.

5. Mitchell, *Holland House*, 232. For an account of Blanco White's role in publishing *El Espagñol*, see Martin Murphy, *Blanco White: Self-Banished Spaniard* (New Haven: Yale University Press, 1989), 61–99, and the letters of Blanco White to Lord Holland, Liverpool University Library.

6. Mitchell, *Holland House*, 220.

7. Halevy, *The Liberal Awakening*, 181.

8. Simpson and Weiner, *Oxford English Dictionary*, 1215. Halevy states: "It was perhaps through the channel of Holland House that the term found its way into the political vocabulary of England" (*England in 1815*, 93). David Manning (*Liberalism* [New York: St. Martin's Press, 1976]) concurs with Halevy's findings and defines liberalism in a way that, unlike L. T. Hobhouse's *Liberalism* (Oxford: Oxford University Press, 1964), shows the importance of its Whig roots.

9. Simpson and Weiner, *Oxford English Dictionary*, 1215.

10. Erdman, "Byron and Revolt," 234–48.

11. Erdman, "Byron and Revolt," 245.

12. Edmund Blunden has argued that the title was taken (he does not say by whom) from a Brussells journal, *Le Liberal*, published under that title from November 15, 1816 to March 31, 1817, and published thereafter under the title *Le Vrai Liberal*, until July 21, 1821. But Byron did not borrow any previous choices ("The Bergami," "Gli," "I Carbonari," and "Hesperides") from periodicals. In fact, his purpose was to distance himself from newspaper editors. He had no need to look to Brussells for a word that he could find circulating among his own revolutionary cronies, the Carbonari.

13. Hunt, *Lord Byron and Some of His Contemporaries*, 15.

14. Nicolson, *Byron*, 23.

15. Eisler, *Byron*, 711.

16. Edward John Trelawny, *Recollections of the Last Days of Shelley and Byron* (1858; reprint, New York: Doubleday, 1960), 157. Trelawny's argument is also taken up by John Cordy Jeaffreson, *The Real Lord Byron* (London: Hurst, 1884), 2:186.

17. Barnette Miller, *Leigh Hunt's Relations with Byron, Shelley and Keats* (New York: Folcroft Press, 1910), 99.
18. David B. Pirie, *Shelley* (Philadelphia: Open University Press, 1988), 4–6.
19. Fred Rosen, *Byron, Bentham, and Greece* (Oxford: Oxford University Press, 1992), 217.
20. Leigh Hunt, "Preface," *The Liberal: Verse and Prose from the South* 1 (1822): vii.
21. Hunt, "Preface," ix.
22. Hunt, "Preface," ix.
23. Hunt, "Preface," ix.
24. Hunt, "Preface," ix.
25. Marshall, "The Catalogue for the Sale of Byron's Books," 140.
26. Grosskurth, *Byron*, 417.
27. Hunt, *Lord Byron and Some of His Contemporaries*, 13.
28. Hunt, *Lord Byron and Some of His Contemporaries*, 13.
29. See George Rudé, *Wilkes and Liberty* (Oxford: Clarendon University Press, 1962) for an overview. More helpful for the present purpose was Stanley Ayling's *George III* (New York: Alfred A. Knopf, 1972), which discusses Wilkes from the perspective of George III.
30. Malcolm Kelsall, *Byron's Politics* (Totowa, N. J.: Barnes & Noble, 1987), 135, 141.
31. Ayling, *George III*, 78.
32. Kelsall, *Byron's Politics*, 141.
33. Alvar Ellegard argues that Junius was Philip Francis and Ellegard's view has been accepted by David McCracken. Ellegard, *Who Was Junius?* (Stockholm: Almquist & Wiksell, 1962); McCracken, preface to *Junius and Philip Francis* (Boston: G. K. Hall & Co., 1979), 140–141.
34. See Malcolm Kelsall's *Byron's Politics*, which views Byron's attitude toward Junius as more positive.
35. Kelsall, *Byron's Politics*, 141.
36. Stuart Peterfreund, in "The Politics of 'Neutral Space' in Byron's *Vision of Judgment*" (*Modern Language Quarterly* 40 [1979]: 275–91) offers a more specific, but I think less convincing, argument than Kelsall. For Peterfreund, Byron's "The Vision of Judgment" recalls Byron's first parliamentary speech and the Tory politicians who responded to it: Byron is Satan (277), Lord Eldon is Michael (282), and Lord Harrowby is Peter (283). Carl Woodring also rejects the equation of Byron and Satan in *Politics and English Romantic Poetry*, 195.
37. David Erdman distinguishes three phases in the movement for reform in "Lord Byron as Rinaldo," 189–229.
38. Kelsall, *Byron's Politics*, 129.
39. Kelsall, *Byron's Politics*, 143.
40. Foot, *The Politics of Paradise*, 241. J. J. Van Rennes, in *Bowles, Byron and the Pope-Controversy* (Amsterdam: H. J. Paris, 1927), points out their many differences of opinion (122). Byron's difference from the radicals is also expressed in his poem to the Luddites,

which he sent to Moore, "principally to shock" Hodgson (*BLJ* December 24, 1816; 5:149). I base my view that the poem is ironic on the line, "And down with all Kings but King Ludd," which is too emphatic to be entirely serious. For a different view, see Erdman, "Byron and Revolt in England," 240, and Malcolm Kelsall, *Byron's Politics*, 1–15.

41. Hunt, *Lord Byron and Some of His Contemporaries*, 24.
42. Hunt, *Lord Byron and Some of His Contemporaries*, 71.
43. Nicolson, *Byron*, 29.
44. Eisler, *Byron*, 296, 469, 296.
45. Thomas Ashton, *Byron's Hebrew Melodies* (Austin: University of Texas Press, 1972), 74.

8

"STILL LET ME LOVE!":
BYRON IN GREECE

> But still, to martial strains unknown,
>   My lyre recurs to love alone.
> Fired with the hope of future fame,
>   I seek some nobler hero's name;
> The dying chords are strung anew,
>   To war, to war, my harp is due . . .
> Love, love alone, my lyre shall claim,
> In songs of bliss and sighs of flame.
>
> "From Anacreon," *Hours of Idleness*

Torn between a life of poetry and a life of action, Byron united both through the erotic liberalism he practiced by fighting and dying for Greek independence. "'Tis time this heart should be unmoved,/Since others it hath ceased to move:/Yet, though I cannot be beloved,/Still let me love!" he wrote in "On This Day I Complete My Thirty-Sixth Year," most likely with Loukas Chalandritsanos firmly in mind. At 36, Byron died as he first imagined he might, when he translated Virgil's Nisus and Euryalus passage as a Harrow schoolboy. Like Nisus, who "sought a foreign home, a distant grave," Byron took some comfort in the company of a young boy of "beardless bloom." Precisely because his own heart was moved in politics as in love, Byron sought "some nobler hero's name" in Greece by remaining faithful to his erotic nature and the politics of feeling it inspired.

By moving from words to actions in Greece, Byron overcame the sin of avarice he feared had beset him in middle age. He left Teresa Guiccioli and Leigh Hunt to devote himself to a public cause. Once he arrived at Cephalonia, however, Byron found himself surrounded by other public-minded men who questioned his liberalism. To contrast Byron's politics with Col. Leicester Stanhope's utilitarianism is to recognize the difference between ancient and modern liberty. I borrow this distinction from Benjamin Constant's suggestive essay, "Ancient and Modern Liberty."[1] Where ancient liberals desired to participate directly in their government, Constant argued, modern liberals competed for commercial markets. Byron was able to appeal to both traditions. He brought a sense of heroic grandeur to the movement for Greek independence, while recognizing that he could only become appointed general of the Western forces in Greece by first volunteering to serve as paymaster for the cause.

Byron's conduct in Greece shows him subtly modifying the ancient liberalism that his classical education and allegiance to the Whigs first encouraged. In fact, Byron's capacity to borrow from the most promising aspects of ancient and modern liberty may help solve dilemmas modern liberals face. While staunchly championing a free press, separation of church and state, and an enlarged role for government, for example, Byron was not content to define liberty negatively, as most modern liberals do. He chose his enemies in George III and Robert Southey, it is true, but he also supported Spanish, Italian, and Greek independence. His willingness to articulate a political creed in his poetry and die in the service of a political cause enabled him to make a lasting example of a gesture, the value of which is still debated.[2]

I

Inspired by a brief visit from John Cam Hobhouse, Byron sailed to Greece, in part, to restore his reputation in England. Suddenly, the same man who begrudged Hunt a weekly stipend of seventy pounds could recount the loss of "8000 dollars" nonchalantly (*BLJ* January 2, 182[3] [1824]; 11:88) as he left Genoa on July 13, 1823 in a chartered vessel with "9 servants—including a doctor specially recruited—five horses, two small cannon, a store of medicines, 10,000 Spanish dollars in cash and bills for a further 40,000."[3] Byron suggested one reason he rejected the persona of Merchant of Venice he had so carefully cultivated while contributing to *The Liberal*. "It is *probable* I shall have to stand partly Paymaster," he wrote to John Bowring. "To say the Truth I do not grudge it—now the fellows have begun to fight *again*" (*BLJ* October 13, 1823; 11:77).

Leigh Hunt has explained Byron's liberality in Greece by noting its public nature. "Lord Byron was not a generous man," he wrote, "and, in what he did, he contrived either to blow a trumpet before it himself, or to see that others blew it for him. . . . As to the Greeks, the *present* of 10,000 was first of all well trumpeted to the world: it then became a *loan* of 10,000£.; then a loan of 6000£.; and he told me in one of his incontinent fits of communication and knowingness, that he did not think he should 'get off under 4000£.'"[4] There is some truth to Hunt's assessment—something quite self-conscious about Byron's decision to assist the Greek cause. Only a late fit of humility or embarrassment prevented Byron from using the three Homeric helmets he had ordered for his departure, two large ones for himself and Trelawny, and a smaller one for Pietro Gamba.[5]

Yet G. Wilson Knight comes to different conclusions about Byron's commitment to Greek independence. Byron "arranged for a supply of medical stores to be purchased and conveyed at his own expense; . . . advanced 4,000 to mobilize the Greek fleet; . . . financed the papers of the liberation; . . . and paid for fortifications for the town of Missolonghi after being named an honorary citizen. William Parry noted that he was 'spending about 2,000 dollars (= 400£.) a week in rations alone.'"[6]

What Hunt could not see was that Byron became avaricious only when he felt his money was being wasted. "I do not grudge any expence for the Cause," he informed Charles Hancock, "but to throw away as much as would equip—or at least maintain a corps of excellent ragamuffins with arms in their hands to furnish [Pietro] Gamba and the Doctor with 'blank books' (see list) broad Cloth—Hessian boots and horse-whips (*the latter* I own they have richly earned) is rather beyond my endurance" (*BLJ* January 19, 1824; 10:95). Protesting perhaps too much, Byron portrayed himself as indifferent to personal glory. "I must muster all the means in my compass as I am paymaster 'pro tempore' and Heaven knows what besides," he wrote to G. Stevens, a customs officer in Arogostoli. In a postscript, he declared his intention to "stick by the Greeks to the last rag of canvas or shirt—and not to go snivelling back like all the rest of them" (*BLJ* January 19, 1824; 11:97).

Byron connected political with erotic freedom during the Greek War of Independence, a fact that Leigh Hunt and William Hazlitt overlooked. Clearly, his attraction to Loukas Chalandritsanos, unplanned and unsought as it was, affected Byron's decision to fight in, rather than merely witness, the Greek war. "If thou regrett'st thy youth, why live?" he asked himself on his 36th birthday, ending his poem with the inevitable answer. "Seek out—less often sought than found—/A soldier's grave, for thee the best;/Then look around, and choose thy ground,/And take thy rest." William Hazlitt experienced an erotic crisis of his own, which he recorded in *Liber Amoris* (1823)[7] and which was not unrelated to the failure of political liberalism after Napoleon, but English society demanded the repression of such desire. Hazlitt, a contributor to *The Liberal*, remained unsympathetic to Byron's activities in Greece, the erotic inspiration for which he was probably unaware. So too Leigh Hunt, married with several children and bitter about the dissolution of *The Liberal*, failed to realize that *eros*, not simply egotism, motivated Byron's liberality.

II

Byron faced harsh criticisms for collaborating with Leigh Hunt on *The Liberal* and for publishing *Don Juan*. No sooner did he leave Leigh Hunt behind, however, than he found another British citizen ready to undertake a minute inspection of his integrity and motives.[8] "Lord Byron possesses all the means of playing a great part in the glorious revolution of Greece," Col. Leicester Stanhope reported to the Greek Committee in London on January 21, 1824. "He has talent; he professes liberal principles; he has money; and is inspired with fervent and chivalrous feeling." But Stanhope added a note of caution. "He will be closely watched and scrutinised by his countrymen, and by the whole world. His fame, like that of other prominent men, must depend on his conduct."[9]

From the moment he met Col. Leicester Stanhope in Greece, Byron disagreed with the utilitarian's approach to freeing that country. Byron criticized Stanhope's "high-flown notions of the sixth form at Harrow or Eton" and had no use for those who preferred arming a country with "a Sunday school to creating an academy of Artilleryship" (*BLJ* February 7, 1824; 10:109). Byron contrasted Leicester Stanhope's idealistic and Benthamite concern with "printing and civilizing expences" (*BLJ* February 7, 1824; 10:109) with William Parry's more practical experience in launching rockets, noting that "Parry complains grievously of the mercantile and *enthusymusy* (as Braham pronounces enthusiasm) part of the Committee." Parry, by contrast, was "a fine fellow—extremely active—and of strong—sound—practical talent" (*BLJ* February 7, 1824; 11:109), just the person to curb Stanhope's more idealistic approach to achieving Greek independence. "Col. Napier and I set him to rights on those points," Byron said of Stanhope, "which is absolutely necessary to prevent disgust, or perhaps return; but now we can set our shoulders *soberly* to the *wheel*, without quarreling with the mud which may clog it occasionally" (*BLJ* October 26, 1823; 11:83).[10]

Stanhope and Byron disagreed vehemently about establishing a free press, as Byron informed Samuel Barff on March 19, 1824.

> From the very first I foretold to Col. Stanhope and to P[rince] Mavrocordato that a Greek Newspaper (or indeed any other) in the *present state* of Greece— might—and probably *would* lead to much mischief and misconstruction—

unless under *some* restrictions—nor have I ever had anything to do with either—as a Writer—or otherwise, except as a pecuniary Contributor to their support on the outset which I could not refuse to the earnest request of the Projectors. Col. S[tanhope] and myself had considerable differences of opinion on this subject—and (what will appear laughable enough—) to such a degree that he charged me with *despotic* principles—and I *him* with Ultra-radicalism.—Dr. Meyer the Editor with his unrestrained freedom of the Press—takes the Freedom to exercise an unlimited discretion—not allowing any articles but his own and those like them to appear—and in declaiming against restrictions—cuts, carves, and restricts—(as they tell me) at his own will and pleasure.—He is the Author of an article against Monarchy—of which he may have the advantage and fame—but they (the Editors) will get themselves into a Scrape—if they do not take care.—Of all petty tyrants he is one of the pettiest—as are most demagogues that ever I knew. (*BLJ* March 19, 1824; 11:138–39)

But Stanhope gives a different impression of the incident which led him to charge Byron with "*despotic* principles." According to Stanhope, the dispute was not philosophical, but practical. Captain Yorke had charged Mavrocordato's government with violating Ionian neutrality. Byron advised Mavrocordato to placate Yorke, but Colonel Stanhope objected to Byron's manner of handling the affair. "In the evening," Stanhope reported to the Committee on January 28,

> Lord Byron conversed with me on the subject. I said the affair was conducted in a bullying manner, and not according to the principles of equity and the law of nations. His Lordship started into a passion. He contended that law, justice, and equity had nothing to do with politics. That may be; but I will never lend myself to injustice. His Lordship then began, according to custom, to attack Mr. Bentham. I said that it was highly illiberal to make personal attacks on Mr. Bentham before a friend who held him in high estimation. He said that he only attacked his public principles, which were mere theories, but dangerous, injurious to Spain, and calculated to do great mischief in Greece. I did not object to His Lordship's attacking Mr. B.'s principles: what I objected to were his personalities. His Lordship never reasoned on any of Mr. B.'s writings, but merely made sport of them. I would, therefore, ask him what it was that he objected to? Lord Byron mentioned his Panopticon as visionary. I said that experience in Pennsylvania, at Millbank, etc., had proved it otherwise. I said that Bentham had a truly British heart; but that Lord Byron, after professing liberal principles from his boyhood, had, when called upon to act, proved himself a Turk.—Lord Byron asked, "What proofs have you of this?"—"Your conduct in endeavouring to crush the press, by declaiming against it to Mavrocordato, and your general abuse of liberal principles."—Lord Byron said that if he had held up his finger he could have crushed the press.—I replied, "With all this power,—which, by the way, you never possessed—you went to the Prince and poisoned his ear."—Lord Byron declaimed against the liberals whom he knew.—"But what liberals?"

I asked: did he borrow his notions of free-men from the Italians?—Lord Byron: "No; from the Hunts, Cartwrights, etc."—"And still," said I, "you presented Cartwright's Reform Bill, and aided Hunt by praising his poetry and giving him the sale of your works."—Lord Byron exclaimed, "You are worse than Wilson and should quit the army."—I replied, "I am a mere soldier, but never will I abandon my principles. Our principles are diametrically opposite, so let us avoid the subject."

If Lord Byron acts up to his professions, he will be the greatest, if not, the meanest, of mankind.—He said he hoped his character did not depend on my assertions.—"No," said I, "your genius has immortalized you. The worst could not deprive you of fame."—Lord Byron: "well, you shall see: judge me by my acts." When he wished me good night, I took up the light to conduct him to the passage; but he said, "What! hold up a light to a Turk!"[11]

To a certain extent, Stanhope and Byron's conflict grew out of the fervor of each Englishman's latest enthusiasm: the one for Bentham's utilitarianism, the other for a life of action.

The irony of this situation was not lost on Byron. "It is odd enough that Stanhope, the soldier, is all for writing down the Turks; and I, the writer, am all for fighting them down," he confided to Pietro Gamba.[12] Stanhope was equally disconcerted, describing Byron disapprovingly as "soldier-mad"[13]: "Lord Byron burns with military ardour and chivalry, and will proceed with the expedition to Lepanto."[14] Byron seemed prepared to follow the chivalric example of Childe Harold he had disowned, and to agree with Madame de Staël that chivalry was, in fact, the military religion of Europe.

I have quoted Stanhope's assessment of Byron's conduct in Greece at such length because their divergent perspectives highlight two distinct traditions of liberalism that were in flux. The evolving philosophy of Jeremy Bentham, John Stuart Mill, and the Radical Reformers, or utilitarians as they called themselves, stressed the important role free institutions (education, a free press, and separation of church and state) play in providing citizens with the tools necessary to acquire and maintain their freedom. "The devising of the right kinds of institutions and their implementation came to be regarded as more important than the formation of character by liberal education," Strauss argues in *Ancient and Modern Liberalism*.[15] Modern liberals take an optimistic view of history, moreover, seeing it as an evolutionary process that illustrates the progress of *human nature*, as Marilyn Butler notes.[16] The preface to Stanhope's *Greece in 1823 and 1824* clearly strikes this theme. There, the editor views the state of Greeks as an inexplicable pause in the advancement of civilization. Greeks "have become the murmuring slaves of a race of uncivilized infidels," while "the modern Greek had degenerated from the talents and magnanimity of his forefathers."[17] Benthamites who believed in progress set out to correct this anomaly.

Modern liberals inherited Bentham's meliorism. Modern liberalism "is historical because it regards the human characteristics as acquired and not as given," Leo Strauss explains.

> It is optimistic and radical; it is "a genuine humanism which is not guilt-ridden"; it is democratic and egalitarian; accordingly it traces the historical changes and hence morality less to outstanding men than to groups and their pressures which "take concrete form in the education activity of the members of the group"; it is in full sympathy with technological society and an international commercial system;[18] it is empirical and pragmatic; last but not least it is naturalist or scientific, that is, nontheological and nonmetaphysical.[19]

Modern liberals define liberty negatively, seeking to protect individual freedom from the mechanizing effects of custom.[20] Economically, they advocate laissez-faire doctrines while socially they protect private liberty.[21] Liberalism finds its more mature expression in Mill's *On Liberty* and his *Autobiography*, where the son of Bentham's editor humanized utilitarian doctrines, stressing the importance of emotions as well as of principles like Bentham's own, the greatest happiness of the greatest number.

But there is another liberal tradition, more ancient than Bentham's and the Westminster reformers' and more closely connected with Greek culture. Ancient liberals invoke their classical ancestry, casting a suspicious eye on attempts to change, or worse, "improve" human nature. Unlike Shelley and Hunt, ancient liberals regard human nature as essentially fixed. In their Christian form, they emphasize the fall of humanity. In metaphysics, they long to return people to what they once were; in Greece they hope to restore the values and literature of that ancient civilization. Stanhope wished to "improve" Greece according to modern, utilitarian notions, while Byron longed to restore it to what it was. "He told me that Capo D'Istria's object was to preserve the Greek character, to which he attributed his success," Stanhope noted. "I said that the progress should be onward, not backward."[22] Byron's admiration for the language and culture of Greece's past, by contrast, guided his desire to free Greece; to a greater extent than Stanhope, he saw himself playing a recuperative role there. Stanhope advocated democracy; Byron (like Marino Faliero) advocated liberty, not "rash equality."

Though he criticized Byron's motives in traveling to Greece, Hazlitt paid tribute to the "long views" of ancient liberals like Byron: "The real, old hereditary nobility and gentry . . . are also men of liberal education; and this is a great point gained." An education like Byron's "accustoms the mind to take an interest in things foreign to itself, to love virtue for its own sake, to prefer fame to life, and glory to riches, and to fix our thoughts on the great and permanent instead of narrow and selfish objects."[23] By praising ancient liberalism, Hazlitt effectively challenged Bentham's tacit endorsement of modern materialism. "The principle on which public institutions ought to be formed is that an office-holder can be expected to subordinate office to personal advantage," Bentham assumed.[24]

Byron rejected such views. He did not believe, like Shelley, that history was an evolutionary process,[25] nor did he view Greek emancipation as "inevitable." They "Who would be free themselves must strike the blow," Byron wrote in *Childe Harold's Pilgrimage* (*CPW* 2:76:721). Most important, Byron was not seduced, as Stanhope was, by the pernicious idea that Greek institutions were somehow superior to Turkish ones. At times, he could manufacture this rhetoric for the consumption of the Greek Committee in London, troping the conflict between Greek and Turk as one between civilization and barbarism, Christianity and Islam. In reality, Byron knew the conflict was not so pure. "At present, there is but little difference in many respects between Greeks and Turks, nor could there be," he confessed to Pietro Gamba. "But the latter (the Turks) must, in the common course of events, decline in power; and the former must as inevitably become better in every sense of the word. The soil is excellent; with skillful tillage and good seeds, we should soon see how rapidly, and in what perfection, the fruits of civilization would rise around us."[26] Byron's agricultural metaphors betray his classical education, for "'Culture' (*cultura*) was ... first used to refer to ... cultivation of the soil and its products," as Leo Strauss explains.[27] Following classical liberals, Byron believed the Greeks must cultivate their soil as assiduously as their minds, nurturing excellence with "skillful tillage and good seeds."

Unlike Stanhope, Byron saw the danger of the modern liberals' tendency to universalize their discoveries, reducing different cultures to a greatest happiness principle or "springs of action" (or even today, to the very principles of democracy). Byron knew that English Tories and colonialists could easily misdirect the virtuous intentions of the radicals. He prided himself on seeing things as they were, regardless of whether such insights conformed to grandiose theories about human behavior. When necessary, this enabled him, despite his ancient liberalism, to speak the language of commerce and incentive, the language of a new generation of liberals led by Jeremy Bentham, David Ricardo, and Adam Smith. "If anything like an equilibrium is to be upheld, Greece must be supported," Byron wrote to the Greek Committee in London.

> Mr. Canning, I think, understands this, and intends to behave towards Greece as he does with respect to the South American colonies. This is all that is wanted; for in that case Greece may look towards England with the confi-

dence of friendship, especially as she now appears to be no longer infected with the mania of adding to her colonies, and sees that her true interests are inseparably connected with the independence of those nations, who have shown themselves worthy of emancipation, and such is the case with Greece.[28]

In this passage, Byron appeals to the calculating modern sensibility by emphasizing English vested interests: "her true interests are inseparably connected with the independence of these nations." At the same time, he invokes the more idealistic language of ancient liberals by alluding to England's "true interests" and stressing that the Greeks are "worthy" of English support. One vocabulary sees nations almost as businesses or trading partners searching for new markets; the other calls nations to a higher destiny by viewing them in terms of their cultural past. One defines virtue extrinsically, as wealth, while the other views it intrinsically, as a good pursued for its own sake.

But although Stanhope was a modern and Byron an ancient liberal, and despite the several differences in principle this entailed, the two managed to agree on political ends. "Byron and Bentham's ideas developed from the same Whig traditions," Fred Rosen observes; "the Harrovian Byron and the Etonian Stanhope, while disagreeing on some points, were in basic agreement on many more."[29] Both advocated a free press in Greece, differing only on how it should be administered. Byron gave money for a free press regardless of its utility—because it was "choiceworthy for [its] own sake"—while Stanhope asked Byron to support a free press *because* of its utility. Byron felt that Greece should be freed first and its citizens' characters improved afterward; Stanhope thought that both could be done at the same time.[30]

Equally trivial were distinctions between Byron and Stanhope's legalism. If Byron was truly an ancient liberal (in Constant's sense), he would have opposed a political system that sought to regulate human behavior externally, through laws. Instead, he would have sought a society that encouraged the growth of character and the pursuit of human excellence, taking a positive and not merely a negative approach to human liberty. In fact, Byron approved of the rigorous legal code used to discipline the Suliotes; three days before his death, he also disciplined a Prussian officer for harming Greek civilians.[31]

The difference between Byron and Stanhope's liberalism, then, may be more apparent than real. Like Stanhope, Byron longed to "do good" and to promote the greatest happiness for the greatest number. His only objection was to "mouth[ing]" about it.

> I shall continue to pursue my former plan of stating to the Committee things as they *really* are—I am an enemy to Cant of all kinds—but it will be seen in

time,—who are or are not the firmest friends of the Greek Cause—or who will stick by them longest—the Lempriere dictionary quotation Gentlemen—or those who neither dissemble their faults nor their virtues.— "I could mouthe" as well as any of them if I liked it—but I reserved (when I was in the habit of writing) such things for verse—in business—plain prose is best—and simplest—and was so—I take it even amongst the antient Greeks themselves—if we may judge from their history. (*BLJ* March 30, 1824; 11:147)

Byron would not call doing good his religion, but this was not out of a failure to respect religion itself. On the contrary, Byron had more faith than Stanhope in the relevance of Christian principles to political liberalism.

The nontheological strain of Stanhope's liberalism formed an important difference between them. In a letter to Bowring, Stanhope revealed his disgust for the superstitions Greek Orthodoxy encouraged: "I attended the church here on Christmas day. The women were all behind the lattices. The ceremony was chiefly mummery. The priests are said to be illiterate and immoral. The people are not very superstitious nor much priest ridden. Education, the press, the translation of the Scriptures, and the collusion of religious opinions, will purify their minds on the most important subjects" (November 13, 1823; 11:62). In line with his views on the importance of a free press, Stanhope thought that reading the scriptures was the surest path to faith. Like Bentham, whose rationalistic zeal in *Not Paul, but Jesus* (1823) led him right out of the faith he professed to defend,[32] however, Stanhope's efforts to approach religion from a utilitarian perspective violated basic tenets of liberalism (the separation of church and state, for example) that he should have been more anxious to defend.

Unlike Stanhope and Bentham, who were "professors of a new religion,"[33] Byron sought to understand the old religion (even Catholicism) on its own terms during his stay in Greece; he did not reduce it to serving as an arm of the state. His conversations with Dr. James Kennedy, a Methodist, are instructive in this respect.[34] If Byron rejected Kennedy's arguments, he did not fail to perform humanitarian acts in Greece that seemed like textbook examples of Christian charity Kennedy would have praised. Byron acted in the spirit of Christianity, for example, by releasing Turkish prisoners "at my own expence" (*BLJ* February 21, 1824; 11:117). Though he believed that money was the Sinew of War, he did not limit his assistance and generosity toward the Greeks to the monetary or even the utilitarian sphere. "Coming to Greece, one of my principal objects was to alleviate as much as possible the miseries incident to a warfare so cruel as the present," he wrote to Mr. Mayer, the English consul in Prevesa. "When the dictates of humanity are in question, I know no difference between Turks and Greeks. It is enough that those who want assistance are men, in order to claim the pity and protection of the meanest pretender to humane feelings. . . . The best recompense I can hope for would be to find that I had inspired the Ottoman commanders with the same sentiments towards those unhappy Greeks who may hereafter fall into their hands. I beg you to believe me" (*BLJ* February 21, 1824; 11:118). Stanhope shared such humanitarianism with Byron, though his brand of it was more secular than the poet's. Outdoing Bentham with his zealotry, Stanhope viewed religion as a barrier to progress.[35] Leigh Hunt and Percy Shelley shared this assessment. Byron, on the other hand, accepted Christian principles of conduct, especially the Christian ethos of the gentleman.

Byron and Stanhope's divergent attitudes toward religion are nowhere more apparent than in their dispute over a motto for an Italian language paper, the *Telegrafo Greco* (*BLJ* March 10, 1824; 11:132). Stanhope, the founder of the paper, wanted the motto to read, "the world our country and doing good our religion" (*BLJ* March 10, 1824; 11:132). For Byron, however, such a narrow, utilitarian view of religion was more blasphemous than Shelley's atheism. "I told the fools of Conductors—that their motto would play the devil, but like all mountebanks—they persisted" (*BLJ* March 10, 1824; 11:134), he wrote to Charles Hancock. Byron worried that an uncensored newspaper would divide Greek forces still further. Stanhope's secular tone would offend Greek nationals. Byron reassured James Kennedy that they "will not turn out either an irreligious or a levelling publication, and they promise due respect to both churches and things" (*BLJ* March 10, 1824; 11:132). In contrast with Stanhope, Byron defined himself as a Christian gentleman. "I suspect that I am a more orthodox Christian than you are," he informed Thomas Moore, "and, whenever I see a real Christian, either in practice or in theory, (for I never yet found the man who could produce either, when put to the proof,) I am his disciple. But, till then, I cannot truckle to tithe-mongers" (*BLJ* April 2, 1823; 10:138).

G. Wilson Knight has attempted to show that Byron lived his life according to Christian teachings and adduces Byron's love of animals, his pacifism, and his selflessness in the fight for national sovereignty in Italy and Greece as examples. Despite the exaggeration of some of its findings, Knight's well-documented book highlights a religious element in Byron's ethos of generosity that distinguishes him from utilitarians and modern day liberals. Byron seemed to understand, implicitly, that the radical doctrines of Shelley, Bentham, and Stanhope posed a greater danger to governments in their initial stages than the religious bigotry they sought to replace. "The opening of *Julian and Maddalo* is a striking reminder of Byron's fundamental seriousness about religion," M. K. Joseph argues,[36] though Terence Hoagwood and Robert Ryan have recently emphasized his skepticism and deism.[37]

Byron took the best from ancient and modern liberalism and offered the world a compelling example of liberal conduct. As a Protestant, he was more tolerant of other branches of Christianity than, for example, his first biographer. In *A Narrative of Lord Byron's Last Journey to Greece*, Gamba saw the struggle for Greek independence quite narrowly:

> There are few either in the Old or the New World, whithersoever the light of civilization extends, who have not proclaimed themselves friendly to the regeneration of Greece. People of all nations, parties, and sects the most opposed to each other, whether in politics or religion, have apparently always been unanimous in the wish of seeing that country liberated from the dominion of the Turks. Who would renounce the name of Christian, and incur the appellation of barbarian?[38]

For Gamba, as for a number of Philhellenes,[39] the "light of civilization" did not extend beyond the portals of a church. Byron, however, took a different view. "In his travels during his younger days," Gamba felt impelled to record, "he had imbibed a greater personal esteem for the character of the Turks than for that of their slaves."[40] As William St. Clair has observed, "Byron almost alone of the Philhellenes of the Greece War of Independence, did not rely on an unspoken assumption of superiority in knowledge and in ability. He tried to inform himself about Greek conditions."[41] Unlike Gamba or Stanhope, Byron insisted on recording his observations exactly as he saw them. He did not attempt to bring them into line with modern liberal assumptions concerning progress and barbarism. Byron saw that Christians could justify colonialism by professing compassion for infidels as easily as Tories could justify their foreign policy by canting about the need to maintain a balance of power.

Byron sought to blend the best of ancient and modern liberalism. From the classical authors he read and translated at Harrow (Plato, Virgil, Plutarch, Polybius), he developed his own ethos of virtue and excellence, and judged modern Greeks by their predecessors. He admired ancient republicanism and borrowed ancient Greek models of effective government. From modern liberals he learned the importance of maintaining political institutions (education, law, a free press) as a safeguard against charismatic tyrants such as Napoleon. Though he ridiculed Bentham as a visionary and criticized the reformers, he supported their programs, however reluctantly, in Greece; ultimately, his opposition to utilitarianism was more rhetorical than substantive.

Numerous factors brought Byron to Greece: Hobhouse's encouragement, boredom with his life in Italy and with the role of *cavalier servente* (*BLJ* August 23, 1819; 6:214), a desire to restore his reputation in England. But once he was there, a fifteen-year-old boy, not Stanhope or Bentham, transformed him from a spectator into an actor. Not the abstract political principles discussed above, but Byron's love for Loukas Chalandritsanos motivated his military involvement in the Greek War of Independence. To make sense of this inspiration, one has only to return to Plato's *Symposium*, which I invoked in the introduction to this study. There, Pausanias argued that male lovers would strive to impress one another with acts of bravery on the battlefield and used the story of Nisus and Euryalus as evidence. As a schoolboy, Byron translated this very episode from book nine of Virgil's *Aeneid*.

> Though few the seasons of his life,
> As yet a novice in the martial strife,
> 'Twas his, with beauty, valour's gift to share—
> A soul heroic, as his form was fair;
> These burn with one pure flame of generous love;
> In peace, in war, united still they move;
> Friendship and glory form their joint reward;
> And now combined they hold their nightly guard.
> (*CPW* 1:77)

Greece was the land of erotic freedom for Byron in 1810, and became so again in 1824, as Stephen Minta has recently shown.[42] Yet shame, perhaps even self-hatred, afflicted Byron in Greece, where he personified his own "Unworthy manhood!," ordering it to "Tread those reviving passions down . . . unto thee/Indifferent should the smile or frown/Of beauty be" ("On This Day," *CPW* 7:28–31).

And it is on this note of Byron as a Janus-faced man—looking backward toward ancient Greece and forward toward a more modern de-eroticized liberalism—that I would like to conclude my study. Partly because Byron's politics was "a *feeling*," he never subscribed to a set of doctrines known as liberalism, but responded to historical events on their own terms and in terms of the individuals who inspired him (*BLJ* January 22, 1814; 4:38).

His meeting with Leigh Hunt in prison was prophetic, for Hunt the political martyr both attracted and repulsed Byron. In 1813, and again in 1821, Hunt played the role of Byron's political conscience. In this study, he has served as a useful gauge by which to measure Byron's growing distance from radicals. With his involvement on *The Liberal* and his expedition to Greece, Byron was a Whig whose aristocratic background significantly colored his political outlook. He attempted to move beyond the metaphors of Whig politics he had learned at Harrow and Cambridge, but neither Hunt's politics of virtue, nor Napoleon's chivalric militarism provided him with an appropriate language to express his political passions. In Italy, Byron identified himself as a "liberal" but even this term was somewhat inaccurate, and based on a linguistic dissonance between Italy and England caused by his exile.

Byron does not conform to modern conceptions of what it means to be a liberal, in part, because he lived in a transitional time, retaining the class pride that Shelley, Hunt, Hazlitt, and others thought often vitiated his political judgment. At Harrow, Byron persuaded his classmates to abandon their plan of burning down the classroom by pointing to the names of their ancestors engraved on the walls. Byron's historical imagination and his Burkean respect for tradition made him proud of what he was and mindful lest a specious theory of progress lead him to abandon his inheritance. He cherished Newstead Abbey and relinquished it only with reluctance. Protestantism, which he could never fully embrace, nevertheless shaped his political imagination.[43] This imagination, synthetic and recuperative, allowed him to make use of ancient liberalism to define a new "liberal awakening." Byron shared with Madame de Staël the daunting task of explaining what liberalism should mean after the French Revolution and during the rise of Napoleon. Even more than Staël, however, he willingly acknowledged the diminished role aristocrats should play as the "king-times" were "fast finishing" (*BLJ* January 13, 1821, *Ravenna Journal*; 8:26).

Byron has often been faulted for his insincerity, for blowing a trumpet before all he did. The accusation, made by Leigh Hunt, is not off the mark. Though Byron's actions were well-advertised, however, this does not mean that they were not genuine. A trumpet was needed in 1824, especially after the Whigs had remained in opposition for the greater part of two decades. Perhaps the best way to accept Byron's self-mythologizing style is to remember the words of another commentator. Benjamin Constant, writing in *Journaux Intimes*, observed that motives in politics were less important than actions. He reasoned that if a politician performs a virtuous action for illiberal reasons, his motives will improve.[44] To a remarkable extent, this is Byron's political record. Egotism may well have led him to deliver his first two speeches in the House of Lords; an affair with Lady Oxford may have prompted him to deliver another in 1813, yet he laid the groundwork for more mature, and perhaps more efficacious, political activity through these half-hearted, muddily motivated acts. In Italy, Byron found new opportunities for political self-expression in 1820 when his love for Teresa Guiccioli and her family encouraged him to join the Carbonari. On his own initiative, he supported Greek independence in 1824, inspired both by the classical ideals of his Harrow education and his love for Loukas Chalandritsanos. To the extent that I have evaluated Byron's motives in this study, I have found his reactions to reformers and radicals wanting. Judged by his actions, however, which was how he wished to be judged, Byron fares quite well. Reversing the inheritance of man he described in "Prometheus," Byron proves himself to be a pure stream from a troubled source, a man whose liberalism sprang from his classical learning and was only transformed into its modern variant at great cost to his most cherished assumptions about hierarchy.

NOTES TOWARD A DEFINITION OF LIBERALISM

Liberalism does not admit of an easy definition today any more than it did in Byron's day. Terms of abuse and praise which Bentham saw as inimical to critical discourse crowd the page.[45] Yet several distinctions are still possible. A set of liberal beliefs might include separation of church and state, freedom of the press, national self-determination, and international free trade. But such doctrines are not very illuminating when listed as political axioms. Since canonical liberal writers rarely referred to themselves as liberals, any attempt to define liberalism (like romanticism) inevitably falls prey to a mistaken hindsight that groups writers according to certain beliefs and principles, rather than according to the language they used to describe themselves or the erotic attractions that inspired their acts of liberal self-sacrifice.

Tories used the word "liberal" to characterize the Spanish liberales (1816) and the more radical members of the Whigs; indeed liberalism itself could be said to have merged out of a crisis in Whig self-representation. The abusive epithet "liberal," as employed by the Tories, recalled the American and French revolutions, the agitation for parliamentary reform, and the fight for Spanish constitutionalism. Liberal ideas benefited from intellectual cross-fertilization, such as the infiltration of Scottish ideas on political economy into Holland House through the education, in Scotland, of such future Whig leaders as William Lamb.[46] Whigs championed the very ideas which displaced them. Carrying forward the Foxite legacy, Lord Holland supported Catholic emancipation and the abolition of the slave trade, and fought for the extension of the franchise. Byron altered the style of championing such ideas, espousing a personal brand of political feeling and self-expression in his poetry and prose that proved immensely popular.

Though he was a Whig, Byron was also a liberal *avant la lettre* who helped shape the principles of the Liberal Party in 1832. Byron championed liberty and national sovereignty even if he could not fully embrace social reforms that would threaten his own livelihood. He was perhaps more comfortable with the revolutionary aspects of liberalism than with its legalistic varieties, and for this reason he preferred Napoleon, Washington, Bolivar, Leonidas, Lord Edward Fitzgerald (the United Irishman), and Lord Cochrane (the radical admiral and M. P. who fought for new republics in South America) to Jeremy Bentham,

Samuel Romilly, or Henry Brougham, whom he despised both intellectually and personally. Byron personalized politics and, in doing so, found himself compared to Napoleon in his own day and to Hitler and Mussolini in ours. Yet Byron has also been the hero of all those (William Morris, John Ruskin, W. H. Auden, Michael Foot) who champion the collectivist branch of liberalism over and against its individualistic varieties. The two need not be irreconcilably opposed, as Nancy Rosenblum has shown,[47] and Byron's ability to fight for Greek independence alongside the Benthamite Colonel Stanhope gives reason for reassurance that cohesion is possible for "liberals" who still dare speak their name.

NOTES

1. Benjamin Constant, "The Liberty of the Ancients Compared with That of the Moderns," in *The Political Writings*, trans. and ed. Biancamera Fontana (Cambridge: Cambridge University Press, 1988), 308–28. Constant draws important distinctions between ancient and modern liberalism. His essay, as Stephen Holmes (*Benjamin Constant and the Philosophy of Liberalism* [New Haven: Yale University Press, 1968]) has shown, was influenced by the two periods in French history during which it was written. He warns against the dangers of excessive political involvement apparent during the French Revolution, but is equally concerned with the atrophy of political life after (and during) Napoleon's reign.

2. Henry Kissinger, *A World Restored: Metternich, Castlereagh and the Problems of Peace, 1812–1822* (Boston: Houghton Mifflin Company, 1957), 16–17.

3. St. Clair, *That Greece Might Still Be Free*, 154.

4. Hunt, *Lord Byron and Some of His Contemporaries*, 72.

5. Marchand, *Byron: A Biography*, 1078, 1081.

6. Knight, *Lord Byron: Christian Virtues* (New York: Oxford University Press, 1953), 185.

7. Jonathan Gross, "Hazlitt's Worshipping Practice in *Liber Amoris*," *Studies in English Literature* 35 (autumn 1995): 707–21.

8. St. Clair, 170. For Stanhope's views on Byron, see Marchand, *Byron: A Biography*, 1166; Nicolson, *Byron*, 205; Leicester Stanhope, *Greece in 1823 and 1824* (New York: Wilder & Campbell, 1825), passim; and Pietro Gamba, *A Narrative of Lord Byron's Last Journey to Greece* (Paris: A & W Galignani, 1825).

9. Nicolson, *Byron*, 205.

10. Described as "a drunk, a bully, and a coward" by Stephen Minta, Parry nevertheless appealed to Byron as a man of action rather than a man of words. Minta, *On a Voiceless Shore: Byron in Greece* (New York: Holt Rinehart, 1997), 250.

11. Nicolson, *Byron*, 209. Fred Rosen notes that this letter does not appear in manuscript. Rosen, *Byron, Bentham, and Greece*, 203.

12. Gamba, *Narrative*, 133.

13. Stanhope, *Greece in 1823 and 1824*, 64.
14. Stanhope, *Greece in 1823 and 1824*, 65.
15. Leo Strauss, *Ancient and Modern Liberalism* (New York: Cornell University Press, 1968), 21.
16. Marilyn Butler, *Romantics, Rebels, and Reactionaries* (Oxford: Oxford University Press, 1982), 153.
17. Stanhope, *Greece in 1823 and 1824*, vi.
18. Clearly, Godwin, Shelley, and Hunt do not meet Strauss's criteria here. Indeed, Sheldon Wolin, in *Politics and Vision: Continuity and Innovation in Western Political Thought* (Boston: Little, Brown and Co., 1960), shows us how Strauss's definition of modern liberalism may be inadequate, a result of lumping together democratic radicalism and liberalism. In fact, liberalism "had its roots in the period before the French Enlightenment.... [Unlike Shelley and Hunt,] David Hume and Adam Smith recognized the limits of reason and the pervasiveness of irrational factors on man and society" (293). I follow Strauss's distinction, because it allows me to differentiate, at least provisionally, between Byron's liberalism and the radicalism of Shelley, Hunt, and Bentham.
19. Leo Strauss, *Ancient and Modern Liberalism*, 14.
20. For a seminal essay distinguishing between positive and negative liberty, see Isaiah Berlin, "Two Concepts of Liberty" in *Four Essays on Liberty* (New York: Oxford University Press, 1969). See also Janet Radcliffe Richards, "Enquiries for Liberators," in *The Skeptical Feminist: A Philosophical Enquiry* (Boston: Routledge & Keegan Paul, 1980), 66–67. For recent definitions of liberalism that largely exclude literary works, see L. T. Hobhouse (Oxford: Oxford University Press, 1964); David Manning (New York: St. Martin's Press, 1976); David Sidorsky, ed. *The Liberal Tradition in European Thought* (New York: G. Putnam's Sons, 1970); Guido de Ruggiero, *The History of European Liberalism*, trans. R. G. Collingwood (Gloucester: Peter Smith, 1981); and John Rawls, *Political Liberalism* (New York: Columbia University Press, 1993).
21. Mitchell, *Holland House*, 121. At Holland House, Foxite principles of the 1780s and 1790s were combined with the scientific approach to political economy taught at Scottish universities. Barred from the grand tour of the continent because of the Napoleonic wars, men like William Lamb and Lord John Russell brought back to Holland House the lessons in political economy they had learned at Edinburgh University under tutors like Dugald Stewart and John Millar.
22. Stanhope, *Greece in 1823 and 1824*, 9.
23. William Hazlitt, "Advice to a Patriot," in *The Collected Works of William Hazlitt*, ed. A. R. Waller and Arnold Glover (London: J. M. Dent & Co., 1902), 3:21. For interesting differences between Hazlitt's and Byron's attitudes toward social class, see David Bromwich, *Hazlitt: The Mind of a Critic* (New Haven: Yale University Press, 1983), passim.
24. Wolin, *Politics and Vision*, 281.
25. Ernest Lovell points out that "egocentric as Byron was, he never once accepted the myth of man's perfectability." Lovell, *Byron: Record of a Quest* (New York: Macmillan, 1949), 240–41.

26. Gamba, *Narrative*, 3.

27. Strauss, *Ancient and Modern Liberalism*, 3.

28. Gamba, *Narrative*, 207–09.

29. Rosen, *Byron, Bentham, and Greece*, 204, 199.

30. Elizabeth Longford and Harold Nicolson underscore the more ridiculous aspects of Stanhope's approach to achieving Greek independence, but William St. Clair, while conceding this point, shows how effective Stanhope could be at implementing his plans. Longford, *The Life of Byron* (Boston: Little, Brown and Company, 1976), 198–200; Nicolson, *Byron: The Last Journey;* St. Clair, *That Greece Might Still Be Free*.

31. In several letters (*BLJ* March 8, 1824; 11:129; March 30, 1824; 11:145; April 1, 1824; 11:150–51), Byron portrays the law in positive terms, a position that contrasts with his rejection of law and legal measures during his separation from Annabella.

32. James E. Crimmins, *Secular Utilitarianism: Social Science and the Critique of Religion in the Thought of Jeremy Bentham* (Oxford: Clarendon Press, 1990), 14.

33. Williams, *Keywords*, 276.

34. Joseph, *Byron the Poet*, 305–08.

35. Crimmins, *Secular Utilitarianism*, 30.

36. Joseph, *Byron the Poet*, 305.

37. Hoagwood, *Byron's Dialectic*; Ryan, *The Romantic Reformation* (Cambridge: Cambridge University Press, 1998).

38. Gamba, *Narrative*, 2.

39. St. Clair, *That Greece Might Still Be Free*, 165.

40. Gamba, *Narrative*, 2.

41. St. Clair, *That Greece Might Still Be Free*, 167.

42. Stephen Minta, *On a Voiceless Shore: Byron in Greece* (New York: Holt Rinehart, 1997).

43. In *Byron and Greek Love*, Crompton stresses Byron's paganism and does not give due weight to his Christian values. For a different view, see W. Paul Elledge, "Immaterialistic Matters: Byron, Bogles, and Bluebloods," *Papers in Language and Literature* 25 (spring 1989), 280, and McGann, *Fiery Dust*, 251.

44. Stephen Holmes, *Benjamin Constant*. Constant "argued that public deceit can have an educative or reformatory function: men become by habit what they first wish to seem by hypocrisy." See also Guy Howard Dodge, *Benjamin Constant's Philosophy of Liberalism: A Study in Politics* (Chapel Hill: University of North Carolina Press, 1980).

45. Crane Brinton, *English Political Thought in the 19th Century* (New York: Harper & Row, 1962), 43.

46. John Millar was William Lamb's tutor at Edinburgh. Mitchell, *Lord Melbourne*, 46–48. The works that helped to spread Scottish ideas about political economy include Smith's *Wealth of Nations*; Jeffrey's *Edinburgh Review*; John Millar's *Observations Concerning the Distinction of Ranks in Society* (1771) and the *Historical View of the English Government* (1787); and Dugald Stewart's *Elements of the Philosophy of the Human Mind* (1792, 1814, and 1827). See D. Forbes, "Scientific Whiggism: Adam Smith and John Millar," *Cambridge Journal* 7, no. 2 (1954): 35–55.

47. Rosenblum, *Another Liberalism*, 189.

Afterword

BYRON AND THE LIBERAL IMAGINATION IN AMERICA

During the 1988 presidential campaign, President Ronald Reagan and Vice President George Bush repeatedly attacked Democratic candidate Michael Dukakis for being a liberal. In the months preceding the election, I watched Dukakis stumble and then fall into a rhetorical void as he found himself incapable of defending the liberal tradition in American politics.[1] More recently, Bill Clinton has also sought to distance himself from the term liberal, defining himself instead as a "New Democrat."

Liberalism never quite recovered from the 1988 election. Perhaps no event in American politics more clearly illustrates the transformation this word has undergone. When Ronald Reagan denounced liberals, after all, he had in mind the New Deal policies advocated by Franklin Roosevelt. What Reagan refused to acknowledge was that before Roosevelt's presidency, Americans identified liberalism with free trade and laissez-faire economic policies, the very policies Reagan campaigned for and saw his successor, George Bush, perpetuating. The debate between Dukakis and Reagan over the "L-word" (by which the word "liberal" came almost shamefully to be known), then, was really a quarrel within the liberal tradition itself: Reagan could disown this tradition only by feigning ignorance of the historical meaning of the word he dismissed. "Liberalism's greatest success has been in America," Bertrand Russell argues, "where, unhampered by feudalism and a State Church, it has been dominant from 1776 to the present day, or at any rate to 1933."[2]

Yet modern liberals created a space for Reagan's narrow view of liberalism by imposing restrictions upon their own political vocabulary. What many Americans called liberalism between 1933 and 1989 was really a form of socialism, a

189

word in disrepute in the United States since the Cold War.[3] It is a hard thing to believe in a set of principles that dare not speak their name. One result of such a circumstance can be found in the evasive strategies employed by Lionel Trilling's *The Liberal Imagination* (1950). Sharply rejecting Marx even in such fictional works as *The Middle of the Journey*, Trilling defined a politics of the left palatable to those suspicious of American communists.[4]

More than any previous study, *The Liberal Imagination* did much to create a space for liberalism during the Cold War. Trilling achieved this feat through a remarkable repudiation of conservatism. Liberalism, Trilling agreed, was the only game in town. With the McCarthy era just around the corner, Trilling could dismiss conservativism as an ideology that rarely expressed itself in ideas "but only in action or in irritable mental gestures which seek to resemble ideas."[5] Yet a decade later, William Buckley essentially agreed with Trilling's assessment of liberalism's dominance of the American political landscape. Buckley characterized liberals as "the dominant voice in determining the destiny of this country."[6] In the absence of what he perceived as respectable political adversaries, Trilling invoked John Stuart Mill's name to encourage liberals to "approach liberalism in a critical spirit."[7] What is striking about Trilling's book, however, is his tendency, evident in the very title he chose for his study, to retreat from the world of action and define liberalism from the standpoint of literature. Even within a literary context, Trilling's definition of the liberal imagination was a selective affair, made possible by those he included (Wordsworth, James, Hawthorne), but even more significant, by those he chose not to include (Byron, Shelley, Hazlitt, and Dreiser): writers with revolutionary political commitments.

Other critics of Trilling's generation and after have also responded to the Cold War, consciously or not, by imagining a more quiescent liberalism than the liberal tradition itself might warrant, one based on the verse of Wordsworth and Coleridge, rather than on that of Byron and Shelley. In emphasizing the first generation of romantic writers at the expense of Byron, critics have reversed the literary judgment of posterity, but only at the price of finding their definitions of romanticism, and thus their definitions of liberalism, woefully incomplete, just as in Ronald Reagan's attempts to define liberalism.

I have tried to recover another tradition of liberalism that has received scant positive attention since World War II. This is the tradition upheld by Byron. Byron's liberalism is problematic, but this fact is tied to the complexity of Byron's liberalism. From the very beginning of his literary career Byron's status as a Lord complicated his relationship to the liberal awakening he helped to bring about. Byron's own contemporaries—Sir Walter Scott,[8] Leigh Hunt,[9] and William Hazlitt[10]—doubted the sincerity of his liberal beliefs; Stanhope, a utilitarian, knew that Byron's heroic individualism had no place in the Enlightenment system of Jeremy Bentham.[11] Even the Chartists and working-class radicals who received political inspiration from Byron's verse, such as Thomas Cooper and George Julian Harney, may have mistaken psychological for political rebellion in his protagonists and in Byron himself.[12] In this century, Bertrand Russell found Byron troubling politically, more likely to be conducive to the fascist politics of the 1940s than corrective of it.[13] Perhaps only acknowledgment of Byron's bisexuality, examined in interesting detail by Louis Crompton and Susan Wolfson, will revive his reputation among certain members of the literary left.

As early as 1950, Lionel Trilling hoped to restore liberalism to its complexity by rescuing the term from the progressive simplifications it had undergone. What I have tried to show in this study is that this complexity appears not only in literature but in Byron's letters. "The subject (truth) of poetry [for Byron] was not the poetic process itself," Jerome McGann has written, not "truth as imagination, in the Romantic formulation—but the human world of men and women in their complex relations with themselves, each other, and their environment, both natural and cultural."[14] I have tried to show how an understanding of Byron's engagement with the culture of Regency England, with its risky conjunction of *eros*, dandyism, and liberalism, can complicate American attitudes toward political life in helpful ways. Drawing from his eighteenth-century predecessors like John Wilkes, Charles James Fox, and Richard Sheridan, Byron crafted a humanistic, as opposed to abstractly theoretical, brand of erotic liberalism which offers a helpful counterexample to the cant produced by the Cold War and sexual McCarthyism.

COLD WAR LIBERALISM: AN AMERICAN PERSPECTIVE

To fully consider the debt liberals owe to Byron's example, I would like to conclude by showing what he might have contributed to American liberalism during the Cold War. My method of investigating the relative neglect or misreading of Byron during the Cold War, in other words, leads to an inevitable question. What credit can the conservative mind properly claim for ending the Napoleonic War in 1815 or the Cold War in 1989? What criticisms and suggestions offered by Byron in 1815 and by the peace movement in the 1960s might color how one views conservative accomplishments in 1815 and 1989? My comments will be necessarily brief and sketchy, but they should show that Byron's poetry and prose offer genuine alternatives to the political wisdom current during the Cold War. Here again, Byron's denunciation of "cant" provides the most potent weapon against political hypocrisy, whether practiced by Robert Southey, Lord Castlereagh, Henry Kissinger, or Richard Nixon.

KISSINGER AND CASSANDRA: A WORLD RESTORED

Henry Kissinger argued that the nineteenth-century legislators maintained a peace that lasted from the Congress of Vienna until World War I. His doctoral dissertation, the revisionist study *A World Restored*,[15] like his *Diplomacy*, celebrates Metternich's and Castlereagh's accomplishments. Surprisingly, most critics take Metternich to be Kissinger's hero. In fact, Kissinger saw the limitations of both diplomats quite clearly. But it was Castlereagh's peculiar brand of congress diplomacy that offered Kissinger the most instructive model for his own diplomatic career. And it was to Great Britain that Kissinger most often looked in searching for a strategy for American foreign policy. "We are confronted by the traditional problem of an 'island' power," he wrote of the United States in *Nuclear Weapons and Foreign Policy*. "Of Carthage with respect to Rome, of Britain with respect to the Continent—that its survival depends on preventing the opposite land mass from falling under hostile control."[16]

Much like Castlereagh, who served as British foreign secretary from 1812 to 1822, Kissinger conducted American foreign affairs, as head of the National Security Council (1969–75) and as secretary of state (1973–77). In the same way that Castlereagh forged alliances with Austria against France and continued to police Europe after Napoleon's capture, Kissinger pursued China as an ally in military action against Vietnam long after public support for the war had evaporated. Like Castlereagh's congresses in Chatillon, Chaumont, and Vienna, Kissinger's secret mission to China, his policy of detente with the Soviet Union, and his shuttle diplomacy with leaders in the Mideast assured the U.S. an ongoing dialogue with adversaries and allies it had many reasons to distrust. Like Castlereagh, who advocated Britain's policy of nonintervention in the internal affairs of other states, Kissinger was criticized for refusing to make civil rights an issue in his pursuit of detente. Like Castlereagh, Kissinger found himself charged with prosecuting an amoral foreign policy, one not rooted sufficiently in principle but in realpolitik. If Castlereagh did not bother to distinguish between the relative morality of restoring a Bourbon or Napoleon to the French throne as Metternich did, Kissinger did not consider the morality of the Vietnam war at all and rejected the views of critics that this war was an imperialist campaign. Both men were solitary figures[17] who can be construed as having betrayed their own people— Castlereagh by enforcing brutal measures on the Irish and Kissinger by compromising Israel's national security to maintain detente with Brezhnev during the Yom Kippur War. Castlereagh appeased Napoleon in the Convention of Cintra, while Kissinger found himself dubbed a "Chamberlain disguised as a Churchill"[18] because of his lenient policy toward the Soviet Union.

Given the obvious similarities between Castlereagh's career and Kissinger's, one wonders why Kissinger did not, from the very outset, find a less controversial foreign diplomat to emulate. The answer, I think, lies in the tragic sense of history first outlined in *A World Restored*:

> The statesman is therefore like one of the heroes in classical drama who has had a vision of the future but who cannot transmit it directly to his fellow-men and who cannot validate its "truth." Nations learn only by experience; they "know" only when it is too late to act. But statesmen must act as if their intuition were already experience, as if their aspirations were truth. It is for this reason that statesmen often share the fate of prophets, that they are without honour in their own country, that they always have a difficult task in legitimizing their programmes domestically, and that their greatness is usually apparent only in retrospect when their intuition has become experience. The statesman must therefore be an educator; he must bridge the gap between a people's experience and his vision, between a nation's tradition and its future.[19]

The statesman must be an educator. Through this subtle maneuver, Kissinger makes the link between Castlereagh and himself explicit. Henry Kissinger, the Harvard professor of government, will improve upon Castlereagh's model by educating the public about his subtle diplomacy. The gods sometimes punish us by granting our wishes too completely, as Kissinger was fond of saying.

Yet the gods and Kissinger's allusions to Greek tragedy expose the ambiguity at the heart of Kissinger's diplomatic career: the tension between his role as adviser and actor, professor and secretary of state, prophet and hero. In the early part of his career, Kissinger saw himself as a prophet in the biblical sense, a voice crying aloud in the wilderness. A German Jewish refugee who had narrowly escaped Hitler's revolutionary war, Kissinger had a vision of the future that he could not communicate to incumbent presidents Truman and Eisenhower. He wrote scholarly articles for *Foreign Affairs*, but he was, in fact, a Cassandra figure. Leaders solicited his advice but rarely took it. All of this changed with the publication of *Nuclear Weapons and Foreign Policy*, the book Kissinger wrote for the Council on Foreign Relations.

In this ground-breaking book, Kissinger suggested foreign policy initiatives that resembled the tragic plots he so cherished in Greek drama. He did not resign his tragic vision; he simply gained an audience for it. Based on the assumption that nuclear war with the Soviet Union was not winnable, Kissinger advocated a series of "limited wars" that could not result in complete victory. Designed to curb Soviet expansion, Kissinger's proposal for limited war ultimately replaced John Foster Dulles's policy of massive retaliation, especially after Dulles's policy proved so unsuccessful in the Suez Canal crisis. When Americans resisted Kissinger's modernized version of Castlereagh's balance of power diplomacy, he blamed America's lack of tragic experience. The country's penchant for complete solutions, for vanquishing enemies without the fear of being similarly vanquished, was typical of an island power, he argued. "Though we have known severe hardships, our history has been notably free of disaster," he wrote.

> to many of our most responsible men, particularly in the business community, the warnings of imminent disaster sound like the Cassandra cries of abstracted "egg-heads." . . . Secretaries George M. Humphrey and Charles E. Wilson . . . may know in their heads, but they cannot accept in their hearts, that the society they helped to build could disappear as did Rome or Carthage or Byzantium. . . . The irrevocable error is not yet part of the American experience.[20]

Kissinger's sense of tragic plotting leads him to write himself into the American political script as a cross-dressing Cassandra, an abstracted "egg-head" who must educate Secretaries Humphrey and Wilson with a chapter borrowed from Aristotle's *Poetics*. Kissinger remained true to his tragic definition. The statesman must be an educator. But what if the lessons Kissinger meant to impart to the United States were themselves flawed? What if this particular prophet was wrong?

In studying the great period of cabinet diplomacy—the age of Metternich, Castlereagh, and Talleyrand—Kissinger hoped to find solutions to twentieth-century problems in the writing of his doctoral dissertation. What is remarkable is the extent to which twentieth-century issues influenced Kissinger's understanding of that time period. This twentieth-century bias is evident in the first sentence of *A World Restored*. "It is not surprising that an age faced with the threat of thermonuclear extinction should look nostalgically to periods when diplomacy carried with it less drastic penalties, when wars were limited and catastrophe almost inconceivable."[21] Kissinger's fear of "catastrophe"—the term comes from Greek drama—is characteristic. Kissinger sought to avoid the catastrophe of thermonuclear war. For this reason, he looked back nostalgically to the nineteenth-century diplomats who arranged a lasting peace. In doing so, however, he unwittingly romanticized their achievements, condemning the United States to the same kind of unacceptable compromises Castlereagh's diplomacy initiated: congress diplomacy, detente, protracted limited wars, and "peace at any price." Perhaps more significant, at least for historians, he distorted the value of Castlereagh and Metternich's accomplishments.

PROMETHEUS, GEORGE WASHINGTON, AND OTHER REVOLUTIONARIES

Kissinger's twentieth-century bias in treating the political events Byron lived through is never more apparent than in his use of the Prometheus legend. For the romantic poets, Prometheus was a hero. In the same way that he revised these poets' assessment of Castlereagh's accomplishments, Kissinger reversed their judgment on Prometheus.

> For many centuries, the legend of Prometheus, who sought to steal the secret of fire from the gods and who was punished by being forced to spend the rest of his life chained to a rock, has been the symbol of the penalties of presumptuous ambition. It was not understood that the punishment inflicted on Prometheus was an act of compassion; it would have been a much more severe penalty had the gods permitted their fire to be stolen. Our generation has succeeded in stealing the fire of the gods and it is doomed to live with the horror of its achievement.[22]

First of all, Kissinger's account of the Prometheus legend is inaccurate. Prometheus did not "seek" to steal fire from the gods; he did steal it. That is why he is chained to a rock. Second, he is not a symbol of "the penalties of presumptuous ambition." As disinterested an observer as Edith Hamilton comments that Prometheus "has stood through all the centuries, from Greek days to our own, as that of the great rebel against injustice and the authority of power."[23] In his introduction to *Prometheus Unbound*, Shelley explained that his hero was "the type of the highest perfection of moral and intellectual nature, impelled by the purest and the true motives to the best and noblest ends."[24] Byron praised Prometheus directly: "Thy godlike crime was to be kind,/ To render with thy precepts less/The sum of wretchedness" (*CPW* 3:35–37). Even Napoleon paled in comparison. Prometheus "in his fall preserv'd his pride,/And, if a mortal, had as proudly died!" ("Ode to Napoleon Buonaparte," *CPW* 3:265).

Kissinger's misreading of Prometheus as a failed revolutionary allows him to see Jupiter as a legitimate sovereign, not unlike George III or Louis XVI. Prometheus becomes like any other failed revolutionary: Napoleon, Hitler, Mao Tse-tung, or Stalin. By pretending that Prometheus was unsuccessful— that he only "sought to steal the secret of fire from the gods" but did not succeed—Kissinger intends to heighten the tragic dimension of man's scientific discovery. Like Mary Shelley's Frankenstein, Kissinger's twentieth-century American man finds himself doomed to his nuclear achievement. The "Modern Prometheus," from the subtitle of Mary Shelley's novel, is a scientist punished by having his wishes granted too completely; he gives man the curse of nuclear power because, unlike Kissinger's Prometheus, no one "prevented" him from doing so.

The root of Kissinger's conservative reading of the Prometheus story lies in his definition of rebellion. "What is a revolutionary?" he asks in chapter 10 of *Nuclear Weapons and Foreign Policy*. His answer would equate French advocates of liberty during the French Revolution with Hitler's curtailment of civil and religious freedom in the late 1930s. In order to define the Soviet Union as a revolutionary power and the United States as part of a legitimate order, moreover, he omits mentioning America's revolutionary struggle for independence against a legitimate power, Great Britain.[25]

Throughout *A World Restored*, Kissinger praises legitimacy at the expense of revolution without sufficiently historicizing these terms. Specifically, he errs in assuming that one cannot support revolutions in specific situations without being a "revolutionary" in a permanent sense. Kissinger defines a revolutionary power as one that can "never be reassured."[26] Because all the "revolutionary" powers Kissinger mentions were defeated in battle, it seems clear that they do not have the luxury of defining themselves or their purpose. To merely claim that they could "never be reassured" hardly answers the question about what made them "revolutionary" to begin with. In fact, Kissinger's definition of revolutionaries empties the term of all local historical and cultural content. He sees in the world a struggle between legitimacy and revolution and opts always for the status quo. Worse still, he calls such diplomacy visionary.

But Byron, who was equally suspicious of tumultuous changes in a social system, was not a revolutionary in this sense. He supported the French Revolution and Napoleon's campaign (in his "Ode to Napoleon Buonaparte"), until it became obvious that Napoleon had betrayed the revolution for which he fought. George Washington, not Napoleon, was Byron's true hero in this poem. And in suppressed stanzas, Byron celebrated George Washington as a conqueror who resisted the temptations of kingship and made "man blush there was but one" (*CPW* 3:19:266). Yet George Washington, not to mention Byron, does not receive more than three pages of treatment in Kissinger's eight-hundred-page study of diplomacy. A mere poet might have shown Kissinger that greatness could be found, not in the men who betrayed their country's principles by propping up "legitimate" powers, but in those, like Prometheus and Washington, who had the courage to lead democratic revolutions and renounce the temptations of dictatorship, the corruption of power.

If Kissinger's *A World Restored* argues that Castlereagh and Metternich were the true visionaries of their time period, *Diplomacy* suggests that Kissinger and Nixon should be remembered in a similar way. Not the peace activists, Kissinger argues in *Diplomacy*, but the cold warriors deserve credit for bringing peace in Vietnam. Indeed Kissinger received the Noble Prize for Peace, a mere year after the Christmas bombings. And Richard Nixon, when asked how he wished to be remembered, replied in a word that is now emblazoned on his tomb: "peacemaker." After numerous books of revisionary history and a eulogy by his secretary of state, Nixon seems likely to achieve that goal, though he ended the war in Vietnam five years later than he promised.

At Nixon's funeral, Kissinger praised the president he had served for his realistic assessment of America's geopolitical interests, his skillful use of balance of power diplomacy. The analysis was the same he had offered of Castlereagh and Metternich's struggle when he wrote his doctoral dissertation. "Conservatism in a revolutionary situation must fight revolution anonymously," Kissinger wrote, "by what it is, not by what it says."[27] Metternich, who described himself as a man of prose, not of poetry, would have agreed. But even Metternich, who enjoyed reading Byron's *Childe Harold's Pilgrimage*, recognized better than Castlereagh or Kissinger the importance of public opinion. "Public opinion," wrote Metternich in 1808, "is one of the most powerful weapons, which like religion, penetrates the most hidden corners where administrative measures lose their influence; to despise public opinion is like despising moral principles.... Public opinion requires a cult all its own.... Posterity will hardly believe that we regarded silence as an effective weapon in this, the century of words."[28] The mere weight of Robert Southey's published writings on George III, of Kissinger's memoirs of the Nixon administration, will not be decisive. Ultimately, the court of public opinion, what Nixon called "the silent majority," will decide for itself the value of its statesmen's accomplishments.

How much would Byron have relished the solemn pieties that governed Nixon's funeral, the cant and posturing. In "The Vision of Judgment," he mocked a similar, all too human tendency, to mourn the death of deeply flawed leaders. "And when the gorgeous coffin was laid low," he wrote of George III's burial, "It seem'd the mockery of hell to fold/The rottenness of eighty years in gold" (*CPW* 6:10:80). His attitude toward Kissinger's hero, Lord Castlereagh, was similarly uncompromising:

> Of the manner of his death little need be said, except that if a poor radical, such as Waddington or Watson, had cut his throat, he would have been buried in a crossroad, with the usual appurtenances of the stake and mallet. But the minister was an elegant lunatic, a sentimental suicide; he merely cut the

"carotid artery" (blessings on their learning), and lo! the pageant and the Abbey! and "the syllables of dolour yelled forth" by the newspapers, and the harangue of the coroner in an eulogy over the bleeding body of the deceased (an Anthony worthy of such a Caesar) and the nauseous and atrocious cant of a degraded crew of conspirators against all that is sincere or honourable.[29]

Byron's *ad hominem* voice speaks powerfully to liberals at the beginning of the twenty-first century, filling the vacuum left by Michael Dukakis and Bill Clinton. For dandies and liberals alike, Byron has shown that he is still very much in fashion. He did not receive a Westminster funeral, "the pageant and the Abbey!" Long before his own burial, however, when the empty carriages of the landed gentry passed by his open casket—honoring him but refusing to be guilty by association—he registered his fame where it most counts, in the court of public opinion. He was not silent in the century of words.

NOTES

1. For a contemporary account of that failure, see Meg Greenfield, "Redefining Liberalism," *Newsweek,* October 31, 1988, p. 82; George Will, *Newsweek,* October 24, 1988, p. 62.

2. Russell, *A History of Western Philosophy,* 600.

3. For a summary of the type of liberalism Ronald Reagan meant to attack, see Michael Oakeshott, *Rationalism and Politics* (Oxford: Oxford University Press, 1962), xxiii.

4. For a sympathetic account of Trilling's criticism of liberalism from within, contrasted with the reactionary criticism of liberalism during the 1988 election, see Benjamin DeMott, "Rediscovering Complexity," *The Atlantic Monthly* (August, 1988): 74.

5. Lionel Trilling, *The Liberal Imagination: Essays on Literature and Society* (Garden City, N.Y.: Doubleday, 1950), ix.

6. William Buckley, *Up From Liberalism* (New York: Free Press, 1957), xvii.

7. Trilling, *Liberal Imagination,* xii.

8. Scott wrote of "Byron's ridiculous pretence of Republicanism" in Roland E. Prothero, *The Works of Lord Byron* (New York: Octagon Books, Inc., 1966), 2:376n.

9. See Hunt, *Lord Byron and Some of His Contemporaries,* passim.

10. William Hazlitt, *The Spirit of the Age* (1824), quoted in Michael Foot, *The Politics of Paradise,* 80. See Howe 10:77.

11. Nicolson, *Byron,* 147.

12. Manning, *Reading Romantics,* 211. See also Andrew Rutherford, "Byron the Best Seller," in *Byron Foundation Lecture* (Nottingham: University of Nottingham, 1964), which argues that Byron's Eastern tales were "exciting without [being] radically disturbing" (20), and Daniel Watkins, *Social Relations in Byron's Eastern Tales,* which sees the autonomy of the Byronic hero as a sign of Byron's liberal bourgeois individualism. Michael

Foot, by contrast, makes a compelling case that Byron's influence on Chartist leaders and radical politicians was even more important than Shelley's. Foot, *Politics of Paradise*, 388.

13. Russell, *A History of Western Philosophy*, 747.
14. McGann, *Don Juan in Context*, 160.
15. Henry Kissinger, *A World Restored: Metternich, Castlereagh and the Problems of Peace, 1812–1822* (Boston: Houghton Mifflin Company, 1957).
16. Henry Kissinger, *Nuclear Weapons and Foreign Policy* (New York: Council on Foreign Relations, 1957), 269.
17. Kissinger, *A World Restored*, 205.
18. *Who is Mr. Kissinger?* (Whitestone: Griffon House Publishing, 1980), 24.
19. Kissinger, *A World Restored*, 329.
20. Kissinger, *Nuclear Weapons and Foreign Policy*, 426.
21. Kissinger, *A World Restored*, 1.
22. Kissinger, *Nuclear Weapons and Foreign Policy*, 65.
23. Kissinger, *Nuclear Weapons and Foreign Policy*, 65
24. *Shelley's Poetry and Prose*, ed. Donald Reiman and Sharon B. Powers (New York: W. W. Norton & Company, 1977), 133.
25. Kissinger, *Nuclear Weapons and Foreign Policy*, 316.
26. Kissinger, *A World Restored*, 2.
27. Kissinger, *A World Restored*, 9.
28. Kissinger, *A World Restored*, 16–17.
29. "Preface to Cantos VI–VIII," in T. G. Steffan, E. Steffan, and W. W. Pratt, *Lord Byron: Don Juan* (New York: Penguin, 1973), 262.

BIBLIOGRAPHY

MANUSCRIPT SOURCES

John Murray Archives, London
Joseph Blanco White Papers, Liverpool University Library
Lamb Papers, British Library
Lovelace Collection, Oxford University
Meyer Davis Collection, University of Pennsylvania

PUBLISHED SOURCES

Abrams, M. H., et al. *The Norton Anthology of English Literature*. 6th ed. Vol. 2. New York: W. W. Norton & Company, 1993.
Airlie, Countess. *In Whig Society*. London: Hodder and Stoughton Ltd., 1921.
Alighieri, Dante. *Inferno*. Trans. Allen Mandelbaum. Berkeley: University of California Press, 1980.
Altman, Janet Gurkin. *Epistolarity: Approaches to a Form*. Columbus: Ohio State University Press, 1982.
Anderson, Benedict. *Imagined Communities*. New York: Verso, 1983.
Arac, Jonathan. *Critical Genealogies*. New York: Columbia University Press, 1988.
Arnold, Matthew. "Byron." In *Essays in Criticism: Second Series*. Reprinted in *Matthew Arnold: Selected Prose*, ed. P. J. Keating. New York: Penguin Books, 1970.
Ashton, Thomas. *Byron's Hebrew Melodies*. Austin: University of Texas Press, 1972.
Asiatic Researches: Comprising History and Antiquities, the Arts, Sciences, and Literature of Asia (1788–1839). 10 vols. New Dehli: Cosmo Publications, 1979.
Ayling, Stanley, *George III*. New York: Alfred A. Knopf, 1972.

Babbitt, Irving. *Rousseau and Romanticism*. New York: AMS Press, 1978.

Bakhtin, Mikhail. *Rabelais and His World*. Trans. Helene Iswolsky. Bloomington: Indiana University Press, 1984.

Bal, Mieke. *Reading "Rembrandt": Beyond the Word-Image Opposition*. Cambridge: Cambridge University Press, 1991.

Barnes, Donald Grove. *George III and William Pitt, 1783–1806*. New York: Octagon Books, 1965.

Barton, Anne. *Don Juan*. Cambridge: Cambridge University Press, 1992.

Beaty, Frederick L. *Byron the Satirist*. De Kalb: Northern Illinois University Press, 1985.

Beckford, William. *Vathek: The English Translation by Samuel Henley (1786)*. Ed. Robert J. Gemmett. New York: Scholars' Facsimiles & Reprints, 1972.

Behrendt, Stephen C. *Shelley and His Audiences*. Lincoln: University of Nebraska Press, 1989.

Benson, Nancy A. "Hero and Narrator in Byron's *Don Juan*: A Piagetian Approach." *Centennial Review* 28–29 (1984–85): 48–57.

Berlin, Isaiah. *Against the Current: Essays in the History of Ideas*. New York: Viking Press, 1955.

———. *Concepts and Categories: Philosophical Essays*. Ed. Henry Hardy. New York: Viking Press, 1950.

———. "Two Concepts of Liberty." In *Four Essays on Liberty*. New York: Oxford University Press, 1969.

Berrong, Richard M. *Rabelais & Bakhtin: Popular Culture in Gargantua and Pantagruel*. Lincoln: University of Nebraska Press, 1986.

Besser, Gretchen Rous. *Germaine de Staël Revisited*. New York: Twayne Publishers, 1994.

Bhabha, Homi K. "DissemiNation: Time, Narrative, and the Margins of the Modern Nation." In *Nation and Narration*, ed. Homi K. Bhabha, 291–322. New York: Routledge, 1990.

———. *The Location of Culture*. New York: Routledge, 1994.

Bissell, R. Ward. *Orazio Gentileschi and the Poetic Traditionin Caravaggesque Painting*. University Park: Penn State University Press, 1981.

Blackstone, Bernard. "Byron and the Republic: The Platonic Background." In *Byron: Poetry and Politics: Seventh International Byron Symposium, 1980*, ed. Erwin A. Sturzl and James Hogg. Austria: University of Salzburg, 1981.

Blainey, Anne. *Immortal Boy: A Portrait of Leigh Hunt*. Philadelphia: University of Pennsylvania Press, 1968.

Blake, William. *Blake: Complete Writings*. Ed. Geoffrey Keynes. Oxford: Oxford University Press, 1957.

Blann, Robinson. *Throwing the Scabbard Away: Byron's Battles against the Censors of Don Juan*. New York: Peter Lang, 1991.

Blessington, Lady. *Conversations with Lord Byron*. Ed. Ernest Lovell, Jr. Princeton: Princeton University Press, 1968.

Bloom, Harold, ed. *George Gordon, Lord Byron*. New York: Chelsea House Publishers, 1986.

Bloom, Harold, and Lionel Trilling, eds. *Romantic Poetry and Prose.* Oxford: Oxford University Press, 1973.
Blum, Carol. *Rousseau and the Republic of Virtue:The Language of Politics in the French Revolution.* London: Cornell University Press, 1986.
Blunden, Edmund. *Leigh Hunt and His Circle.* New York: Harper & Brothers Publishers, 1930.
———. *Shelley:A Life Story.* Oxford: Oxford University Press, 1965.
Borst, William A. *Lord Byron's Pilgrimage.* New York: Archon, 1948.
Bostetter, Edward E. "Byron and the Politics of Paradise." *Publications of the Modern Language Association* 75 (1960): 571–77.
———. *The Romantic Ventriloquists.* Seattle: University of Washington Press, 1975.
Boswell, John. *Christianity, Social Tolerance, and Homosexuality.* Chicago: University of Chicago Press, 1980.
Bowles, W. L., ed. *The Collected Works of Alexander Pope.* Introduction by W. L. Bowles. London: John Murray, 1806.
———. *The Invariable Principles of Poetry: In a Letter Addressed to Thomas Campbell, Esq.; Occasioned by Some Critical Observations in His Specimens of British Poets, Particularly Relating to the Poetical Character of Pope.* London: Longman, 1819.
Boyd, Elizabeth French. *Byron's Don Juan:A Critical Study.* New York: Humanities Press, 1958.
Briggs, Asa. *William Cobbett.* Oxford: Clarendon Press, 1967.
Brightfield, Myron F. *Scott, Hazlitt, and Napoleon.* Los Angeles: University of California Press, 1943.
Brinton, Crane. *English Political Thought in the 19th Century.* New York: Harper & Row, 1962.
———. *Political Ideas of the English Romanticists.* Oxford: Oxford University Press, 1926.
Brissenden, R. F. *Virtue in Distress: Studies in the Novel of Sentiment from Richardson to Sade.* New York: Harper & Row Publishers, 1974.
British Museum General Catalogue of Printed Books. Vol. 38. London: Trustees of the British Museum, 1966.
Brock, W. R. *Lord Liverpool and Liberal Toryism 1820 to 1827.* London: Frank Cass & Company, 1967.
Bromwich, David. *Hazlitt:The Mind of a Critic.* New Haven:Yale University Press, 1983.
———. "Keats and Politics." *Studies in Romanticism* 25 (summer 1986): 200–25.
Brooks, Peter. *The Novel of Worldliness: Crebillon, Marivaux, Laclos, Stendhal.* Princeton: Princeton University Press, 1969.
Broughton, John Cam Hobhouse, Baron. *Recollections of a Long Life:With Additional Extracts from His Private Diaries.* Ed. Lady Dorchester. 6 vols. New York: AMS Press, 1968.
Brown, Norman. *Sexuality and Feminism in Shelley.* Cambridge: Harvard University Press, 1979.
Brown, Wallace. "Byron and English Interest in the Near East." *Studies in Philology* 34 (1937): 55–64.

204   Bibliography

———. "English Travel Books and Minor Poetry about the Near East, 1775–1825." *Philological Quarterly* 16 (1937): 249–71.

———. "The Popularity of English Travel books about the Near East, 1775–1825." *Philological Quarterly* 15 (1936): 70–80.

Browne, E. G. *A Literary History of Persia*. 4 vols. New York: Scribner, 1902.

Bryant, Arthur. *The Age of Elegance: 1812–1822*. New York: Harper & Brothers Publishers, 1950.

Buckley, William. *Up From Liberalism*. New York: Free Press, 1957.

Burke, Edmund. *A Philosophical Enquiry into the Origin of Our Ideas of the Sublime and Beautiful*. Ed. J. T. Boulton. Notre Dame, Ind.: University of Notre Dame Press, 1968.

———. *Reflections on the Revolution in France and Thomas Paine, The Rights of Man*. New York: Doubleday, 1989.

Burnett, T. A. J. *The Rise and Fall of a Regency Dandy: The Life and Times of Scrope Berdmore Davies*. Boston: Little, Brown and Company, 1981.

Burrow, J. W. *Whigs and Liberals: Continuity and Change in English Political Thought*. Oxford: Clarendon Press, 1988.

Butler, Judith. *Bodies That Matter: On the Discursive Limits of Sex*. New York: Routledge, 1993.

———. *Gender Trouble: Feminism and the Subversion of Identity*. New York: Routledge, 1990.

Butler, Marilyn. *Burke, Paine, Godwin, and the Revolution Controversy*. Cambridge: Cambridge University Press, 1984.

———. *Jane Austen and the War of Ideas*. Oxford: Clarendon Press, 1987.

———. *Romantics, Rebels, and Reactionaries*. Oxford: Oxford University Press, 1982.

Buxton, John. *Byron and Shelley: The History of a Friendship*. New York: Harcourt, Brace & World, 1968.

Byron, George Gordon, *The Complete Miscellaneous Prose: Lord Byron*. Ed. Andrew Nicholson. Oxford: Oxford University Press, 1991.

———. *Don Juan*. Ed. Leslie Marchand. Boston: Houghton Mifflin Company, 1958.

———. *Lord Byron: Don Juan*. Ed T. G. Steffan, E. Steffan, and W. W. Pratt. London: Penguin, 1957.

———. *Lord Byron: The Complete Poetical Works*. Ed. Jerome McGann. 7 vols. Oxford: Clarendon Press, 1980–93.

———. *Lord Byron's Letters and Journals*. Ed. Leslie A. Marchand. 12 vols. Cambridge: Harvard University Press, 1973–82.

———. *The Poetical Works of Byron*. Ed. Robert F. Gleckner. Boston: Houghton Mifflin Company, 1975.

———. *The Works of Lord Byron*. Ed. Richard Henry Stoddard. 16 vols. Boston: Francis A. Niccolls & Co., 1900.

———. *The Works of Lord Byron: Letters and Journals*. Ed. Rowland E. Prothero. 16 vols. New York: Charles Scribner's Sons, 1901.

Byron, George Gordon, and Leigh Hunt. *The Liberal: Verse and Prose from the South*. 4 vols. Salzburg: Salzburg Institute, 1978.

Calder, Angus. *Byron.* Philadelphia: Open University Press, 1987.
Calvert, William J. *Byron: Romantic Paradox.* New York: Russell & Russell, 1962.
Cameron, Kenneth, ed. *Romantic Rebels: Essays on Shelley and His Circle.* Cambridge: Harvard University Press, 1973.
———. *Shelley: The Golden Years.* Cambridge: Harvard University Press, 1974.
Campbell, Thomas. *Specimens of the British Poets; with Biographical and Critical Notices, and an Essay on English Poetry.* Vol. 1. London: John Murray, 1819.
Cannon, Garland. *The Life and Mind of Oriental Jones: Sir William Jones, the Father of Modern Linguistics.* Cambridge: Cambridge University Press, 1990.
Cantemir, Demetrius. *The History of the Growth and Decay of the Ottoman Empire.* 1756.
Carr, Raymond. *Spain: 1808–1939.* Oxford: Clarendon Press, 1966.
Carson, Anne. *Eros the Bittersweet: An Essay.* Princeton: Princeton University Press, 1986.
Carretta, Vincent. *George III and the Satirists from Hogarth to Byron.* Athens: University of Georgia Press, 1990.
Cash, Arthur Hill. *Sterne's Comedy of Moral Sentiments: The Ethical Dimension of the Journey.* Pittsburgh: Duquesne University Press, 1966.
Castle, Terry. *Masquerade and Civilization: The Carnivalesque in Eighteenth-Century English Culture and Fiction.* Stanford: Stanford University Press, 1986.
Castronovo, David. *The English Gentleman: Images and Ideals in Literature and Society.* New York: Ungar Publishing Company, 1987.
Cecil, Lord David. *The Young Melbourne.* New York: Bobbs-Merrill, 1954.
Cervantes Saavedra, Miguel de. *Don Quixote.* Trans. J. Cohen. New York: Penguin, 1950.
Chandler, James. *England in 1819: The Politics of Literary Culture and the Case of Romantic Historicism.* Chicago: University of Chicago Press, 1998.
———. "The Pope Controversy: Romantic Poetics and the English Canon." In *Canons,* ed. Robert von Hallberg. Chicago: University of Chicago Press, 1984.
Cheatham, George. "Byron's Dislike of Keats' Poetry." *Keats-Shelley Journal* 32 (1983): 20–25.
Chew, Samuel P. *Byron in England.* New York: Charles Scribner's Sons, 1924.
———. *The Dramas of Lord Byron: A Critical Study.* New York: Russell & Russell, 1964.
Chezy, A. L. *Medjnoun et Leila poeme traduit du persan de Djamy.* Paris: L'Imprinerie de Valade, 1807.
Christensen, Jerome. *Lord Byron's Strength: Romantic Writing and Commercial Society.* Baltimore: Johns Hopkins University Press, 1993.
———. "Marino Faliero and the Fault of Byron's Satire." In *George Gordon: Lord Byron,* ed. Harold Bloom, 149–65. New York: Chelsea House Publishers, 1986.
———. "Perversion, Parody, and Cultural Hegemony: Lord Byron's Oriental Tales." *South Atlantic Quarterly* 88 (summer 1989): 570–88.
———. "Setting Byron Straight: Class, Sexuality, and the Poet." In *Literature and the Body: Essays on Populations and Persons,* ed. Elaine Scarry. Baltimore: Johns Hopkins University Press, 1988.
———. "Theorizing Byron's Practice: The Performance of Lordship and the Poet's Career." *Studies in Romanticism* 27 (winter 1988): 477–90.

Cline, C. L. *Byron, Shelley and Their Pisan Circle*. Cambridge: Harvard University Press, 1951.
Clubbe, John, and Ernest Lovell. "Dramatic Hits: Napoleon and Shakespeare in Byron's 1813–1814 Journal." In *British Romantics as Readers: Intertextualities, Maps of Misreading, Reinterpretations, Festschrift for Horst Meller*, ed. Michael Gassenmeier, Petre Bridzun, Jens Martin Gurr, and Frank Eric Pointner, 271–294. Heidelberg: Universitätsverlag C. Winter, 1998.
———. *English Romanticism: The Grounds of Belief*. De Kalb: Northern Illinois University Press, 1983.
Colley, Linda. *Britons Forging the Nation*. 2d. ed. New Haven: Yale University Press, 1964.
Cone, Carl B. *The English Jacobins: Reformers in Late 18th Century England*. New York: Charles Scribner's Sons, 1968.
Constant, Benjamin. *Political Writings*. Trans. and ed. Biancamaria Fontana. Cambridge: Cambridge University Press, 1988.
Connelly, Willard. *The Reign of Beau Brummell*. New York: Greystone Press, 1940.
Cooke, Michael G. *The Blind Man Traces the Circle*. Princeton: Princeton University Press, 1969.
Cox, Jeffrey N. *Poetry and Politics in the Cockney School: Keats, Shelley, Hunt and their Circle*. Cambridge: Cambridge University Press, 1998.
Crimmins, James E. *Secular Utilitarianism: Social Science and the Critique of Religion in the Thought of Jeremy Bentham*. Oxford: Clarendon Press, 1990.
Crompton, Louis. *Byron and Greek Love: Homophobia in 19th-Century England*. Berkeley: University of California Press, 1985.
Daly, Kirsten. "'Worlds beyond England': *Don Juan* and the Legacy of Enlightenment Cosmopolitanism," *Romanticism* 4, no. 2 (1998): 189–202.
Dawson, P. M. S. *The Unacknowledged Legislator: Shelley and Politics*. Oxford: Clarendon Press, 1980.
DeMott, Benjamin. "Rediscovering Complexity." *The Atlantic Monthly* (August, 1988): 74.
Derry, John W. *Castlereagh*. New York: St. Martin's Press, 1976.
———. *Charles James Fox*. New York: St. Martin's Press, 1972.
De Silva, D. M. "Byron's Politics and the History Plays." In *Byron: Poetry and Politics: Seventh International Byron Symposium*, 1980, ed. Erwin A. Sturzl and James Hogg, 113–37. Austria: University of Salzburg, 1981.
D'Herbelot, Barthelemy. *Bibliothèque Orientale ou Dictionnaire Universel*. 4 vols. Paris: J. Neaulme and N. van Daalen, 1777.
Dickinson, H. T. *British Radicalism and the French Revolution, 1789–1815*. Oxford: Basil Blackwell, 1985.
Dietze, Gottfried. *Liberalism Proper and Proper Liberalism*. Baltimore: Johns Hopkins University Press, 1985.
Dodge, Guy Howard. *Benjamin Constant's Philosophy of Liberalism: A Study in Politics*. Chapel Hill: University of North Carolina Press, 1980.
Dollimore, Jonathan. *Sexual Dissidence: Augustine to Wilde, Freud to Foucault*. Oxford: Clarendon Press, 1991.

Donelan, Charles. *Romanticism and Male Fantasy in Byron's Don Juan: A Marketable Vice.* London: Macmillan Press; New York: St. Martin's Press, 2000.

Dover, K. J. *Greek Homosexuality.* New York: Random House, 1978.

Dowden, Wilfred S. "Byron and the Austrian Censorship." *Keats-Shelley Journal* 4 (winter 1955): 67–75.

Duffy, Edward. *Rousseau in England: The Context for Shelley's Critique of the Enlightenment.* Berkeley: University of California Press, 1979.

Eagleton, Terry. *Literary Theory.* Minneapolis: University of Minnesota Press, 1983.

———. *The Rape of Clarissa: Writing, Sexuality and Class Struggle in Samuel Richardson.* Minneapolis: University of Minnesota Press, 1982.

Ehrman, John. *The Younger Pitt: The Years of Acclaim.* London: Constable, 1969.

Eisler, Benita. *Byron: Child of Passion, Fool of Fame.* New York: Alfred A. Knopf, 1999.

Elfenbein, Andrew. *Byron and the Victorians.* Cambridge: Cambridge University Press, 1995.

Eliade, Mircea. *The Encyclopedia of Religion.* New York: MacMillan, 1987.

Elledge, W. Paul. "Immaterialistic Matters: Byron, Bogles, and Bluebloods." *Papers in Language and Literature* 25 (spring 1989): 280.

Ellegard, Alvar. *Who Was Junius?* Stockholm: Almquist & Wiksell, 1962.

Elliott, R. C. *The Power of Satire: Magic, Ritual, Art.* Princeton: Princeton University Press, 1960.

Elwin, Malcolm. *Lord Byron's Wife.* London: Macdonald, 1962.

Endelman, Todd. *Radical Assimilation in English Jewish History, 1656–1945.* Indianapolis: Indiana University Press, 1990.

Erdman, David. "Byron and Revolt in England." *Science & Society* 11 (1947): 234–48.

———. "Byron and 'The New Force of the People.'" *Keats-Shelley Journal* 11 (1962): 47–64.

———. "Byron's Stage Fright: The History of His Ambition and Fear of Writing for the Stage." *ELH* 6 (1939): 219–45.

———. "Lord Byron and the Genteel Reformers." *Publications of the Modern Language Association* 56 (1941): 1065–94.

———. "Lord Byron as Rinaldo." *Publications of the Modern Language Association* 57 (1942): 189–231.

Fischer, Doucet. "Countess Guiccioli's Byron." *Shelley and His Circle* 7, no. 20 (1986): 373–486.

Fleming, Anne. *Bright Darkness.* London: Nottingham Court Press, 1983.

Fletcher, Richard M. *English Romantic Drama, 1795–1843: A Critical History.* New York: Exposition Press, 1966.

Foot, Michael. *The Politics of Paradise.* New York: Harper & Row, 1988.

Forbes, D. "Scientific Whiggism: Adam Smith and John Millar." *Cambridge Journal* 7, no. 2 (1954): 35–55.

Forsberg, Roberta. *Madame de Staël and the English.* New York: Astra Books, 1967.

Foxon, David. *Libertine Literature in England: 1660–1745.* New York: University Books, 1965.

Frank, Judith. "'A Man Who Laughs Is Never Dangerous': Character and Class in Sterne's *A Sentimental Journey.*" *ELH* 56 (spring 1989): 97–124.

Franklin, Caroline. *Byron's Heroines.* Oxford: Clarendon Press, 1992.

———. "Cosmopolitan Masculinity and the British Female Reader of *Childe Harold's Pilgrimage.*" In *Byron the European: Essays from the International Byron Society.* Ed. Richard A. Cardwell, 105–126. Lewiston: Edwin Mellen Press, 1997.

Fuess, Claude M. *Lord Byron as Satirist in Verse.* New York: Russell & Russell, 1964.

Fuss, Diana. *Inside/Out: Lesbian Theories, Gay Theories.* New York: Routledge, 1991.

Gamba, Pietro. *A Narrative of Lord Byron's Last Journey to Greece.* Paris: A & W Galignani, 1825.

Gassenmeier, Michael, and Norman Platz. *Beyond the Suburbs of the Mind: Exploring English Romanticism.* Essen, Germany: Verlag Die Blaue Eule, 1987.

Gellner, Ernest. *Nations and Nationalism.* Ithaca: Cornell University Press, 1983.

———. *Nationalism.* Ed. David Gellner. New York: New York University Press, 1997.

Girouard, Mark. *The Return to Camelot: Chivalry and the English Gentleman.* New Haven: Yale University Press, 1981.

Gleckner, Robert F. *Byron and the Ruins of Paradise.* Baltimore: Johns Hopkins Press, 1967.

Graham, Peter. *Byron's Bulldog: The Letters of John Cam Hobhouse to Lord Byron.* Columbus: Ohio State University Press, 1984.

———. *Don Juan and Regency England.* Charlottesville: University Press of Virginia, 1990.

Grebanier, Bernard. *The Uninhibited Byron: An Account of His Sexual Confusion.* New York: Crown Publishers, 1970.

Greenberg, David. *The Construction of Homosexuality.* Chicago: University of Chicago Press, 1988.

Greenfield, Kent Roberts. *Economics and Liberalism in the Risorgimento: A Study of Nationalism in Lombardy, 1814–1848.* Baltimore: Johns Hopkins University Press, 1965.

Greenfield, Meg. "Redefining Liberalism." *Newsweek,* October 31, 1988.

Grierson, Herbert. *The Background of English Literature and Other Essays.* New York: Penguin, 1925.

Gross, Jonathan David. "Byron and The Liberal: Periodical as Political Posture." *Philological Quarterly* 72 (fall 1993): 471–85.

———, ed. *Byron's "Corbeau Blanc": The Life and Letters of Lady Melbourne.* Houston: Rice University Press, 1997.

———. "Hazlitt's Worshipping Practice in *Liber Amoris,*" *Studies in English Literature* 35 (autumn 1995): 707–21.

Grosskurth, Phyllis. *Byron: The Flawed Angel.* New York: Houghton Mifflin, 1997.

Gutwirth, Madelyn. *Madame de Staël, Novelist.* Champagne: University of Illinois Press, 1978.

Hagstrum, Jean H. "Byron's Songs of Innocence: The Songs to Thyrza." In *Eros and Vision: The Restoration to Romanticism,* 197–192. Evanston, Ill.: Northwestern University Press, 1986.

———. *Sex and Sensibility: Ideal and Erotic Love from Milton to Mozart.* Chicago: University of Chicago Press, 1980.
Halevy, Elie. *The Growth of Philosophical Radicalism.* Trans. A. D. Lindsay. London: Faber & Gwyer, 1928.
———. *A History of the English People: England in 1815.* Trans. E. I. Watkin and D. A. Barker. New York: Peter Smith, 1949.
———. *A History of the English People: The Liberal Awakening (1815–1830).* Trans. E. I. Watkin. New York: Peter Smith, 1949.
Hamilton, Edith. *Greek Mythology.* New York: Penguin, 1969.
Hampson, Norman. *A Social History of the French Revolution.* London: Routledge & Kegan Paul, 1963.
Hansard's Parliamentary Debates. London: T. C. Hansard, 1820.
Harby, Clifton, ed. *The Bible in Art: Twenty Centuries of Famous Bible Paintings.* New York: Covics Friede, 1936.
Harper's Dictionary of Classical Literature and Antiquities. Ed. Harry Thurston Peck. New York: American Book Company, 1923.
Haslett, Moyra. *Byron's Don Juan and the Don Juan Legend.* Oxford: Clarendon Press, 1997.
Hayden, John O., ed. *William Wordsworth: The Poems.* 2 vols. New Haven: Yale University Press, 1977.
Hazlitt, William. *The Collected Works of William Hazlitt.* Ed. A. R. Waller and Arnold Glover. 12 vols. London: J. M. Dent & Co., 1902.
———. *The Complete Works of William Hazlitt.* Ed. P. P. Howe. 20 vols. New York: AMS Press, 1967.
———. *London Magazine* 3, no.18 (June 1821): 593–607.
———. *The Venetian Republic: Its Rise, Its Growth, and Its Fall.* New York: AMS Press, 1966.
Henderson, Ernest P. *Symbol and Satire in the French Revolution.* New York: G. P. Putnam's Sons, 1912.
Herold, J. C. *Madame de Staël: Mistress to an Age.* New York: Harmony Books, 1958.
Hinde, Wendy. *Castlereagh.* London: Collins, 1981.
Hirschkop, Ken. "Bakhtin and Cultural Theory." In *Bakhtin and Cultural Theory*, ed. Ken Hirschkop and David Shepherd. Manchester: Manchester University Press, 1989.
Hoagwood, Terence. *Byron's Dialectic: Skepticism and the Critique of Culture.* Lewisburg: Bucknell University Press, 1983.
Hobhouse, L. T. *Liberalism.* Oxford: Oxford University Press, 1964.
Holmes, Richard. *Shelley: The Pursuit.* London: Quartet Books, 1976.
Holmes, Stephen J. *Benjamin Constant and the Philosophy of Liberalism.* New Haven: Yale University Press, 1968.
Holst, H. Von. *The French Revolution: Tested by Mirabeau's Career: Twelve Lectures on the History of the French Revolution.* Vol. 1. Boston, 1894. Vol. 2. Chicago: Callaghan & Company, 1894.
Horace. *Horace: Satires, Epistles, and Ars Poetica.* Ed. H. Rushton Fairclough. Cambridge: Harvard University Press, 1978.

Howes, Alan B., ed. *Sterne: The Critical Heritage*. London: Routledge & Kegan Paul, 1974.
Hulme, T. E. "Classicism and Romanticism." In *Critical Theory since Plato*, ed. Hazard Adams, 355–63. Irvine: Harcourt Brace Jovanovich, 1971.
Hunt, Leigh. *The Autobiography of Leigh Hunt with Reminiscences of Friends and Contemporaries*. 2 vols. New York: Harper & Brothers, 1850.
———. *The Feast of the Poets, with Notes and Other Pieces of Verse*. London: James Cawthorn, 1814.
———. *Leigh Hunt's Political and Occasional Essays*. Ed. Lawrence and Carolyn Houtchens. New York: Columbia University Press, 1962.
———. *Lord Byron and Some of His Contemporaries; with Recollections of the Author's Life, and His Visit to Italy*. London: Henry Colburn, 1828.
Isbell, John. *The Birth of European Romanticism*. Cambridge: Cambridge University Press, 1994.
Jami, Mullana Abdulrahman. *Analysis and Specimens of the Joseph and Zulaikha, a Historical-Romantic Poem, by the Persian Poet Jami*. Trans. S. Robinson. London: Williams and Norgate, 1873.
———. *The Book of Joseph and Zuleikha, Historical Romantic Persian Poem*. Trans. Alexander Rogers. London: David Nutt, 1892.
———. *Joseph und Suleicha; historisch-romantisches Gedicht aus dem Persischen des Abdurrahman Dschami*. Trans. Franz Rosenzweig. Vienna: Anton Schmid, 1824.
———. *Yusef and Zulaikha: A Poem by Jami*. Trans. R. T. Griffith. London: Trubner & Co., Ludgate Hill, 1882.
Jarrett, Derek. *Pitt the Younger*. New York: Charles Scribner's Sons, 1974.
Jeaffreson, John Cordy. *The Real Lord Byron*. 2 vols. London: Hurst, 1884.
Jesse, Captain. *Beau Brummell*. London: Grolier Society, 1844.
Johnson, Claudia. *Jane Austen: Women, Politics, and the Novel*. Chicago: University of Chicago Press, 1988.
Johnson, Edward Dudley Hume. "Don Juan in England." *ELH* 11 (1944): 135–53.
———. "Lord Byron in *Don Juan*: A Study in Digression." Ph.D. diss., Yale University, 1939.
———. "A Political Interpretation of Byron's 'Marino Faliero.'" *Modern Language Quarterly* 31 (1942): 417–25.
Johnson, R. Brimley, ed. *Shelley-Leigh Hunt: How Friendship Made History*. London: Ingpen and Grant, 1928.
Johnstone, Charles. *Chrysalis, or the Adventures of a Guinea*. London, 1760.
Jones, William. *The Collected Works of Sir William Jones*. New York: New York University Press, 1993.
———. *Laili Majnun, A Persian Poem of Hatifi*. Calcutta: M. Cantopher, 1788.
———. *The Letters of Sir William Jones*. Ed. Garland Cannon. 2 vols. Oxford: Clarendon Press, 1970.
Jordan, Frank, ed. *The Romantic Poets: A Review of Research and Criticism*. 4th ed. New York: Modern Language Association of America, 1985.
Joseph, M. K. *Byron the Poet*. London: Victor Gollancz, 1966.

Kaiser, Walter. *Praisers of Folly: Erasmus, Rabelais, Shakespeare.* Cambridge: Harvard University Press, 1963.
Kant, Immanuel. *Critique of Judgment.* Trans. Werner S. Pluhar. Indianapolis: Hackett Publishing Company, 1987.
Keach, William. "Cockney Couplets: Keats and the Politics of Style." *Studies in Romanticism* 25 (summer 1986): 182–94.
Kelly, Linda. *Juniper Hall.* London: Weidenfeld & Nicolson, 1991.
——. *Richard Brinsley Sheridan: A Life.* London: Pimlico, 1998.
Kelsall, Malcolm. "Byron and Wordsworth: European Cosmopolitanism and English Provincialism." In *Byron the European: Essays from the International Byron Society.* Ed. Richard A. Cardwell, 91–104. Lewiston: Edwin Mellen Press, 1997.
——. *Byron's Politics.* Totowa, N.J.: Barnes and Noble, 1987.
——. "Hamlet, Byron and 'an Age of Despair.'" In *Beyond the Suburbs of the Mind: Exploring English Romanticism,* Ed. Michael Gassenmeier and Norman Platz. Essen, Germany: Verlag Die Blaue Eule, 1987.
Kenner, Hugh. *The Counterfeiters: An Historical Comedy.* Baltimore: Johns Hopkins University Press, 1985.
Kierkegaard, Søren. *Either/Or.* Trans. Walter Lowrie. 2 vols. Princeton: Princeton University Press, 1974.
Kissinger, Henry A. *Diplomacy.* New York: Simon & Schuster, 1994.
——. *Nuclear Weapons and Foreign Policy.* New York: Council on Foreign Relations, 1957.
——. *A World Restored: Metternich, Castlereagh and the Problems of Peace, 1812–1822.* Boston: Houghton Mifflin Company, 1957.
——. *Years of Renewal.* New York: Simon & Schuster, 1999.
Knight, G. Wilson. *Lord Byron: Christian Virtues.* Oxford: Oxford University Press, 1953.
——. *Lord Byron's Marriage: The Evidence of Asterisks.* New York: Macmillan, 1957.
Knolles, Richard, ed. *The Turkish History, and its Continuation* by Sir Paul Rycaut, 1687–1700.
Koestenbaum, Wayne. *Double Talk.* New York: Routledge, 1989.
Koran. Trans. N. J. Dawood. London: Penguin, 1956
Kroeber, Karl. *British Romantic Art.* Berkeley: University of California Press, 1986.
——. *Ecological Literary Criticism: Romantic Imagining and the Biology of Mind.* New York: Columbia University Press, 1994.
——. "Romantic Historicism: The Temporal Sublime." In *Images of Romanticism,* ed. Karl Kroeber and William Walling, 149–65. New Haven: Yale University Press, 1978.
Laclos, Pierre Choderlos de. *Les liaisons dangereuses.* Trans. Lowell Bair. New York: Bantam Books, 1968.
——. *Les liaisons dangereuses.* Trans. Richard Aldington. New York: Signet, 1962.
Lang, Cecil. "Narcissus Jilted: Byron, Don Juan, and the Biographical Imperative." In *Historical Studies and Literary Criticism,* ed. J. J. McGann. Madison: University of Wisconsin Press, 1985.

Langles, Louis Mathieu. *Contes, fables et sentences, tires de differens auteurs du poeme de Ferdoussy, sur les rois de Perse.* Paris: Royez, 1788.
Lansdowne, Richard. *Byron's Historical Dramas.* Oxford: Oxford University Press, 1992.
Leask, Nigel. *Romantic Writers and the East.* Cambridge: Cambridge University Press, 1992.
Levinson, Marjorie. *Keats's Life of Allegory: The Origins of a Style.* Oxford: Blackwell, 1990.
———. "A Question of Taste: Keats and Byron." In *Rereading Byron: Essays Selected from the Hofstra University's Byron Bicentennial Conference,* ed. Alice Levine and Robert N. Keane, 187–204. New York: Garland, 1993.
Lewis, Charlton, and Charles Short, eds. *A Latin Dictionary.* Oxford: Clarendon Press, 1955.
Lewis, Wilmarth Sheldon, and Joseph W. Reed, Jr., eds. *Horace Walpole's Correspondence with the Walpole Family.* 46 vols. New Haven: Yale University Press, 1946–73.
Lim, Paulino. *The Style of Lord Byron's Plays.* Austria: Salzburg University Press, 1973.
Little, Douglas. "Byron and the Eunuch Muse." *Keats-Shelley Journal* 25 (1976): 24–25.
Logan, James V., John E. Jordan, and Northrop Frye, eds. *Some British Romantics: A Collection of Essays.* Columbus: Ohio State University Press, 1966.
Longford, Elizabeth. *The Life of Byron.* Boston: Little, Brown and Company, 1976.
Looper, Travis. *Byron and the Bible: A Compendium of Biblical Usage in the Poetry of Byron.* Metuchen: Scarecrow Press, 1978.
Lovejoy, Arthur O. *Essays in the History of Ideas.* New York: G. P. Putnam's Sons, 1948.
Lovell, E. *Byron: Record of a Quest.* New York: Macmillan, 1949.
———. *His Very Self and Voice: Collected Conversations of Lord Byron.* New York: Macmillan, 1954.
Macaulay, Thomas. *Critical, Historical and Miscellaneous Essays by Lord Macaulay.* 6 vols. New York: Sheldon and Company, 1860.
MacDonald, Daniel J. *The Radicalism of Shelley and Its Sources.* New York: Phaeton Press, 1969.
Mack, Anne, and J. J. Rome. "Marxism, Romanticism, and Postmodernism: An American Case History." *South Atlantic Quarterly* 88.3 (autumn 1989): 605–32.
Maertz, Gregory, ed. *Cultural Interactions in the Romantic Age: Critical Essays in Comparative Literature.* Albany: State University of New York Press, 1998.
Manning, David J. *Liberalism.* New York: St. Martin's Press, 1976.
Manning, Peter J. *Byron and His Fictions.* Detroit: Wayne State University Press, 1978.
———. *Reading Romantics.* New York: Oxford University Press, 1990.
Mannix, Daniel P. *The Hell-Fire Club.* London: Four-Square, 1961.
Marchand, Leslie. *Byron: A Biography.* 3 vols. New York: Alfred A. Knopf, 1957.
———. *Byron: A Portrait.* Chicago: University of Chicago Press, 1970.
———. *Byron's Poetry: A Critical Introduction.* Boston: Houghton Mifflin, 1965.
———. "Narrator and Narration in *Don Juan,*" *Keats-Shelley Journal* 25 (1976): 26–42.
———. "Review of Byron and Greek Love." *Keats-Shelley Journal* 45 (1986): 190–93.
Margetson, Stella. *Regency London.* New York: Praeger Publishers, 1971.
Marshall, William. "The Catalogue for the Sale of Byron's Books." *The Library Chronicle of the Friends of the University of Pennsylvania Library* 34 (winter 1968): 24–50.

———. *Byron, Shelley, Hunt and The Liberal.* Philadelphia: University of Pennsylvania Press, 1960.
———. *The Structure of Byron's Major Poems.* Philadelphia: University of Pennsylvania Press, 1962.
Maurois, Andre. *Byron.* New York: D. Appleton and Company, 1930.
———. Introduction to *Les liaisons dangereuses,* by Pierre Choderlos de Laclos. New York: Bantam, 1989.
May, Gita. *Stendhal and the Age of Napoleon.* New York: Columbia University Press, 1977.
Mayne, Ethel Colburn. *Byron.* New York: Charles Scribner's Sons, 1924.
———. *The Life and Letters of Anne Isabella Lady Noel Byron: From Unpublished Papers in the Possession of the Late Ralph, Earl of Lovelace.* New York: Charles Scribner's Sons, 1929.
McCracken, David. *Junius and Philip Francis.* Boston: G. K. Hall & Co., 1979.
McGann, Jerome. *Don Juan in Context.* Chicago: University of Chicago Press, 1976.
———. *Fiery Dust: Byron's Poetic Development.* Chicago: University of Chicago Press, 1968.
———. "'My Brain Is Feminine': Byron and the Poetry of Deception." In *Byron: Augustan and Romantic,* ed. Andrew Rutherford. New York: St. Martin's Press, 1990.
———. *The Romantic Ideology.* Chicago: University of Chicago Press, 1983.
———. *Social Values and Poetic Acts: A Historical Judgment of Literary Work.* Cambridge: Harvard University Press, 1988.
———. *Towards a Literature of Knowledge.* Oxford: Clarendon Press, 1989.
Medwin, Thomas. *Medwin's Conversations of Lord Byron.* Ed. Ernest J. Lovell, Jr. Princeton: Princeton University Press, 1966.
Meisel, Martin. "Pictorial Engagements: Byron, Delacroix, Ford Madox Brown." *Studies in Romanticism* 27 (winter 1988): 551–62.
Melbourne, Lady. "To Lord Byron," Add. MSS, 45547, f.70 (October 19, 1814), *Lamb Papers,* British Library, London.
Melikian, Anahid. *Byron and the East.* Beirut: American University of Beirut, 1977.
Mellor, Anne K. *English Romantic Irony.* Cambridge: Harvard University Press, 1980.
Mellor, Anne K., and Richard E. Matlak. *British Literature: 1780–1830.* New York: Harcourt Brace College Publishers, 1996.
Merquior, J. G. *Liberalism: Old and New.* Boston: Twayne Publishers, 1991.
Michasiw, Kim Ian. "The Social Other: Don Juan and the Genesis of the Self." *Mosaic* 22 (spring 1989): 29–48.
Midrash Rabbah. Trans. H. Freedman. London: Soncino Press, 1939.
Mignot, Vincent. *The History of the Turkish, or Ottoman Empire.* Trans. A. Hawkins. 4 vols. London, 1787.
Mill, John Stuart. *Autobiography.* Boston: Houghton Mifflin Company, 1969.
Miller, Barnette. *Leigh Hunt's Relations with Byron, Shelley and Keats.* New York: Folcroft Press, 1910.
Minta, Stephen. *Byron in Greece.* New York: Holt Rinehart, 1997.
Mitchell, Leslie. *Holland House.* London: Duckworth, 1980.

———. *Lord Melbourne*. Oxford: Oxford University Press, 1997.
Moers, Ellen. *The Dandy: Brummell to Beerbohm*. New York: Viking Press, 1960.
Monkhouse, Cosmo. *Life of Leigh Hunt*. London: Walter Scott, 1893.
Montagu, Lady Mary Wortley. *Works*. 5 vols. 1803.
Montesquieu, Baron de. *Persian Letters*. 1721. Trans. C. J. Betts. New York: Penguin, 1973.
———. *The Spirit of Laws*. Trans. and ed. Anne M. Cohler, Basia Carolyn Miller, Harold Samuel Stone. New York: Cambridge University Press, 1989.
Moody, Jane. "'Fine Word, Legitimate!': Towards a Theatrical History of Romanticism." *Texas Studies in Literature and Language* 38 (fall/winter 1996): 223–44.
Moore, Doris Langley. *The Late Lord Byron: Posthumous Dramas*. Philadelphia: Lippincott's, 1957.
———. *Lord Byron: Accounts Rendered*. London: John Murray, 1974.
Moore, John. *Zeluco: Various views of human nature, taken from life and manners, foreign and domestic*, 2 vols. London: A. Strahan and T. Cadell, 1789.
Murphy, Martin. *Blanco White: Self-Banished Spaniard*. New Haven: Yale University Press, 1989.
Nicolson, Harold. *Byron: The Last Journey*. New York: Archon Books, 1969.
Nixon, Richard. *Beyond Peace*. New York: Random House, 1994.
Oakeshott, Michael. *Rationalism and Politics*. Oxford: Oxford University Press, 1962.
O'Connor, Maura. *The Romance of Italy and the English Political Imagination*. New York: St. Martin's Press, 1998.
Ogle, Robert. "The Metamorphosis of Selim: Ovidian Myth in *The Bride of Abydos* II." *Studies in Romanticism* 20 (spring 1981): 21–31.
Oliver, Robert T. *Four Who Spoke Out: Burke, Fox, Sheridan, Pitt*. Syracuse: Syracuse University Press, 1946.
Opeloye, Muhib. "The Account of Joseph (Yusuf [A. S.]) in the Qur'an and the Bible." *Hamdard Islamicus* 18, no. 3 (1985): 85–96.
O'Toole, Fintan. *A Traitor's Kiss: The Life of Richard Brinsley Sheridan*. New York: Farrar, Strauss, Giroux, 1997.
Palache, John Garber. *Four Novelists of the Old Regime: Crebillon, Laclos, Diderot, Restif de la Bretonne*. New York: Viking Press, 1926.
Paolucci, Henry. *Who Is Mr. Kissinger?* Whitestone: Griffon House Publishing, 1980.
Parker, David. "The Narrator of Don Juan." *Ariel* 5, no. 1 (1974): 49–58.
Paston, George, and Peter Quennell. *"To Lord Byron": Feminine Profiles, Based upon Unpublished Letters; 1807–1824*. New York: Charles Scribner's Sons, 1939.
Peterfreund, Stuart. "The Politics of 'Neutral Space' in Byron's *Vision of Judgment*." *Modern Language Quarterly* 40 (1979): 275–91.
Phy, Allene Stuart. *Mary Shelley*. San Bernardino, Calif.: Borgo Press, 1988.
Pinto, Vivian. *Byron and Liberty*. New York: The Folcroft Press, 1969.
Pirie, David B. *Shelley*. Philadelphia: Open University Press, 1988.
Plamenatz, John. "Liberalism." In *Dictionary of the History of Ideas*, ed. Philip P. Wiener. New York: Charles Scribner's Sons, 1973.
Plato. *Plato: The Symposium*. Trans. and ed. Alexander Nehemas and Paul Woodruff. Indianapolis: Hackett Publishing Company, 1989.

Plummer, Kenneth, ed. *The Making of the Modern Homosexual.* Totowa, N.J.: Barnes and Noble, 1981.
Pocock, J. G. A. *The Machiavellian Moment.* Princeton: Princeton University Press, 1975.
———. *Politics, Language, and Time, Essays on Political Thought and History.* New York: Atheneum, 1971.
Pomeau, Rene. *Laclos et le libertinage.* Paris: Universitaires de France, 1983.
Praz, Mario. *The Flaming Heart.* Gloucester: P. Smith, 1966.
———. *The Romantic Agony.* Trans. Angus Davidson. 2d ed. Oxford: Oxford University Press, 1954.
Prest, John. *John Russell.* New York: Macmillan, 1972.
Priestley, J. B. *The Prince of Pleasure and His Regency, 1811–20.* New York: Harper & Row Publishers, 1969.
Purkayastha, Pratyush Ranjan. *The Romantics' Third Voice: A Study of the Dramatic Works of the English Romantic Poets.* Salzburg, Austria: Salzburg University Press, 1978.
Quennell, Peter. *Byron in Italy.* New York: Viking Press, 1941.
———. *Byron: The Years of Fame.* Hamden: Archon Books, 1967.
Raab, Felix. *The English Face of Machiavelli.* London: Routledge & Kegan Paul, 1964.
Rabelais, François. *Gargantua et Pantagruel.* Trans. J. M. Cohen. New York: Penguin Books, 1986.
Rashi. *The Metsudah Chumash: A New Linear Translation.* Trans. Avrohom Davis. Hoboken, N.J.: KTAV Publishing House, 1994.
Rawls, John. *Political Liberalism.* New York: Columbia University Press, 1993.
———. *A Theory of Justice.* Cambridge: Harvard University Press, 1971.
Raymond, Dora Neil. *The Political Career of Lord Byron.* New York: Henry Holt & Co., 1924.
Reid, Stuart J. *Lord John Russell.* London: Sampson Low, Marston & Company, 1895.
Reilly, Robin. *William Pitt the Younger.* New York: G. P. Putnam's Sons, 1979.
Reiman, Donald, ed. *The Romantics Reviewed: Contemporary Reviews of British Romantic Writers.* 5 vols. New York: Garland Press, 1972.
Rennes, J. J. Van. *Bowles, Byron and the Pope-Controversy.* Amsterdam: H. J. Paris, 1927.
Rich, Adrienne. "Compulsory Heterosexuality and Lesbian Existence." In *Women, Sex, and Sexuality,* ed. Catherine R. Stimpson and Ethel Spector Person. Chicago: University of Chicago Press, 1980.
Richards, Janet Radcliffe. "Enquiries for Liberators." In *The Skeptical Feminist: A Philosophical Enquiry,* 66–67. Boston: Routledge & Keegan Paul, 1980.
Richardson, John. *Dictionary, Persian, Arabic, and English; to which is prefixed, a dissertation on the languages, literature and manners of Eastern Nations.* 2 vols. Oxford, 1777.
———. *A Dissertation on the Languages, Literature, and Manners of Eastern Nations* [Richardson on Eastern Nations]. 2 vols. Oxford: Clarendon Press, 1778.
Ridenour, George. "The Mode of Byron's Don Juan." *Publications of the Modern Language Association* 79 (September 1964): 442–46.
———. *The Style of Don Juan.* New Haven: Yale University Press, 1960.
Roberts, Michael. *The Whig Party.* New York: Macmillan, 1939.
Robertson, J. Michael. "Aristocratic Individualism in Don Juan." *Studies in English Literature* 17 (autumn 1977): 639–55.

———. "The Byron of *Don Juan* as Whig Aristocrat." *Texas Studies in Language and Literature* 17 (winter 1976): 709–24.

Robinson, Charles E., ed. *Lord Byron and His Contemporaries: Essays from the Sixth International Byron Seminar*. Newark: University of Delaware Press, 1982.

Roddier, Henri. J. J. *Rousseau en Angleterre au XVIIIe siecle*. Paris, 1950.

Root, Christina M. "History as Character: Byron and the Myth of Napoleon." In *History and Myth: Essays in English Romantic Literature*, ed. Stephen C. Behrendt, 149–66. Detroit: Wayne State University, 1990.

Rosbottom, Ronald C. *Choderlos de Laclos*. Boston: Twayne Publishers, 1978.

Rosen, Fred. *Byron, Bentham, and Greece*. Oxford: Oxford University Press, 1992.

Rosenblum, Nancy L. *Another Liberalism: Romanticism and the Reconstruction of Liberal Thought*. Cambridge: Harvard University Press, 1987.

Roth, Cecil, ed. *Encyclopedia Judaica*. Jerusalem: Keter Publishing House, 1971.

Rousseau, Jean-Jacques. *Julie ou la nouvelle Heloise*. Paris: Garnier Freres, 1973.

Rousseau, Samuel. *The Flowers of Persian Literature: Containing Extracts from the Most Celebrated Authors in Prose and Verse; with a translation into English: being a companion to Sir William Jones' Persian grammar to which is prefixed an essay on the language and literature of Persia*. London: Rousseau, 1801.

Rudé, George. *Wilkes and Liberty*. Oxford: Clarendon Press, 1962.

Ruggiero, Guido de. *The History of European Liberalism*. Trans. R. G. Collingwood. Gloucester: Peter Smith, 1981.

Ruhtra. "To the Memory of Charles Skinner Matthews." *Morning Chronicle*, December 6, 1814.

Russell, Bertrand. "Byron and the Modern World." *Journal of the History of Ideas* 47 (1947): 24–37.

———. *A History of Western Philosophy*. New York: Touchstone, 1972.

Rutherford, Andrew. *Byron: A Critical Study*. Stanford: Stanford University Press, 1961.

———. "Byron the Best Seller." In *Byron Foundation Lecture*. Nottingham, England: University of Nottingham, 1964.

———. *Byron: The Critical Heritage*. New York: Barnes and Noble, 1970.

Ryan, Robert. *The Romantic Reformation*. Cambridge: Cambridge University Press, 1997.

Saccio, Peter. *Shakespeare's English Kings: History, Chronicle, and Drama*. New York: Oxford University Press, 1977.

Sadler, Michael T. H. *The Political Career of Richard Brinsley Sheridan*. Oxford, England: B. H. Blackwell, 1912.

Said, Edward. *Beginnings: Intention and Method*. New York: Columbia University Press, 1985.

———. *Orientalism*. New York: Pantheon, 1978.

Sale, George. *Preliminary Essay to the Koran*. 1734. New York: Garland, 1984.

Sales, Roger. *English Literature in History: 1780–1830; Pastoral and Politics*. London: Hutchinson, 1983.

Samuel, Maurice. *The Gentleman and the Jew*. New York: Alfred A. Knopf, 1952.

Schaub, Diana. *Erotic Liberalism*. Lanham, Md.: Rowman & Littlefield, 1995.

Scott, Jonathan, ed. "Introduction" to *The Arabian Nights: Tales, Anecdotes, and Letters*. 6 vols. London: Cadell and Davies, 1800.

Scrivener, Michael. "'Zion Alone Is Forbidden': Historicizing Antisemitism in Byron's *The Age of Bronze*." *Keats-Shelley Journal* 43 (1994): 75–97.
Sedgwick, Eve Kosofsky. *Between Men: English Literature and Male Homosocial Desire*. New York: Columbia University Press, 1985.
———. *Epistemology of the Closet*. Los Angeles: University of California Press, 1990.
Seidel, Michael. *Satiric Inheritance*. Princeton: Princeton University Press, 1982.
Sewall, Richard B. "Rousseau's First Discourse in England." *Publications of the Modern Language Association* 52 (September 1937): 908–11.
Sha, Richard. *The Verbal and Visual Sketch in Romanticism*. Philadelphia: University of Pennsylvania Press, 1998.
Shapiro, Ian. "J. G. A. Pocock's Republicanism and Political Theory: A Critique and Reinterpretation." *Critical Review* 4 (summer 1990): 433–71.
Sharafuddin, Mohammed. *Islam and Romantic Orientalism: Literary Encounters with the Orient*. London: New York: Tauris, 1994.
Sharp, Michael Stewart. "'Freedom's Battle': War and Revolution in Byron's Major Poetry." Ph.D. diss., University of Wisconsin, 1985.
Shattuck, Roger. *Forbidden Knowledge*. New York: St. Martin's Press, 1996.
Shaw, D. L. "Byron and Spain." *Renaissance and Modern Studies* 32 (1988): 45–60.
Shelley, Mary. *The Last Man*. Ed. Anne McWhir. Peterborough, Ontario: Broadview, 1996.
Shelley, Percy. *Shelley's Poetry and Prose*. Ed. Donald Reiman and Sharon B. Powers. New York: W. W. Norton & Company, 1977.
———. *Shelley's Prose*. Ed. Fred Jones. 2 vols. Oxford: Clarendon Press, 1964.
Shilstone, Frederick W. *Byron and the Myth of Tradition*. Lincoln: University of Nebraska Press, 1988.
Sidorsky, David, ed. *The Liberal Tradition in European Thought*. New York: G. P. Putnam's Sons, 1970.
Simpson, J. A., and E. S. C. Weiner, eds. *The Oxford English Dictionary*. 20 vols. 2d ed. Oxford: Clarendon Press, 1989.
Smiles, Samuel. *A Publisher and His Friends: Memoir and Correspondence of the Late John Murray*. 2 vols. London: John Murray, 1891.
Smith, E. A. *Lord Grey: 1764–1845*. Oxford: Clarendon Press, 1990.
Soderholm, James. "Annabella Milbanke's 'Thyrza to Lord Byron.'" *The Byron Journal* 21 (1993): 30–42.
———. *Fantasy, Forgery, and the Byron Legend*. Lexington: University Press of Kentucky, 1996.
Southey, Robert. *Letters from England: By Don Manuel Alvarez Espriella, Translated from the Spanish*. Ed. by Jack Simmons. London: Cresset Press, 1951.
St. Clair, William. *That Greece Might Still Be Free: The Philhellenes in the War of Independence*. New York: Oxford University Press, 1972.
Staël, Madame de. *Germany*. Ed. O. W. Wight. New York: Derby and Jackson, 1859.
———. *Madame de Stael: On Politics, Literature, and National Character*. Ed. Morroe Berger. New York: Doubleday, 1964.

Stanhope, Leicester. *Greece in 1823 and 1824.* New York: Wilder & Campbell, 1825.
Sterne, Laurence. *A Sentimental Journey through France and Italy.* Ed. Graham Petrie. New York: Penguin, 1967.
Stout, George Dumas. *The Political History of Leigh Hunt's Examiner.* St. Louis: Washington University Press, 1949.
Stowe, Harriet Beecher. *Lady Byron Vindicated.* New York: Haskell House Publishers, 1970.
Strauss, Leo. *Ancient and Modern Liberalism.* New York: Cornell University Press, 1968.
Strickland, Margot. *The Byron Women.* London: Peter Owen, 1974.
Sturzl, Erwin A. and James Hogg, eds. *Byron: Poetry and Politics. Seventh International Byron Symposium, 1980.* Salzburg, Austria: University of Salzburg, 1981.
The Arabian Nights Entertainments, also an introduction and notes illustrative of the religion, manners, and customs of the Mahummedans. Trans. Jonathan Scott. 6 vols. London: Longman, Hurst, Rees, Orme, and Brown, 1811.
Thelander, Dorothy R. *Laclos and the Epistolary Novel.* Geneva: Library Droz, 1963.
Thomas, Gordon Kent. *Lord Byron's Iberian Pilgrimage.* Utah: Brigham Young University Press, 1983.
Thomis, Malcolm I. *The Luddites: Machine Breaking in Regency England.* New York: Shocken Books, 1972.
Thompson, E. P. *The Making of the English Working Class.* New York: Pantheon, 1964.
———. *The Romantics.* Oxford: Oxford University Press, 1997.
Thompson, James M. *Napoleon Buonaparte.* Oxford: Basil Blackwell, 1988.
Thompson, James R. *Leigh Hunt.* Boston: Twayne Publishers, 1977.
Thompson, Stith. *Motif-Index of Folk-Literature.* 6 vols. Bloomington: Indiana University Press, 1955.
Thorslev, Peter. *The Byronic Hero: Types and Prototypes.* Minneapolis: University of Minnesota Press, 1962.
———. "Post-Waterloo Liberalism." *Studies in Romanticism* 28 (fall 1989): 437–61.
Thrall, Miriam. *Rebellious Fraser's.* New York: AMS Press, 1966.
Tillyard, Stella. *The Aristocrats: Caroline, Emily, Louisa and Sarah Lennox, 1750–1832.* London: Chatto & Windus, 1994.
Trelawny, Edward John. *Recollections of the Last Days of Shelley and Byron.* 1858. New York: Doubleday, 1960.
Trilling, Lionel. *Beyond Culture: Essays on Literature and Learning.* New York: Viking Press, 1965.
———. *The Liberal Imagination: Essays on Literature and Society.* Garden City, N.Y.: Doubleday, 1950.
Trueblood, Paul. *Byron's Political and Cultural Influence in Nineteenth-Century Europe: A Symposium.* London: Macmillan Press, 1981.
———. *Lord Byron.* Boston: Twayne Series, 1968.
Trumbach, Randolph. "Erotic Fantasy and Male Libertinism in Enlightenment England." In *The Invention of Pornography: Obscenity and the Origins of Modernity, 1500–1800,* 253–82. New York: Zone Books, 1993.

Turner, James G. "Lovelace and the Paradoxes of Libertinism." In *Samuel Richardson*, ed. Margaret Doody and Peter Sabor. Cambridge: Cambridge University Press, 1991.
Usher, Howard. *The Owners of Melbourne Hall*. Derby, England: J. H. Hall & Sons, 1993.
Vallentin, Antonina. *Mirabeau*. Trans. E. W. Dickes. New York: Viking Press, 1948.
Vassall, Henry Richard, 3rd Lord Holland. *Further Memoirs of the Whig Party*. Ed. Lord Stavordale. London: John Murray, 1905.
Vassallo, Peter. *Byron: The Italian Literary Influence*. New York: St. Martin's Press, 1984.
Versini, Laurent. *Laclos et la tradition: Essais sur les source et la technique des Liaisons dangereuses*. Paris: Librairie Klincksieck, 1968.
Vital, Anthony. "Lord Byron's Embarrassment: Poesy and the Feminine." *Bulletin of Research in the Humanities* 86, no. 3 (1983–85): 269–90.
Voisine, Jacques. *Jean-Jacques Rousseau en Angleterre a l'epoque romantique: Les ecrits autobiographiques et la legende*. Paris: Didier, 1956.
Wagner, Peter. *Eros Revived: Erotica of the Enlightenment in England and America*. London: Secker and Warburg, 1988.
Walpole, Horace. *The Yale Edition of Horace Walpole's Correspondence*. Ed. W. S. Lewis. 48 vols. New Haven: Yale University Press, 1937.
Waters, Lindsay. "The 'Desultory Rhyme' of *Don Juan:* Byron, Pulci and the Improvisatory Style." *ELH* 45 (1978): 429–42.
Watkins, Daniel P. *Sexual Power in British Romantic Poetry*. Gainesville: University Press of Florida, 1996.
———. *Social Relations in Byron's Eastern Tales*. Rutherford, N.J.: Fairleigh Dickinson University Press, 1987.
Weeks, Jeffrey. *Sex, Politics, and Society: The Regulation of Sexuality since 1800*. London: Longman, 1981.
White, J. B. "Letters from Lord Holland." Liverpool Mss. University of Liverpool Library. Liverpool, England.
White, Newman Ivey. *Shelley*. 2 vols. London: Secker & Warburg, 1947.
Whitmore, Allen Perry. *The Major Characters of Lord Byron's Dramas*. Austria: Salzburg University Press, 1974.
Wiener, Howard. "Byron and the East: Literary Sources of the 'Turkish Tales.'" In *Nineteenth Century Studies*, ed. Herbert John Davis, William Clyde De Vane, and Robert Cecil Bald, 89–129. New York: Greenwood, 1968.
Wilkes, Joanne. *Lord Byron and Madame de Stael: Born for Opposition*. London: Ashgate, 1999.
Will, George. *Newsweek*, October 24, 1988, p. 62.
Willcox, William B., and Walter L. Arnstein. *The Age of Aristocracy: 1688 to 1830*. 4th ed. Lexington, Mass.: D. C. Heath and Company, 1983.
Williams, Raymond. *Culture and Society*. New York: Columbia University Press, 1958.
———. *Keywords: A Vocabulary of Culture and Society*. New York: Oxford University Press, 1976.
Wintrop, Norman. *Liberal Democratic Theory and Its Critics*. London: Croom Helm, 1983.
Wolfson, Susan. "Couplets, Self, and *The Corsair*." *Studies in Romanticism* 27 (winter 1988): 491–515.

———. *The Questioning Presence*. Ithaca, N.Y.: Cornell University Press, 1986.

——— "'Their She Condition': Cross-Dressing and the Politics of Gender in Don Juan." *ELH* 54 (fall 1987): 585–617.

Wolin, Sheldon. *Politics and Vision: Continuity and Innovation in Western Political Thought*. Boston: Little, Brown and Company, 1960.

Woodring, Carl. *Politics in English Romantic Poetry*. Cambridge: Harvard University Press, 1970.

Woodward, E. L. *Three Studies in European Conservatism: Metternich, Guizot, the Catholic Church in the Nineteenth Century*. London: Constable & Co. 1929.

Wordsworth, Jonathan, Michael C. Jaye, and Robert Woof. *William Wordsworth and the Age of English Romanticism*. New Brunswick, N.J.: Rutgers University Press, 1987.

Wu, Duncan. *Romanticism: An Anthology*. 2d ed. London: Basil Blackwell, 1998.

Yohannan, John D., ed. *Joseph and Potiphar's Wife in World Literature: An Anthology of the Story of the Chaste Youth and the Lustful Stepmother*. New York: New Directions, 1968.

———. "The Persian Poetry Fad in England, 1770–1825." *Comparative Literature* (1952): 137–160.

Young, Ione Dodson. *A Concordance to the Poetry of Byron*. 4 vols. Austin, Tex.: Best Printing Company, 1975.

Young, Wayland. *Eros Denied: Sex in Western Society*. New York: Grove Press, 1964.

Zegger, Robert E. *John Cam Hobhouse: A Political Life, 1819–1852*. Columbia: University of Missouri Press, 1973.

INDEX

Abdullah (Hatifi), 58
Ada (daughter of Byron and Annabella Milbanke), 89, 93–4,
Agaddah, 59
Albany Chambers. *See* Melbourne House (Albany)
Allegra (daughter of Byron and Claire Clairmont), 164
Almack's, 16
Anderson, Benedict, 95–6
aristocratic liberalism: Byron and Staël, 10, 184; Byron's gay narrator in *Don Juan*, 130; Byron's revolutionary definition of, 6; Carbonari, 153–164; and gentlemanly comportment, 31, 110, 126n18; in *Marino Faliero*, 115, 112–124; Pope-Bowles controversy, 101–112
Arnold, Matthew, 12n17, 106
Auden, W. H., 186

Bhabha, Homi, 95
Bakhtin, Mikhail, 26
Baldwin, William, 36, 38
Bankes, William, 47
Bayard, 87

Beckford, William, 73n15, 76n47, 148
Bentham, Jeremy, and Byron's disdain for, 185; materialism, 178; *Not Paul, But Jesus* (1823), 180; printing press in Greece, 174–77
Berlin, Isaiah, 11, 13n23
Bessborough, Lady Henrietta Frances (Henrietta Spencer; Lady Duncannon; "Lady Blarney"), 33
Beuve, Sainte, 92
Bible. *See* Old Testament; New Testament
Blackwood's Edinburgh Magazine, 101, 103
Blessington, Lady, 82
Bloom, Harold, 131
Boccaccio, 139
Boethius, 141
Bolivar, Simon, 185
Bonaparte. *See* Napoleon Bonaparte
Bowles, William, 101–112, 129
Brougham, Henry Peter, 97n13, 98n14, 155
Brown, Charles Armitage, 153; "Shakespeare's Fools," 159
Brummell, Beau, 9, 16–17, 26, 28n9
Buckley, William, 190
Burdett, Sir Francis, 155, 157, 167

221

Burke, Edmund, 18; *Reflections on the Revolution*, 24, 87
Burns, Robert, 89, 110
Bush, George, 189
Bute, Lord, 161
Butler, Judith, 132
Butler, Marilyn, 176
Byron, sixth Baron (George Gordon Noel): aesthetic and political views, 112–124; avarice (pose of), 165–167, 172; deism, 181; erotic liberalism and, 5–9, 11, 33–36, 50, 55, 89, 107, 191; generosity, 172; love of animals, 181; pacifism of, 181; parliamentary career and, 26, 119; radicalism and, 149n2, 155, 160–64, 162, 169n40, 187n18; Satanic school of poetry, 162; skepticism, 181
Byron, works: "[Bout rimés from Seaham]," 53n47; "The Bride of Abydos" 1, 10, 55, 57-65, 71, 75n26, 80, 81, 82; "The First Kiss of Love," 2; "By the Rivers of Babylon," 65; *Childe Harold's Pilgrimage* (cantos 1 and 2), 1, 4, 16, 32, 35, 64, 85, 87, 178; *Childe Harold's Pilgrimage* (cantos 3 and 4), 49, 80, 83, 85, 91, 92, 94, 197; "Childish Recollections" (1806), 5; *The Corsair*, 10, 21, 23, 25, 156; *Don Juan*, 4, 5, 9, 32, 35, 66–72, 129–148, 174; *English Bards*, 21, 89; "Epigrams on Lord Castlereagh," 159; *The Giaour*, 79, 81; *Heaven and Earth*, 155; *Hebrew Melodies*, 9, 49, 53n47, 55, 65; *Hints from Horace*, 5; *Hours of Idleness*, 89; "Lines to a Lady Weeping," 21, 22, 25, 156; "Love and Death," 146; *Manfred*, 5, 8, 49; *Marino Faliero*, 1, 10, 51n13, 101, 112–124,164, 177; "Ode to Napoleon Buonaparte," 118, 195, 198; "Ode to the Framers of the Frame Bill," 18; "On This Day I Complete My Thirty-Sixth Year," 146; Pope-Bowles Controversy, 1, 10, 101–112, 156; *Sardanapalus*, 164; *The Siege of Corinth*, 53n47; *The Vision of Judgment*, 9, 11, 146, 153–167, 169n36, 197; *The Age of Bronze* (1822), 5, 9; *The Lament of Tasso*, 7; *The Liberal*, 1, 5, 35, 124, 153–167, 183; *The Two Foscari*, 164; "There's Not a Joy the World Can Give," 2; *"Waltz: An Apostrophic Hymn,"* 5; *Werner*, 155

Calvinism, 65
Campbell, Thomas, 102
Canning, George, 17, 28n9, 97n5
cant, 105–106, 109, 157, 179, 191, 197-8
Carbonari, 6, 7, 11, 16, 27, 121, 153, 156, 184
Carlton House, 32
Cartwright, John, 16, 18, 20, 22, 156
Carson, Anne, 2, 12n5
Castle, Terry, 147
Castlereagh. *See* Stewart, Robert, Lord Castlereagh
Castlereagh, Lady, 16
Catholic emancipation, 8, 9, 18–19, 49, 162, 185. *See also* parliamentary reform
cavalier serventissmo, 147
Cervantes, Miguel de: *Don Quixote*, 37, 49, 66, 87, 135
Chalandritsanos, Loukas: Aristocratic liberalism and, 130; Byronic self-improvement and, 3, 8, 11; Byron's poetry, 146–48, 171; inspires Byron's participation in Greek war, 8, 11, 173, 183–84
Chandler, James, 125n9
Charles I, 65
Charles IV, 86, 154
Charlotte, Princess, 23; "Lines to a Lady Weeping" and, 22–23, 25, 156
Chatterton, Thomas, 89
Chew, Samuel, 101, 115, 127n28

Chezy, A. L., 57
chivalry, 87–88
Christensen, Jerome, 54n51, 131, 144
Churchill, Charles, 33
Cintra, Convention of, 84
Cicero, 27, 124
Clare, Lord, 2, 3, 133, 166
Clarke, Edward, 59
classical education, 108
Clinton, William Jefferson: sexual generosity, 8; liberalism, 198; New Democrats, 189. *See also* liberalism
Cockney Poets, 101, 103, 109, 111, 157. *See also* Leigh Hunt; John Keats
Coke, John, 75n35
Cold War, 2, 12, 190–91
Colley, Linda, 18, 100n79
Constant, Benjamin, 11, 83, 87, 172, 179, 184; "Ancient and Modern Liberty," 13n23, 172, 186n1; *Journaux Intimes*, 184
conservatism, sexual, 10
cosmopolitanism: aristocratic, 85; Benjamin Disraeli and, 79–80; Byron's liberalism and, 4, 8, 10, 35, 79–81, 83, 85–86, 94–6; *Childe Harold* and *De l'Allemagne* and, 83–86, 92, 94–96, 99n60; *Don Juan* and, 55, 72; *eros* and, 72; libertinism and, 4–6, 8; Madame de Staël, 80–88; pedantry and, 84; 105–6; Pope-Bowles, 106–7; Robert Southey and, 72; self-contradictory, 85–88, 94–95
Cottins, Madame, 106–7
Courier, 23, 24, 155, 156
Cowper, William, 89
cricket, 103–4
Crompton, Louis, 11, 13n,21, 131, 191

dandies & dandyism, 17, 31, 191, 198
Dante Alighieri, 81, 139
Dashwood, Sir Francis, 32, 33
Davies, Scrope, 16, 17, 32, 143

De Broglie, Victor, 83
D'Eresby, Lady Willoughby, 16
Delawarr, Lord, 41, 133
Devonshire House, 32, 33
D'Herbelot, 57-8, 74n18, 76n47,
Dickens, Charles: *Bleak House*, 160
Dionysus, 71
Disraeli, Benjamin, 79–80; *Vivian Grey*, 79
Don Juan, characters in Byron's, 67
Dukakis, Michael, 189, 198

Edinburgh Review, 84, 88, 109
Edleston, John, 3, 152n57
Eisler, Benita, 148, 157, 167n1
El Espagñol, 153–54
Elfenbein, Andrew, 131, 134, 150n21
Elgin, Lord, 27, 89
Emerson, Ralph Waldo, 6
epistolary novels, 35, 48–50
Erdman, David, 113
eros: and Byron, 5, 35–36; *Childe Harold*, 93, 94, 174; cosmopolitan and religious, 72; defined, 2–4, 72, 93; Eastern cultures, 79; generosity, 55; liberalism, 7, 174, 191; libertinism, 1–3; *philia*, 62, 94, 191; Plato's *Symposium*, 2; political integrity, 35–36; Sappho's lyric poetry, 5; Tasso, 7-8; Wordsworth's "Tintern Abbey," 93–94
erotic liberal, 6–7, 8
erotic liberalism: *Childe Harold's Pilgrimage*, canto 3, 89; defined, 7, 9, 10; dialectic with libertinism, 36, 50; epistolary novels, 34; Harold's active moral voice, 89; honesty about passions, 35; humanistic, 191; Joseph story and, 55; "The Lament of Tasso," 7; *The Liberal*, 5; resisting ideology, 11; sexual generosity, 107; shown in Byron's death in Greece, 171; susceptibility to beauty, 7

Erskine, Lord, 28n9, 117, 123, 127n34
Euripides, 69

feeling: absence of, 83; cosmopolitanism and, 84; "feminine," 39, 46; frequency of use in *Childe Harold*, canto 3, 92, 94; and libertinism, 10; sexual, 36; in Staël, 91–96, 185; in Tasso, 7. *See also* politics of feeling
Ferdausi, 57
Ferdinand VII, 27, 154
Fielding, Henry: *Joseph Andrews*, 55, 67, 69, 72
Fitzgerald, Lord Edward, 185
Foot, Michael, 2, 15, 31, 186
Fox, Charles James: and Catholic emancipation, 19; classical literary tastes of, 103; contributor to Brummell's album, 28n9; and Lord Holland, 16, 154; as model/countermodel for Byron, 33, 191. *See also* Sheridan, Richard Brinsley
Francis, Monks of St., 32
French revolution, 162

Gamba, Pietro, 120, 173, 176, 178
Garrick, David, 4
gay narrator in *Don Juan*, 129–148, 130
Gellner, Ernest, 95
Gentileschi, Orazio: "Joseph and Potiphar's Wife," 64, 75n35
George III, 9, 32, 158, 160–163, 172
George IV (Prince of Wales; Prince Regent), 10, 17, 25, 33, 65, 158
Gifford, William, 24
Gillray, James, 33
glukipikron, 2
Gleckner, Robert, 132
Glenarvon: Lady Oxford (Lady Mandeville), 41, 52n29, 52n35, 121–2, 148
Goethe: on Byron, 8; Percy Shelley translates for *The Liberal*, 159; Staël on, 84, 86; *Wilhelm Meister*, 81

Graham, Peter K.: pantomime, 140; preface to *Don Juan*, 151n27; Southey's *Letters from England*, 77n55;
Greek independence, 1, 8
Grenville, Lord, 119
Grey, Charles, 33, 167
Grosskurth, Phyllis, 53n48, 159, 168n1
Guiccioli, Teresa: and Angiolina in *Marino Faliero*, 120; and Byron, 1, 3, 144, 147, 171; leads Byron to join Carbonari, 6, 184
Gutwirth, Madelyn, 80

Hafiz, 57
Hagstrum, Jean, 11
Hampden Club, 156
Haslett, Moyra, 66
Hazlitt, William: ancient liberalism, 11, 177–8; on Byron's insincere liberalism, 9, 36, 130, 177, 184, 190; erotic crisis of, 173; French revolution in verse, 103; *The Liberal*, 153, 159, 164, 173; *Liber Amoris*, 173, 186n7; "My First Acquaintance with Poets," 160; "On the Spirit of Monarchy," 160; Pope-Bowles controversy, 104–6, 156; "*talks pimples*," 164; *The Venetian Republic*, 119, 130, 153, 159
Heine, Heinrich, 84
Hervey, Mrs., 83
Hitler, Adolf, 193, 195–6; and Byron, 186
Hobhouse, John Cam (Lord Broughton): advises Byron in Italy, 6, 140, 143, 147, 166, 172; and Byron's Greek adventure, 3, 172, 182; and Byron's view of Whigs, 19, 108, 112; and Byron's wedding and exile, 47, 85; and dandies (Brummell, Matthews), 17, 147; and *Don Juan*, 135, 143; Erskine, radicalism, and, 124, 125, 127n34, 155; Medmenham monks, 32; Newgate and Westminster, 22, 117-119, 123–124; on Staël, 82, 97n8
Hodgson, Francis, 45–46

Index

Hogg, Thomas Jefferson, 153
Holland, Lord, and: "Bride of Abydos," 63; Byron's political career, 16, 18, 21, 23, 25, 155, 185; Byron's preface to "The Corsair," 23; Catholic emancipation, 185; classical literary tastes, 103–4; Spanish liberalism and *El Español*, 153–5
Holland House, 48, 82, 153–4
Holy Alliance, 26–27
Homer, 81, 137
homoeroticism, 11, 149
Horace, 138, 140
Howard, Frederick, 90
Hume, David, 4
Hunt, Henry, 155
Hunt, John, 160
Hunt, Leigh: Byron emulates and turns away from, 25–27, 31, 99n47, 107, 129, 177, 181; Byron visits in jail, 10, 15, 21–3, 26–27, 183; Cockney school, 101, 103, 109, 114, 156–7; misreads Byron's liberalism, 130, 157, 172–4, 181, 183–4, 190; and Percy Bysshe Shelley, 159, 166; Pope-Bowles controversy, 109, 111–2; Pym and Hampden, 22, 25, 129, 130; as Skimpole in Dickens's *Bleak House*, 160; and Wordsworth's politics of feelings, 24
Hunt, Leigh, works: *The Dogs*, 159; *Examiner*, 10, 32, 157; *The Feast of the Poets*, 24; *Lord Byron and Some of His Contemporaries*, 160; *The Liberal*, 5, 36, 38, 129, 153–167, 172, 174; *The Story of Rimini*, 164; *See also* Byron (Works: *The Liberal*)
Hunt, Henry ("Orator"), 11,155

Isbell, John, 88, 96n4

Jami: "Bride of Abydos," 57-64; Byron draws on plot and imagery of, 10, 55; Koran (Joseph story), 10, 55–56, 58–59, 61, 63, 69; translations of, 57-58, 74n24, 77n54; "Yusef and Zuleika," 10, 55–70
Jefferson, Thomas, 8
Jefferies, Lord, 18
Jersey, Lady, 16
Johnson, E. D. H., 103, 125n2
Johnson, Samuel: *Rasselas*, 56
Jones, Sir William, 57
Joseph, M. K., 24
Jews: Byron and, 9, 63, 64, 66–72, 167
Judaism: Abraham, 71; circumcision, 71–2
Junius, 160–162

Keats, John: Cockney school, 101–3, 109; defies Pope, 101–112; "Eve of St. Agnes," 164; poetic system of, 102, 109, 124, 126; social class, 103, 114
Kelsall, Malcolm, *Byron's Politics*: on Byron's liberalism, 31, 125n2, 130; on Byron's radicalism, 2, 15, 17, 28n25, 30n45
Kennedy, Dr. James, 180
Kennedy, John F., 8
King, Jr., Martin Luther, 8
Kinnaird, Douglas, 156, 165–67
Kissinger, Henry: balance of power, 193–8; *Diplomacy*, 192, 197; influenced by Castlereagh, 12, 192–8; and John Foster Dulles, 194; misreads Prometheus legend, 195–198; *Nuclear Weapons and Foreign Policy*, 192, 196; self-perceived peacemaker, 197; *A World Restored*, 192, 197. *See also* Stewart, Robert (Lord Castlereagh)
Knight, G. Wilson, 115, 173, 181
Koran (Qur'an), and: Byron's reading of Joseph story, 61, 62–63; Byron's "The Bride of Abydos," 59, 61–64, 69, 72; circumcision, 71, 77n53; *Genesis*, 58; Jami's "Yusef and Zuleika," 55–64, 58, 59; Persian poetry and stories, 10, 55, 58
Kroeber, Karl, 24

226 Index

Laclos, Pierre Choderos de, 4, 10, 39, 45. *See also Les liaisons dangereuses*
Lamb, Lady Caroline: on Byron as Laclos's Valmont, 40–8; Byron's affair with, 31, 37, 122–3, 144, 148; Staël on Byron and, 80, 91. *See also Glenarvon*
Lamb, William, 28n9
Lang, Cecil, 131
Leask, Nigel, 63
Leigh, Augusta: Ada and, 94; Byron's affair with, 22, 42, 93, 166–7; Lady Melbourne advises Byron about, 65, 137
Leigh, Medora, 100n65
Les liaisons dangereuses: Byron imitates epistolary style of, 40–50, 49; Byron's knowledge of, 52n24, 87; condemns libertinism, 4, 35; endorses male eroticism, 34
liber, 5
liberal: aristocratic and cosmopolitan, 6, 79, 130; Byron's use of, 5–7; Castlereagh's use of, 154; defined, 5; *El Espagñol* and English usage, 79, 154; libertine, 31, 123; radical, 155, 160; Southey's use of, 7, 154; Staël and, 1, 10, 80–81
liberales: abusive epithet used by Tories, 185; Spanish political party, 154
liberal arts education: first recorded use of "liberal," 5; facilitates libertinism, 48
liberal party (1832), 1, 185
liberalism: ancient vs. modern, 11, 172, 176, 178, 184; anti-nationalism, 80; aristocratic, 6, 10, 110, 115, 101–124, 126n18, 130, 153–164, 184; charismatic and personal, 8, 19, 84, 95; Christian gentleman's, 93, 110, 181; Cold War, 191; cosmopolitan, 4–6, 10, 79, 95–6; conservative aesthetics, 101, 108; definition of, 5–7, 185–6; free speech, 85; French Revolution, 124, 184; historical figures (Constant, Blanco White, Lord John Russell), 154, 172, 184; libertinism, 48–50; literature (Hazlitt, Staël, Trilling), 173, 79–96, 187n20, 11, 190; *Marino Faliero,* 112–124; nationalism and militancy, 79–81, 118; politicians (Mirabeau, Napoleon, Reagan, Roosevelt), 124, 84, 189–190, 189; political scientists (Buckley, Strauss, Rosenblum, Russell), 176, 186, 189, 198n6; post-Napoleonic, 173; post-Waterloo, 153; self-destructive, 116; "*the South*" of Europe, 158; Spanish derivation, 79; Whigs, 6, 168n8. *See also* aristocratic liberalism
liberality, 164; *eros* motivates Byron's, 174
libertine, 1, 23, 35, 65, 120, 121–124
libertinism: betrayal of patriarchy, 122, 124; *Childe Harold,* 89, 93; chivalry, 87–88; class privilege, 50, 87–89; *eros* and, 1, 3, 50; historical precedent for, 3–4, 10, 21, 65 (Charles I); Joseph story, 55–72; liberalism, 48–50; licentiousness, 31–2, 33, 107; literary precedent, 6, 43–44, 49; political importance of, 48–50; *Marino Faliero,* 120–22, 124
liberty, 172
Liverpool, Lord, 35

Macaulay, Thomas, 49, 54n52
Manning, Peter, 29n34, 29n40, 30n40, 115–16, 128n42, 128n46, 149n13
Marchand, Leslie, 32, 126n18, 130
Marshall, William, 135, 160
Matthews, Charles Skinner, 131, 132–33, 134, 136, 138, 147
Mavrocordato, 175
McGann, Jerome, 53n37, 53n47, 57, 89, 108, 132, 191
Medmenham Abbey, 32
Melbourne House (Albany, before 1792), 64, 75n35

Melbourne House (Whitehall, after 1792), 32, 48, 75n35
Melbourne, Lady: advises Byron on "Lines to a Lady Weeping," 24–25; arranges Byron's marriage, 35; criticizes Staël, 80–81; correspondence with Byron, 2, 53n42, 55, 100n65, 145; hostess, 48; Lady Pinchbeck, 32, 137; Madame de Merteuil, 35–41, 40; Gentileschi's "Joseph and Potiphar's Wife," 64, 75n35
Metternich, 86, 121, 192, 194
Milbanke, Annabella (Lady Byron): Byron's sexual history with, 138, 142; as Clarissa Harlow, 39–47; as Madame de Tourvel, 39–47; and moral selfishness, 107; reforms Byron, 3, 9, 39–47, 49, 65, 142; Staël to reconcile Byron with, 83
Milbanke, Judith (Lady Noel), 46, 166
Mill, John Stuart, 176, 190; *Autobiography*, 177; *On Liberty*, 177
Milton, John, 137
Minta, Stephen, 11, 183
Mirabeau, Comte de, 124
Monbron, Louis Charles Fougeret de: *Le Cosmopolite*, 5, 85
Montagu, Lady Wortley, 102
Montesquieu, Baron de, 9, 57, 72, 77n55, 142
Moore, Doris Langley, 131
Moore, Thomas, 22, 85; Byron explains poetry to, 25, 26, 81, 146; *The Liberal*, 156–7, 165; and Sheridan,19, 20
Morris, William, 186
Morning Chronicle: "Lines to a Lady Weeping," 23, 27; *Marino Faliero*, 119; "To the Memory of Charles Skinner Matthews, Esq.," 132–3, 134, 147
Murray, John: Byron condescends to, 105, 126n14; Byron explains *Marino Faliero* to, 113–114; Byron's letters to, 82, 164; and *Don Juan*, 137, 164, 166;
"politics of feeling," 92; publishes "Lines to a Lady Weeping," 25

Napoleon Bonaparte: Byron's admiration for, 22, 26–27, 31, 88, 99n47, 185; Byron's criticism of, 9, 80–86, 91; failure of political liberalism after, 173; Stael's criticism of, 80–86, 91, 184; Whig collaboration with, 162
Narbonne, Louis Comte de, 87
Nathan, Isaac, 9,10, 55, 60, 65
nationalism: Alexander Pope and English, 103; Byron and Staël on, 10, 81, 84, 85, 86, 95; English and French, 85; same-sex love, 144; Staël cultivates German, 88
Necker, M., 89
neoclassicism, 101–114
Newstead Abbey, 18, 32, 44, 184
New Testament, 8
Nicholson, Andrew, 103
Nixon, Richard, 192, 197

Old Testament, 8, 55, 59, 61, 63, 76n50; Adam, 62, 71; Cain, 61; Daniel, 67; Genesis, 58, 63, 66, 68; King David, 63, 67; Jacob, 67; Joseph, 10, 55, 55–65, 66–72, 76n51; Noah, 61, 67, 71; Psalm *137*, 10, 65, 162
orientalism, 56
O'Toole, Fintan, 19, 33
Otway, Thomas, 114, 119
Ovid, *Heroides*, 60
Oxford, Lady (Jane Scott): Byron's infatuation with her daughter, Ianthe, 89; Byron's political career, 22, 31, 36, 37, 184; cross-writing, 45, 52n29; and Lady Caroline Lamb, 41, 42, 45, 52n29; Lady Mandeville (*Glenarvon*), 41; *Les liaisions dangereuses*, 52n29; Potiphar's wife, 57, 64;
Oxford, Lord (Edward Harley): nicknamed Potiphar, 57, 64

Paine, Thomas, 123, 156
Parry, William, 174, 186n10
Perceval, 33
Petrarch, Francesco, 81, 84
Petronius, 131
Phèdre, 88
philia, 2, 62, 94
Phillips, Thomas, 63
Pitt, William, 18, 33
Plato: Byron's reading of, 9, 182; charismatic Alcibiades and, 8; *eros* and, 2; homoeroticism and, 136, 138–39; *scala d'amore* and, 138; *Symposium*, 2–3, 8, 136, 138–39
politics of feeling: Greece, 171; Leigh Hunt and, 27; libertinism and, 10, 32–33, 35;
poetry and, 1, 16, 21–7, 80, 85, 92, 94
Pope, Alexander, 101–112, 124, 129; *Rape of the Lock*, 156
Potiphar, 57, 64. See also Lord Oxford
Potiphar's wife, 57, 62–64, 75n35
pluralism, 63
Prince Regent. See George IV
Prometheus, 7, 184, 195–198
Pulci, Luigi: *Il Morgante Maggiore*, 159

Quarterly Review, 109

Rabelais, François: Byron's free speech and, 25; Byron's lists and, 66; motto at Abbey of Thelème, 32; writing and physicality, 138
Racine, Jean: *Phèdra*, 69
radicalism: Byron and, 149n2, 155, 160–64, 162, 169n40, 187n18; effective leadership,117-120; libertinism and, 124; Robert Southey, 162–64
Reagan, Ronald, 189
Rees, Michael, 28n8
reform, parliamentary: Byron's speech on, 16; Whigs and, 108, 155, 160–64

Ribbing, Adolf Ludwig Count, 87
Ricardo, David, 178
Richardson, Samuel, 4; *Clarissa*, 34–5, 39–40, 48; *Sir Charles Grandison*, 4
Romilly, Samuel, 155; Byron's antipathy for, 186
Roosevelt, Franklin, 189. See also liberalism
Rosèn, Fred, 11, 157-8, 179
Rosenblum, Nancy, 96; collectivist and individualistic liberalism, 186
Rousseau, Jean Jacques: *Julie, ou La nouvelle Héloïse*, 34–35, 43; praised by Byron, 89, 92; read by Byron, 9; "Sentimental Anatomy," 107; *The Social Contract*, 34; as subject for *The Liberal*, 159
Rousseau, Samuel, 57
Rushton, Robert, 167
Ruskin, John, 186
Russell, Bertrand: Byron's fascism, 9, 13n19, 191; liberalism in U.S., 189
Russell, Lord John,154, 187n21
Rutherford, Andrew, 132

Sade, Marquis de, 4
Sadi, 57-8
Sale, George, 58, 63, 73n15
Sandwich, John Montagu, Earl of, 32, 33
Sappho, 2, 88
Scott, Sir Walter, 9, 106, 130, 190
Scrivener, Michael, 13n18
self-mythology: Byron and Staël, 10, 90–92; Constant and Byron, 184
Selwyn, George, 32
sentimentalism in: *Clarissa*, 34–35; epistolary novels, 31–50, 53n37; *Julie, ou La nouvelle Héloïse*, 34–35; *Les liaisons dangereuses*, 40–50
sexual McCarthyism, 191
Shakespeare, William: and Alexander Pope, 102; *Julius Caesar*, compared with *Marino Faliero*, 112; *The Merchant*

of Venice, 165, 167, 172; *Much Ado about Nothing*, 5; and social class, 114
Shelley, Mary: *Frankenstein*, 196; *The Last Man*, 15, 31, 143; *The Liberal*, 159–160
Shelley, Percy Bysshe: atheist, 159, 164, 181; influences Byron, 83, 113, 130, 190; *The Liberal* and, 157-9, 164; *Prometheus Unbound*, 195
Sheridan, Richard Brinsley: influences Byron, 9, 15, 18–21, 26, 191; personal life of, 32, 33; political leader, 124, 162, 167
Sidmouth, Lord, 33, 35
Smith, Adam, 178
Soderholm, James, 52n31, 152n57
Southey, Robert: Byron's attacks on, 67, 81, 143, 172, 163, 192; Castlereagh's use of "liberal" precedes, 154; failed cosmopolitanism of, 72; *Letters from England*, 71–2; radicalism of, 162–164; *Thalaba the Destroyer*, 56; "A Vision of Judgement," 160–161
St. Clair, William, 148, 182
Staël, Madame de, and: Benjamin Constant, 184; "The Bride of Abydos," 80–81; Byron's politics, 2, 9, 79–96, 184; *Childe Harold*, 5, 80, 88; chivalry, 176; cosmopolitanism, 4, 79–96; *Considerations on the Principal Events*, 95; *Corinne*, 4,10, 80, 84, 88, 90, 95; *De l'Allemagne*, 4,10, 80–96, 83, 176; *Delphine*, 91, 95; French neoclassicism as despotism, 84; liberal politics of, 8, 80, 142; *On Literature Considered in its Relationship*, 95
Stanhope, Col. Leicester: Byron contrasted with, 172, 174–6; Byron's motives in Greece, 174–6, 178; Greek nationalists, 181, 182; modern liberalism, 11, 172, 174, 177, 179
Sterne, Laurence: libertinism of, 4, 32–33, 35–39; *A Sentimental Journey*, 36–39, 46; *Tristram Shandy*, 20, 36–38, 49

Stewart, Robert (Lord Castlereagh): Byron's criticisms of, 9, 35, 67–68, 83, 140, 157–9, 192; Henry Kissinger's view of, 76n45, 193, 195, 197; "liberal" as abusive epithet, 7; 154–55; private life of, 33, 140. *See also* Lady Castlereagh
Stothard, Thomas, 60–61
Stowe, Harriet Beecher, 142
Strauss, Leo, 11, 176, 178,187; *Ancient and Modern Liberalism*, 176

Talleyrand, 42, 83, 92, 194
Tasso: *Jerusalem Liberated* 7
Thélème, Abbey of, 32
Thorslev, Peter, 148; post-Waterloo liberalism and, 153
Tory party, 155, 161
Townshend, John, 28n9
Trilling, Lionel, 11, 131, 191, 198n4; *The Liberal Imagination*, 11, 190; *The Middle of the Journey*, 190

utilitarianism: Bentham, Mill, and radical reformers and, 11, 176, 191; Leicester Stanhope and, 11, 172, 174

Virgil, 81, 137, 183
Voltaire, 89

Wagner, Peter, 9n
Walpole, Horace, 51n13, 114, 147
Washington, George: Byron admires, 185, 195–198
Watkins, Daniel, 148
Webster, James Wedderburn, 42, 166
Webster, Lady Frances, 31, 43, 57, 64–65, 121–2
Wellington, first duke of (Arthur Wellesley), 16, 84, 158, 159
Whigs: Beau Brummell and, 16; Byron and, 21, 25, 27, 161–62, 185; literary taste and, 103, 109; Neapolitan revolution and, 120, 124

Index

Whitbread, Samuel, 95
White, Joseph Blanco, 154
Whitehall. *See* Melbourne House, Whitehall
Whitehead, Paul, 32
Wiener, Harold, 57, 73n10 & 15,
Wilde, Oscar, 129
Williams, Raymond, 12n13; 31
Wilkes, Joanne, 10, 80, 84
Wilkes, John: Byron and, 160–163; libertinism and, 4, 33, 191; Medmenham Abbey and, 32, 50n6
Winckelmann, Johann Joachim, 142
Wolfson, Susan, 77n52, 131, 191
Woodring, Carl, 29n30, 127n35
Wordsworth, William: Byron's criticisms of, 24, 67, 72; Cold War liberals and, 11, 190; "Tintern Abbey," 93; "The Thorn," 135

Zambelli, Lega, 166

ABOUT THE AUTHOR

Jonathan David Gross received his Ph.D. from Columbia University, where he was a president's fellow. He has edited *Byron's "Corbeau Blanc": The Life and Letters of Lady Melbourne* (Houston: Rice University Press, 1997) and published essays on Hazlitt and Napoleon. He served as a Mayer Fund fellow (1994) at the Huntington Library and is currently an associate professor in the Department of English at DePaul University.